ID0984731

Guilford Technical Community College
1958–2008

Guilford Technical Community College
1958–2008

Creating Entrepreneurial Partnerships
for Workforce Preparedness

Dr. Lee W. Kinard, Jr.

CAROLINA ACADEMIC PRESS
Durham, North Carolina

Library of Congress Cataloging-in-Publication Data

Kinard, Lee.
 Guilford Technical Community College, 1958-2008 : creating entrepre-
neurial partnerships for workforce preparedness / by Lee W. Kinard, Jr.
    p. cm.
 Includes bibliographical references and index.
 ISBN 10: 1-59460-558-0 / ISBN 13: 978-1-59460-558-1 (alk. paper)
 1. Guilford Technical Community College--History. 2. Academic-indus-
trial collaboration--North Carolina. 3. School-to-work transition--North
Carolina. 4. Career education--North Carolina. I. Title.

 LD6501.G85K56 2008
 378.756'62--dc22

2008005282

Carolina Academic Press
700 Kent Street
Durham, NC 27701
Telephone (919) 489-7486
Fax (919) 493-5668
www.cap-press.com

Printed in the United States of America

To the dedicated faculty and staff
of GEIC, GTI and GTCC.

The goal of the Community College System must be as comprehensive as the needs of our students are. If this is not understood, then it is our duty to make it clear, so that it will be understood. We must support policies which will open all of these doors to all of the people who can walk through them with any degree of promise to themselves and to the State.

William Dallas Herring, 1992

The publication of this book was funded by Wachovia.
The GTCC Foundation, Inc. graciously acknowledges Wachovia's
generosity in financing this tribute to GTCC's 50th Anniversary.

Contents

CONTENTS

List of Photographs and Illustrations

Foreword

An insightful philosopher notes that one of the most rewarding experiences available to human beings is the opportunity to participate in creating a productive enterprise before all the fundamental parameters of the project have been established, tested, and studied to death so that anybody can replicate the process. This was the challenge GTCC founders pursued in 1958 when, as representatives of government, business, and education, they partnered to compile the study that launched GTCC's embryonic forerunner, the Guilford Industrial Education Center.

This history traces the progenitor's venture to establish a basic training center through a meticulous recounting of trials, tribulations, and intense and acrimonious debates. It enables the reader to observe how boards of diverse and politically appointed individuals partnered to cope with the capricious industrial transition that roiled the Piedmont Triad during the second half of the 20th century and haunted the state into the millennium. It further represents the most comprehensive effort that has been mounted in decades to dispel the widespread stereotypical, often dismissive attitude that tends to relegate North Carolina's community colleges to second-rate educational status even though the system accepts more than 800 thousand students a year.

Imagine for a moment, what agency, other than the state's 58 community colleges, could North Carolina depend on to train, retrain, and motivate masses of ambitious, tax paying residents to sustain the economic infrastructure of a progressive state. While it is reasonable to assume that most community colleges developed similarly, what sets "Guilford County's most unique educational institution" apart on its 50th anniversary is the extensive range of successful, entrepreneurial partnerships, and programs that emerged from its founding fundamental relationship between representatives of government, education, and industry.

While GTCC may have struggled to define itself and its mission during its first quarter-century, the last twenty-five years have proven immeasurably rewarding for the citizens of Guilford County. In thanking the Wachovia Foundation for funding this history, I am honored to note that GTCC has succeeded as an educational institution by adhering to society's noble aim to "set free and develop the capacity of human individuals without respect to race, sex, class, or economic status."

Don Cameron
President, GTCC
April 3, 2008

Preface

Writers have often proclaimed that "history is another country;" I interpret that to mean that those who have personally experienced, in this case, the creation of an institutional setting, are arguably licensed to describe the phenomenon in the context of their association with observable and documented facts and events. When GTCC President Don Cameron asked me to compile a narrative commemorating the Institution's fifty-year commitment to workforce preparedness, he authorized me to report what I discovered and prioritized based on my study of the events and incidences involving the evolution of the institution since 1958.

What follows is a description of the significant phenomena that contributed to the incremental development and ultimate success of one of the world's premier community colleges. I crafted the project from public and institutional documents, records, and publications, most notably the extensive and complete minutes from the various boards of advisors and Trustees, several historical monographs, an exceptional oral history, and impressions compiled from my half-century personal and professional association with the Institution. It is important to note that I was professionally and personally acquainted with many of the newspaper reporters who wrote about the College, including Jerry Bledsoe, Richard Benton, Owen Lewis, and Wilson Davis.[1]

My relationship with GTCC dates from 1958 when, as the host and founding producer of "The Good Morning Show" (WFMY-TV, CBS, Greensboro-High Point-Winston Salem), I interviewed the founders of the Guilford Industrial Education Center (GIEC). Across the ensuing decades, I invited Trustees, faculty, staff, and students to appear on the "Good Morning Show" and produced inestimable segments explicating the Institution's programs and projects. I hired at least two GTCC graduates to work at WFMY-TV. When I decided to complete my college education at UNCG in 1971, I attended (GTI) as recommended by the UNCG registrar, to achieve transfer competency in

Algebra I and II. GTCC honored me on several occasions by inviting me to deliver the major commence address as well as numbers of addresses at the department and program level. Following my retirement from WFMY-TV (1999), I joined GTCC as Executive Assistant to President Donald W. Cameron (February 2000) to market his most ambitious project, the immensely successful Larry Gatlin School of Entertainment Technology.

The daunting challenge to produce this study of workforce preparedness in Guilford County could not be accomplished in isolation from the industrial history of the county and the state. The story begins with the mid-century efforts of Governor Luther Hodges and the General Assembly to industrialize a state second only to Texas in the numbers of small farms maintained by tenant farmers. GTCC's institutional development parallels the evolution of the North Carolina Community College System from its genesis under the State Board of Education in 1963 to the establishment in 1979 of the State Board of Community Colleges, which assumed governance of the system on January 1, 1981.

As a multi-faceted initiative, workforce preparedness originated with the mid-twentieth-century initiatives to industrialize North Carolina by (1) increasing literacy through a system designed to provide basic and compensatory education for adults. This concept (2) would ideally introduce laborers to a series of practical instructional exercises designed to increase their technical skills provided by (3) a series of industrial education centers, technical and community colleges offering a maximum of two years' training beyond the high school. For citizens uninterested in attending the state's four-year colleges and universities, this plan offered preparation for productive careers in a variety of industries. Revolutionizing industrial productivity through workforce preparedness in a rural state heavily dependent on recycling fibrous plants into consumer products would presumably broaden the manufacturing sector to produce more sophisticated and profitable products that would elevate the standard of living while insuring the state's fiscal and productive vitality.

"The Deep River Covenant," referencing the stream that topographically separates Guilford County's two largest cities, High Point and Greensboro, as it passes through historic Jamestown a few miles west of GTCC's main campus, is an authorial concept that frames the consensual integrity of the Trustees who have guided and supported the Institution's destiny. The "covenant" is an unarticulated agreement in principle that enabled powerful business, professional, civic, social, and political leaders, some with distinct territorial interests, to set aside personal agendas to build and guide an institution committed to workforce preparedness and economic development for the betterment of Guilford County.

This convention evolved organically some ten years after the school opened following a series of strident and widely publicized philosophical debates. This covenant is unique to Guilford County and remains a model for future civic cooperation and creating settings for future institutions. Since its inception as the Guilford Industrial Education Center, the Institution's various boards have been chaired by ten men and one woman: Zaph Rochelle (GIEC, 1958–63); H. Frank Starling (GTC, 1967–69); John T. Davis, Jr. (GTI, 1969–81); Frank W. York (GTI-GTCC, 1982–84); J. William McGwinn, Jr. (1984–87); Dr. Stuart B. Fountain (1987–92); Charles A. Greene (1992–95 and 1998–2001); James F. Morgan (1995–98); J. Patrick Danahy (2001–04); David S. Miller (2004–07); and Shirley M. Frye (2007–).

GTCC's unbridled success as a comprehensive community college is further attributable to an entrepreneurial series of educational, industrial, and governmental partnerships that established its international reputation for workforce preparedness and economic development. At 50, GTCC is firmly committed to training highly skilled technicians to reinforce the Piedmont Triad's new industrial clusters in biotechnology, nanotechnology, transportation-supply-train logistics, health care, and other futuristic twenty-first century programs.[2]

From its humble beginning as North Carolina's "first training school, established through the cooperative efforts of education and industry" (1955), to the opening of the (Piedmont) Guilford Industrial Education Center (GIEC, 1958), through its maturation as Guilford Technical Institute (1965), to its flagship status as a comprehensive community college (1983) with an international reputation, GTCC is still, as former president Dr. Luther E. Medlin proudly proclaimed in 1972, "Guilford County's most unique educational institution."[3]

Acknowledgments

I am indebted to GTCC President Donald W. Cameron for assigning this project and assisting in its completion. Its presumed clarity rests with the editing expertise of Dr. Judy Cheatham, Professor of English at Greensboro College. My GTCC colleague Jane M. Pendry, College Liaison for the Early Middle Colleges, burned the midnight oil to get the manuscript in an acceptable state for publication. Dr. Cameron's Executive Administrative Assistant Marcia McClaren aided with research documentation and technical support. Thanks to Maria Collozzi in the President's Office for clerical assistance.

Members of the GTCC President's Council provided critiques and valuable information including executive vice presidents Dr. Marshall "Sonny" White and Cuyler McKnight; vice presidents, Rae Marie Smith, Dr. Kathy Baker Smith, and Leroy Stokes and his staff including Philip King and Bob Plain. James S. "Jim" Belk, Executive Director of the GTCC Foundation; Jean Jackson, Human Resources Director; and Jacqueline Greenlee, Director of Development, were extremely helpful in compiling and interpreting data and information. Thanks to Margot Horney and Melissa McKinney in the Foundation office and stalwarts Mitzi Ellis, Cheryl Hemric, Coretta Montague, Travis Hyatt, and Wilson Davis in the Marketing and Information department.

The data supplied by Karen Ritter, Tonya England, and Laura Altizer in Institutional Research contributed measurably to understanding the statistical state of the institution. Thanks to my mentor Dr. Carolyn Schneider, Division Chair Arts & Sciences, and to her colleagues Division Chairs Shanna Chastain, Ken Rowe, Mary West, Ed Frye, Anne Hockett, and Dr. Beverley Gass, Dean of the Learning Resource Center. This history could not have happened without the cooperation of the excellent LRC staff including GTCC archivist Belinda Daniels Richardson for her compilation of GTCC's extensive archives, including early documents, a complete record of the Board of Trustees meetings, photographs, video material, and other official institutional records. Thanks also to LRC staff Marc Lehman, Matilda Kirby Smith, and George Machen.

I am further indebted to Roy A. Carter for *A History of GTI: 1958–71* and to Associate Professor of Communication and Fine Arts Shelly Lutzweiler for her Oral History Series and monographs on the Guilford County TB Sanatorium, the Gazebo, and the Iddings house. Other references are included in the Bibliography and Appendix. I would like to thank one of North Carolina's major historians and one of my former professors Dr. Allen Trelease (UNCG), for reminding me of the "fine line that separates history and journalism."[1] I owe a tremendous debt to former and present UNCG School of Education professors Dale Brubaker, Fritz Mengert, David Purple, and Svi Shapiro for their inspiration and guidance.

I also thank the staff of Carolina Academic Press for their assistance.

In reminding the reader that I have written what seemed important to me about GTCC, its students, and supporters, I take full credit for the errors that may have occurred.

Lee Kinard, November 5, 2007

Introduction

We define the community college as *any institution regionally accredited to award the associate in arts or the associate in science as its highest degree.* That definition includes the comprehensive two-year college as well as many technical institutes both public and private.[1]

Arthur M. Cohen
Florence B. Brawer

An Industrial Snapshot

Twentieth-century historians attribute the 19th-century industrialization of Guilford County to six basic factors: (1) the railroad network that inspired (2) energetic, able, and technically minded visionaries to establish an industrial base with (3) local capital. The economic vitality that enabled existing industries (4) to breed new enterprises as (5) entrepreneurs demonstrated a remarkable agility to change with consumer demand. Eventually, the combination of these factors (6) nurtured the creation of a wide range of small businesses employing 250 or fewer that secured, to the extent possible, the economic foundation of the county.[2]

The state's earliest industrialists, like Michael Schenck, who built the state's first cotton mill in Lincoln County (1813), were often Scots-Irish and German immigrants who knew how to funnel the power from fast-moving streams into profitable tanneries and grist mills. As William Powell (1989) reports, isolated settlements in the Piedmont forests depended on a service economy driven by self-taught weavers, carpenters, coopers, wheelwrights, wagon makers, tailors, blacksmiths, hatters, and rope makers. A century and a half later, the state's community colleges were still struggling to elevate the skills of the descendants of the state's seminal "mechanics," what I refer to as the "hands" people who played a vital role in the development of North Carolina's material culture.[3]

While the Great Depression diminished North Carolina's manufacturing power in the early 1930s, a quick recovery in 1935 enabled the state to sustain its ranking as the leading industrial state in the Southeast and the nation's largest producer of textiles, tobacco products, and wooden furniture. At the onset of World War II (September 1, 1939), Guilford County's 243 manufacturing plants were employing 25,123 production workers. By 1947, 410 plants were employing 26,172 production workers. Cone Mills, Burlington Mills, J. P. Stevens, and Guilford Mills formed part of a Guilford County textile industry that was annually injecting over $155 million into the economy.[4] When Lorillard arrived in Greensboro (1954) to produce cigarettes, 509 plants in Guilford County employed 33,045 workers. By October 1945, High Point's prosperity seemed assured by the presence of 202 plants; by early 1946, 2,500 jobs were available in the city and 66 new manufacturing plants were slated to open before year's end.

While GTCC's predecessor, the Guilford Industrial Education Center (GIEC), was in the planning stage (1957–58), the launch of Sputnik I on October 4, 1957, spurred a national frenzy to overcome the Russian advantage in science and technology. Explorer I, the first American satellite, was launched into space on January 31, 1958, followed by Vanguard I and Explorer 3 in March. However brilliant, the galactic glitter of these celestial successes was shadowed by the realities of a national recession when unemployment reached a postwar high of nearly 8 percent (5.5 million men and women) before the economy rebounded at the end of 1958. Guilford County's labor force totaled 103,600 of whom 5,700 or 5.5 percent were unemployed. Of the 97,900 folks working every day, 83,250 were nonagricultural wage and salaried workers (excluding domestics), 10,350 were self-employed, unpaid family workers, or working as domestics in private households, and 4,300 labored in agriculture.[5]

As the GIEC prepared to open in the fall of 1958, employment at Lorillard had skyrocketed to 2,200 and the company was searching for 125 maintenance men. Guilford County ranked first in the state in new and proposed industries, first in the growth of its labor force, and first in a labor force that was engaged in trade and industrial pursuits.[6] North Carolina's industrial education centers were nobly and strategically created to increase the technical skills of unskilled laborers. Observably, the target population for this training had no great admiration for education. They represented a class of workers GTCC founder and Board chair Zalph Rochelle characterized as "poor louts" in a luncheon speech to Asheboro Rotarians (see Chapter 7).[7]

Embedded Illiteracy

While North Carolina may have been the Southeast's manufacturing giant in the late 1950s, it was a perilous roost as industrialists rushed to train their workforce to master new manufacturing techniques. Corporate survival depended on a producer's ability to create a wide range of products from furniture and textiles to plastic bottles and distilled cedar oil, plus the technology to protect the United States during the Cold War. The desperate need to increase literacy and upgrade workforce skills was clearly apparent to lawmakers in the 1955 North Carolina General Assembly, who created a nine member State Board of Higher Education. The group's first Chair, D. Hidden Ramsey, advocated the development of tax supported public junior (community) colleges, but the possibility of any attempt to combine college parallel or transferable courses and vocational training in these new institutional settings flared into an ongoing controversy.[8]

Workforce preparedness was not restricted to North Carolina. From a national perspective, it was accepted that modern industrialization depended on a massive educational initiative to increase the literacy and upgrade the skills of America's workers. Community colleges were visualized as the providers of an *intermediate educational curriculum* that would bridge the perceived gap in educational training and opportunities between high schools and four-year colleges and universities. In North Carolina that vision was fraught with serious cultural challenges that persisted through the 20th century.[9] At publication, researchers were still concerned with the fate of the state's "less educated" workers who lost well-paying jobs when the decline of traditional manufacturing was exacerbated by an influx of illegal immigrants.[10]

The root causes of North Carolina's literacy problem are traceable to the rapid decline of rural tenancy that forced minimally educated farm laborers to search for entry level manufacturing jobs and, in many cases, migrate to the municipalities where those industries were located. Displaced tenant farmers provided a large pool of struggling laborers grasping for survival and eager to work in factories at prevailing wages. Thus, when industry modernized and expanded following Word War II, the literacy gap among their employees forced employers to search for a means to upgrade the technical skills and employable traits of their workforce.[11]

The High Point industrialists and educators who partnered to establish an embryonic training school on English Street in the mid 1950s recruited students who were raised to believe that their survival depended on brute strength. Born with a stubborn reliance on subsistence farming, manual labor, and self-taught mechanical trades, many of these students had shunned rote-afflicted classrooms and dropped out of school to take production jobs in furniture, tobacco, and textile factories. The factory aristocracy[12] was thrilled to welcome them for decades until modern technology rendered unskilled labor ineffective. Market demands for full fashioned hosiery and elegant furniture crystallized the mission of the (future) North Carolina Community College System by exacerbating the need to systemize occupational education beyond the high school to train adults.[13]

The industrialization of North Carolina did not result in a population of well-to-do factory workers, but most were able to find jobs. In 1970 when more than 1,745,900 North Carolinians were employed in non-agricultural jobs, hourly textile wages averaged $2.35; tobacco, $3.19; furniture, $2.41; paper $3.27; and electronics $2.61.[14] However, when labor costs dramatically increased in the 1980s and 90s, textile makers moved production out of the U.S. leaving thousands of minimally skilled workers unemployed. And when the major tobacco companies were no longer able to evade the health issues associated with their products and forfeited enormous sums in retribution, this pressure, in conjunction with plant modernization, mergers, and acquisitions, disenfranchised even more workers. The idolized furniture industry endured its share of mergers and acquisitions before the foreign — mainly Asian — flexibility to produce quality products at lower costs sent many American furniture manufacturers scurrying across the Pacific leaving thousands of unemployed North Carolinians in the wake of their migration.[15]

These economic challenges could be viewed as the predictable processes of capitalistic evolution from one product to another, from one manufacturing stage to another, but that analogy dismisses the human factor involved in industrial transitions that only a unique institution like GTCC could address. The economic security of North Carolina's marginally educated "hands-on" production workers, many the product of rural tenancy, was always problematic. The challenge confronting the African-American laborer in Guilford County was even more precarious considering the minimal opportunities available to people of color in the late 1950s.[16] A series of vocational training centers appeared to be the most convenient and economical way to retrain the state's workers to cope with new manufacturing techniques, but the process that resulted in the eventual creation of the North Carolina Community College System is a complicated muddle of state and local educational initiatives.[17]

The North Carolina Community College System

Dean B. Pruette, a former superintendent of the High Point Public Schools and one of GTCC's founding fathers, once proudly proclaimed that "the beginning of the entire movement for North Carolina's system of community colleges and technical institutes began in High Point and came through the hole of a sock."[18] While many local industrialists probably agreed with Pruette, the system actually evolved through a series of evolutionary steps beginning with the establishment of a tuition free, public junior college in Buncombe County in 1927.[19]

Twenty years later following World War II a number of "off campus temporary centers," sponsored by the North Carolina College Conference, opened to serve the influx of returning World War II veterans. Two of these became permanent institutions; Mecklenburg College opened in Charlotte in 1949 to serve African-Americans and later merged with the Central Industrial Education Center to form Central Piedmont Community College. The "off campus" centers in Asheville, Charlotte, and Wilmington were called community colleges since they offered more occupational courses than junior colleges and operated without state aid and supervision.[20]

The Greensboro Chamber of Commerce fostered the Greensboro Evening College to provide courses for non-traditional students at non-traditional hours. As C. Van Woodward (1993) noted, "The voice of the South in the 1950s had become the voice of the chamber of commerce in the era of the 'Bull Dozer Revolution.'"[21] To achieve accreditation, the center merged with Guilford College to become its Greensboro Division. By merging professional degree programs with its liberal arts curriculum, the Quaker institution assured its solvency by institutionalizing one of the first adult education programs in the country.[22]

The third developmental stage involved the necessity to institutionalize the orderly management of these "community colleges." After turning aside an initial proposition in 1953, the General Assembly relented and passed the first so-called Community College Act in 1957. It empowered member institutions to operate under the supervision of the State Board of Higher Education, to have independent trustees, and to receive state and local aid. This legislation authorized a half-million dollars for manpower development through a bill introduced by Guilford County Democratic representative Ed Kemp, an eventual GTCC founder, to develop ten industrial education centers including the GIEC that evolved into GTCC.[23]

The 1963 General Assembly extensively revised (G.S. 115A, later changed to 115D) this dual and wasteful system of community colleges and industrial education centers in two steps. Institutions in Asheville, Wilmington, and Charlotte were converted to four-year colleges while existing and future public community colleges, technical institutes, and industrial education centers were melded into the Department of Community Colleges, an arm of the State Board of Education. Local independent trustees were empowered to govern these institutions with state and local funding. The final step in the systematic governance process occurred in 1979 when the General Assembly established the State Board of Community Colleges effective January 1, 1981.[24]

The Guilford Industrial Education Center

The GIEC evolved from a successful training center established in 1955 by High Point sock and furniture makers in association with the High Point Public Schools. Operating in a rented building on English Street in High Point, the sock maker's looping classes graduated 204 workers in three years. A knit machine fixing course graduated 120 in two years and 50 students had registered for a class in cutting and sewing contingent on the program's expansion to the Guilford Industrial Education Center in Jamestown. Upholstery classes sponsored by furniture makers had graduated 34, who were immediately employed, and signed up 50 more for another six-month course.[25]

The Piedmont Industrial Education Center Project Committee (PIECPC, 1957–58), chaired by Clarence Edward "Ed" Kemp, cited the success of the English Street project as proof that Guilford County desperately needed a manpower training facility. A feasibility survey forecast an immediate need for 1,021 workers in a range of industrial trades including power sewing (237), machining (97), weaving (80), upholstering (79), and looping (72). At least 518 supervisors indicated a willingness to participate in regular supervisory development programs. The projected center was also expected to draw from a pool of 3,176 high school juniors and seniors enrolled in Guilford County's three school systems (1,468 boys, 1,708 girls).[26]

The High Point leaders who had been instrumental in establishing the English Street classes presented their proposal for an industrial education center to the Guilford County Board of Commissioners on November 14, 1957. In keeping with the Commissioners desire to find a need for the county's derelict TB hospital, they recommended locating the future Industrial Education Center in the shuttered Guilford County Tuberculosis Sanatorium at the eastern edge of Jamestown. In addition to the City Councils, Chambers of Commerce, and Junior Chambers of Commerce (Jaycees) in High Point and Greensboro, the proposal was heartily endorsed by the Furniture Manufacturers Association, the Hosiery Manufacturers Association, and Piedmont Associated Industries. [27]

On March 17, 1958, the commissioners officially offered the former TB sanatorium property in Jamestown, valued for insurance purposes at $1,000,000, as a site for the center. They pledged to fund, operate, and maintain the facility and graciously offered $30,000, exclusive of State reimbursements, to finance needed alterations and renovations. The State Board of Education approved the commissioners' plan to establish the Guilford Industrial Education Center on April 3, 1958, now celebrated as GTCC's Founders' Day.[28] The organization of the GIEC culminated on May 3, 1958, with the appointment of an advisory committee to assist and advise the boards of education in Greensboro, High Point, and Guilford County in operating the facility.[29]

GIEC, GTI, GTCC

GTCC's substantial uniqueness is directly attributable to its evolution as an ongoing partnership among education, industry, and government. The GIEC's founding Executive Director and six succeeding presidents have managed the institution with differing degrees of commitment, vision, and administrative skills. To their everlasting credit, each appears to have done his best with the resources at his command. They can be categorized as founders, shapers, sustainers, nurturers, and entrepreneurs. Executive skills aside, there were occasions, particularly during the painful, formative years, when the Institution might have failed for lack of leadership had it not been for the enduring dedication of faculty and staff. An entire volume could be devoted to the self-sacrificial persistence of this sister- and brotherhood that former Executive Vice President Marshall "Sonny" White commended as GTCC's "Disciples of Hope." A legion stayed the course during their entire careers despite poor pay and tedious working conditions. Lamentations aside, they believed in the spirit of the institutional mission to help students succeed to the extent of their individual desire to develop personal skills and productive careers. These stalwarts, and their colleagues at the other 57 institutions, are the heart and soul of the North Carolina Community College System.

Much of GTCC's success is attributable to the generally consistent support of the Guilford County Board of Commissioners. Given that Guilford is historically one of the most fractious counties in North Carolina the commission's confirmation of GTCC's annual budget has seldom wavered or sunk to abject partisanship.[30] History may judge their wisdom in denying GTCC the Carolina Circle Mall as a Greensboro campus, but this debatable decision eventually enabled the College to build an entirely new facility that may provide an even bigger boon to the northern and eastern sections of the county. The Commissioners' endorsement of GTCC bond campaigns, while not always unanimous, has been of inestimable value in attracting the support of more than 60 percent of the voting electorate.

Members of GTCC's openly political Board of Trustees appointed by the Governor, the Guilford County Board of Commissioners, and the Guilford County Schools Board of Education have compiled an exemplary record of service. Indeed, their history is a governance model for consensus and cooperation between women and men of differing political persuasions, educational philosophies, racial and ethnic backgrounds, and professional and personal interests. At publication, Shirley M. Frye has become the first African-American and the first female to serve as Board chair. Suffice it to say, you would have to have lived in Guilford County for fifty years to understand the quality of the Board's leadership given the competitive nature of the area's two major cities and the often unbridled egos of their respective leadership cadres.

The prevailing negative in this history is the self-indicting reluctance of the North Carolina Legislature to adequately fund the Community College System.[31] That fault may be slowly moderating in the first decade of the twenty-first century as North Carolina struggles to replace its traditional manufacturing industries with futuristic entrepreneurial clusters. Piedmont legislators, long lost in the power trade off between eastern and western cliques, finally gained a measure of strength due in part to enormous campaign contributions to Democratic governors Hunt and Easley.[32] By the beginning of the new century, Guilford's legislative delegation began to reap the benefits of their competence, longevity, leadership, and personal negotiating skills.[33]

A Chronological Structure

This project organically organized itself into three major sections devoted to (1) the development of the Guilford Industrial Education Center and its subsequent elevation to Guilford Technical Institute (1958–71), (2) the evolution of a rapidly growing and somewhat loosely organized enterprise, into a tightly organized accredited institution (1971–91),[34] culminating in (3) "The Entrepreneurial Presidency of Dr. Donald W. Cameron." Beyond the history of workforce preparedness in Guilford County 1958–2008, the major themes include the challenge to elevate literacy by providing basic and compensatory education to adults; the evolving struggle to pace the needs of the workforce with technology by offering timely, productive vocational and technical training in addition to promoting economic development and civic leadership while sustaining and enlarging on a variety of business-industry-education partnerships.

The Guilford Industrial Education Center welcomed its first students to Jamestown during the formative years of the civil rights struggle in the aftermath of Brown vs. Board of Education (1954). Its history parallels the recession that marked the post Korean War period, the Cuban Missile Crisis, the assassination of President John F. Kennedy, and the Vietnam War. By the time President Donald Cameron was inaugurated in 1991, the Cold War had ended and the United States had gone to war in the Middle East where its forces remain at publication.

N.C. State Representative Clarence Edward "Ed" Kemp, Chairman
Piedmont Industrial Education Center Project Committee

Bruce B. Roberts, Director
Guilford Industrial Education Center
1958–1965

Dr. Dean B. Pruette
Superintendent
High Point Public Schools

Zalph Rochelle, Chair
GIEC Advisory Board 1958–1963
Chair, GTI Trustees 1963–1967

Guilford TB Sanatorium "Old Main" and its two wings.

The Guilford County TB Sanitorium
Jamestown site of the Guilford Industrial Education Center 1958.

Section I

Creating a Unique Institution
1958–62

Chapter 1

The Guilford Industrial Education Center: 1958–62

If only some school wuz nearby where they would teach my boys wheels, screws, and valves! Then they would study and not be slaves to the soil.[1]

An Unknown Mother Interviewed in the 1930s

Loopers and Toe Boys

Someone suggested that High Point, North Carolina, incorporated May 26, 1859, "was built in defiance of all the laws of commercial, industrial, political, and social gravitation." Like other towns in the north central Piedmont,[2] the city was born in the "wood era of the 19th century"; but when W. J. and T. F. Wrenn, John H. Tate, and E. A. Snow scanned the hardwood forests, they envisioned tables, chests, and chairs where others had seen only spokes, wagons, and tool handles. The High Point Furniture Company, Inc. they launched with $9000 in 1889 produced three piece bedroom suites for $7.50 and beds for 75 cents. High Point was soon destined to become "the furniture capital of the world".[3]

A few decades later in 1904, the industrial threads of the textile industry enveloped the Furniture City when John Hampton Adams and James Henry Millis began producing black hose in a partnership that matured into the largest hosiery manufacturer in the world. Thanks to Adams-Millis, High Point became "the furniture and hosiery capital of the world" in the 1950s.[4] The new industrial plants streaming endlessly on line during this period of exceptional industrial growth demanded more skilled labor than diversified occupation programs in the public high schools could provide. The problem of productive labor was compounded in High Point by an abundance of older, unskilled individuals who were not adequately trained to earn a living in the emerging technological environment. The sock makers' desperate need for a technically skilled workforce soon generated a partnership between industry and education that seeded an internationally renowned community college.

GTCC owes its birth in 1958 to the sock and furniture maker's crucial need for "loopers" and "toe boys." Hosiery manufacturing was mechanized except for the final process; the closing of the hole at the toe of a sock still had to be done by hand. Few workers were attracted to the slow, tedious process that was hard on the eyesight. Frustrated by their inability to recruit loopers and tired of distributing bundles of socks to cottage loopers across the city, the manufacturers shared their dilemma with High Point City School officials to see if the Diversified Occupations program could provide a solution.

Superintendent Dean Pruette and his Diversified Occupations Coordinator Bruce Roberts partnered with the hosiery industry to open a looping school in a $35 per month rented building on English Street. The manufacturers agreed to furnish the equipment and the school officials committed to administer the program and recruit an instructor. Fortunately, the instructor they hired was familiar with a new looping technique that, while still done by hand, was vastly quicker.[5]

The looping school piqued the interest of the Furniture City Manufacturers Association whose members needed power sewers for their upholstery departments. They visualized an intensive off-site training program to replace their traditional reliance on a supply of trainable "toe boys." "Toe boys" were the entry-level employees assigned to keep sewers supplied with the springy Mississippi Delta moss (toe) used as "filler" for upholstered products; "toe-boys" carted the moss from the loading dock to the upholstery department. Those who demonstrated more potential were trained in-house as power sewers, but that scheme failed to keep up with the demand for sewers as business increased. The furniture makers used the "looping" school as a model for the sewing school they opened in an annex at the English Street facility. The success of this small training center convinced the manufacturers to quest for a larger training facility at the same time a major initiative to industrialize North Carolina was underway in Raleigh.[6]

Governor Luther Hodges (1954–61) and members of the North Carolina General Assembly were seeking to improve the skill level of the state's workforce at the same time the Guilford County commissioners were deliberating the future of the county's abandoned TB hospital in Jamestown. This convergence of industrial and governmental initiatives leading to the creation of GTCC's embryo was almost too good to be true. Freshman state representative Clarence Edward "Ed" Kemp (Democrat) of High Point[7] was the youngest member of the North Carolina General Assembly in 1957 when House Speaker Kemp Dalton chose him to introduce a separate appropriations bill requesting funding for ten industrial education centers including, hopefully, one for Guilford County.

Aware that separate appropriations bills rarely made it through the General Assembly, the Speaker ordered Kemp to cautiously shepherd the $500,000 measure through the committee process until it reached the floor where it ultimately passed in conjunction with the somewhat misnamed Community College Act of 1957.[8] The Guilford County commissioners used the $50,000 they received to establish the first of the state's new industrial training centers in the former Guilford County TB Sanatorium on the eastern edge of historic Jamestown. On April 3, 1958, the State Board of Education approved the "Proposal for the Establishment of an Industrial Education Center," thereby establishing for Guilford County's 191,057 residents the training facility that evolved into Guilford Technical Community College.[9]

Representative Kemp chaired the Advisory Committee charged to assist and advise Guilford County's three public school boards in organizing and operating the center.[10] The committee moved quickly to establish a precedent for developing partnerships with professional and industrial organizations that defined the institution's productive history. The Piedmont Chapter of the American Society of Tool Engineers (ASTE) accepted an invitation to help design and plan a new shop for metal and machine operator courses and the Western Electric Company consented to help the College develop an electronics workshop and classroom.[11]

A Place of Hope Revisited

The Guilford Industrial Education Center (GIEC) was officially institutionalized on June 12, 1958,[12] on the grounds of the former Guilford County TB Sanatorium. The complex occupied a rolling wooded lot that formed part of a tract of 89.12 acres owned by the county and situated north of US Highways 29 A and 70 A on the eastern outskirts of Jamestown.[13] Ironically, the hospital that was built to help tubercular patients convalesce in the 1920s was transformed at mid-twentieth century into a recuperative technical center at which citizens could reinvent their skills and learn productive trades. The Institution emerged from a 1917 commitment by the State Board of Charities and Public Welfare to care for "the dependent, the defective, the delinquent and the seriously ill," which authorized any county to build and maintain a tuberculosis hospital by bond issue and special tax.[14]

The tuberculosis hospital that prominent Greensboro residents had discussed as early as 1916 to combat the invidious disease known as "the Men of Death" opened January 1, 1924. It expanded through the years to serve a maximum of 140 patients in 1936. When tremendous advancements in the prevention and treatment of the disease greatly reduced its threat, the hospital's Board recommended closing the facility. About 40 convalescents were transferred to the McCain Hospital in Moore County and the hospital was shuttered in September 1955. The hospital was never "a place to die," but a facility to help its patients return to a more productive life; GTCC maintains that tradition in its original footprint to this moment in time.[15]

Jamestown: 1958

When the Building and Grounds Department of the Guilford County Schools arrived to renovate the main buildings for the Guilford Industrial Training Center in 1958, three years of disuse and the elements had taken their toll. "Oh! My Lord!" Ed Kemp's first impression of the facility was one of utter dismay: "The buildings still looked pretty good, but hadn't been used in I don't know how many years; they were in a poor state of repair, dirty, floors were in bad shape."[16] Old Main, a 36,129 square-foot brick veneer structure with two story wings, was remodeled to provide classrooms and administrative offices with $50,000 from the county and numerous donations from business and industry. Bruce Roberts, who directed the Center from 1958 until it became GTI in 1965, reminisced about the school's opening on its twentieth anniversary in 1978:

> We opened in the fall of 1958 with about 42 students who transferred from the High Point program (on English Street). They studied knitting machine fixing, upholstery, and upholstery cutting and sewing. Our first staff consisted of six individuals including myself. Facility-wise, we had the former hospital's administrative building, two adjoining hospital wings, and a two story nurses' residence. I lived on campus in the house once occupied by the hospital administrator.[17]

Roberts neglected to mention that his wife Rachel, with whom he lived in the former home of sanatorium director Dr. M.D. Bonner, spent three days sweeping out Old Main before the start of classes.[18] Oral history interviews with early instructors suggest that the first students were often disadvantaged, poorly educated dropouts, many of whom were marginally socialized. During the 1960s the Center participated in a program promoted by Governor Terry Sanford to rehabilitate delinquent citizens recommended by probation officers, a program that aroused mixed sentiments among the faculty and staff.[19] Subjective observations aside, the Center was deemed a success at the end of 1959 when 593 students had enrolled in six courses and the staff had increased from an original cadre of three administrative personnel and three instructors to eleven full-time and ten part-time instructors. Machinery Hall with its 15,050 square feet was the first shop-building constructed on the Jamestown Campus. Completed in 1959 at a cost of $103,000, it cost approximately $7 per square-foot.[20]

The curriculum expanded in 1959–60 to include Automotive Mechanics, Machine Shop, Plumbing and Sanitation, Sheet Metal and Welding. Air Conditioning, Refrigeration and Industrial Chemistry were added in 1960–61; a variety of other programs were offered to special groups on an "as needed" basic. A Cooperative High School Program, introduced in 1959, provided vocational education for high school juniors and seniors as an integral part of their high school curricula. Completers received two units of high school credit. The GIEC enrolled 1,212 students for the spring 1961 semester and 225 for the following summer session. By this time, the state had allocated $60,000 to purchase tools and equipment to support courses in auto mechanics, welding, air conditioning, refrigeration, textiles, and heavy machinery.[21]

MDTA: 1962

The Federal Manpower Development and Training Act (MDTA), a gigantic workforce training program, broadened the Center's training mission by enabling it to offer an extensive series of programs. The measure was created to reduce unemployment and meet manpower needs by training unemployed individuals in communities without enough qualified applicants to fill the available business and industry jobs. The GIEC trained job applicants recruited by the Employment Security Commission (ESC) for jobs required by local industries.

The first MDTA programs were stenography, mechanical drafting, and air-conditioner mechanic training. Programs were eventually conducted as needed in over twenty separate job skills, including upholstery, sheet metal, welding, auto mechanics, restaurant cook, dental hygienist, chemist assistant, furniture wood-working, cashier-checker, and dental assistant. During the eight-year period ending June 30, 1970, over 1,600 trainees participated in 61 institutional programs; the MDTA produced more than 1,000 successful completers. This exceptionally productive federal program further benefited the school by providing administrators an opportunity to start programs that would have otherwise been impossible.[22]

A Question of Equality

The GIEC opened in concert with the New South ideal of industrial expansion at the same time the struggle to end racial segregation in the public schools enveloped North Carolina and Guilford County. Following the 1954 Supreme Court Brown vs. Board decision, token integration of the three public school systems in Guilford County began a long, often litigious, journey through the courts: Greensboro (1957), High Point (1959), and Guilford County 1965[23]. African-American activists were understandably concerned about the admission requirements of the Guilford Industrial Education Center from the moment the school was established.

The Guilford County Council of Negro Parents and Teachers Association asked E. P. Pearce, the Assistant Superintendent of the Guilford County Schools, in a letter dated September 10, 1958, for assurance that "an area school for technical training in Guilford County established by the State Department of Vocational Training and the County Board, would be open to all youth of the area served, so long as they meet the entrance requirements." When their query went unanswered, they posted a second and more politically strident letter (December 1, 1958): "We understood that State and Federal Funds are being used for the purchasing of equipment and other needs and we are assuming that this Institution will be open to all young citizens who meet the standards for admittance." Pearce responded three weeks later (December 23, 1958):

> At the present the program of industrial training in Guilford County is in its beginning stage and embodies only a small number of course offerings, which are designed primarily for adults. Problems of transportation and suitable schedule arrangements have made it virtually impractical to institute a countywide training program for high school students at this time. This matter is being studied and it is hoped that some solution will be forthcoming soon.[24]

Thirteen months later, February 1, 1960, the civil rights struggle intensified across Guilford County. Four African-American students from the North Carolina Agricultural and Technical College (now North Carolina A & T State University) sat down at the *Whites Only* lunch counter at the downtown Woolworth and refused to leave when denied service. On February 11, students from High Point's William Penn High School staged the civil rights movement's first non-college student protest when they sat-in at the South Main Street Woolworth lunch counter. [25]

A year and a half later, members of Greensboro's African-American community, who were tenaciously questioning educational employment practices, asked to appear before the GIEC advisory committee. Three members of the Greensboro Citizens Association (GCA) were subsequently invited to attend a "called meeting" of the committee on October 12, 1961. The organization's chairman reportedly asked GIEC chairman Ed Kemp to explain the background and policies governing the Guilford Industrial Education Center thus prompting this exchange:

> Chairman Kemp went into detail to explain the development of industrial education centers, the financial assistance, governmental backing, and policy-making procedures. Mr. Taylor was given an opportunity for comment and went into a detailed discussion of theological ethics and the personal persecution of his own boyhood and adult life.

> Mr. Allen, at this point, asked Mr. Taylor, "Just what is your problem?" Mr. Taylor did not voice a problem at this time, except that the "Board should be civil." Much later in Mr. Taylor's comments, the only concrete objection was that a picture should not be required on an application and that a job opportunity need not be available as a prerequisite to industrial training.

> Chairman Kemp advised Mr. Taylor that the picture situation would be considered, but the latter request was a policy set forth by the State Board of Education under which all centers operated.

> Mr. Taylor and his committee were thanked for coming and were cordially dismissed. A discussion ensued concerning the requirement of a picture and Mr. (W. H.) Marlette moved that we no longer require a photograph to be attached to an application blank. Mr. (John) Hardin seconded and the motion was carried.[26]

The Greensboro Citizens Association left with what might be considered a major moral victory considering that racial protests were seldom immediately successful. Tough confrontation provided an opportunity for African-Americans to apply with impunity at the young Institution; the acceptance of African-Americans in GIEC training programs was a moot point if employers were unwilling to hire them. Historian William Chafe (1980) discussed the implications of this perceived pattern of segregated employment that allegedly prevailed in Greensboro and Guilford County in the 1960s, and the reluctance of companies, institutions, and boards to voluntarily desegregate. Describing the appearance of the Greensboro Citizens Association before the Center's advisory committee, he portrayed the "catch-22" policies of the GIEC as an example of discrimination:

> Out of 1,212 students enrolled at the Industrial Education Center in Guilford County, only two were black. When the Greensboro Citizens Association, a black protest group, demanded to know why Negro applicants

were being rejected, the staff responded that the Institute accepted only those who could prove they had a job waiting for them when training was complete. Since the Negro applicants could not secure promised positions from employers, they were turned down for training. The vicious cycle was completed, of course, when editorial writers then explained away the black employment situation by saying that Negro young people had not taken advantage of the technical training available to them.[27]

It is unclear if dropping the admission requirement for a photo to accompany an application to the GIEC affected the enrollment of applicants. When the advisory committee discussed the number of "colored persons" who had "expressed an interest in training at the Center" on March 21, 1962, the group was surprised that since the last Board meeting on October 12, 1961, "each person who had asked for an application and was given one, had not returned it." The Greensboro Citizens Association could have been "testing the water," a common protest strategy during the civil rights struggle.[28]

A wealth of civil rights' era literature deals with the history of the movement in Guilford County, but as the protests continued, particularly in Greensboro, the major focus was on white businesses, restaurants, movie theaters, transportation, and restroom facilities. While the public school integration issue seethed on one level, one administrator suggested (1963) that "the integration issue was not a relevant issue as far as community college educators were concerned." According to Winfred L. Godwin, director of the Southern Regional Education Board, "while community colleges would increase higher educational opportunities for the Negro, it would be a serious and tragic distortion of the community college purpose to view it as the institution primarily for Negroes." However, segregation was becoming an issue closely aligned with federal funding and, in time, the community college would prove to be an invaluable source of skills training for African-Americans.[29]

The GIEC 1958–63

Five years after its inception, the GIEC employed seven administrative personnel, twenty full-time instructors, and sixteen part-time instructors; an expanding curriculum offered twelve vocational programs; additional courses provided on an "as-needed" basis included adult pre-employment training, skills-upgrading, and training for supervisory personnel and firemen. The changing technology of the era led to the creation of an evening program in keypunch and computer operations using IBM equipment in the Guilford County Tax Office.[30]

This period of Institutional growth is characterized by the creation of industrial, educational, and political partnerships with the singular goal of improving workforce productivity. The success of the GIEC is attributable to a variety of tangible and intangible factors beginning with the experience and character of the Institution's founders: hardnosed, practical industrialists, wily politicians, and committed educators with connections and clout who created a training center to upgrade worker productivity on the plant floor. Retrospectively, the creation of the Guilford Industrial Education Center in a climate of cooperation among business, government, and education may have been the county's finest moment; the incentive was the communal sharing of industrial profits; the fact that skills could improve the quality of life for the workers and their families had yet to resonate from a pastoral hillside in Jamestown.

GIEC Profile 1958–63

Year	Students	Faculty	Staff	Programs
1958–59	50–593	3	3	6
1959–60		11 FT 10 PT		11*
1960–61		20 FT 16 PT	7	14
1961–62				17*
1962–63				23*
*10 of these 23 programs including the MDTA courses were provided as needed.				

For its first year of operation (1958–59), the GIEC's enrollment increased ten-fold at a cost to the state and the county of $109,375.

1958–59 GIEC Expense Budget

Guilford County		$30,000.00
State		79,375.00
Total		$109,375.00
Capital Expenses		
Machinery Hall And Renovation		$75,000.00*
Instructional Supplies		$1,500.00**

* Wiggs, pp. 22-24.
** Carter, p. 6

Chapter 2

1963–65: From GIEC to GTI

North Carolina's system of 'comprehensive' community and technical colleges, sometimes characterized as a coordinated confederation, is the outgrowth of a legislated marriage in 1963 between an existing network of industrial education centers and a seminal system of public junior colleges.[1]

The Department of Community Colleges

The *Act to Promote and Encourage Education Beyond the High School* (1963) created the Department of Community Colleges as an agency of the State Board of Education. The Guilford Industrial Education Center was one of 19 similar centers transferred from the Department of Trade and Industrial Education to the new department along with two community colleges and eight units in which clusters of extension classes were offered. This action, institutionalizing the GIEC, vested its local control in an eight-member Board of Trustees split between appointees from the Guilford County School Board and the Guilford County Commissioners. Their eight-year terms were initially staggered to rotate two positions every two years.[2]

Policy-making continuity was assured for the new Institution when three veterans of the Industrial Education Center Project Committee and the GIEC Advisory Board were named Trustees. By appointing Ed Kemp, Zalph Rochelle and John R. Foster to the new GIEC Board, the county's governing bodies established a precedent to grow the Institution through institutional boards composed mainly of white males with extensive experience in business and politics. Their expertise as advocates for workforce training and fiscal responsibility would soon be tested in the rapidly changing social and technological climate that inevitably defined the future of the GIEC and its institutional successors. On September 9, 1963, the new Board elected Zalph Rochelle Chairman and James L. Williams Vice Chairman; the GIEC director, 34-year-old

Bruce B. Roberts, was selected Secretary and named as an ex-officio member of the Board.[3]

Percy Sears

The most historically significant Trustee appointed in 1963 was Greensboro resident and Guilford County commissioner Percy H. Sears. Known as "Mr. Republican," this socially committed politician, who worked as a manufacturer's representative and real estate developer, exerted a tremendous influence on the College for 31 years and 10 months from September 1963 to June 30, 1995. Shortly after taking his seat, Sears informed his colleagues that the Guilford County Commissioners were prepared to allocate $250,000 to build a Furniture Institute at the Center.[4] The penchant for detail that characterized Sears' lengthy tenure emerged when he declared that he would like to see "a record kept on each student for three to five years after completion (of their program) in order to see what was being accomplished." His perceptive suggestion that, "each instructor work with a committee from the type of industry he represents," probably prompted the development of the program advisory committees that have contributed tremendously to GTCC's successful program partnerships with business and industry. Sears advocacy for the Institution included every facet of its operation: construction, landscaping, grounds-keeping, parking, and student transportation.[5]

Furniture Hall: 1963

Assured of support from the county commissioners, now that Percy Sears was aboard, the Trustees moved to employ Greensboro architect J. Burton Wilder to design the Furniture Institute, which evolved into Furniture Hall in 1965. The *High Point Enterprise* strongly endorsed this enterprise by encouraging the commissioners to "furnish an adequate structure to make the furniture institute the outstanding such training project in the nation."[6] Architect Wilder envisioned an entirely new campus beginning with a stage-by-stage demolition of Old Main, then housing the school's administrative offices and many of its classrooms; the back of the building would be razed first to make room for the new Furniture Institute. The scheme projecting eleven new buildings established a precedent for grouping the major structures on the Jamestown campus on the high ground formerly occupied by the hospital complex.[7]

1963: Mertys W. Bell Library

The Center's library began operating in the administration building on a 20 hour a week, two nights a week schedule on January 14, 1963. By the time the facility celebrated National Library Week in April 1964, it housed more than 1,200 reference and technical books toward a goal of attaining 10,000. Nearly 11,000 visitors checked out almost 3,700 items in its first fifteen months. Mertys Bell, for whom the library was eventually named, described the early collection as "one of the best of its sort in the county." The collection was mainly comprised of technical and reference works associated with the Center's instructional programs. Aware that the library had quickly outgrown its makeshift quarters, Center director Bruce Roberts made its expansion a top priority.[8]

Enrollment: 1963–65

The GIEC grew steadily through 1963–64 by enrolling 1,710 students in trade (vocational) education and 295 in the technical curriculum. By the beginning of the 1964–65 academic year, the Center had trained over 7,000 people; classes were filled to capacity with 1,035 students in technical, distributive education, trade, practical nursing, and adult education classes. Construction began on Furniture Hall (September 1964) and its 1965 opening would predictably further boost enrollment. [9]

Programs: 1963–65

The GIEC did not function apart from the anxieties and challenges of the escalating Cold War and its associated national defense issues. A course for Civil Defense Shelter managers was one of the more intriguing subjects taught in 1963. Fallout shelters became a government prerogative after the 1962 Cuban Missile Crisis; though most were designated in public buildings, alarmed and energetic citizens erected shelters on their personal property, stocking them with survival supplies. A Radiation Safety Officer from Duke University taught the 40-hour Shelter Management course and the students attending from a 10-county area concluded the program by spending a night in a fallout shelter.

GTCC's immensely successful Adult Basic Education (ABE) program is traceable to a 1964 extension program that offered basic education courses in reading and writing to 82 adults at High Point's Chavis YMCA.[10] Percy Sears was ecstatic when the county commissioners passed along federal funds to promote adult education, a cause he championed. Consistently searching for money to alleviate Guilford County's literacy gap and supporting the Equal Opportunity Act (EOA), Sears was a stickler for fiscal responsibility and requested a quarterly report detailing enrollment and financial information.[11]

Business Education and Commercial Art and Advertising Design were added to the curriculum in 1965. The first mention of a "practical nursing course," eventually established in 1965, occurred during the July 22, 1964, Board session. High Point Hospital officials were interested in providing a one-year program for nursing candidates as an alternative to their three-year program; the GIEC would teach the theoretical courses and the hospital would provide the clinical experience.[12] In seven productive years, the GIEC evolved into an educational institution recognized for service to youth, adults and industry in Guilford County. Its maturation provides an intriguing study of how workforce preparedness initiatives succeed when community leaders understand the necessity for training and retooling and then react by forming partnerships with education, industry and government.

Expansion: GIEC-GTI 1965

Financing programs in the Community College System, a major theme in this study, is an ongoing challenge because the institutions are prohibited from using state funds to start them. Funding is based on full-time equivalent formulas paid in arrears and not always in full. By early 1965, a persistent concern with the Center's fiscal restraints convinced the Board to consider the financial advantages inherent in upgrading to a technical institute. Dr. I. E. Ready, Director of the Department of Community Colleges, briefed the Trustees on the differences between industrial education centers and technical institutes in July 1964. The arguments for expansion were obvious: the expanding enrollment mirrored a rapidly escalating need to train students to fill job vacancies in the county's industrial plants; classes were at capacity with prospective students waiting for vacancies to enroll; with the clincher being that by the nature of their mission, technical institutes were funded at a higher rate than industrial education centers.[13]

An impressive series of Board decisions in April–May 1965 dramatically improved the opportunities for workforce training in Guilford County. The initial transformation occurred on April 2, 1965, when the Board unanimously authorized Chairman Rochelle to petition the State Board of Education to elevate the Center to a technical institute within North Carolina's 34-unit network of community colleges, technical institutes, and industrial education centers. This new status, making the school eligible for federal and state funds, was actually the second of three steps mandated by North Carolina's Higher Education Act of 1963 to enable industrial education centers to expand to community college status,[14] which included college transfer possibilities for students—a possibility deemed unnecessary by the elitist editors of the *Greensboro Record*: "The Guilford facility, in reaching the second step (technical institute), has no urgent need to expand into the liberal arts field. The county has seven other colleges that have amply taken care of that."[15]

Few affluent residents would have supported the comprehensive community college concept at that time but, in retrospect, Guilford's prospective college students were as worthy of a low cost alternative to the local private colleges and state universities as were the residents of neighboring Alamance, Davidson, Randolph, and Rockingham counties, all of which possessed comprehensive community colleges. Ironically, we know now that a comprehensive community college could have made a major difference in the lives of thousands of Guilford County students by providing economical, comparable quality college transfer courses. From a fiscal point of view, liberal arts courses, which were relatively inexpensive to schedule, would have provided a source of revenue to finance the more expensive nursing and dental programs. In the context of the period, many people were unaware of the community college mission in higher education.

The crux of the original argument centered on the supposition that adding the college parallel (transfer) liberal arts programs, specific to the curriculum of a comprehensive community college, would diminish the original mission of the industrial education center to train skilled workers for the technical trades.[16] In addition, there were widespread, generally unsubstantiated fears that, "community colleges" might transition into private junior colleges and on to four-year institutions negating the need for an occupational-vocational institution to train skilled industrial workers. The line in the sand on GIEC's expansion to a comprehensive community college was eventually drawn between Board Chair Zalph Rochelle's dogged insistence on technical training to provide skilled labor for the county's factories, possibly to thwart union intrusion into High Point's furniture plants and a future president's vision of GTI as a comprehensive community college, or as some observers speculated, "Jamestown University."[17]

A Change in Leadership

The Board interviewed Dr. Herbert F. Marco, Dean of Academic Affairs at the Cumberland Technical Institute in Maryland as a possible successor to

GIEC co-founder Bruce Roberts on April 2, 1965; Roberts had directed the Center since its inception in 1958. Marco, an exceptionally credentialed and experienced administrator, appears to have been the sole contender for the position; the minutes do not reveal a reason for replacing Roberts, or a list of candidates under consideration. When the State Board of Education accepted Robert's resignation in May, officials said he had requested to be relieved because of illness, but planned to remain on the faculty in an administrative capacity.[18] According to Mrs. Roberts, it was understood from the beginning of the Marco administration that Roberts would leave the school. The Board was still dealing with the issue of Robert's relationship with the school on July 20, 1965, when chairman Rochelle revealed that he had written a letter to Mr. and Mrs. Bruce Roberts "declaring them *persona non grata* on the campus."[19]

This letter evidently ended a lengthy professional relationship between two of GTCC's founding fathers; it could possibly have been an eviction notice to Roberts, then occupying the house the Board wished to remodel for Marco.[20] Whatever the reason(s) for his departure, his contribution as the Institution's founding director remains untainted and his 1978 comments published with those of Rochelle, Kemp, and others on the founding of the Guilford Industrial Education Center in "Decades of Development," are devoid of bitterness.[21]

Dr. Herbert F. Marco

After voting to become a technical institute at the historic session on April 2, 1965, the Board offered Dr. Herbert F. Marco the directorship of the Guilford Industrial Education Center effective May 2, 1965. A scientist and engineer with degrees from Cornell, Syracuse, and Yale, and a decorated World War II bomber pilot, Dr. Marco served on the team that established the Air Force Institute of Technology in Ohio. The experience he accrued directing that project through the accreditation process to a doctoral granting institution presumably prepared him to mold a fledgling technical institute into a first class institution. "Sputnik," and the resulting space race between the U.S and the Soviet Union, guided Marco into the missile and rocket industry and inevitably to the National Aeronautics and Space Administration where he worked in research and development. While he may have been an abrupt, abrasive tactician, GTI was presumably fortunate to have an experienced academic of his caliber.[22]

In view of Board's intention to maintain the school as a technical institute, as opposed to transforming it into a comprehensive community college, hiring Marco may not have been the best decision. The minutes reveal that, from the moment of his acceptance, Marco had a broader view of adult education than some of the Trustees:

> Dr. Marco stated a challenge to offer to adults something more mean-ingful to their lives (presumably than technical training) and mentioned a course in government for better understanding by the people. Percy Sears stated that they (the Trustees) want to stick to the industrial in-terest and mentioned the EOA (Economic Opportunity Act) pointing out that the Board needs to discuss the EOA program with Dr. Marco.[23]

Marco's vision of a civics course with its liberal implications and Sears' al-liance with Rochelle to maintain the industrial training mission, grounded the debate two years later when Marco battled publicly with Board members over his proposal to advance the school to community college status. In 1965, the Board was ecstatic, if not desperate for personnel reasons, over the opportu-nity to employ an administrator with broad technical experience as well as academic credentials. With the Center becoming Guilford Technical Institute (GTI), Marco was promoted from Director to President and the county com-missioners were asked to supplement his pay, renovate a residence for him, and pay his moving expenses.[24]

The State Board of Education, with the concurrence of the Department of Community Colleges, approved Marco's presidency after only four days as Director and the expansion of the GIEC to Guilford Technical Institute on May 6, 1965. The decision authorized the school to offer technical, trade, gen-eral adult, and community service programs as well as award the Associate in Applied Science degree in technical curricula. The decision also paved the way for Governor Dan K. Moore to appoint four new Trustees, increasing Board membership to an even dozen, to guide the school toward a greater destiny as Guilford County's unique educational institution.[25]

While Dr. Marco would not be inaugurated as the first president of Guil-ford Technical Institute for more than a year, he appeared confident and solidly in control at his first presidential Board meeting on Tuesday, June 8, 1965. He outlined a series of new accounting procedures, introduced new faculty, and specified several maintenance initiatives for the campus. The Trustees com-mended his presentation and, noting that High Point was "sold on the pro-gram," suggested that "Dr. Marco needs to speak in Greensboro." Western Elec-tric CEO, W. O. Conrad, indicated that he would pass the word along to the Rotary Club, by far the most important civic club in the city. Whatever Marco might have accomplished in answer to this assignment was undoubtedly negated in a week-long series of investigative articles by *Greensboro Daily News* reporter Jerry Bledsoe (February, 1967). For a variety of reasons, selling the College to Greensboro during its first fifty years proved to be a major challenge for the Institution's leadership.[26]

GTI: Greensboro 1965

Guilford County may not be unique as a county in the United States, but it must rank high on the list of most fractious. The contentious historical relationship between Greensboro and High Point has been documented to a degree by twentieth-century historians.[27] Some argue that GTI figured prominently in this feud between the two cities. For example Greensboro considered GTI a High Point project; the institution was founded in High Point by High Point educators and businessmen who directed the Board for almost ten years. The main campus was located in Jamestown, a rural community at the eastern edge of High Point with strong ties to that city's leaders. GTI programs relegated to Greensboro were installed in second-hand school buildings and other generally unattractive locations; none of the Greensboro programs approached signature status.

The lack of a positive Greensboro image of GTCC across more than 40 years is ironic given the prestigious list of inaugural Board members who resided in the city: W. O. Conrad, Western Electric; John R. Foster, Odell Mill Supply; Russell F. Hall, Wysong & Miles; Percy Sears, the indomitable entrepreneur; H. Frank Starling, Cone Mills, Inc.; and James L. Williams, Blue Bell, Inc. These skilled executives directed high profile companies with positive public images and most of their successors from the Gate City were high profile leaders. However, GTI's industrial training mission could not distinguish the school in a city blessed with a boutique assortment of liberal arts institutions. Not until the Board chairmanship of former Cone Mills CEO Pat Danahy (2001–04) did GTCC make the first major step toward selling the College to Greensboro by building in 2005 the East Wendover Campus. In fact, the ramifications of this project in answer to the careless omission of the College from the 1999 "McKinsey Report," an economic survey commissioned by a consortium of Greensboro foundations, is a major topic in Chapter 28.[28]

Summary

President Marco confidently expected to enroll 400 full-time students for the 1965–66 academic year; he further believed he had a good chance of getting at least $250,000 of the $323,000 budget he had requested. On July 20, 1965, he told the Board that the Department of Community Colleges had verbally approved the former center's vocational programs in Auto Mechanics, Furniture Upholstery, Welding, Knitter-Fixer, Drafting, and Cosmetology. Technical Curriculum programs receiving verbal approval included Electrical Technology, Mechanical Technology, Furniture Engineering, Business Administration, Medical and Executive Secretarial Courses, Practical and Registered Nurse Programs, and the Dental Assistant and Dental Hygienist Programs. Marked by its expansion to Guilford Technical Institute, the naming of its first president, and an inaugural visit from N.C. Governor Dan K. Moore rank the summer of 1965 as one of the most exciting periods in the Institution's history; however, as Marco and his Board soon discovered, expansion is often problematic and subject to growing pains.[29]

Dr. Herbert F. Marco
President GT 1965–1967

1967 Upholstery Class (LR) Steve Farabee, Levon Hazelton, Randall Chandler, James Ledbetter, Dewitt Nelson, Grayson Weaver, Tony McNeal, and Ronnie Prevate.

1967 Knitter Fixing Class (LR) Randy Myrick, Ray Allen, Arthur Smith, Randy Rich, Harold Barber, Harold R. Robertson, and Bobby Caulder.

1967 Sheet Metal Class (LR) Steve Ward, Clifton Robertson, Rex Evans, Barry Friddle, Danny Edwards, and Instructor A.M. Covington.

Virginia Bangiola, seen here with Art Department Chair Ralph E. Calhoon, received the first Associate in Applied Science Degree awarded by GTI on May 22, 1966.

Graduates at GTI's first commencement, Sunday, June 11, 1967.

Section II

The Marco Administration
1965–1967

Chapter 3

Growing Pains

Keep in mind that hundreds of deserving students are being turned away from four-year colleges and universities for various reasons. These students must not be denied an education or treated as second class citizens.[1]

Herbert Marco, GTI President

Dedication Day: August 19, 1965

Planning for the dedication of GTI occupied the Board and staff in the weeks following the May 6, 1965, decision that expanded the training center to a technical institute. Since Governor Dan K. Moore was scheduled to speak, the invitation list included Guilford County's significant political, business and media representatives. On the eve of the event, Marco's announcement that more than 600 applications had been received for the 1965 fall term prompted this magnanimous editorial endorsement.[2]

> The Institute deserves all the support it can get from the county. It will become an increasingly important factor in Guilford's pursuit of new industry. The availability of labor is an essential part of any industrial expansion program, but it doesn't do much good to have labor available if there is no place to train it.[3]

"The sun is shinning, things look good for the Institute." August is not the Piedmont's most stable weather month. Sweltering heat and humidity greeted Governor Moore when he arrived on the Jamestown campus for the 3:00 P.M. ceremony. Recalling the two hot Democratic gubernatorial primaries waged against Greensboro Federal Judge L. Richardson Preyer, Moore assured the audience of approximately 300 that he had forgotten the blistering campaigns

27

and proceeded to stress the need for unity, education, action, and cooperation to support the state's industrial development:[4]

> A state can rise no higher than the abilities of its people. The ignorant, the illiterate, the unskilled worker, the school dropout; these failures of our educational system are often failures in our social and economic system.
>
> Guilford Technical Institute and other institutions of this type offer solutions to these problems. They allow North Carolinians to develop their abilities.
>
> This is no time for apathy. This is a time for action. This is a time for all North Carolinians to unite on all levels, township, city, county, and state, to recognize the needs of industry and economic development and to meet those needs.[5]

The celebration concluded with the dedication of Furniture Hall, a 30,040-square-foot shop built for $263,000 ($8.75 per square foot), and the recognition of four new Board members allocated by virtue of the school's expansion to a technical institute. The high profile appointees represented a variety of industries; Cone Mills executive H. Frank Starling worked for the world's largest denim manufacturer; John T. Davis, Jr., soon succeeded (1967) his father as president of Davis Furniture Industries, Inc.; Robert O. Kistler was a Boren Clay Products executive; and John W. Thompson presided over the Thompson-Arthur Paving Company.

Program Update: 1965–66

At the beginning of the GTI era, 20 full-time and 20 part-time faculty taught 290 full-time students, 145 in the evening programs; 90 high school students were enrolled as were a number of special students in art and supervisory training courses.[6] They were supported by four administrators and seven clerical personnel.[7] The curriculum included nine technical programs leading to the Associate in Applied Science (AAS) degree; ten one-year vocational programs, adult education classes, extension courses, supervisory personnel development training, and a variety of one-time courses conducted through the Manpower Development and Training Act (MDTA). Biology and physics labs in the Health Science building, formerly the nurses' home, were pronounced fully equipped and available to students in the Dental Hygiene and Dental Assistant programs paid for and equipped through the MDTA and supervised by the Institute.[8] Plans were underway to broaden the college experience by creating a series of student awards and establishing a Recognition Day.

The Institution's lengthy association with Cosmetology began when GTI assumed responsibility for the vocational program previously operated by the Greensboro Public Schools. Cosmetology remained at the McIver School, 643 West Lee Street, in Greensboro until its relocation to Furniture Hall in June 1968. GTI also adopted the Practical Nursing program formerly operated by the Greensboro Public Schools and the Moses H. Cone Memorial Hospital.[9] Beyond these acquisitions, the Institute's admission standards were revamped to conform to a Department of Community Colleges directive requiring students to be eighteen years of age or high school graduates; this move presumably terminated the Cooperative High School Program (Est. 1959) then enrolling 90 students.[10]

The State of the Institution

Chairman Zalph Rochelle and Russell Hall were the sole Board members present to welcome Governor Moore's four new appointees to their first session on September 15, 1965. Since six Trustees did not constitute a quorum, Rochelle deferred the business agenda and asked President Marco to brief the new Trustees on the state of the Institution.

The president seized on this topic to ask the Trustees to immediately consider expanding the Institute to a community college in order to have a "licensed nursing program." His intention to view the technical institute designation as a short step on route to community college status was clearly on the table. Chairman Rochelle did not open the floor for discussion on Marco's request and ended the session by congratulating the president on the organizational progress accomplished during his first two months as CEO.

In fact, GTI faced major academic and spatial challenges; ninety percent of the school's students had failed recent mathematics and English tests (September 10–11, 1965), a situation Marco attributed to "the high schools and the homes," still a valid excuse forty years later. Only one advanced English class was on the schedule with the majority of the students enrolled in remedial or developmental courses. Added to the faculty to meet the enrollment increase, four new teachers taught classes staggered from 7:15 A.M. until 10 P.M.

While space for programs was near capacity in some areas, Marco determined that parking was *the* major problem at the Institute. Echoing Percy Sears' concern that the front lawn was being ruined, he suggested creating parking spaces along the railroad tracks at the rear of the campus on land deemed unsuitable for classrooms. Emotional arguments aside, the ongoing "Jamestown campus parking issue" begs for a practical, reasonable analysis that would have possibly provided for new construction nearer the Greensboro-High Point Road with strategically incorporated peripheral parking softened by creative landscaping. However, the belief that the "beautiful front lawn and the pines and crepe myrtles" should be preserved had been institutionalized. Forty years later, GTCC president Don Cameron, who was still wrestling with the issue, characterized the "parking problem as a walking problem."[11]

Organized Labor

Attendance at the October 12, 1965, Board meeting improved measurably as Zalph Rochelle gaveled 11 of 12 Trustees present to re-elect him unanimously for another term as chairman. Given the harmonious atmosphere, it would have been difficult to foresee this unanimity collapsing and emblazoning media headlines within two years. The Trustees listened as President Marco summarized a series of apparently contentious conversations with various unions in the Greensboro area who were seeking the school's help to train apprentices according to union rules. These unions wanted GTI to pay the instructors hired by the unions to teach unsupervised programs set up under union criteria.

When Marco refused to accommodate their unreasonable demands, the union spokesmen presumably threatened to go over his head and take their proposal to the Department of Community Colleges. As the Board discussed the political implications of this strong-arm tactic, Board member and High Point College President Dr. Wendell Patton argued that the implementation of union apprenticeship training was an administrative decision and the Board should confine itself to policy; his suggestion that, "if the unions wanted to appeal Marco's decision they could appear before the Board," evolved into a unanimously approved motion. There were apparently no repercussions to Marco's refusal to consider the union's proposition and the issue disappeared. Apprenticeship opportunities were eventually instituted years later through a series of industrial partnerships negotiated by the College and area CEOs.[12]

No industrialist in Guilford County was prepared to take a union threat lightly considering that rumblings of unionization plagued them at least until 1975. If, as rumored, Zalph Rochelle was indeed the "furniture czar" charged to hold off the unions, he had every reason for vigilance.[13] The first major move to organize furniture workers in High Point occurred in March 1906 when the city's furniture makers fired employees belonging to a "fledgling union," and gave their jobs to non-union employees. Thirteen years later, in August 1919, a series of wildcat strikes precipitated the "worst upheaval" in the history of the southern furniture industry. Non-union workers sympathized with the strikers and the governor was called on to mediate the crisis; a closed shop was out of the question, but management promised not to retaliate and accepted the principle of collective bargaining.[14]

Wage cuts and deteriorating working conditions triggered a major strike in High Point's hosiery mills in 1932, but this was settled congenially, presumably without involving the national unions. During the violent labor incidents that rocked the Carolinas in 1934, "flying squadrons" of Textile Workers Union of America members descended on mills in the county where they were repulsed by loyal workers and national guardsmen. Almost 100 textile mills in the state closed on September 3, 1934, when workers joined a nationwide walkout. The strike at the Highland Mill in High Point lasted 13 weeks in a dispute that ended only in response to an appeal by President Franklin Delano Roosevelt on September 23, 1934. As Elizabeth Wheaton (1987) pointed out, "Anti-unionism in North Carolina is as much a way of life as textiles and tobacco."[15]

College Transfer: The 1965 Debate

The public perception of GTI, and the issue of language describing "college level courses" and "transferable credits," dominated a long segment of the lengthy October 12, 1965, Board session. Vice-chair James L. Williams wondered, "if recent newspaper releases and other publicity" were erroneously leading the general public to believe "that the Institute offers courses on the same level with a liberal arts college, when in fact these students would not be able to transfer to another (4-year) institution and receive academic credit for courses taken at the Institute."

Dr. Marco replied that, "the Institute's catalog states that it is entirely up to the receiving institution to determine whether or not a student can transfer credits earned at the Institute;" he did not believe the catalog was at fault for stating that GTI offered "college level courses in such fields as English and mathematics." Marco argued that this "philosophy" was backed by the State Board of Education and the Department of Community Colleges; he further claimed that GTI's instructors were "as fully qualified to teach these courses as any employed by a liberal arts college."

Dr. Patton challenged Marco by pointing out that "inasmuch as the Institute is not accredited, (by the Southern Association of Colleges and Universities, SACS), it should not use the phrase transferable credits." At this point, Chairman Rochelle reminded the Trustees "that the basic purpose of the Board of Trustees and the administration is to run a good school and to train people for industrial growth in this area." Rochelle believed these instructional objectives were being accomplished and observed that, "while the confusion (over college-level courses, or transferable credits) was not new, it could be attributed to "wrong publicity." He reminded the Board that students were enrolled to study toward an Associate in Applied Science degree and reiterated that "the Institute is in no way competing with the liberal arts colleges." Vice Chair Williams wanted the issue settled on the spot, but Rochelle tabled any discussion of "transferable college credits" to the November 9, 1965, Board session prompting the inclusion of this disclaimer in the minutes:

> Some statements and suggestions were made by Dr. Wendell Patton, which were inadvertently omitted from the minutes (of the October 12, 1965, meeting). More specifically he (Patton) requested that Dr. Marco obtain statements from accredited colleges and universities in North Carolina as to whether or not they would allow credit for work completed at Guilford Technical Institute. Dr. Marco replied that these arrangements would be made when a Guilford Technical Institute graduate would request a transfer. He has already discussed this matter with two college presidents and this was their recommendation.[16]

Patton was not in attendance at the November 9, 1965, Board session when a lengthy letter Marco had written him (November 1, 1965), attempting to clarify the catalog language regarding "transferable credits," was inserted in the minutes. Marco argued that because the Institution was qualified to award the Associate in Applied Science Degree and was recognized by the American Association of Junior Colleges, "it teaches many courses which necessarily must be at the college level." He dispelled Patton's concern that vocational courses might be considered transferable, implying that, "it is doubtful that any graduate of our technical programs would apply for transfer credits to a liberal arts college, but they, in all probability, would go to another technical school or university."

> The receiving institution would consider each transfer request separately and accept or reject it accordingly, even though our curriculums were accredited by all associations. But our course credits are transferable to all community and technical institutes in our system, according to the Chairman of the State Board of Education. All this you already know. In

addition, we are cooperating closely with the University's dental school in case some of our students should desire to go on to a baccalaureate. We have been tentatively accepted by the Auburn Community College in New York State for transfer purposes. Similar arrangements are being made or will be made with other institutions such as Guilford College and NC State University for our outstanding students. We are a brand new technical institute and, as you know, we must be in operation for some time before we can seek accreditation by out-of-state agencies. The only commitment which we can effect is that transfers will be made on an individual basis.[17]

The crux of Marco's argument rests with the possibility that individual colleges and universities would consider accepting transfer credits from GTI on an individual basis; but the combative advocate for community college status proceeded to argue that, "no institution in our country has a monopoly on the English language, American government, mathematics and other *basic* educational courses." Reluctant to end on a conciliatory note, he admonishes the High Point College President to; "Keep in mind that hundreds of deserving students are being turned away from four-year colleges and universities for various reasons. These students must not be denied an education or treated as second class citizens." [18]

This exchange was the opening round in a debate that was only resolved in 1983 when GTI was awarded comprehensive community college status and expanded to Guilford Technical Community College. Marco, the abrasive academic visionary, had challenged two strong opposing forces that would align against GTI's quest for community college status: Board members determined to maintain the focused technical training mission of the Institution and the county's private liberal arts colleges who were convinced they would lose students to GTI should the Institution adopt a college transfer program. Dr. Patton, an administrator with a huge stake in the latter issue, resigned from the Board in August 1966.[19]

Tech Talk

One product of Marco's desire to enhance GTI as a student-oriented Institution resulted in the introduction of a student newspaper in November 1965. The inaugural *Tech Talk* headlined the school's first student body election when Luther Seawell was elected President; Lance Maners, Vice President; Janie O'Ham, Secretary; and Jan Upchurch, Treasurer. According to the publication, GTI's female students, the "girls" of that era, were interested in sports activities including bowling and golf. The "boys" enjoyed playing football on campus, but practice sessions between classes were discontinued for lack of insurance to compensate students for injuries. The students' interest in sports was also tempered by their practical recognition that late afternoon classes and jobs conflicted with practice. The introductory *Tech Talk* alluded to a high degree of school spirit on campus with contented students enjoying the collegiality of their brand new technical institute. [20]

Precis

Herbert Marco may have swept his eyes across the picturesque Jamestown campus at the end of 1965 revelling as much in the facility's growth as in its promise for the future. He may have mused over the temper of his Board and the undercurrent of emotion attending the issue of "transferable credits." At the same time, he may have been formulating a strategy to jumpstart the Institute toward designation as a community college with an even broader vision of a "Jamestown University."[21] No one can doubt Marco's empathy for workers who he believed needed civic instruction beyond narrow vocational and occupational training to make their lives successful, or demean his concern for the plight of those students turned away without recourse from four-year institutions. Considering that his inauguration was five months away (May 22, 1966) and that his philosophy aligned him against a powerful Board, he might have wondered if the event would actually occur or what impact his philosophy would have on his career. As the forthcoming months proved, he was not a man to lead a "second rate institution."

Chapter 4

A Second-Rate Institution, or a Provisional Open Door?

One of the main reasons for wanting to become a community college is to do all we can to encourage industry by making an education available to children of people who are moving into this area with new industry.

Herbert Marco

January 1966: Program Update

1966 emerged as the most contentious year in the Institution's brief existence as Herbert Marco attempted to achieve community college status and thus avoid the stigma of remaining "a second rate institution."[1] It soon became apparent that his broader concept of the Institute exceeded the practical expectations of the industrialists on his Board. This was the major issue confronting the school's leaders during a furious period of growth that taxed the Institute's facilities and financial resources. The year's top priorities included winning a spot for GTI on a proposed bond issue, planning new construction, and confronting the issues extending from a rapid increase in programs and student enrollment. Some of the most historic Board meetings in GTCC's history were conducted during the 1966 calendar year.

To attract public interest, GTI introduced 17 new extension courses in January 1966, including a broad range of "how-to" topics from personal income tax, wills, trusts, and deeds, to "Know Your Automobile," a course specifically designed for women at risk of being duped by disreputable auto mechanics. The ongoing creation of short-term courses and new programs—and the necessity to market them—spurred the Trustees to discuss how to efficiently advertise classes during an era when the newspapers consented to print the schedules for free, at least once. Zalph Rochelle and John Davis volunteered to raise money for radio commercials, but the creation of a marketing department was not broached.

A Fundamentals Learning Laboratory, coordinated by Mary I. Breeze, opened to provide individual instruction with programmed materials. This learning system enabled students to prepare themselves in any subject from grade school through high school and, following the required examinations and equivalency tests, qualify for a high school diploma presented by the Guilford County Schools. Adult basic education classes offering reading, writing, and arithmetic through the eighth-grade were taught at YMCAs in Greensboro and High Point.

The institution profited in program development thanks to grants from the Manpower Development and Training Act (MDTA). These federal dollars supported carpentry, masonry, and Nurses' Aide classes at A & T College (now North Carolina A&T State University) in Greensboro. A $379,095 MDTA grant implemented the Dental Hygiene and Dental Assistant programs and $62,000 funded the Chemical Assistant program; an MDTA sheet metal course began with 20 students in January 1966. During this same period, the College was training more than 100 employees for the Gilbert and Barker Company (Gilbarco), the major gasoline pump maker that relocated to Guilford County from New England.[2]

Facilities: 1966

GTI's physical plant included four buildings when the Jamestown campus expanded to approximately 46 acres in 1966. "Old Main," the former hospital's major building, housed the library, administrative offices, bookstore, student lounge, commercial art labs, a textile machine laboratory, and classrooms. Health Science's biology and clinical practice labs and classrooms occupied the former nurses' home, while air-conditioning, automotive, electrical, machine tool, and welding shops and a chemistry lab were lodged in Machinery Hall.[3] Furniture Hall contained upholstery and woodworking shops, classrooms, a student lounge, and faculty offices. The demand for space prompted the Board to consider adding a second floor to Machinery Hall, seeking space in the McIver and Central public schools in Greensboro, and asking the county commissioners "to dedicate all county lands around the present Technical Institution for the Institute's use."[4]

The physical plant priorities included a new library-classroom building and a cafeteria, but maintaining the aging sanatorium structures threatened to drain the school's meager financial resources. Extensive repairs, including some critical ones, were needed, but budget concerns halted improvements to grounds and buildings for the remainder of the year. Wearing his twin sombreros as county commissioner and GTI Trustee, Percy Sears emerged as a powerful advocate when funding contingencies challenged the Institution.[5] Early in 1966, he suggested that the Board should start thinking about the architectural style of the buildings planned for the campus since there was a possibility of taking a $500,000 bond issue to the voters in April. Chairman Rochelle suggested adhering to the style of the administration building, the sanatorium's venerable "Old Main." The new Machinery Hall and Furniture Hall were flat roofed in contrast to the old hospital structures, leading Marco to suggest that additional floors could be added, but that form of expansion never occurred.[6]

Expansion and Subterfuge

Percy Sears and Herbert Marco presented GTI's case for inclusion in a proposed school bond issue to a joint meeting of the Guilford County Commissioners and the county's three school boards on February 7, 1966. Sears told the panel that 1,200 students were occupying all the available space at GTI including the new Furniture Hall and remodeled rooms in the former hospital buildings; classes were staggered from 7 o'clock in the morning until 10 o'clock at night to accommodate the influx of students. Marco pleaded for additional land, a library, a cafeteria, and more classrooms to cope with an escalating enrollment. The presentations resonated with the assembled policy makers who approved $500,000 for the Institute as part of an April referendum.

What appeared to be a positive financial boost for the school quickly soured as the proposed bond issue cracked the Board's usually consistent solidarity: High Point College President Dr. Wendell Patton emphatically refused to support the expansion of GTI to a comprehensive community college. Dr. Patton said,

> I want to go on record as being opposed to the bond issue because of plans to change the status of the Technical Institute to a Community College and cast my vote NO in favor of its being placed on the County referendum pertaining to this matter.[7]

Patton's objections did not deter the majority decision to pursue community college status, and the Board quickly moved to accomplish this objective (February 8, 1966). Percy Sears suggested that Marco and Trustees Zalph

Rochelle, John Davis, and Frank Starling form a strategy committee to consult with Director Ready at the Department of Community Colleges before submitting the expansion proposal to the governor. Board Chair Rochelle, ever the defender of the school's technical-training mission, chimed in with a reminder from the Board's executive committee: "If the status of the Institute changed, the name Guilford Technical Institute should be retained as Guilford Technical Institute and Community College."

Marco responded that he had briefed Ready about the expansion in a recent telephone conversation and recounted his rationale:

> One of the main reasons for wanting to become a community college is to do all we can to encourage industry by making an education available to children of people who are moving into this area with new industry.[8]

Community college status would also funnel more money to the library, fund additional staff, earn students the right to transfer credits, and prevent the school from becoming what it apparently was in Marco's estimation, "a second rate institution." Marco added that State Attorney General Wade Bruton had ruled that GTI could become a community college without submitting its expansion to a public referendum.

Topics introduced during this historic Board session involving the increasingly disaffected Trustee Dr. Wendell Patton rebounded in confrontation and correspondence through August 1966. Patton was specifically offended by Percy Sears' suggestion that the Board consider withholding a public announcement of the Institute's desire to become a community college until the bond issue had been decided; Sears' suggestion that if the bonds passed, the State Board would be less inclined to question GTI's ambitious expansion, elicited this response from Patton in a February 15, 1966, letter to Marco:

> The thing that disturbs me particularly is the apparent attempt to get the bond issue passed before the public is told that an attempt may be made to become a community college. I hope you understand why I feel that I cannot be a party to such subterfuge.[9]

Patton was additionally irked by Chairman Rochelle's announcement that GTI had been granted membership in the American Association of Junior Colleges.[10] In a letter (May 16, 1966) he indicated that recognition and accreditation as a junior college did not command any prestige or authority. Patton's argument reflected on the following statement attributed to Jesse R. Barnet, Assistant to the Executive Director, AAJC:

This Association is not an accrediting body, nor does membership in the American Association of Junior Colleges in any way imply accreditation of the Institution by this Association.[11]

From the moment of his appointment to the Board, there are indications that Patton was professionally displeased with Marco's opportunistic stretch toward community college status and any strategy associated with that objective. Marco's initiative to expand the Institute, and threaten High Point College's enrollment with college transfer courses, contradicted the promise tendered to Patton by the county commissioners when they appointed him to the Board that "a community college would never be considered for this area." By the time he resigned on August 9, 1966, Patton had ample reason to consider Marco's attempt to expand a violation of these principles.[12]

March 8, 1966

The creation of the GTCC Foundation, Inc., in 1966 provides a brief but positive break from the dissension smoldering around the community college expansion. The forerunner of today's prestigious organization was chartered and approved by North Carolina's legendary Secretary of State Thad Eure effective February 18, 1966. GTI's twelve Trustees subsequently voted to appoint themselves as full directors on the Foundation Board and empowered themselves to appoint eight additional members to one year terms.[13]

April 12, 1966

Expansion to a community college was only one of the growth issues confronting the Board in 1966; the necessity to establish a temporary branch in Greensboro was crucial to the Institute's mission. There were two possibilities for the location: a former factory site and an abandoned school building. Greensboro classes were already taught at various locations presumably convenient to students, but the need to expand services to the city was a crucial issue, if only to take some program pressure off the burdened Jamestown campus. The era of expanding transient facilities in Greensboro was about to commence, and for a variety of reasons 37 years would pass before Guilford Technical Community College broke ground for its first totally new campus on East Wendover Avenue.[14]

The tremendous gift GTI received from the citizens of Guilford County on April 12, 1966, softened the conversion controversy that began to affect the Institute during this crucial year. On a $14 million bond issue, a light turnout of voters approved school construction in the county including $500,000 for GTI. The margin was 11,282 to 2,048, assuring the construction of a new library-classroom building. Their approval forecast a boost in the tax rate in Guilford County, from 2 to 5 cents per $100 property evaluation by the 1971–72 fiscal year.[15]

Countdown to Controversy

The accounting procedures instituted by Marco's administration more clearly defined GTI's fiscal operations beginning with the first quarter of 1966 when the president reported that the March payroll totaled $60,000. On the credit side of the ledger, the Institute was on track to receive around $1.0 million from the MDTA programs that had already paid the school approximately $2.0 million.[16] The possibility that GTI would soon expand to a community college attracted a flurry of press attention and bold headlines in the weeks preceding the Institute's first presidential inauguration on May 22, 1966. Board Chair Rochelle stated his position clearly for the *Greensboro Record:*

> We're very happy being a technical institute. Our job is to furnish technicians and we're glad to have that job. It takes seven technicians to keep one professional man going and we're filling a real need.[17]

Having clarified the Institute's technical mission and his awareness of the additional funding and prestige that would accompany GTI's designation as a comprehensive community college, Rochelle emphasized his obsession with the school's name:

> Actually, we have no choice (of becoming a community college) if we are to fill the needs of the community. But it is not the Board's desire to change the name of the Institute. It will still be a technical institute and will be known as Guilford Technical Institute and Community College.[18]

Regardless of the mission to train industrial technicians, the Board had to consider expanding the Institute to a community college in light of the necessity to train nurses; the State Board of Nursing refused to license registered nurses trained at a technical institute. Admitting that an RN program "should have been started a year ago," Rochelle pledged to establish one as soon as possible and cited two additional reasons for seeking community college status: the fact that GTI was not getting its share of federal money and the necessity to make it easier for the Institute's students to transfer their credits. But he stopped short of endorsing a comprehensive college transfer program:

> The Board of Trustees has no intention of becoming a liberal arts college; the only thing we intend to teach in the liberal arts is what courses our students need to become good technicians.[19]

The *Greensboro Record* subsequently endorsed "GTI's surprising plan" to achieve community college status:

> It (the College) would not embark on a program of liberal arts instruction but would continue to specialize in the training of technicians. There would be some marked advantages, however. For one thing a student would find it easier to transfer his credits to another college. For another, the school would be able to snare a larger portion of federal money. But the chief reason is the need for registered nurses. In the community college, the training of nurses would become a major part of the work. Since the N. C. Board of Nursing won't license nurses trained at a technical institute the only way the school can help meet the growing need for nurses is through a change in its legal classification.[20]

The *Record's* editorialist concluded with an insightful prediction: "If the Trustees are successful in their petition, the Institute can become a major educational force in what is already one of the state's foremost centers of higher learning."[21] For better or worse, the expansion issue had provoked the outpouring of "publicity" GTI's Board had long coveted. The editorial appeared the day before Chairman Rochelle posted two important letters, one to Governor Dan Moore and the other, an extensively detailed argument promoting GTI's expansion, to Dallas Herring, chairman of the State Board of Education.[22]

The governor was informed that Herring and Dr. Ready, Director of the Department of Community Colleges, had visited GTI and "were greatly cheered and impressed by the progress made in the past year and the full utilization of our buildings and equipment." Though the forthcoming debate would be bitter, interestingly the letter to Governor Moore specifies the Trustees' near-desperation to gain "college" status by foregoing many benefits usually accompanying the higher status:

> Dr. Herring encouraged us to make application as soon as possible for a change in status from technical institute to community college. As stated in the attached letter, and in keeping with the promise made to you, we are not asking for additional funds that normally go with a college parallel curriculum. As a matter of fact, our emphasis will be upon terminal courses here rather than the first two years of university training.

As we explained to you in your office, there are many courses which are vital to this community that we cannot teach since we are a technical institute. Chief among them is registered nursing. Another reason why this is imperative that the word "college" be appendaged to our name is to make good our promises to the Gilbarco families who are moving to this area. Local enrollments at local colleges have been completed and are closed. [23]

We can operate as a college under the monies allotted to us in our present budget. We respectfully ask you to confirm our request with the State Board of Education.

Rochelle's letter to State Board of Education Chair Herring reiterated the Trustees' decision to forego the $500,000 allotted to new community colleges and assured Herring that:

Our emphasis will be on technical-vocational training to meet industrial needs and to teach skills to the non-high school graduate as well.

Rochelle then proceeded to enumerate ten arguments for GTI's expansion that reflect a cultural picture of mid 1960s Guilford County and the values and judgment of the Institute's Trustees and administrators. Probably this language was President Marco's:

1. Of the 3,460 high school graduates this June over half are young women. The large majority will not continue their education because of various reasons, first of which is that Guilford Technical Institute is not a community college; secondly the local four-year colleges are already filled and are not taking additional applicants. One such college has accepted only seventeen local residents, another less than one hundred. These young women are entitled to continue their education fully as much as men.

2. All men do not make good machinists, metal workers, or upholsterers. Many do not have manual ability, but do have mental agility. These persons must be encouraged to go into their chosen field of education — to make a start at least — here at home. We still need merchants, doctors, lawyers, office workers as much as we need sheet metal workers.

3. Medicare is here and so are the aged. For varied unintelligible reasons, technical institutes are not permitted to have a Registered Nurse curriculum even though excellent clinical facilities are available at several hospitals in the area — and despite the fact that this is a great

need throughout the State. Hospitals are closing wards and whole floors because of the lack of registered nurses.

4. Library assistants are in demand, an excellent vocation for a young woman, but we are stymied because we do not award the Associate in Arts degree and our educational credits are not transferable for further education, if desired, because we are not a community college.

5. General Education courses, or liberal arts curriculum, cannot be authorized for technical institutes despite the high quality of its faculty for these courses are reserved for the community college. We still need mental growth in all areas whether baker, butcher, lawyer or doctor for better understanding of peoples and for better government.

6. Guilford County is the second most populous county in the State, a close second to Mecklenburg, if not larger at this time. The counties north and south of Guilford are much smaller. One to the north has only 965 high school graduates this June, and the one to the south has 1,200. Yet, these two counties each have a community college. In order to justify their classrooms, they are depending upon the young people from Guilford County. This is not just, nor fair to the Guilford community, its local investment in GTI and its young people.

7. Guilford County has given more in money, time, land, and buildings to the North Carolina Community College System than any other county—over $2,500,000. No federal or state money is included in this sum. Further, it has given local financial support for several years.

8. Even the small community college can get federal funds under Title I because of their college status, whereas a rapidly growing Institute such as Guilford (GTI) cannot.

9. In cooperation with the Governor's Total Development Program, we are training over 100 machinists and metal workers currently to keep commitments made to the new industries by the Governor. We are also obligated to the families, the young men and women, moving into the State. They must a permitted to obtain at least their first year of college education here and to transfer those credits later.

10. According to the Attorney General of the State of North Carolina, the State Board of Education may convert Guilford Technical Institute to a community college (P. I15A–23—General Statutes) at their discretion. We ask for that privilege, for the people have demonstrated their continued interest by the recent (April 12) $500,000 bond issue for Guilford Technical Institute, their willing support from the

> County General Funds, their attendance at Guilford Technical Institute public functions, and continued, very favorable press.
>
> In summary, the Trustees of Guilford Technical Institute respectfully request the State Board of Education to upgrade our status to community college now, even on a provisional basis, until the next General Assembly, so that we may meet the industrial, health, and educational needs of our community and truly OPEN THE DOOR to all who seek to be useful citizens.[24]

The issue of community college status was semantically complicated, though sanely negotiable in spring 1966, but the two men who could do the most for the school were on the verge of drawing furrows in the red clay of the Piedmont needing only a specific provocation to raise the level of conflict and contention. Board Chair Rochelle was willing to forego state funding to get federal funding even on a provisional basis, while his president was concerned with educating workers in the civic skills and expanding the range of employment for women. Both men based their arguments for community college status on the need for a nursing program and higher educational opportunities for an undisclosed number of prospective students moving to Greensboro with a major manufacturer of service station equipment, but they were never on the same page. One wanted a sampling of transferable courses to reinforce the future for promising technicians; the second envisioned a liberal arts cafeteria line for the more ambitious students who could not find a place in Guilford County's six liberal arts institutions.

Chapter 5

What's in a Name?

It is more than a change of name; it is changing the nature and intent of the Institute just as much as we did when we changed from an Industrial Education Center to a Technical Institute.[1]

Dr. Wendell Patton, GTI Trustee
President, High Point College

Sunday, May 22, 1966:
The Inauguration of Herbert F. Marco

With the music of the Ragsdale High School Band echoing across the hills and vales of eastern Jamestown, a robed procession led by GTI Board Chair Zalph Rochelle wound beneath the campus pines to inaugurate the Institution's first president. More than a year had elapsed (May 6, 1965) since Dr. Herbert Francis Marco, described by the *High Point Enterprise* as "a man of unusual energy and ideas," had joined GTI from his post as Dean of Academic Affairs at Allegheny Community College in Cumberland, Maryland.

Commercial Art Department Chair Ralph E. Calhoun greeted the inaugural audience of approximately 400 on behalf of the faculty while Steve York represented the student body. Dr. Ralph Jolly, the President of Greensboro College, delivered the opening address with its complimentary appraisal of Dr. Marco's leadership skills. Jolly cautioned the audience to be wary of what he termed "the over-centralization of education in the state," a concern probably shared by many struggling private colleges as they observed the legislature building a new, competing system of two-year institutions.

In his inaugural address, GTI's first president characterized the Institute as "the College who comes home to the student," reminding his audience that, unlike the county's other institutions of higher education, GTI was truly *their* college: "This is your opportunity. You, your children, do not have to leave home to gain a college education. It is right here and the cost is so little." He lauded the dramatic increase in enrollment, from approximately 400 to more than 1,200, that followed the school's expansion from industrial education center to technical institute. Citing the prevailing "knowledge explosion" then sweeping the continent, Marco reiterated GTI's primary objective to train technicians and "semi-professionals" and pledged to "not neglect the general education so necessary to the mental growth of all individuals." A week after more than 63,000 protesters marched to the Washington Monument to pledge to vote for only anti Vietnam War candidates, the decorated World War II Air Force veteran framed patriotism as a major theme of his administration:[2]

> We believe in Americanism. We believe in our way of life and we support it. Consequently, all candidates for a diploma or degree from this Institute must take a course in American government and citizenship before he can graduate. There is no room on this campus for communists and draft dodgers, or for anyone who does not believe in our way of life and in our Constitution.[3]

The 1960s represent one of the most fragile and potentially destructive periods in the 20th century history of the United States of America; this nation, the leader of the free world, was locked in the most intensive survival period of the Cold War struggle with the Soviet Union. Its leaders were mesmerized by the escalating conflict with a communist regime in Vietnam and socially distracted by the civil rights struggle rending the county's social fabric. In a period when American values were questioned on every front, Herbert Marco, a member of "America's Greatest Generation," was determined to see that GTI's students were instructed in the principles of the nation's founding fathers.

His address outlined three institutional objectives for GTI:[4]

> (1) To raise the general level of education and quality of its students; for it is through knowledge that a nation becomes great, a community becomes prosperous, and the people learn to sponsor good government; (2) To develop good graduates—useful in the community, the government, and industry; (3) To inculcate citizenship in all its students.

> Love of county is important. It is absolutely necessary if we are to maintain our way of life. What good will we gain if we train people in the sciences and skills only to have them turn against us—to destroy our freedoms—to destroy our homes—our families and our country. Citizenship is just as important as, or even more important than, a technical skill.

Marco's philosophical affinity for positioning citizenship above workforce preparedness continued to distance him from the practical need for skilled technicians visualized by the industrialists who served GTI as its Trustees. After a year on the job, he had not deviated from the principles he expressed the day he was hired; that April 2, 1965, he characterized the position as "a challenge to offer adults something more meaningful to their lives, a course in government for better understanding by the people." Percy Sears had quickly reminded him that the Trustees wanted to stick to the industrial interest; attracted by the additional money, programs, and the transferable credits community college status commanded, Marco was still determined to pursue an elevated mission for the Institution.

In 1966, when Guilford County's industrial future depended on upgrading the literacy and skills of a marginally educated labor force challenged by mechanization, a strategic plan to specifically address this issue did not appear as a major priority in Marco's Presidential address. When U.S. factory workers took home an average of $91.80 a week, and Russia and the U.S. were jockeying to maintain the balance of power and racing to space, Herbert Marco appeared more concerned about educating workers to cope with the communist threat to American democracy than training them in the new technologies needed to bolster Guilford County's manufacturing future and protect the nation. Not once in his speech during the height of the civil rights movement did he offer to address the plight of Guilford County's African-Americans who, with proper training, represented one of the county's major assets. However, in retrospect, the job at GTI had drawn a highly productive scientist administrator from the edge of space to a struggling vocational school where the needs were more practical and immediate. The new chief executive concluded his inauguration by awarding GTI's first Associate in Applied Science degree to Mrs. Virginia Bangiola, of High Point, a graduate in Commercial Art and Advertising Design.[5]

Proposed: *Guilford Technical College*

Despite the glowing impressions of GTI, Community College Director I. E. Ready and State Board of Education Chair Dallas Herring had presumably conveyed to Board Chair Rochelle following their visit to the Institute, and their apparent endorsement of its expansion to a community college, the conversion Rochelle requested in his May 18, 1966, letter to Herring, was not a done-deal. Thus begins the most controversial period in the early history of Guilford Technical Community College, a drama played out in the Board room and the media.

The first glitch appeared in the June 14, 1966, Board session when Dr. Marco repeated Dr. Ready's suggestion that, "to avoid any legality about (a) referendum for tax support, we (GTI) should not fight for community college status at this time." The issue grew more controversial when Marco added that Ready felt sure that, he could get the Institute's name changed to Guilford Technical College in the event the Board wanted to become a college in name only. Ready's offer contradicted Marco's earlier announcement from Attorney General Wade Bruton, who had ruled that a referendum was not necessary to change the Institute's name and establish its eligibility for additional funding.[6]

Presumably, by merely adding *College* to its name, the Institute could gain approval for a coveted registered nursing program, given that the prerequisite for approval was recognition as a college; however, as a "*college*" in name only, the Institution would not be permitted to offer college transfer programs or to receive the automatic $500,000 allotted to community colleges. Trustee W. O. Conrad, a Western Electric executive, reminded the Trustees that GTI's strength "lies in our vocational and technical programs and we should emphasize these."[7]

Marco assured the Board that "our industrial vocational programs are greater than our technical programs and will not be compromised," after which he returned to his own agenda of creating a college, noting that changing the name of the institute to *Guilford Technical College* would be advantageous because "there are no other technical colleges this side of Raleigh, and we are surrounded by liberal arts colleges." The exchange concluded with the Board voting to accept Ready's suggestion to forego seeking full community college status and settle for the lesser designation.[8] Once again, the Trustees wrestled with the policy of limiting "liberal arts courses" to specific programs and the pressure to add "college" to its name to guarantee approval of certain programs, specifically nursing.

August 2, 1966

During this session, the Board deliberated budget and personnel issues before tackling the next hurdle in its proposed expansion. While the county commissioners had sharply pared the Institute's request for $175,000 for fiscal 1966–67 to $125,000, Percy Sears reassured the Trustees that additional funds would be available for necessary repairs, construction, and emergencies. The commissioners had diverted Marco's request for road repair and parking lot construction funds to the State Highway Commission and postponed an expensive conversion of the school's electrical system.

Beyond its conservative county budget, GTI received a federal grant of $38,222.29 to raise the general level of adult education and a $5,000 Health, Education and Welfare (HEW) grant to support the library. Sixth District Congressman Horace Kornegay notified Marco that grants were available from the Higher Education Facilities Act for Health Sciences, but in order to qualify for a share of the $31 million, an institution was required to have "college" in its name.

The personnel segment of this session touched on the careers of some of the Institution's historic figures. Librarian Mertys Bell resigned to accompany her husband to a new job in Virginia. Fortunately for GTI, Bell eventually returned to the College and remained until retirement. The Board approved the employment of Colonel George A. Finley, an administrator who would play an important role in maintaining the Institute in future troubled times; Wanda Russell was hired as an instructor in Business Education and Kenneth Vaughn as an Instructor in Accounting. The Board additionally approved a presidential request to hire a "colored" supervisor at a salary of $5,400 for nine months.[9]

The issue of Board approval to change the Institute's name to *Guilford Technical College* (June 14, 1966) had resurfaced yet again on August 2; Marco recommended retaining "'Technical, because our objectives are technical." Lecturing the Board on the difference between a technical institute and a community college and noting that several current students would like to transfer their credits, Marco suggested that the College should pursue the previously recommended referendum on expansion to gain additional financing from the county. This suggestion led the Board to ask State Attorney General Bruton to rule on the possibility of retaining the funds allocated to GTI should the school expand to a community college:

> In the event the State Board of Education approves a change from technical institute to community college, with the accompanying change of name, may the proceeds which have been budgeted by the County Commissioners for the maintenance of Guilford Technical Institute be used for the continuation of the same institute under the new name and status, together with bond funds voted by the people of Guilford County at the last referendum (April 1966) for capital improvements for Guilford Technical Institute. [10]

Pending a favorable reply, the Board unanimously decided to submit a request for community college status to Dr. Ready and the State Board of Education by August 4, 1966. Having voted with the majority, High Point College President Wendell Patton restated his reservations about the community college issue by reminding his colleagues:

> It is more than a change of name; it is changing the nature and intent of the Institute just as much as we did when we changed from an Industrial Education Center to a Technical Institute.[11]

The State Board of Education quickly granted approval, but the text of the (August 4, 1966) letter from Dr. Ready authorizing the conversion, and his "name change caveat," created a series of controversial issues that agitated the Institute's Trustees, faculty, staff, and students for more than a year:

> The State Board of Education approves the conversion of Guilford Technical Institute to a community college, with the stipulation that the voters of Guilford County approve, before the beginning of the 1967–68 fiscal year (June 30, 1967), the local financial support required for the converted institution, as provided in G.S. I15A, such conversion contingent on approval of the Governor and Advisory Budget Commission.

> As soon as I am notified of action by the Governor and Advisory Budget Commission, I will let you know.

> The Board members asked me to convey to you their concern about the proposed name, "Guilford Technical Community College," though they leave to the Board of Trustees the final decision in this matter. They have some feeling that technical community college may have the same labeling effect that technical high school has in the past.

> My understanding from your correspondence is that your Board of Trustees is not asking for additional construction funds from the next General Assembly beyond those the State Board is already planning to request.[12]

The initial fallout from the decision approving GTI's expansion to a community college prompted Dr. Patton's resignation from the Board. The High Point College president made his decision known in three letters, the first to Dale Montgomery, Chairman of the Guilford County Board of Commissioners, restates his patented objections to a community college in the county:

> First, with this change in status from a technical institute to a community college offering a basic two-year college program, a very real possibility of conflict of interests develops between my responsibilities as President of a private college and a Trustee of a tax-supported college.

> Secondly, I would like to be able to speak as a private *citizen* in voicing opposition to increasing the tax burden of the citizens of Guilford County by adding a community college to a county, which already has more colleges than any other county in the state. Not *only do we* have a major branch of the University of North Carolina, but a state-supported

technical college as well. In addition to these there are at least four accredited colleges all within the county. Everyone connected with the development of the community college program has stated publicly many times it was not the intent of this program to put these institutions in areas where colleges were not needed.

As you already know, I was told at the time of my appointment to the Board that a community college would *never* be considered for this area and I have been especially concerned over the past 12 to 15 months when it began becoming obvious that careful plans were made for this end. Under these conditions, I do not see how I can make any significant contribution to the welfare of Guilford Technical Institute or carry out the responsibilities assigned to me by the county commissioners when they appointed me to the Board of Trustees.[13]

Patton's resignation presumably removed the most vocal dissenter to community college status from the Board, but when his decision was not immediately acknowledged to his satisfaction, Patton fired off an emotional letter underscoring his dismay to President Marco (August 29, 1966). Marco responded that he was away on vacation when Patton's resignation arrived and assured Patton that "no discourtesy was intended in not answering your letter before this date."[14] Patton's resignation was discussed at an emergency meeting of the Trustees on August 23, 1966, and unanimously accepted. The names suggested to replace him indicated the Board's interest in holding his seat for a representative from another liberal arts institution: Dr. Ralph Jolly, President, Greensboro College; Dr. Otis Singletary, Chancellor, UNCG; Dr. James Ferguson, Vice Chancellor, UNCG; Dr. Lewis Dowdy, President A & T College (now NC A & T State University) were mentioned as possible candidates along with Board attorney Robert Martin.

This emergency meeting was primarily convened to discuss the legal procedures involved in establishing a referendum to enable the voters an opportunity to decide if they approved tax support for GTI as a community college. The timing of the referendum created a discussion that was finally resolved on August 30, 1966, when the Board accepted Percy Sears' advice to ask the County Commissioners to set November 8, 1966, as the date for the vote and stipulated that the tax rate not exceed 5 cents.[15]

September–October 1966: Bursting at the Seams

It quickly became clear that GTI's route to community college status was fraught with a plethora of legal and legislative hurdles. President Marco informed the Board at a special session on September 15, 1966, that the Advisory Budget Commission had deferred action on GTI's quest for community college status to the General Assembly and that Dr. Ready had subsequently recommended postponing a tax referendum for community college status from fall of 1966 to spring 1967.[16]

> Under Chapter 115A of the General Statutes, new or converted institutions must be approved by the State Board of Education, the Governor, and the Advisory Budget Commission. Until approval is secured from all of the above, the institution officially is not approved or converted. Therefore, it would not be proper to plan for any vote of the people for local financial support required or to use the name community college until full approval of all agencies is secured. This will necessarily be after the General Assembly has acted on the budget requests to implement the changes.[17]

Legislative approval was deemed tenuous because the state funds needed to accomplish this change were included in the supplemental "B" budget requests presented by the State Board of Education to the Advisory Budget Commission. Former legislator and GTI Trustee Ed Kemp underscored the precariousness of the situation by reminding the Board that "B" Budget items were difficult to get passed at any time. Acting on his suggestion that "the more strength we can get behind us, the better chance we will have," the Trustees decided to lobby their local legislators by inviting them to a briefing dinner sometime after the November 8, 1966, election.[18]

While the drive to press GTI's advancement to community college status dominated the Board meetings throughout 1966, administrative and operational issues expanded and intensified. The dollar purchased phenomenally more in 1966, but the maintenance of buildings, grounds, and parking lots, the purchase of equipment, the scarcity of space, the demands for new programs, and the lack of contingency funds challenged the institute's leaders. Marco asked the Board for permission to close registration in mid-September 1966 because the institute was at full capacity. He was actually conducting classes in his home and contemplating establishing a "twilight school" at Ragsdale High School just across Highway 29A from the Institute.[19]

A month later (October 11, 1966), the president reported a preliminary count of 1,600 enrolled students, compared to 250 a year earlier. The full-time enrollment had almost tripled from 171 to 500. Dental Hygiene was operating at capacity with 60 students; 42 students were enrolled in what Marco called "a full nursing program" (apparently in reference to another program other than the vocational program in Practical Nurse Education established in 1965.)[20] The president's attempt to institute a nursing program had flared into a controversial exchange with the Department of Community Colleges in January 1966.

According to Marco, a student in GTI's Public Service Program had called a member of Ready's staff concerning the school's "Registered Nursing Program."[21] Details about that conversation and a letter to the presumed student from a staff member at the system office indicating that GTI did not have an RN program reached the Board of Trustees much to the displeasure of its members and President Marco. Marco assured Ready that GTI did not have a RN program but planned to begin one in the fall of 1966. He did admit, however, that students presumably preparing for a nursing career were enrolled in the Public Service Administration curriculum. The incident prompted the following memo from Board Chair Rochelle:

> All personnel are instructed to refrain from making personal contact, or directing others to do so, with the members of the Board of Trustees or members of the Community College System headquartered in Raleigh on matters pertaining to the Institute without the express knowledge and permission of the chief administrative officer of the Guilford Technical Institute or its future equivalent. Violators of this policy are subject to disciplinary action or dismissal.[22]

Questions surrounding the nursing program would emerge publicly in early 1967, as one of the growth issues confronting the Institute, in a *Greensboro Daily News* series written by Jerry Bledsoe.[23] The Trustees did approve a Nursing Agreement with the Moses H. Cone Memorial Hospital on November 9, 1966, and the school was later permitted to establish a refresher course for RNs.

Expansion remained the foremost topic in 1966. Anticipating the school's eventual Public Safety Complex, Percy Sears suggested that the school needed a central place to train rural firemen and law enforcement officers as opposed to delivering training at station sites throughout the county. The Jamestown campus parking lots, walks, and drives were upgraded and four prisoners were each paid 50 cents an hour to perform maintenance chores. Trustee and County Commissioner Sears alleviated the president's concern about paying for this inexpensive labor with the news that the County had over a million-plus surplus dollars and the Institute could request additional funds after the general election on November 8, 1966.[24]

Marco may have breathed a sigh of relief at the possibility of improving the school's fiscal infrastructure with a windfall from the county, but it was the last positive financial report he would hear for weeks. State auditors were headed to GTI expecting to finish their examination in five days, but the accounting morass they discovered kept them in Jamestown for six weeks. Their inventory of recommendations unleashed a controversy that played out in the Board room, at executive committee meetings, and in the press. Thus began the most disruptive period in the history of the Institution publicly pitting the Chairman of the Board against the President of GTI in a confrontation that did not bode well for either man, or for Guilford Technical Institute.[25]

Chapter 6

The Gathering Storm

That there is a conflict between (President) Marco and at least some of the Trustees is apparent. It appears to center on who is running GTI, Marco or the Trustees.[1]

November 9, 1966

The first visible evidence of escalating organizational and fiscal tension between Board Chair Rochelle and GTI administrators emerged during a crucial session on November 9, 1966. With six of twelve Trustees present, Rochelle, citing the Board minutes as a public and legal record, blistered Board secretary Reba Embry for improperly documenting the minutes of the previous session by not including several relevant letters. He lectured Embry about her responsibility to the Board and, while she was permitted to continue recording the minutes, the Board named Trustee Robert Kistler as its official secretary at its December 13, 1966, session. The tone of the minutes Embry faithfully recorded underscores Rochelle's determination to establish a more professional, business approach to conducting the Institute's business and documenting the Board sessions. The motivation for his aggressive approach emerged when he asked for a motion to allow the state auditors to see the Institute's books and records including those maintained by the GTI Foundation.

> Mr. Robert Kistler made the motion that we (the Board) cooperate to the fullest extent with any authorized governmental agency and specifically instruct Dr. Marco to furnish all records to the North Carolina State Auditors, answer their questions, and instruct his subordinates to furnish information and answer questions necessary to this audit, including an audit of the Guilford Technical Institute Foundation funds.[2]

55

Following the motion's unanimous approval, Rochelle rushed to establish a policy, effective immediately, whereby only the Board could transfer funds between accounts. Percy Sears footnoted this new policy by reminding his colleagues that only the county commissioners could approve transferring county funds from one account to another. Copies of the minutes from the November 9 session and those of the GTI Foundation were ordered forwarded to Raleigh to assure the State Auditor that GTI was fully committed to complying with his review of the Institute's finances.[3]

If President Marco was perturbed by the impending state audit, it did not deter him from broaching the question of creating an athletic program. The students apparently wanted a basketball team but, since the Institute lacked the estimated $1,500 to finance the project, admission would have to be charged at the games. The Board tabled the issue after Percy Sears noted that money collected from taxpayers could not be used to fund an athletic program. A basketball team may have placated some disaffected students, but the Institute was facing enough financial challenges without incurring an additional burden.[4]

There was some good news. The Board of Trustees recommended unanimously that the county purchase a 71-acre parcel of land for $70,000 that would nearly double the size of the Jamestown campus. They additionally approved a design for the proposed library classroom building financed by the $500,000 April 1966 bond issue. This structure (Business Careers) would eventually house the administrative offices during the period between the razing of "Old Main," the last sanatorium structure, and the construction of the Medlin Campus Center.[5]

December 13, 1966

Rumors of labor unrest and preliminary recommendations from state auditors dominated the December Board session. Disgruntled employees shared their dissatisfaction over the Institute's holiday vacation schedule with Trustee James L. Williams, who reported that 26 were threatening to strike. The schedule in question provided approximately ten days vacation for nine-month employees and three days, or basically, two long weekends for 12-month employees. The issue was tabled to allow President Marco time to discuss the problem with the agitated employees and report to the Board. There is no record that reporters were in attendance at this meeting, but *Greensboro Daily News* journalist Jerry Bledsoe later chronicled "discontent and grumbling among both faculty and students at the school" in his five-part series on GTI

("Turmoil on the Campus," February 5–9, 1967); according to Bledsoe, "rumors about all sorts of incidents, mostly unprovable (sic) filtered out to the press" during this period.

> Students and teachers told reporters they didn't like "the way the school was being run. Everybody was sort of afraid," said an ex-student. "It just doesn't have the atmosphere of a college," said a girl now attending classes.

> Most of those who were unhappy blamed GTI President Dr. Herbert Marco for their discontent.[6]

The State Auditor's Report

Employee and student dissatisfaction with GTI was compounded by a plethora of recommendations (audit exceptions) enumerated in a December 8, 1966, letter from State Auditor Henry Bridges. Beginning with Accounts Receivable, GTI was cited for the lack of a formal policy regarding the over-charging, collection, and refunding of student fees and the maintenance of required documents. Bridges faulted the administration for failing to address these audit exceptions for the fiscal year ending June 30, 1965, during the preceding 18 months. He advised the Institute to set up formal "accounts receivable" records for students and recommended the adoption of policies enforcing the payment of accounts before students were allowed to continue in class, take examinations, graduate, or receive a transcript.

Marco took the high road concerning the state audit with a response that "no money had been found missing," but there was no glossing over the auditors' censure of a hodgepodge of funds and special accounts that did not conform to acceptable accounting methods or appear in the official financial records of the institute. Reforms were encouraged to formalize the management of cash receipts, the operations of the furniture shop, and the cosmetology program GTI inherited from the Greensboro Public Schools in 1963. The auditors were initially unaware that GTI managed the cosmetology school and its finances. They were sharply critical of the Institute's failure to comply with a previous request to fully disclose the funds associated with this operation and recommended a thorough revamping of its financial operations.

The Board was encouraged to comply with statutes governing GTI's various budgets and warned that additional recommendations were forthcoming. The imperative to correct this multitude of fiscal discrepancies was reinforced by Chairman Rochelle following a meeting between the auditors and the

Board's Executive Committee. According to Rochelle, the auditors "made more recommendations on this audit than on all the audits of the (Guilford) county schools this year."[7] The Board's Executive Committee recommended immediate compliance with the recommendations and invited the auditing team to return in two months to check on the implementation of the process. In what could be interpreted as a "slap on the wrist" for promoting expansion, Rochelle recommended, on behalf of the Executive Committee, that the Board, the President, and the Staff of GTI cease referring to the Institute as a "college" until community college status was achieved. The administration was additionally ordered to change the campus sign proclaiming the school's motto, *Your College, Your Opportunity*. Issues extending from this nearly three-hour marathon were carried over to a special called meeting on December 21, 1966.[8]

December 21, 1966

Chairman Rochelle convened this session to further formalize the fiscal and personnel operations of the Institute. The lengthy agenda listed the recommendations submitted by the auditors and the actions necessary to comply with the exceptions. In addition to distributing a copy of the December 8, 1966, letter from state auditor Henry Bridges to president Marco detailing the panel's extensive recommendations, Rochelle passed out a list of twenty unaccounted-for capital items, mostly sewing machines, receipted by the school's former director, Bruce Roberts, and valued at $690. The Board ordered business manager Wade Johnson to find out what happened to the missing capital items and report back.[9]

The chairman initiated a new era of fiscal responsibility and accountability by instructing Johnson and bookkeeper Ruth Harvey to report their compliance progress to the Board. They were ordered to furnish the Trustees with the funding transfers necessitating Board approval; and, while they would continue to report to the President on operations and administrative matters, Johnson and Harvey were henceforth responsible to the Board on legal issues and matters related to state and county laws. They were additionally authorized to discuss any questions they might have about the legality of any Board action with the state's auditors.

President Marco rebutted the audit exceptions by arguing that the Community College System was growing so quickly that GTI was not alone in its accounting struggles; Board Chair Rochelle dismissively responded that the Board expected Johnson and Harvey to take immediate action on the audit recommendations including hiring an additional person to work in the business office. When the President replied that the school was a half-person over the personnel budget and without funds to pay another employee, Rochelle reminded him "that it was up to the administration to find out how to pay someone and bring their recommendation to the Board."

Upon reflection, this session may have marked the beginning of the end of the Marco administration. It did not bode well for Marco's future when the Board created a grievance procedure that enabled faculty and students to speak with the Trustees in a manner that, presumably, would not undercut the president's authority. James Williams chaired this small group consisting of Trustees Robert Kistler and John Foster with Marco serving ex-officio. Reporter Jerry Bledsoe, one of three journalists attending the session, reported "several sharp exchanges between Rochelle and Marco during the meeting." Rochelle was quoted as telling a reporter that "the results of that meeting had stripped Marco of some of his authority," a statement Marco later refuted.[10]

The embattled President could not excuse the exceptions attesting to haphazard bookkeeping, missing capital items, the absence of a formal policy allowing for the disposal of assets, and the administration of various bank accounts. The accounting process lacked proper supervision and it appears from the minutes that neither the Board nor the administration had a realistic grasp of the Institute's fiscal status. Confronted with this administrative nightmare, Marco defended his management of the Institute.

> I have talked personally to several of the top officials in the state headquarters for the community colleges. I am glad to report that every confidence was expressed in my administration. They know our rapid expansion, as well as in other colleges and institutes in the system, made methodology antiquated and difficult to follow, short cuts and improvisions (sic) had to be made. The Raleigh headquarters again expressed confidence that in due time all the loose ends will be tied. They are not alarmed, nor vindictive, for they appreciate the problems under which we are working.

In moving to accept Marco's statement as his official reply to the state audit, Trustee William Conrad assured the President of his vote of confidence and the Board unanimously approved the motion to insert Marco's statement into the minutes.

Trustee James Williams reported that he and Chairman Rochelle had responded to faculty and staff dissatisfaction with working conditions at GTI first noted on December 13 by meeting with the employees and distributing a "job satisfaction survey." The instrument offered employees an opportunity to express their opinions about the administration, relationships with colleagues and attitudes toward salary and regulations. Williams assured the Board that the questionnaire would not be divided between faculty and staff.[11] Marco was not asked to report on any discussions he may have conducted with the disgruntled employees, nor did he volunteer any information.

As the meeting drew to a close, it was obvious that the negative audit from Raleigh had not weakened the local support for Guilford Technical Institute. The Board and the county officials who partially funded the school were confident it would succeed. Percy Sears announced that, as a show of support, the County Commissioners had complied with the Board's request and optioned 71 acres adjacent to the Jamestown campus for future expansion. Sears, determined to see the Institute prevail, reported that the commissioners had strategically redirected these funds from other sources because they "felt it was worth it," an admirable move considering the fiscal discrepancies plaguing the Institute.

Rochelle's aggressive management of the session occurred in the presence of three local journalists whose attendance indicated the level of interest questions about GTI's operations had attracted across the county; James Hawkins represented the *High Point Enterprise* and reporters James Wagner and Jerry Bledsoe, the *Greensboro Daily News* and *Greensboro Record*. Rochelle graciously recognized the reporters while noting that, "the school is a public institution and it will thrive on the reports it gets from the press," a remark that in time, he probably wished to recant. He offered to buy the reporters' breakfast and promised to send them notices of future Board meetings.

Trustee William Conrad picked this moment to reveal that:

> It had been reported to him that some member of the Board had made the statement to a reporter, and it had been announced over the radio, that the Board was dissatisfied with the (Marco) administration. He (Conrad) stated that he would like to go on record that he was satisfied with the administration and the statement that had been made did not express his opinion.

> Mr. Rochelle informed the Board that this statement had been made by the reporter after the running of a taped interview with him (Rochelle) and he had called the station and the statement had been cut after he asked them not to run it after his tape. Mr. Rochelle also stated that he was not dissatisfied with the management (of the College).

This interchange elicited a motion from Robert Kistler that the Board give Dr. Marco a unanimous vote of confidence. The motion was supported by the nine members present including Chairman Rochelle who assured the President that he wanted Marco to build "an educational institute second to none" and encouraged him to spend his time promoting the Institute and hiring faculty. [12]

Growth and Challenge

The final Board session of 1966 may have concluded on a conciliatory note; however, the professional embarrassment extending from the obvious evidence of fiscal mismanagement and poor supervision was not casually dismissed by this group of highly respected businessmen and civic leaders. Combined with developmental and maintenance costs, the fundamental accounting problems extending from GTI's rapid institutional growth created a management nightmare for administrators. The 1965–66 Board minutes reference dozens of operational crises that demanded financing ranging from basic infrastructure improvements to equipment needed to support the curriculum. Rochelle admitted that the school survived on money from various sources: "if we couldn't scrounge it out of some government agency, we'd hit industry. A lot of times industry kept it growing."[13]

The decision to convert a decrepit TB sanatorium into a college campus was a blessing and a curse; while it removed a derelict facility from the county commissioner's agenda and provided the fledgling Guilford Industrial Education Center a base of operations, its crumbling buildings demanded extensive maintenance, repair, and remodeling; its roads and parking areas were never designed to handle the traffic that flocked to the campus. At the same time, enrollment growth, which was what the Institute was really all about, was phenomenal. GTI budgeted for 621 students in the fall of 1966 when 747 registered for curriculum courses and 122 for extension classes. The Institute solved the cost of this burgeoning enrollment only because funds were diverted from a sister institution that did not get into a new building on time.[14]

Of course, GTI's success in terms of attracting students was not unique. In fact, growth of two-year institutions across the state was so great that Dr. I. E. Ready, Director of the Department of Community Colleges, applauded the success of North Carolina's commitment to fill the educational-training gap beyond high school with a crash program to develop two-year schools by noting that:

> People are beginning to accept the fact that it is just as honorable and valuable to attend the community colleges and institutes as what have been considered the 'prestige' colleges and universities. [15]

In 1966, the Community College System, operating under the State Board of Education, included 12 community colleges, 17 technical institutes, and an industrial education center at Jacksonville.[16]

Journalists Jim Hawkins, *High Point Enterprise*, and Jerry Bledsoe, *Greensboro Daily News*, were again in attendance when the Trustees gathered on

January 17, 1967, to hear President Marco provide the most detailed financial report submitted to the Board during his administration. The school's 1966–67 operating budget with approximately 2,000 students enrolled, included $366,783 in state funds and $129,500 in county funds.

The student population was burgeoning with 989 (FTE) compared with 0 (FTE) in spring 1965 and 540 (FTE) in the fall of 1965. Federal funds derived from the MDTA programs were reported as $1,261,696.[17] The Board approved a refresher course for registered nurses and a dental assistant program to begin in March 1967.[18]

What the minutes do not reflect is an acrimonious exchange reported by Bledsoe involving Marco, business manager Wade Johnson and Rochelle regarding those surplus sewing machines discovered missing during the state audit. When Johnson was asked for his report on the sewing machines requested by the Board at its December session, he replied that he didn't have it.

> Marco told the Trustees that Johnston worked for him and he (Marco) reported on the machines himself. Commissioners (Trustees) reminded Johnston that he worked for the Board and they expected him to do what they instructed him to do. Marco muttered loud enough for reporters to hear: "He doesn't work for you, he works for me."[19]

Rochelle and Marco began their public duel less than three weeks after this exchange as the Board Chair, who had given Marco free reign to run the school, attempted to regain control of the Institute. Marco's statement attributing many of his administrative and operational problems to the rapid growth of GTI and the Community College System was a valid observation. Both were an expansive work in progress in an era of major social change, and both were struggling to refine their respective identities and missions. For example, late in 1966, the state board attempted to clarify the distinctions among institutions in the system to address perceptions of "federal discrimination" and its inequities due to labeling by the U. S. Office of Education (USOE).

This federal "labeling" process may explain why Marco labored so diligently to have "college" inserted in the institution's name. As Wiggs (1988) pointed out, "Certain USOE grant programs distinguished between 'colleges,' 'community colleges' and 'technical institutes.'" And some programs, which limited funding for community colleges and excluded funding for technical institutes, were screening out North Carolina's institutions according to labels as opposed to actual classifications. In an effort to quell this inequity, the Board issued this clarification:

> In North Carolina, both community colleges and technical institutes offer two-year technical programs. In both types of institutions, any given

technical program is identical in content and standards. The name of the institution has nothing to do with the quality of the associate in applied science degree awarded.

There are 12 community colleges and 17 technical institutes in North Carolina. None of these should be under pressure to seek a name change and a broadening of functions in order to secure Federal aid in meeting local needs for any technical programs.

The community colleges and technical institutes in this state are alike except for the college parallel program offered by community colleges.[20]

Clearly, technical programs in both types of institutions were alike and certain courses from each program in each institution could be transferred. There is no indication that Marco shared this resolution, which might have mooted the name-change wrangle, with his Board, but he did ask to have the following "Formal Policy Statement" inserted into the minutes. It reiterated the principles inherent in the creation of an "intermediate system of higher education" and emphasized the State Board of Education's determination to prevent ambitious citizens from subverting the Community College System by using a community college as a springboard to develop a four-year institution.

The Community College System has been established to fill an educational opportunity gap between the high schools and the four-year colleges and the university system. The filling of this gap requires open door admission of both high school graduates and of others who are eighteen years old or older but are not high school graduates. The provision of educational opportunity for this broad range of student ability and needs requires a broad range of curriculum offerings, including college level, high school level, and for some elementary level studies.

The carrying out of this responsibility assigns a unique role to the institutions in the Community College System, which role is fundamentally different from the more selective role traditionally assigned to four-year colleges and universities. Because of this, for a community college to aspire to become a four-year college would not represent normal growth, but would destroy the community college role and replace it with an entirely different type of institution.

The State Board of Education is completely committed to maintaining the unique, comprehensive role of the institutions in the Community College System, and is opposed to any consideration of a community college as an embryonic four year college.[21]

The document, inserted into the minutes without discussion during the January 17, 1967, session, may have contributed to the public debate between Rochelle and Marco that flared in the press after the chairman delivered a fiery diatribe at the Asheboro Rotary Club on February 4, 1967. Rochelle, who prominently served as Vice President of the State Association of Community College Trustees, charged from the podium that, "North Carolina's vocational and technical institutes have gone college crazy and are in danger of being wrecked because of it."

Claiming that the "desire to change vocational and technical schools to two-year community colleges has got in our blood veins and is running rampant across our state," he accused technical institute presidents and trustees of being

> Enamored by the idea of being college people. It sounds good, there's glory to it, there's esteem to it, but there is also danger to it. After all, if we are going to be college professors, if we are all going to be college board members, if we are all going to be college presidents, why in the dickens should we worry about teaching some poor lout out there how to fix a machine?

According to Jerry Bledsoe, who covered the event,

> Rochelle also warned that the community colleges could be 'deceiving the public' by turning out students who think they have two years of college education, 'when actually what they have is two years of post-graduate high school.' Community college graduates might find themselves 'not equipped' to transfer to four year colleges and universities.

Rochelle reminded his audience that vocational and technical schools were created to solve the high school dropout problem and train less educated people to earn a living—principles he felt would be threatened if the schools became community colleges. Rochelle demanded protection for the vocational and technical programs, and encouraged the legislature to continue the present community colleges system as a blend of vocational and technical schools suggesting that, "If junior colleges were needed in some areas they should be established under the State Board of Higher Education." Rochelle's outburst occurred while GTI's petition for community college status was awaiting legislative approval, but the Board Chair declined to say if he would actively oppose the move.[22]

Asked to comment on Rochelle's remarks, Marco estimated that GTI had a 50–50 chance of attaining community college status while conceding that Rochelle's opposition "would throw a lot of difficulty in our way."[23] He played the gender card in an era when it was just becoming popular by arguing that community college status would allow GTI to offer more programs than were then available for women and assure the safety of the current curriculum: "We will not give up any of our vocational-technical programs. In fact, we will strengthen them."[24] Rochelle's Rotary Club speech and Marco's reaction appeared the day before the *Greensboro Daily News* began publishing Bledsoe's controversial "Turmoil on the Campus" series, probing the origin of GTI's problems and speculating on its future. Within five months, the multi-faceted, near ruinous philosophical debate between two strong personalities resulted in the resignation of GTI President Herbert F. Marco and the eventual departure of founder and Trustee Zalph Rochelle.

Chapter 7

Turmoil on the Campus

Zalph Rochelle leaned back in his High Point office chair and began to talk about Guilford Technical Institute. "This is the story," he said, "of a little bitty egg grown into a good sized rooster." What he didn't mention was that the hatching process was quite turbulent. It even ruffled the tail feathers of the mother hen, the GTI Board of Trustees of which Rochelle is chairman.[1]

GTI: "A Rooster from a Tiny Egg"

Thus begins part one of Jerry Bledsoe's February 1967 examination of GTI's institutional integrity and its ability to train Guilford County's workforce. Serious questions about fiscal management and the style and quality of leadership exhibited by the President and Board Chair had suddenly eclipsed three years of phenomenal growth when the Institute's budget quadrupled to $1.5 million and the enrollment to nearly 2,000. The media expose, accompanied by the public debate between Trustees and administrators over the question of community college status, pictured a thriving institution conflicted by narrow personal agendas, impetuous decision-making and a poor choice of language.

Bledsoe's articles are significant for the information they provide about the Institute, information that does not appear in the cryptic Board session minutes. The series could not have had a more resounding introduction than Rochelle's Asheboro outburst and his reference to the school's potential students as "louts."[2] With due respect to this practical-minded founding father, without whom there would probably be no GTCC, this stereotypical branding of Guilford County's factory workers as oafs and ruffians clearly delineated the cultural chasm that separated the laboring class from middle and upper class industrialists who represented the New South aristocracy in central North Carolina and throughout the South.[3]

The state's textile, furniture, and tobacco manufacturers, who were histor-ically responsible for attracting workers from secondary schooling by offering marginal wages and subsidized housing, discovered, with the onset of mech-anization, that they had cut off their noses to spite their faces. Modern tech-nology had rendered their workforce dysfunctional. The myth that youngsters could drop out of school in the eighth grade and make a living in the mill had succumbed to the electronic whisper of modern technology. The Community College System was the most economical route to train workers to fix knitting machines and upholster furniture, but it is highly unlikely that the manufac-turers who founded the Guilford Industrial Education Center were interested in diluting their practical training mission with conceptual courses that could awaken an individual's awareness of a greater opportunity for intellectual growth in a region long conflicted by labor unrest.

Chairman Rochelle's inflammatory remarks that community college status would "wreck vocational programs and they would die on the vine," was ill conceived. College transfer programs inevitably became the "cash cow" insti-tutions relied on to underwrite the more expensive nursing, dentistry and technical programs. The ensuing struggle among GTI's Board Chair, the Trustees, and the president, over the issue of community college status, is as crucial to understanding latter twentieth-century industrial assumptions about workforce development versus intellectual growth as it is to observing the mat-uration of GTCC and the North Carolina Community College System.

The 1967 turmoil was merely the first round in a continuing struggle fu-eled by the paranoia that technical training for one set of students could pos-sibly be threatened in co-existence with a two-year liberal arts curriculum. Frankly, Guilford County citizens should have clamored for a community col-lege transfer program that would have provided more opportunities for ad-mission to the first two years of a liberal arts education at a cost far below that of the universities and private colleges. Arguably, a "walk-in" college transfer program established in downtown High Point in the late 1960s could have rev-olutionized the city's educational history given that its only four-year institu-tion was a small, church-affiliated college.[4]

The bitter philosophical struggle between Rochelle and Marco should not diminish the character or commitment of either man, nor should it taint the devotion of the industrialists and politicians who partnered to create—on the fly—an embryonic educational institution to train under-prepared workers. Given the pressure Rochelle appeared to be under to help the Institute suc-ceed for Guilford County and particularly for High Point, he probably should be forgiven his refusal to tolerate GTI's expansion to a comprehensive com-munity college in 1967.

Bledsoe's introductory report reviewed the Institute's history and set the stage for succeeding articles by questioning the school's ability to provide a quality education given that its growth in students and funding had quadrupled in four years.[5] The second article, "The Problem at GTI: Who Is Running the School," focused on the previously discussed six-week state audit that left the Institute's administration and its Board reeling from numerous exceptions to sloppy bookkeeping, the absence of required records, poor supervision and floating pools of money not regulated by the Board. Rochelle summed up the lack of leadership by confessing that, "his Board had been acting more like the Board of Trustees of a garden club than a school" and pledged to rejuvenate the panel.

While Marco and Rochelle were divided over whether rapid growth or a rampant disregard for accounting procedures were to blame for the disastrous audit, the chairman rested his case on poor presidential leadership citing "a lack of communications and a lack of pulling things together at GTI." [6] With the crux of their disagreement smoldering on power and principle, the question was clear; with the fate of the Institute's future governance at stake, who could best lead GTI, a strong Board or a strong president, and was there space for compromise?

"Mrs. X's" case themed Bledsoe's third article: "A Course in Futility: Certificate, But No Job" implied that job placement might not be an option for all of GTI's graduates. "Mrs. X's" story begins at the Employment Security Commission office where she learns that the Federal Manpower Development and Training Act (MDTA) will pay her to attend school while she trains to become a chemical assistant with an opportunity to earn as much as $95 a week. This financially strapped, pregnant, 29-year-old mother of 4 and caregiver to a totally disabled husband, was working as a nurse's aide when she enrolled. Eleven of 21 students, 3 men and 8 women, reportedly finished the class. All of the men and one of the women found employment as chemical assistants, but the remainder did not, either because there were no jobs or because they were women. Rochelle explained the MDTA process whereby the Employment Security Commission recruited candidates to train for positions requested by industries and paid acceptable students to attend classes conducted by GTI; these procedures led completers to assume that a job was guaranteed.

The chemical assistant course Mrs. X and her colleagues took reportedly cost the taxpayers $23,199; $2,109 for each student trained, or $7,733 for each job filled. An Employment Security Commission official was quoted as saying, "Some (courses) have been quite effective and some have not; it's very complicated." Running the MDTA programs enlarged the Institute's curriculum and attracted funding, but their effectiveness was apparently problematic.

Bledsoe reported that since 1961 the MDTA had paid for about 35 courses at GTI at a taxpayer cost of $1.5 million. The programs had trained draftsmen, stenographers, bricklayers, carpenters, auto mechanics, body repairmen, nurses' aides, cooks, and sheet metal workers all at the request of local business and industry.

Bledsoe's fourth article, "GTI Offered Courses, but Lacked Authority," questioned the school for offering nursing and dental hygiene programs that had not been approved by the state, a move Chairman Rochelle termed, "a colossal blunder."[7] Bledsoe quoted the following description from GTI's *1965–66 Catalogue.*

> The associate in applied science degree will be awarded upon successful completion of this program, and graduates will be eligible to take the state board examinations for licensure as a registered nurse.

> But that course would never produce a registered nurse. The school had no authority to offer the program and school officials knew it. [8]

Thirteen young women reportedly paid their fees in the summer of 1965 and began classes to work toward a RN degree. They were aware that the course had not been accredited, but President Marco had confidently assured the women that "it was a sure thing, just a matter of time." The Board minutes for July 20, 1965, provide a clue to what might have happened in this instance, noting that:

> 'verbal approval' was given for a list of technical courses by the Department (of Community Colleges) in Raleigh including practical and registered nurse programs, and programs in dental assisting and dental hygiene.

According to Bledsoe, Dr. Marco elaborated on the professional and public support for the programs and indicated that the

> Full cooperation of the three major local hospitals has been secured and this program is expected, along with the dental hygienist program, to form an important part of our courses of study. [9]

Bledsoe reported that the presidential optimism was badly misplaced:

> Classes dragged on through one quarter, into a second. Despite the repeated assurances of Dr. Marco, the students had begun to worry. They were not taking courses they knew they should be taking if they were to become nurses. No provision had been made for any study work at a hospital. Finally, at the urging of a faculty member, the students called the Community College Division of the State Board of Education and learned that, 'we were not then nor ever would be accredited. We were

wasting our time.' The students were advised not to go any further in the course.[10]

Determined to get some answers, they phoned GTI Board members including County Commissioner Percy Sears and Board Chair Zalph Rochelle. The callers labeled the responses to their calls "unsympathetic."

> The administration, they said, took a letter they had received from the state board confirming their fears and did not return it.

> Actually, GTI Board members were quite concerned about the situation. They went to Raleigh with a hurried bid to get community college status for GTI to save the course. It was not saved, however, and the girls had wasted their time. They were not even refunded their fees.[11]

Two archived letters regarding the nursing question include one written on January 17, 1966, to Mrs. Charles Ward of Thomasville from Louise Bryant, the Educational Supervisor of the Associate Degree in Nursing Program in the Department of Community Colleges at the State Board of Education. Bryant wrote Ward that,

> A curriculum for an associate degree program in nursing at Guilford Technical Institute has not been approved by either the State Board of Education and/or the North Carolina Board of Nursing.[12]

She encouraged Ward to contact an administrator at GTI, or a member of the Board to discuss "the future status of the program in which you are enrolled" and mentioned Percy Sears' name. Bryant's letter and Ward's presumed follow-up calls to Sears and Rochelle created a reactive furor indicating that Rochelle was unaware that Marco had assured the students the course would be approved.

On January 20, 1966, Rochelle vehemently responded to Dr. I. E. Ready at the Department of Community Colleges that the Board had full confidence in President Marco's performance. He assured Ready that Marco regularly reported "on the status of all programs and future plans," and accused the state office of exceeding their authority by corresponding with the nursing students and suggesting that they discuss their grievances with the Board.

> Recently an incident occurred which is contrary to good professional ethics and I am sure that you will agree that steps should be taken so this type of thing will not occur again. A student in our Public Service Program called a member of your staff concerning the Registered Nursing Program. The student received a letter in return to confirm a telephone conversation. I am enclosing this letter for your information.

The points that we object to are as follows:

Your staff should know that we do not have a Registered Nursing Program.

On January 5, Dr. Marco wrote Mrs. Bryant requesting assistance in filling out the required forms for the Registered Nursing Program which we have hopes of starting next fall.

At no time has the Board of Trustees or the administration of the Institute accepted any student in a Registered Nursing Program. The students, who are preparing themselves for a nursing career, either here or elsewhere, are in our Public Service Administration curriculum.

In view of the above facts, we feel that members of your staff exceeded their authority in going over your and Dr. Marco's heads in recommending that the dissentient student contact members of the Board of Trustees. This is not a good administrative practice or policy. It is the consensus of this and other similar institutions that the members of your staff are there to help us, not to oppose us, nor to cause dissension among the student body, faculty or staff.[13]

The following day, January 21, 1966, Rochelle wrote President Marco.

At your first opportunity, will you read the following statement to the members of your faculty and staff to govern all personnel connected with Guilford Technical Institute, and will you make this statement a part of the rules and regulations of the Institute?

All personnel are instructed to refrain from making personal contact, or directing others to do so, with the members of the Board of Trustees or members of the Community College System headquartered in Raleigh on matters pertaining to the Institute without the express knowledge and permission of the chief administrative officer of the Guilford Technical Institute or its future equivalent.

Violators of this policy are subject to disciplinary action or dismissal.

Please inform me when this statement of policy is delivered to the personnel and include it in the records of the Board of Trustees.[14]

Rochelle's obvious embarrassment in the nursing case was not assuaged by Bledsoe's description of poor academic advising in the case of 20 dental hygienist students. In 1965, they took courses for credit in a presumably non-existent program they were reportedly told could be transferred to the dental hygiene program as soon as it was approved. According to Bledsoe:

When the program did come through (1966), after 10 months of work on the part of local officials, it was a federally sponsored course under the Manpower Development Training Act (MDTA). The students were surprised to learn the courses they had taken would have to be repeated. The credits they had been promised they could transfer could not be transferred.[15]

Six students continued in the program while a few switched courses and the remainder dropped out. Now, almost two years later, the Institute was embroiled in a controversy involving these high profile programs that were fueling President Marco's frantic struggle for community college status. Chairman Rochelle attributed the nursing and dental "blunders" to an inclination "to move ahead too fast." Bledsoe surmised that the frantic request for community college status in 1966, approved by the State Board of Education and forwarded to the General Assembly, was a hurried strategy to "save a nursing course which could not otherwise be credited," but continued with this pattern of poor planning by noting that "other courses have also been announced and then dropped or delayed."[16] Bledsoe wrote:

> Last fall, for example, local newspapers carried an announcement from Dr. Marco that a course in highway landscaping and beautification was to be held. Graduates would supposedly find work with the State Highway Department. That course isn't going on either. And won't be. 'Plans had not been completed before the announcement was made,' Rochelle said. Fortunately, no students began classes to become highway beautifiers before plans fell through. No announcement was ever made that the course was cancelled.[17]

There is no denying that the Institute was remiss in communicating the message that this specific program had been cancelled. It was originally a part of the Governor's New Industry Training Program to train supervisors and foremen to work in the Federal Highway Beautification Program. Rochelle informed the Board on May 10, 1966, that this one year vocational training program was supposed to bring $3.0 to $4.0 million to the state, but there is no extant record of a reason for its cancellation.[18] The Board Of Trustees and administration were both at fault for having failed to establish dependable lines of communication with the public and the media from the Institution's inception.

GTI: Two Men in a Struggle

The problems roiling GTI during this period were directly attributable to the Board's "hands-off" policy following Marco's assumption of the presidency. While the power struggle between the Board Chair and the President intensified after the state audit in late 1966, there is no indication that the Board and the administration attempted to find a positive resolution to their obvious differences. Bledsoe's fifth article argued that the line in the sand between GTI's leaders rested on the distinction between a technical institute and a vague interpretation of a community college as a traditional junior college foundation for a four-year college. He concluded that, "the (junior) college is already there hiding behind the title of a technical institute;" a conclusion that may have been fueled by campus gossip about "Jamestown University." In the middle of the muddle of this confounding controversy exacerbated by Rochelle's rants, the Board was still focused on expansion:[19]

> GTI is a junior college in everything but name and it may have that soon. Trustees have asked the legislature to allow the technical institute to become a community college this session.[20]

On the plus side, community college status would purportedly gain the Institute $405,000 in state funds for desperately needed capital improvements, plus a larger state budget for additional teachers, and the possibility of more federal grants. The publicity generated by Bledsoe's series prompted High Point College and Guilford College to oppose the proposed expansion on the basis that GTI was bound to become a four-year liberal arts institution and attract their potential students with lower tuition, a fear Rochelle attempted to squash as this interview with Bledsoe reveals:

> 'We're not interested in being a college, as such,' says Rochelle. 'We want to give the average guy who can't afford these other colleges a working education.'

> 'Actually,' Bledsoe wrote, 'Rochelle isn't interested in GTI becoming a college at all. His desire to give the average guy a way to learn to earn a living has brought him almost to the point of leading the opposition to community college status for GTI.'[21]

Recounting Rochelle's remarks to the Asheboro Rotarians that community college status would destroy a technical institute's vocational programs, Bledsoe implied that "a serious split could develop among Board members over the matter," even as he noted that the struggle between Rochelle and Marco could be deeper than their differences over community college expansion."[22] The day "2 Men in a Struggle" appeared (Thursday, February 9, 1967), Bledsoe reported that Marco and his Board had been summoned to a (February 16, 1967) Raleigh conference with Dr. I. E. Ready, director of the Department of Community Colleges, and Dallas Herring, Chairman of the State Board of Education.

Herring denied any knowledge of a controversy and characterized the meeting as an opportunity "to discuss an urgent matter in the light of developments" as a "normal procedure, a private conference between the institutional representatives and us."[23]

The relationship between Rochelle and Marco flared to a more argumentative level when the chairman accused the administration of an inclination to secrecy and a failure to admit mistakes. He suggested that "an open door policy where the public is entitled to know anything and everything about Guilford Technical Institute would go far in correcting individual problems."[24] Restating his opinion that the school should remain a technical institute and charging that it was not being run to its maximum effectiveness, Rochelle intimated in a published report that the Raleigh meeting would include the question of whether GTI should continue under the leadership of Marco and the Board:

> If the Board runs the school so that we can welcome reporters, auditors, observers from state departments and the public, we will automatically correct the individual problems that have had so much publicity recently.[25]

Beyond intimating that Marco could be fired, Rochelle's objectives for GTI included establishing a greater feeling of security for the faculty by instituting contracts to establish their terms of employment and reviewing the school's vocational programs to attract "the guy who doesn't have a chance." He was firmly convinced that GTI's attempt to achieve community college status was a step toward becoming a four-year college and was broadly skeptical about the future of community colleges in a competitive match up with established four-year colleges and universities.[26] However, his opposition to expansion in February 1967 does not mesh with the arguments for the broader status he posted to Dallas Herring, Chairman of the State Board of Education, and Governor Dan Moore on May 18, 1966. That correspondence requested a change in status from technical institute to community college with the stated rights and privileges of that designation.

A close review of the Herring letter indicates that it may have been drafted by Marco since the arguments presented for community college status appear to be more his than Rochelle's. The author pleads for expansion as a way to help educate young women who can't get into local four-year colleges. He additionally argues that conversion will assist young men who do not have manual ability, but are mentally agile and could be prepared for various professional careers. The letter additionally addresses the need for registered nurses, "which can't be trained at technical institutes and library assistants requiring an Associate in Arts degree." Item 5 of Rochelle's petition for the change in status addresses the liberal arts curriculum.

General education courses, or liberal arts curriculum, cannot be authorized for technical institutes despite the high quality of its faculty—for
those courses are reserved for the community college. We still need mental growth in all areas whether baker, butcher, lawyer or doctor for better understanding of peoples and for better government.[27]

This letter, and Rochelle's remarks nine months later that, "where GTI can
be of service the most is to teach people to make a living and acquire skills
which contribute to industrial growth, which in turn, will attract more industry," appear to define different philosophies.[28] Two headstrong humanitar-
ians appear irrevocably divided; the industrialist is committed to seeing unskilled laborers learn to earn in a technical environment while the educational
administrator's determination to liberalize the curriculum implies that his
agenda could provide an alternative to the county's private colleges. On a personal level, Marco kept his mouth shut even when Rochelle exposed his bias
by charging that "all technical institute presidents would rather be college presidents because there's more glory and esteem to it."[29]

By mid February 1967 the GTI Trustees were secretly meeting and Rochelle
was accusing the state of "creating a string of half-pint Mickey Mouse colleges
that aren't capable of producing quality graduates in either academic, vocational, or technical fields;" GTI Trustee W. O. Conrad was clamoring for
Rochelle's resignation and the question of technical institute versus community college status was beginning to resemble a Valentine massacre placing a
fledgling institution committed to training Guilford County's workforce at
risk.[30]

Chapter 8

A Mickey Mouse College?

The state is creating a string of half-pint, Mickey Mouse colleges that aren't capable of producing quality graduates in either academic, vocational, or technical fields—they don't fit well in the same bed.[1]

Zalph Rochelle, GTI BOT Chair

A Question of Stewardship

The turmoil surging from three crucial meetings between February 13–17, 1967, involving GTI Trustees vexed the school and county for months. The drama premiered with a so-called "unity" session involving eight Trustees and excluding Board Chair Rochelle. Termed by some a "secret session," it preceded the regular monthly Board meeting and a mandated summit with the State Board of Education. Contention between Trustees became public when Rochelle's claim that he had not been invited to the "unity" session was refuted by Trustee W. O. Conrad. Rochelle countered that he had been asked to call an "off the cuff" meeting, but refused because he didn't want to meet without the press in attendance and then charged that the meeting "appeared to be an attempt to oust him as chairman." Unity, secret, or off-the-cuff aside, whatever happened at the Monday night meeting influenced Bill Conrad to write a letter four days later demanding Rochelle's resignation.[2]

Eight of GTI's eleven Trustees gathered for the so-called "secret" meeting in the Blue Bell, Inc., office of vice-chair James L. "Jimmy" Williams; in addition to Rochelle, Ed Kemp and Frank Starling did not attend the meeting.[3] Williams closed the session to the press with the excuse: "All we're having is a very informal little get-together. We're having no formal meeting. We're having no press present, and it's just that simple." This strategy forced the public to rely on speculative press reports including quotations from those attending as to what issues might have been discussed. Beyond debating the proposal for community college status, the Board reportedly discussed "'implications and innuendos' that recent statements and actions by Rochelle 'might not be serving the best interest of the Board';[4] it is highly probable that Trustee Conrad, who had been researching the Board minutes, chose this moment to question the legality of Rochelle's re-election as Board chairman."

> Rochelle said after the Monday meeting (February 13, 1967) that he was elected at a meeting of the Trustees in July 1966. There are no minutes of a July meeting and several Board members said they could not remember one. One Trustee said there could have been a meeting at which there was not a quorum. Another said he seemed to recall a meeting at which Rochelle was elected after being nominated by Williams.
>
> Rochelle maintained that he had been legally elected, but could no longer be sure it was in July (1966). Rochelle said nobody had questioned his chairmanship at an official Board meeting.[5]

Rochelle was determined to retain his chairmanship until July 1, 1967, and pledged to fight any attempt to unseat him. The minutes, maintained by Dr. Marco and his secretary, do not record a meeting of the GTI Board of Trustees in July 1966; however, the Board's executive committee including Zalph Rochelle, W. O. Conrad, Percy Sears, and Marco did meet July 14, 1966; also attending were Board attorney Robert Martin and George Rottman, building consultant for the Guilford County Schools. The minutes for this meeting and those signed by Rochelle for the remainder of the year do not record his re-election as chair. Since Rochelle was determined to have the minutes precisely reflect the business of the Board, it is highly unlikely that he would have allowed his election to pass undocumented. For the record, Rochelle and Vice Chairman Williams were last re-elected to their positions on October 12, 1965.[6]

The GTI Board session on Valentine Day morning 1967 at the Howard Johnson Restaurant apparently proceeded in a civil atmosphere even though Rochelle was clearly aware that the majority who attended the previous evening's "unity" meeting were committed to community college conversion. The press gallery included Jerry Bledsoe, *Greensboro Daily News;* Jim Wagner and Dot Benjamin, *Greensboro Record*; Jim Hawkins, *High Point Enterprise*; D'Etta Barnhart, WGHP-TV Channel 8; and Don Frazier, WNOS Radio. For much of its existence, the fledgling Institution had benefited from positive press coverage, but the audit exceptions and the conversion issue were generating widespread public attention elevating the contentious state of affairs at GTI to Guilford County's number one news story. As might be expected, the press quotes following the session were far more provocative than the staid Board minutes.

Several topics introduced at the session posed major implications for the future of the Institution; not the least of which was Percy Sears' motion that the Board move its meetings to the Institute and invite the school's administrators to report on activities in their various departments. It was the inquisitive Sears' strategy to broaden the communications stream in a setting where Board members could ask questions about the Institute's specific operations from the employees who implemented their policies. Unfortunately, the move to meet on the Jamestown campus did not happen in this era, but when it did occur it remained an incisive policy that continues to this day. Classroom space was a major topic during the session even as the planning for the present day Business Careers building was going forward. Sears, who, as history proved, was ahead of his time in championing institutional growth, suggested renting mobile classroom trailers, a proposal that incited Marco to ask for ten to solve his scheduling problems.

Rochelle, who had seized on the school dropout issue to reinforce his stonewall defense of GTI's technical programs, asked Marco to explain the statutes pertaining to admitting 16- to 18-year-old dropouts. The chairman contended that the admissions requirements set by state law were designed to discourage students from quitting high school to enter technical institutes. Never one to mince words, he labeled "getting them (dropouts) off the street corners and into the classrooms a good investment for the county" and pushed the issue for the remainder of his tenure on the Board.[7]

Inevitably, Western Electric executive Conrad, who had emerged as the most vocal advocate for conversion to community college status, broached the meeting's major topic by suggesting that the Board reaffirm the position stated in its May 1966 letter to Dr. Dallas Herring, Chairman of the State Board of Education, seeking approval of comprehensive community college status for GTI to meet the various needs of its constituents.

Conrad charted his presentation to illustrate how a comprehensive community college could successfully embrace an industrial education center, a technical institute, and an adult basic education program in concert with a two-year liberal arts program. The presentation was calculated to convince the Board that GTI's technical programs were not at risk through expansion because stopping or side stepping programs without the approval of the State Board of Education was impossible.[8]

Following Conrad's explanation, the Board members reiterated their intention to continue offering vocational and technical programs in the event GTI was granted conversion and approved his motion with a voice vote that did not include one from the chairman. James Wagner (*Greensboro Daily News*) wrote,

"Rochelle did not participate in the voice vote taken Tuesday. He heard a chorus of 'ayes' and ruled the motion approved without asking for 'nay' votes." The next few weeks would prove that Conrad was exceptionally prepared to "sell" any audience on the benefits of converting GTI to a community college and that Zalph Rochelle was just as determined to squelch the idea.[9]

Dorothy Benjamin's report proclaiming the Board's decision to "go for broke" and seek community college status appeared that afternoon in the *Greensboro Record.* Rochelle was quoted as repeating his overwhelming fear that conversion would adversely affect the Institute's technical and vocational training and ignore the 16- to 18-year-old dropouts. He repeated his embedded belief that the discrepancy in funding between technical institutes and community colleges was prejudicial and predicted that inserting "college" into its name would completely alter the culture of GTI:

> I don't see why a technical institution can't have full status like a college. The people we serve need a practical, technical education to earn a living. A well-run technical institution ought to be as good as a liberal arts school. I've been fearful we might neglect the technical and vocational aspects.[10]

Rochelle believed that a liberal arts program at GTI would interact favorably with the four-year colleges and universities in Guilford County, but his overriding fear was its assumed threat to the Institute's technical and vocational programs; as he put it, "They don't fit well in the same bed."[11] The depth of his concern can be further attributed to his distrust of Marco's "college" agenda. Clearly, he did not believe Marco would protect GTI's technical and vocational programs, which comprised the county's workforce preparedness aorta. Of course, if the state and county failed to fund the conversion, a liberal arts program at GTI was a moot question. In the meantime, the Institute desperately needed the money that community college status would provide to create more learning space.[12] Rochelle's stubborn defense of technical programs may have isolated him from his Board, but his argument was not invalid, nor was he alone in his contention.

More than a year later (November 1968), the Department of Community College's Industrial Education Director George L. Howard resigned because of philosophical differences with several of the Department's mainstream initiatives. His comments presumably renewed the debate over which state agency should be responsible for new industry training (NIT). According to Howard,

> The (community college) system started out as a system of industrial education centers but has gotten into the business now of college parallel work. It is almost impossible for a man who is a community college president to wear both hats—academic and technical.[13]

Howard was among those highly placed state officials, including Chairman J. W. "Willie" York of the State Board of Conservation and Development, who believed that "higher education was not the universal prescription for all ills, and that job training must be offered for the unskilled."

February 14, 1967, was a long day in the frenetic life of Zalph Rochelle. Frustrated that three-fourths of his Board had met without him the previous evening, he gaveled the dissidents into session at 8:00 A.M. at the Howard Johnson Restaurant in High Point. He concluded his boisterous Valentine twelve hours later by haranguing the General Assembly, the State Board of Education, and the Department of Community Colleges in the Sky Room of the Southern Furniture Exposition Building in High Point. When he carted his bully pulpit to a meeting of the High Point Chapter of the American Business Clubs that evening, he escalated the conversion debate because he believed that the funding pattern for technical institutes was a calculated strategy to prevent them from starting additional programs, including health science, which would greatly benefit Guilford County.

The passionate industrialist presented a compelling argument for focusing on technical training for Guilford County's workforce, and the region's laborers were fortunate to have his advocacy. Leveraging his dual positions as GTI Board Chair and Vice President of the State Association of Community College Trustees, he challenged the General Assembly to "initiate an in-depth study to determine the effectiveness of North Carolina's Community College System." He reportedly charged that pressure from the State Board of Education's community college division was rushing trustees of vocational and technical institutes to seek "college" status, thereby creating "a string of half-pint, Mickey Mouse colleges that aren't capable of producing quality graduates in either academic, vocational, or technical fields—they don't fit well in the same bed."[14]

He claimed that "trustees of technical and vocational schools were being 'constantly bludgeoned over the head'" to seek college status; that technical institutes were denied money and not allowed to teach certain technical courses, such as health sciences, unless they became community colleges. This process, according to Rochelle, that places "tremendous pressure" on the Boards to seek college status. He urged the General Assembly to fund vocational and technical schools on the same level as community colleges and accredit them to teach the technical programs their designation prohibited them from teaching.[15]

He blamed the State Board of Education for restricting the enrollment of 16- to 18-year-old dropouts in vocational and technical institutes by requiring "elaborate and discouraging procedures for their admittance" and ratcheted up his evangelistic pitch to exclaim: "The state has now clobbered the dropout in the teeth; we need to eliminate this fantastic waste of young manpower."[16] Rochelle challenged the legislature to appoint a group of "outside consultants" to study the status of North Carolina's community colleges and encouraged the American Business Club chapters in the state to lobby for legislative action to change the Community College System so that technical institutes would not be forced to become colleges to qualify for additional money and programs.

Guilford County's three major newspapers prolifically editorialized on the brewing debacle over community college status for GTI even as Governor Dan Moore's 1967–68 budget confirmed that conversion was not imminent. His 58.7 percent ($45.7 million) increase for the Community College System recommended upgrading Wayne County Technical Institute to a community college, but it did not mention GTI. Clearly the Institute needed to right its course before it expanded, and the *Greensboro Daily News* credited Bledsoe's series with exposing the Institute's principal problems:

> They center on seeming failure by the Institute's administrators, in time of expansion to deal fairly and intelligently with students and faculty. Part of this failure is due to hasty growth and ill advised ambition. But a good deal more may involve organically poor administration and a clash of personalities among Trustees and administrators.[17]

The paper challenged the State Board of Education to prevent "poor management and controversy from destroying what its own officials consider one of the four more important institutions in the (community college) system."[18] In its February 15, 1967, afternoon edition, *The Greensboro Record* congratulated the state for vetoing the conversion even as the editor vehemently denounced GTI's Board for its lack of stewardship and Marco for his presidential ineptitude. The *Record* joined its sister publication, the *Greensboro Daily News*, in challenging the State Board of Education and GTI's additional funding sources, the federal and county governments, to examine the Institute's performance before allowing it to convert to a college:

> Neither community nor state will be well served by a title, whatever it may come to be, which the Jamestown school does not merit. Prudence and vision dictate that foundations be secured before superstructures are erected.[19]

Wallowing in a milieu compounded of contention, mismanagement, and accusations of illegalities, the GTI Trustees met with the State Board of Education in Raleigh on February 16, 1967. They learned from Chairman Dallas Herring that the Department of Community Colleges was sending a "task force" to GTI to work with the Institution in whatever areas needed help. The institutional disorder did not prevent GTI's Trustees from pursuing the conversion issue. It did, however, force them to consider either waiting for expansion until they could improve their dysfunctional operation or remaining a technical institute for the present while seeking special authorization and funds from the General Assembly to give courses in registered nursing and dental hygiene.

Seven members were in favor of applying for college status immediately with the alternative of requesting implementation of the health science programs, should the conversion initiative fail. Trustees Rochelle, Kemp, Davis, and Starling voted to seek the health programs thereby reaffirming the split that emerged at the previous Monday's secret meeting. On this occasion, furniture executive John T. Davis joined the minority faction. The Board refused to take "no" for an answer on the conversion issue and again asked the State Board of Education to "'do the best it can' to get college status for GTI 'as soon as possible.'"[20]

Knowing that only the GTI Board could fire the Institute's president, Rochelle took advantage of the Raleigh conference to demand that President Marco be relieved of his duties because of ineffective leadership. His loss of confidence in Marco presumably stemmed from the administrative irregularities revealed by the state audit, but their differing philosophies on the mission of the school surely fueled his demand. Trustee Bill Conrad defended Marco, who won a unanimous vote of confidence from the 11 Trustees present including Rochelle; in an ironic twist of allegiance Rochelle was quoted as saying "that he voted confidence in Marco, because 'as long as he is president I have to give him support.'"[21]

Guilford County citizens learned from the media that the schism between Trustees had widened even further when a letter written by Conrad calling for Rochelle's resignation became public. Conrad based his case on the grounds that neither Rochelle nor vice-chair James Williams had been legally elected for the year beginning July 1, 1966. As noted earlier, there is no written record of any election for Board Chair or vice-chair in July 1966. Rochelle, believing that the attempt to oust him was based on his criticism of GTI's operation, replied that "he had been elected to serve until July 1, 1967, and intended to do so and would fight any move to oust him."[22]

State Senator Ed Kemp, one of the institution's founders and a Trustee, solved that crisis with a "clear and firm" opinion from Attorney General Wade Bruton that "officers of the Board of Trustees are duly qualified until duly qualified successors are named."[23] Rochelle kept his seat even though the minutes clearly substantiate that that "no election of Board officials had occurred since October 1965, when Rochelle and vice-chair James Williams were elected." Conrad accepted the legal decision and dropped his demand for Rochelle's resignation, guaranteeing that the chairman would remain in office until at least July 1, 1967.

Kemp sought to end the conflict between Rochelle and Conrad on a positive note by affirming that "he didn't see any need for major dissension on the Board of Trustees over the matter of who the officers are at this particular time adding, 'the school is more important than any personality involved.'"[24] Rochelle promised to appoint a nominating committee "in due time." This issue aside, there was no indication that the strained relationship between President Marco and Board Chairman Rochelle had abated. The questions that demanded addressing as the state task force prepared to travel to Jamestown revolved around the leadership and managerial competencies of the Institute's president, his philosophical differences with the Board Chair, and a clear definition of what constituted a comprehensive community college as opposed to a "Mickey Mouse College."[25]

Chapter 9

Battles and Leaders

The State Board of Education is justified in sending a task force to Guilford Technical Institute to help 'strengthen and improve' its management. The Jamestown atmosphere of clashing personalities, divided Trustees, and secret meetings needs to be cleared.[1]

February 1967

When it investigated Guilford Technical Institute in 1967 the Department of Community Colleges was administered by the State Board of Education. Allan Markham, who headed the department's institutional evaluation and accreditation division, brought his team to Jamestown on Monday, February 27, 1967. The task force of professional educators, twelve men and a woman, was charged to "strengthen and improve" conditions at the school. Its members were assigned to interview personnel, study reports, examine the curriculum and make recommendations. While the panel would presumably meet with the Board at some time during the process, to avoid additional fragmentation and dissension among the Trustees they did not plan to interview individual members.[2]

The core of the controversy gripping the Institute centered on the persistent, divisive fear that conversion to community college status would destroy GTI's primary function as a vocational and technical training facility. It remained to be seen if the dissident groups in the Board room could actually sit down face to face and resolve their anxieties with a set of agreeable principles. Meanwhile, the squad of experts from Raleigh was primed to look over their shoulders. Dr. Ready initially believed the task force could complete its first visit in less than three days but intimated that return visits were possible before the committee filed its report. The comprehensive nature of the investigation is verified by the expertise attributed to individual task force members;

they were familiar with every internal operation including adult education, college parallel programs, construction and facilities, curriculum, vocational and technical programs, health occupations, and the Manpower Development and Training Act.[3] GTI's external relationship with the public and the press was also a prime target for study; as Dr. Ready noted, "We believe the people of Guilford County should be kept fully informed about the operations of this Institution. We believe in open communications."[4]

The task force members began their visit by meeting with the staff and faculty, but President Marco was obviously determined not to let the investigation disrupt the Institute's operations. He "moved ahead as rapidly as possible" to build programs like Dental Assisting (then under MDTA), that could strengthen his case for conversion. He encouraged potential students to apply at the Employment Security Commission offices for preliminary screening and testing and appointed a panel of dentists to select 20 potential candidates for the high profile program.[5]

"GTI Needs a Straightening"[6]

Retrospectively, February 1967 marks the first public exposure of student and faculty life at GTI. Prior to the disastrous audit in late 1966 and the furor over community college conversion, faculty and student issues were as impervious to the media as they were to the Board's agenda. Faculty issues involving terms of employment, remuneration and benefits discussed in previous chapters, increased as the school expanded. Beyond a few disparate notes in the minutes relevant to sports teams and the tentative introduction of "Tech Talk," student life was not a major topic at Board meetings. During the GIEC period, the director could demonstrate Institutional credibility by issuing staid statistics reflecting the numbers of adult workers trained; individual student achievement became more important with the transition to Guilford Technical Institute and the enrollment of more traditional age college students.

While Jerry Bledsoe's comprehensive and controversial series exposed the negative dimension of student experiences related to certain programs, the conversion issue inspired a proactive stance by the Student Government Association and the faculty. A letter supporting conversion submitted to State Board of Education Chairman Dallas Herring by English instructor Charlene Hall and 25 colleagues elicited this response:

> I concur with the view that a fully comprehensive institution is needed
> and that apparently the philosophy of total education, which is the foun-

dation of this movement, has not been understood by critics of Guilford Technical Institute.

The State Board of Education and the Department of Community Colleges will take immediate steps to assist the Institution in the improvement of this situation. Meanwhile, I commend the staff and faculty for the responsible stand they have taken during these difficult days.

Our state constitution says, "The people have a right to the privilege of education and it is the duty of the state to guard and maintain that right." This shall be our goal as we endeavor to help you in this situation.[7]

Herring's position on conversion, reflected by the decisions of the State Board of Education's administration of the Department of Community Colleges, is a matter of public record, but it is more difficult to identify GTI's "critics," unless we consider Chairman Rochelle, conversion's most vocal opponent, and Bledsoe and his fellow journalists. GTI Student Body President Tom Duncan's letter to Herring at the height of the February 1967 media exposé includes an SGA petition endorsing conversion. Duncan optimistically portrays the breadth of student spirit at GTI, a communal willingness to learn, and the potential role of the Institute's students as community leaders. Describing the school as "the only opportunity for some" and "a second chance for others," his letter and petition suggests widespread student support for conversion and its benefits including additional funding and program expansion.[8]

A week later, Duncan posted a similar letter to State Representative Hargrove Bowles, Jr., emphatically denying Bledsoe's charges of "campus turmoil and an over-all attitude of unrest and disappointment."

Such statements are not true! As a result, up to this point the public has been given slanted truths and incomplete information. We considered fighting the press, but such a battle would have gained us little and would have increased the controversy. Thus we have waited calmly for the newspapers to present their views. During this time, we have gathered our forces. We feel it is time to voice our opinions about the issue.[9]

Duncan assured Bowles that 75 percent of GTI's student body supported the conversion to community college. Some students stated their opinions in letters to the editors of Guilford County's newspapers. Welding student Jack Marshall, who was pleased with his course work and his instructor, "a fine patient teacher," suggested that GTI's students be allowed to vote on the conversion issue.[10] Another welding student's experience was less than positive; Paul C. Ward believed wholeheartedly in the mission of GTI but terminated his

course when the numbers of students accepted exceeded the instructor's capability to teach the entire class due to space, time and equipment limitations.
He wrote that:

> Guilford Technical Institute is needed, even if it has not met standards in
> the past. It is simply up to industry to demand, and students to expect,
> adequate facilities to be used by competent instructors.[11]

March 14, 1967

When the GTI Board convened for its regularly scheduled session, the furious debate over the Institute's performance and its future had been raging
in the press for more than a month; the Chair had lost confidence in the President and the Trustees were seriously divided. The Board regained its full 12
member strength when the county commissioners selected the first African-
American to sit on the Board of Trustees, Greensboro educator Vance Chavis,
to replace Dr. Wendell Patton, who had resigned over the conversion issue.
Trustee John Thompson's unanimously approved resolution asking Western
Electric executive W. O. Conrad to continue on the Board suggests that Conrad, who had demanded Rochelle's resignation as chairman may have been on
the verge of resigning, or leaving the Board at the end of his term in June.
Thompson's successful resolution, with the press observing, suggests that the
Board was endeavoring to emphasize its reunification.[12]

The Trustees spent much of the session processing the documents necessary to finance and construct the new classroom-library building before giving the floor to William Marley, the local Manpower Development and Training Act (MDTA) Coordinator. Marley proceeded to explain the purpose of
the federal Act in response to Bledsoe's critical articles on the training program's alleged shortcomings. He reassured the Board that the MDTA had
been created to train the unemployed and fill the community's workforce
needs and that the MDTA training GTI provided was based on job-needs surveys conducted by the Employment Security Administration. At the time 330
students were reportedly enrolled in seven courses: dental hygiene, stenography, on-the-job training, dental assisting, auto mechanics, building maintenance, and a carpentry apprentice program.[13] Five programs designed to train
dropouts for positions as diverse as cashier-checker, welding, small engine repair, upholstery, and food service were slated to begin within the month.[14]
Since conversion was still on the table, the Board unanimously decided to
meet with the Guilford County Delegation to the General Assembly in
Raleigh on March 22, 1967.

The Blessing of a Veto for the Future of GTI

Six days before the caucus, the *Greensboro Record* punctured the Board's expectations by counseling the Trustees to spend the next two years remedying the Institution's problems and restoring its foundations.

> Guilford Technical Institute, however valuable the upgrading may be, is simply not yet prepared for community college status. No scrutiny of the state report is required in support of that conclusion. There has been testimony enough in the clash of Trustees with Trustees and of chairman with president, in courses announced without authority and canceled without notice, in students' frustration in accreditation, in administrative procedures snarled.[15]

Dr. Ready had advised Trustee John Foster to "abandon any effort at all for community college status," and Percy Sears lamented, "We were licked on the community college thing even before the investigative team came in."[16] Ready restated the obvious, reminding the Board that neither the governor, nor the advisory budget commission, nor the State Board of Education, had requested funding for GTI's conversion to a community college. GTI's chances of becoming a community college during the current session of the General Assembly were characterized as "pretty well zero." In terms of "the people and the funds" working together, that was not happening at the state level and it was not going to happen.

The revival of the ubiquitous "name change" debate that GTI become a "technical college" prompted Dr. Ready, who was not at the legislative briefing, to restate the organization of the institutions administered by the Department of Community College: "The law defines community college, technical institute, and industrial education center and legally there is no provision for anything else. It can't be both a community college and technical institute." While a puzzled Dr. Ready pondered semantic redundancies, W. O. Conrad presented "The GTI Story," one of the most eloquent descriptions of the Institution on record to the Guilford County Legislative Delegation. In his case for naming GTI a "Technical College," Conrad cited the present and future need for a new class of sub-professional technicians to support America's new generation of engineers. Emphatically reminding the legislators that conversion would allow the Institution to "serve the needs of the total population of Guilford County," he closed with this challenge: "We are growing too fast in Guilford County to procrastinate over this kind of decision."[17]

April 11, 1967: "GTI Out to Build Image"[18]

The GTI Board minutes for the April 11 session do not contain a single reference to the discussion to add "college" to the Institution's name, as Jim Hawkins reported in the *High Point Enterprise* on March 23, 1967.

> The issue of college status came up when chairman Zalph Rochelle reported on a meeting which Trustees had with the Guilford legislative delegation and included in it references to "upgrading the Institution." Dr. Ready in his reply reminded Dr. Marco that a change of status must follow an accepted pattern and that Gov. Dan Moore had made "very clear recommendations" that only one new community college (in Wayne County) be approved by the legislature.[19]

According to Hawkins, the thoroughly embroiled Trustees first approved a resolution "to stop talking about college status until the public becomes aware of the needs of the school," then rescinded this directive and emphasized the need to rebuild the "image" of the school in order to encourage enrollment for the fall semester. President Marco was directed to invite public school counselors to GTI for a briefing on the Institute's programs and develop a recruiting brochure. Board approval to hire David Senkpiel as the Director of Student Personnel was another positive step toward upgrading the Institute's services.[20]

April 25, 1967

The GTI Board met in special session eleven days later to finalize the bidding process for the new library-classroom building funded by federal, state, and county governments for $349,554.86 including $160,000 from the GTI bond issue. Even as GTI was securing previously appropriated funds for the desperately needed building, its operational expenses were escalating. Marco warned Guilford County Commission Chairman Dale Montgomery that legislative appropriations would fall short of funding the school's needs and asked the county to consider supplementing faculty and staff salaries and paying for certain administrative and clerical positions recommended by state auditors.[21]

"Healing the Breach"[22]

Dr. Ready distributed copies of his department's task force report when he lunched with the Trustees on May 2, 1967, at the Towne House Restaurant in

High Point. According to Jerry Bledsoe, nine of the panel's 11 recommendations were leveled at the Institution's dysfunctional Board and its disorganized president. The examiners concluded that two major circumstances had caused "the first major loss of confidence in the Institution:" "the split between the Trustees" and "serious administrative weaknesses." [23] They found that the Trustees did not appear to fully understand what a technical institute was, nor were they clear on how the Board should function as the Institutions' local governing body.

The report chastised individual Trustees for discussing Board matters with the press before presenting them to the Board. They were counseled to open their meetings, except for personnel discussions, and censured for failing to establish satisfactory lines of communication between themselves and the public, the faculty, and students. The Trustees were ordered to make decisions as an entity and reminded that individual Trustees could only exercise the authority delegated to them by the Board; they could not arbitrarily act independently.

The administration was censured for a variety of ill-formed decisions instituted out of ignorance or to deliberately by-pass state regulations. Marco's staff was cited for "an abortive attempt" to start a registered nursing program without state approval as well as for establishing a public service curriculum program without state approval; "in which students said they were led to believe their credits could be transferred to other programs." The administration was cited for failure to properly execute a pending proposal to start an associate degree nursing program and to adequately prepare to secure accreditation for the dental hygiene program.[24] The task force recommended a staff reorganization to alleviate problems extending from administrative overloads in some areas and the serious neglect of necessary administrative functions.

The administration's inability to communicate effectively with faculty, students, and the public elicited a variety of recommendations including the need for a new student handbook, the development of an in-service training program to promote staff involvement in curriculum planning, and a strategy to organize advisory committees. GTI was described as "not totally off the track in carrying out its mission, but with problems, all of which cannot be attributed to growing pains." The list of remedies proposed an Institutional self study, a campus master plan, improved record keeping, a space utilization study, and a physical plant upgrade. The ever gracious Dr. Ready, who was stretching to manage a Department of Community Colleges expanding exponentially across the state, offered to "accept a full share of responsibility for any failures that may have come about."[25]

"Heartaches and Rough Places"[26]

On June 5, 1967, President Marco ignored the chairman of his Board and submitted his letter of resignation to Vice Chair James Williams. To establish a positive footnote to his departure, he noted the growth of the Institute "from the least of the institutions in the state to its present position in the top ten" and the graduation of the first recipients of the Associate in Applied Science Degree.

> Despite the adverse publicity concerning the status of the Guilford Technical Institute it serves and has served a very useful function in the growth of the industrial community. It should be allowed to grow under peaceful, harmonious atmosphere for the good of all young people.

> Therefore, since the Institute has climbed out of the morass it was in May 1965 and now has its rightful place in the education sun, my talents are no longer needed in this area. Hence, I am submitting my resignation as President and Chief Administrator, effective, July 1, 1967.[27]

While the Board pondered Marco's resignation, the Institute's graduates lined up in front of Old Main on Sunday, June 11, 1967, for the school's first commencement. The legendary Dr. Bonnie Cone, Vice Chancellor of the University of North Carolina at Charlotte, delivered the charge to twenty-three recipients of the Associate in Applied Science degree. Barbara Jean Pardue (Greensboro) was honored as the most outstanding student and Julian Craig Murphy (Greensboro) received the President's Medal honoring GTI's most outstanding first year student.[28]

Ironically, the Board accepted Marco's resignation at its regularly scheduled session on June 13, 1967, when his nemesis Zalph Rochelle stepped down as Board Chair. Cone Mills executive Frank Starling assumed the chairmanship while W. O. Conrad, a Rochelle opponent and Marco supporter, became vice chairman; Robert O. Kistler was re-elected secretary. John T. Davis, Jr., Davis Furniture Company, High Point, who would become one of the Institutions' legendary advocates (1965–81), was named to replace Conrad as Vice Chairman.[29]

The Trustees graciously voted Dr. Marco their appreciation for "promoting the development and growth of Guilford Technical Institute as a member of the business and educational community of Guilford County," and pledged to continue supporting his initiatives. In a show of harmony Rochelle presented the president a going away gift while praising him for transforming the industrial education center into a technical institute. The outgoing chairman admitted that it was "a process that included a lot of heartaches and a lot of rough places."[30]

Dr. Marco, in taking Guilford Technical Institute from an industrial education center to a technical institute, has made a real contribution to our community. We feel that his enthusiasm has done much to build a foundation on which our institute can grow and we wish him well.[31]

During Marco's tenure enrollment soared from around 200 in 1965 to 2,500 in 1967; vocational and technical programs expanded and the staff grew to number around 30.[32] The school trained 200 workers for Gilbarco, the service station gas pump manufacturer, and enrolled more than 400 students in Manpower Development and Training Act Programs (MDTA). While Marco was packing his bags for a move to Virginia, construction was beginning on GTI's new library-classroom building, and Trustee Percy Sears was suggesting that federal and state funds might be available to construct a health-science building on the Jamestown campus.[33]

Marco's interview with *Greensboro Record* journalist Owen Lewis enabled the beleaguered president to release some of his frustration with the media: "It is not only my feeling, but the feeling of many in this community that the *Greensboro Daily News* badly used Guilford Technical Institute." In an obvious reference to Bledsoe's series, he charged that, "the newspaper articles hurt this institution a great deal" and proceeded to repeat his argument for comprehensive community college status.

I feel that the Community College System is greatly misunderstood by the Guilford community. I have repeated it over and over again that we do not want to become another liberal arts college. That role is being played by the seven senior institutions that serve the same area as Guilford Technical Institute.

Since I am by training, by profession, and by experience, an engineer, industrialist, and educator, I feel very strongly that our (GTI's) role in this community will be in technical and vocational fields to enhance our industrial and professional development.

However there are needs in this community which cannot be met by a technical institute. These are in the field of health sciences and two year terminal courses in the field of general education for many, many young women who do not wish to be auto mechanics, machinists, or sheet metal workers.

I have never once advocated, backed or intimated that we should have a college parallel program at this Institution. This is where I differ from my critics who said I was trying to make this another four-year liberal arts college.

It is a matter of record that at no time did I or my friends on the Board advocate any liberal arts or college parallel program. This is where I think the public was misled by the press. The official records, such as the minutes of the Board meetings, will prove this.

I've stated publicly many times, at my inauguration and at graduations, "we're here solely to meet the educational and training needs of the community and make useful citizens of our students." This goal has been published in catalogs, literature, and all formal statements. [34]

When questioned about the task force's sharp criticism of his administration, Marco offered this explanation:

When I took over GTI in '65, I inherited certain people who were on the staff. At that time I did not receive any additional allotment of staff positions. Consequently, we all had to share the administrative burdens. In that first year, I was not only president, but a night watchman, weekend telephone operator, grounds superintendent, traffic control officer, and handling all the other house keeping functions for which personnel were not authorized by the state or the county. [35]

Marco reviewed the administrative personnel shortfall that forced his administrators to share responsibilities and wear different hats. He indicated that any attempt to strengthen the administration, as suggested by the task force, would have to occur with the existing staff and face the same workload challenges. He repeated his long-standing argument that a comprehensive community college would have more administrative positions;

You don't have to give up vocational programs when you get community college status. The misstatement of the situation has been made in malicious attacks by my adversaries. But there are many people in the community who just want GTI to grow.

Here at GTI we are training more people in more skills than ever before. We have aided this community greatly in improving industrial skills. The articles written in the paper hurt this school and me personally. No recognition was ever given the good work we have done.

I have no argument with the Trustees as a whole, but with one man.

As to the press, he said,

I have no argument with those who report the facts accurately, but with one reporter who has a knack for distorting facts and lifting things out of context. I regret having to leave. This school should be allowed to grow in a good community atmosphere.[36]

Dr. Herbert F. Marco died two years later in Richmond, Virginia, at the relatively young age of 62. At his passing, he was the special assistant for the Virginia Division of State Planning and Community Affairs. There are more questions than answers to the crisis involving his relationship with Chairman Rochelle. They often appear to be echoing the same theme, but their fragmented rhetoric as quoted in the press indicates that the practical industrialist and the philosophic academic were poles apart in their vision for GTI. Marco's invective against Bledsoe is personal and perhaps misplaced since the state task force verified many of the reporter's published charges in their recommendations.

In retrospect, the Board probably should never have hired Herbert F. Marco. They knew from his statement at the time of his employment that he was a liberal educator determined to instill social values in his students, values he deemed just as important, if not more important, than technical skills. It is possible Marco was quickly hired to restore order at the floundering Industrial Education Center. On the Institution's twentieth anniversary, the man he replaced, the founding director of the Guilford Industrial Education Center Bruce Roberts, recalled that, when he left in 1965, "the Center (GIEC) had more than 3,000 students and a staff of approximately 60. Curriculum offerings had been expanded greatly, and we had quite an operation."[37] But Marco described what he inherited from Roberts as a "morass" he encountered in May 1965, when the press reported that only 200 students were enrolled. During the unruly summer of 1967, GTI's founders began drifting from the Institution either into history, or obscurity, as the new Board Chair began searching for a new president, a personable healer to embrace and enhance a unique institution.

Chapter 10

Transition and Revitalization: July–December 1967

GTI, GTI
With our cherished memories
We lift our hearts to thee,
Now, and forever more.
You, our pride, may you bloom and grow,
Bloom and grow forever
GTI, GTI
Bless my alma mater forever.[1]

"I Am an American Day"

One of the more provocative Institutional asides to the turbulent period (November 1966 to June 1967) was the resilience exhibited by GTI students, albeit a "dwindling student body," during this crisis of credibility. While the disenchanted aired their complaints in the media, others passionately defended the Institute in letters to state leaders and the press. The Institution's inaugural "I Am an American Day," espousing those patriotic principles President Marco intoned at his hiring and during his inauguration, reflected his determination to operate and innovate in spite of the investigation.

The unique celebration occurred on May 17, 1967, two weeks after the state task force had released its critical report. Linda Peak described the event in *The Gateway*, the student newspaper edited by Judy Phillips. Bob Poole, the legendary morning voice of WBIG Radio in Greensboro served as master of ceremonies and introduced L. Richardson "Rich" Preyer, one of Guilford County's historical giants of the 20th century. Preyer, an heir to the Vick Chemical Company (Vicks VapoRub and Oil of Olay) fortune, was serving as a superior court judge in 1957 when his ruling allowing five black children to enter the all white Gillespie Park School in Greensboro marked the first time black and white children attended school together in the city. Preyer served briefly on the federal bench and later represented the state's 6th Congressional District. A cookout and games on the Jamestown campus front lawn concluded the "I Am an American Day" festivities, and then the School and its leaders returned to the business at hand, a change of leadership in the administration and the Board room.

> We can't let Zalph Rochelle leave the chairmanship and Dr. Herbert F. Marco the presidency of Guilford Technical Institute without expressing, on behalf of a grateful community, appreciation for their tremendous contributions toward the launching and development of the Institution at Jamestown.
>
> Both men have served GTI as they felt their responsibilities directed. That conflict developed in such a situation was perhaps inevitable, but both contributed a great deal toward the laying of foundations upon which the Board of Trustees is determined to erect now a stronger and better regulated school dedicated to the vocational training for which it was built.[2]

Far from a gratuitous gesture, this editorial in the *High Point Enterprise* was a sincere expression of deep appreciation from a respected newspaper in the unique city that had nurtured the embryonic vocational and technical courses that founded the Guilford Industrial Education Center. High Point's sense of ownership never wavered during the Institution's first fifty years. While the technological and industrial innovation that sparked the beginning of the 21st century created the need for a major new campus in eastern Greensboro, the soul of GTCC steadily resonates in the expanding complex lining the 600 block of South Main Street in High Point and beneath the pines on a Jamestown hillside.

A memento of appreciation former president Marco presumably packed as he prepared to leave Jamestown was Volume I of *Whispering Pines*, GTI's first yearbook. Nine students directed by Barbara Pardue, winner of the "Outstanding Student Award," produced this inaugural forty page hardback. Green lettering on a white background matched the school colors while the content included a variety of pictures depicting campus life, related activities, and this dedicatory message honoring Dr. Marco.

> To the first president of Guilford Technical Institute who has worked conscientiously for the good of the students, and who has helped a great deal in the progress of Guilford Technical Institute; we, the 1967 graduating

class, proudly dedicate the 1967 *Whispering Pines* to Dr. Herbert F. Marco.[3]

Sentiment aside, the Institution faced tremendous challenges in mid-1967; its president had resigned, the founding Board Chair was stepping down, and the State Board of Education and Department of Community Colleges had directed the Trustees to reorganize and revitalize the school. The revision of administrative procedures and the restoration of leadership were two of the Board's paramount objectives. The crisis demanded a cautious search for a chief executive officer who could quell the turmoil and restore respect for the school internally and externally, but during this process, a strong administrator was needed to helm the ship.

The Trustees named Colonel G. A. Finley, Director of Technical and Vocational Programs, as the interim chief administrator. Finley accepted the role, but, having no intention of seeking the presidency, he asked the Board to fill the vacancy "as soon as possible" and submitted a laundry list of conditions. He wanted assurance that any purported "private lines of communication" between members of the staff and faculty and members of the Board would be shut down. He solicited a guarantee that the Institute's technical and vocational programs would continue and requested the assignment of a staff assistant from the Department of Community Colleges to his office before agreeing to temporarily direct the Institute with a salary upgrade to $11,256 (annually). Finley's "conditions" provide a clearer understanding of the operational disorganization plaguing the Institute and his personal intention to forego a leap from the frying pan into the fire.[4]

The prevailing Institutional dysfunction renewed the Board's resolve to manage firmly with more precise attention to fiscal and personnel operations. An ambitious slate of committees was appointed to monitor all aspects of the Institute's operations within the framework of the "Constitution and By-Laws" of the Department of Community Colleges. The Trustees and their interim Chief Administrative Officer immediately partnered to solve challenges involving the dental and cosmetology programs and considered producing a color film on the Institute to address the perceived credibility issue with the community. Within days, Colonel Finley was probably overjoyed to learn that his tenure as interim CEO was a short-lived transition.

July 11, 1967

The Board approved Chairman Starling's motion to delegate the selection of the next president to the "committee for securing a new president for GTI."

While the membership of this committee is not a matter of record, Starling had obviously decided on a single candidate to head the Institute. Within hours, his one-man recruiting mission ended a few blocks from his Cone Mills' office at Greensboro Page Senior High School where Luther R. Medlin was serving as the founding principal. The educator he selected as GTI's second president was a native of High Point and a graduate of High Point College. [5]

Luther Medlin launched his career as teacher and principal in Gaston County where he helped build and operate the Southeast's first Orthopedic School for Crippled Children. After moving to Greensboro in 1943 and serving as the principal of Central School for 15 years, he was chosen to open the city's second high school in 1958.[6] Medlin was positioned to spend the remainder of his career at the Walter Hines Page Senior High School when Frank Starling challenged him to bring his "optimism and foresight" to GTI. He was one of the most popular educational and civic leaders in Greensboro and, as a local editor noted, well respected across the county.

> If Luther Medlin can handle the urgent business of building a first rate technical school, time will take care of the community college issue. Re-establishing the image of GTI may well be the least demanding of his chores. Image cannot fail to flourish if substance is there.[7]

August 8, 1967

When Chairman Starling introduced his hand picked candidate to the Board during their session at the MDTA headquarters in Greensboro, he guaranteed them that, "Luther Medlin is a man the whole community can support wholeheartedly." Medlin, in turn, assured the Trustees that when he reported for duty on September 15, 1967, the Institute would continue on its original mission, and by inference, leave the ambition to convert to a community college behind; "Our immediate job is to do an exceptionally good job with the technical and vocational subjects we have, rather than to plunge into college parallel courses." That statement appeared to stifle any further consideration of applying for comprehensive community college status.[8]

The reports the president-elect heard at that Board session provided him with an understanding of where GTI was at this recovering stage in its history. The Long Range Planning and Building Committee was concerned with relocating the troublesome cosmetology program that had been a source of audit exceptions since the Institute inherited it from the Greensboro Public Schools.[9] Red tape had delayed construction of the new library-classroom building with completion now targeted for late spring 1968. Dr. Arthur Stone was directing the MDTA Dental Hygiene and Dental Assisting programs and Governor Dan Moore had reappointed John W. Thompson, Jr., Thompson-Arthur Paving Company, to another seven-year term on the Board. Thompson chaired the MDTA Program committee at the same time his company was building much needed parking lots for the Institute. The Thompson-Arthur Paving Company submitted invoices totaling $6,500 for constructing new parking lots on the Jamestown campus in September 1967.[10]

President-elect Medlin probably breathed a sigh of relief when Trustee John Davis, chairman of the Board's salary committee, reported that he and Colonel Finley had reviewed the Institute's salary structure and found it within the state guidelines and comparable to that of similar institutes. Medlin, whose salary was $20,000, soon quickly learned that employee morale was one of a number of challenges he faced;

> In spite of what I found upon my first campus visit, a skeletal curriculum with a dwindling student body (about 700) and few remaining staff members, I did see a very real need for GTI. There was an exceptional job market for individuals with certain skills, and there were literally thousands of people in search of a way to obtain these skills.[11]

September 11, 1967

Luther Medlin had not officially reported to work when interim CEO George Finley reported that 382 students had registered for the fall quarter, as compared with 334 in 1966. The increase may have indicated that the citizens of Guilford County had not lost faith in GTI, but the most dramatic business of the session was the Board's acceptance of Ed Kemp's resignation. The founding father of North Carolina's Industrial Education Centers served three two-year terms in the N.C. House (1957–63) and two terms as a state senator (1965–69). As a young representative, he assumed a leadership role in writing and introducing the legislation supporting the innovative network of Industrial Education Centers. Kemp chaired the first Advisory Committee for the Guilford Industrial Education Center and was appointed to GTI's first Board of Trustees. Only the pressure of managing his expanding advertising agency could have convinced him to resign.[12]

In September 1966, the Board's long range planning committee was negotiating with the architectural firm of J. Hyatt Hammond to prepare a master plan for the Jamestown campus. Since future construction depended on this document, the Board voted to allocate $15,000 to the project during the next five years. The Trustees also authorized Colonel Finley to organize the necessary administrative procedure to pursue the construction of the "second new permanent building" on the Jamestown campus, a health/science building that would house the dental, cosmetology and nursing programs. The construction cost for the 22,000-square-foot building estimated at $25 per square foot totaled $550,000.[13]

Reestablishing the GTI Spirit: September 15, 1967

Medlin's administrative goal on a 1967–68 operating budget of $529,023 was to expand the curriculum and seek SACS accreditation, but he initiated his presidency with a grassroots housekeeping project to strengthen faculty, staff and student morale.[14]

> The entire faculty and staff worked evenings and weekends as a maintenance force repairing tile, painting, mopping, and doing everything else that was required. Students were involved in a project to build and upholster chairs and tables for our library. This created a beautiful spirit of unity and cooperation between all of us, and I believe that spirit played a major role in the school's ultimate success in re-establishing itself and its role within the Guilford County community.[15]

Luther Medlin and his wife Helen, a public school principal, appreciated GTI's picturesque Jamestown setting and the necessity for maintenance and amenities; "Our campus, already beautiful," he noted, "is potentially the most beautiful of all the state's community colleges, but it is in desperate need of attention. Attention that will require money."[16] He promptly requested funding for landscaping, maintenance, and parking, but he also looked inside to employ more counselors and spice up the food service.[17]

The new CEO's immediate task was to soothe, as diplomatically as possible, the fallout from the strained relationship between High Point and Greensboro personalities Rochelle and Conrad. As Guilford County historians have noted, "Inter-municipal rivalry has given a special degree of tension to all that happens and has happened" in the county.[18] The combative relationship between High Point and Greensboro had been historically exacerbated by a unique range of business and political personalities perpetually conflicted over individual, municipal, county, and corporate agendas; not the least of which in this case was the fact that GTI was born and nurtured on English Street in High Point.

To GTI's benefit, Medlin's birth city promptly reclaimed her native son when the *High Point Enterprise* named him "High Pointer of the Week."[19] At the same time, his Greensboro admirers wondered why he had chosen to leave a high profile appointment, like Greensboro's new Page High School, for a troubled trade school in rural Jamestown. To his everlasting credit, this visionary educator was brilliantly cognizant of what GTI could mean to the county;

> I think the future of Guilford Technical Institute is perhaps greater than that of any other unit in the state's system of community colleges and technical institutes and I want to be a part of it. Its future is bright. Its services to the youth of the community are unlimited.[20]

Luther Medlin's ties to High Point and Greensboro and his conciliatory leadership style laid the foundation for the "Deep River Covenant," the unspoken consensual convention that united the Board's diverse personalities from Greensboro and High Point to rebuild GTI. More than 30 years later, Board Chair James F. "Jim" Morgan (1995–98) reminded Don Cameron that GTCC was most fortuitously administered by keeping one foot on either side of the Deep River as a way of placating the leadership of the county's largest cities.[21]

October 10, 1967

President Medlin began his first academic quarter in the fall of 1967 with 43 instructors, 32 full-time and 11 part-time. The 1,501 student enrollment included 344 daytime, 857 evening and 300 MDTA. He quickly reorganized his staff to fill the 12 positions allotted by the Department of Community Colleges; Administrative Assistant; Director of Technical and Vocational Programs; Director of Student Personnel, with two Counselors; Director of Adult Education; Director of Extension; a Business Manager with a Bursar and Bookkeeper; plus a Librarian and an Assistant Librarian. The four new staff members Medlin initially hired were Foy E. Hill, Bursar; Richard Waldrop, Vocational and Technical Education Director; Preston Williams, Business Manager; Elizabeth M. Everett replaced secretary Rita Embry.[22]

By filling all of the allotted positions, excepting that of a half-time counselor, Medlin exceeded the $8,900 average salary allowed to community colleges and technical institutes. In July 1967, the State Board of Education had approved an institutional salary schedule that provided for a chief administrative officer range for entry between $9,288 and $13,020 per year with a ceiling of $17,400. The salary for Deans of Instruction ranged from $8,436 to $15,792; from $7,656 to $14,340 for business managers and program directors. The salary for senior clerical positions ranged from $3,326 to $5,380.[23]

The new administrative plan Medlin presented after a mere three weeks in office was designed to maximize leadership and service from faculty and staff. It demonstrated a remarkable appreciation for the community's industrial and business priorities including the need for two-year programs in civil engineering, architectural technology and data processing. Beyond initiatives to strengthen and broaden GTI's curriculum, Medlin identified programs that would occupy the proposed Health-Science building. The obvious choices included the dental programs, cosmetology, a nurses' training program, and laboratories for physics, chemistry and biology. The groundwork was also laid, though perhaps unimaginable at the time, for GTI to eventually have the largest high school in the county when the county's three school boards "approved in principle" a proposal to participate in GTI's adult high school program.[24]

The Board reorganized in the aftermath of a changing of the guard with a commitment to perform at a higher standard. Under Frank Starling's leadership, nine committees were named. Many of these would combine in the future, but in 1967 they included, Personnel, Finance, MDTA Programs, Curriculum, Long Range Planning, Salary, Public Relations, Adult Education and Vocational Training, and Health Service. The Board welcomed two new Trustees when Dr. William Hinson was appointed to complete Ed Kemp's term and William Beerman replaced Vice Chairman W. O. Conrad. Chairman Frank Starling appointed John T. Davis Jr. to succeed Conrad as Vice Chairman insuring that the shared leadership of the Board between Greensboro and High Point remained intact.

The Trustees continue to explore the acquisition of certain MDTA programs including dental hygiene and dental assisting that were potentially targeted to transfer from federal to state control. The operational cost to GTI was estimated at $71,000 for Dental Hygiene and $35,125 for Dental Assisting, not including equipment. These federally financed programs were two of the Institute's most successful with the director Dr. Arthur Stone reporting that all 14 of the latest dental hygiene graduates passed their State Boards and that all but one passed the National Boards.

November 14, 1967

The accomplishments effected by the Board during this session rank among the most important enacted in the first decade of the Institution's existence. However, the review of the bids for a surplus three-quarter ton truck provide an interesting aside to the more pressing issues when Tommy Burnett's high bid of $15 topped George Greene's $12 and David Thompson's $10. Architect Hyatt Hammond presented his master plan for the campus and drawings defining the proposed Health-Science building. The Trustees subsequently resolved to apply for a grant of $563,000 from the State Board of Education to construct the 30,256-square-foot facility.

The building and remodeling campaign Medlin mounted was balanced by the Board's resolution to seek full accreditation from the Southern Association of Schools and Colleges (SACS) and add a two-year Electronic Data Processing program to the curriculum by the 1968 fall quarter. The financial documents archived with the minutes from October 31 — November 30, 1967, provide the most comprehensive extant fiscal profile of the Institution to date.[25] The Curriculum and Adult Education and Vocational committees boosted the curriculum by unanimously recommending that the Board reactivate Manufacturing Technology and Civil Technology and add a two-year program in Architectural Drafting and Design.[26] During this period of intense activity October–December 1967, the GTI Foundation Board reported a balance of $1,810.05.[27]

December 12, 1967

The Board turned again to the possibility of establishing a registered nursing program following President Medlin's thorough review of the topic with the Department of Community Colleges (DCC). Former President Marco's poorly executed pursuit of a nursing program had publicly embarrassed the Institute and contributed to his departure, but on this occasion the DCC suggested that Medlin reengage the process by partnering for clinical space with a local hospital. To this end, Chairman Starling reactivated the Nursing Committee and named Zalph Rochelle to head a panel composed of Dr. William Hinson, James Williams, and Percy Sears. Federal funding to support the program was also problematic, but Medlin was confident that assistance from the Health and Educational Facilities Act (HEFA) might be possible by July 1968. The Board also decided to request state funds to transfer the MDTA-financed Dental Hygienist program to GTI.[28]

Vacations, Holidays, and Staff Organization

Luther Medlin was clearly a people person and evidence of his open management style is observable in his commitment to strengthen personal and institutional relationships within the campus community. He addressed personnel issues by publishing an "Official Holiday and Vacation Schedule" on November 28, 1967. The plan enabled 12 month employees to earn one day of vacation per month and accumulate a maximum of 20 days with presidential approval. Employees who worked 9 months, but fewer than 12 were permitted to observe the same holiday and vacation schedule as full-time curriculum students; that is, from the final date of the spring quarter until the beginning of the fall quarter. Employee holidays included New Year's Day, Easter Monday, Independence Day, Labor Day, Thursday and Friday for Thanksgiving, and five working days at Christmas including Christmas Day, if it fell in the Monday–Friday period.[29]

The organizational chart Medlin published on December 4, 1968, clearly delegated the operational management of the Institute to four major directors including the Administrative Assistant, Director of Student Personnel, Business Manager, and Director of Instruction.[30] For an administrator who had reported to work on September 15, Luther Medlin's year end report to the Board of Trustees is admirable for the energy and zeal he had devoted to completely revitalizing GTI's public perception and reorganizing its internal operations.

His strategy to elevate the Institute's image involved publicizing all facets of its operations and introducing prominent and official members of the Guilford County community to its campus, staff, and faculty. He and Helen greeted and informed more than 400 guests including Trustees, staff, faculty, county commissioners, teachers, administrators, and friends of the school at several open houses. He welcomed the community college presidents to Jamestown and maintained a rigorous schedule of public speaking appearances.

Medlin's perception that GTI could become the county's foremost economic developer inspired him to host a delegation representing an out-of-state industry considering relocating to the Triad. The State Advisory Committee on Dental Hygiene selected him to chair a special committee to study staff needs and training. His public relations initiatives included entertaining members of the Vocational and Technical Education Committee of the Greensboro Chamber of Commerce as well as the superintendents of the county's three public school systems and addressing the High Point Chamber of Commerce.

Summary

The first six months of 1967 historically characterize GTI's darkest period. A year that began with an embarrassing series of newspaper articles documenting alleged deficiencies in operation and administration and the public conflict between president and Board Chair ended harmoniously and beneficially for the county and the Institute. GTI's fiscal maturity is most obvious, but the personal and professional relationships that must energize any successful organization are evidenced by Luther Medlin's innate ability to transfer his vision into direct action in the various segments of the operations.

There was no obvious attempt to halt operations and regroup when the Medlins moved to Jamestown. Guided by the second president's administrative finesse and control, the Institution righted its operations even as it expanded its programs. A number of occupational extension programs were instituted to serve local industry, including supervisory training for 24 employees of Cone Mills, a cooperative work-study program with Bell Telephone Laboratories, on-the-job training in Knitting Machine Fixing, an intensive sixteen-week program conducted jointly with the National Tool and Die Association, and a six-week refresher course for inactive registered nurses. Finally, the agonizing year droned into history and Guilford Technical Institute began its revitalization to match the vision of its founders by proceeding to train an exceptional workforce for Guilford County in a variety of skills.[31]

Jamestown Campus with the LRC and the west wing of the Medlin Campus Center 1975.

H. Frank Starling
Chair Trustees 1967–1969

Dr. Luther R. Medlin
President GTI 1967–1975

John T. Davis
Chair Trustees 1969–1981

Library-Classroom-Administrative Building

Section III

The Medlin Presidency
1967–75

Chapter 11

1968: Striving for Significance

I knew about Guilford Technical Institute, but like so many others, I thought of it as a small, somewhat insignificant operation on the western edge of Greensboro near Jamestown and High Point. Few paid GTI much attention in those days and perhaps they overlooked its potential.[1]

Luther Medlin, 1978

Facilities and Financing

GTI's Board of Trustees worked as diligently in 1968 to support the College as any Board in the Institution's first decade, but producing a quorum appeared a problem when only half of the members attended the first session of the New Year on January 9. While Vice Chairman Davis held the written proxies of Chairman Frank Starling and Dr. William Hinson, who were "unavoidably absent," a question about the legality of these documents prompted a unanimously approved motion to request a ruling on the appropriate use of proxies from the county attorney.[2]

The proxy issue did not deter the six Trustees present from pursuing an ambitious construction program that occupied them and the administration throughout this pivotal year. Their first order of business was to approve $15,000 to furnish and suitably equip the auditorium in the Library-Classroom building, which would also house the Institute's administrative offices. They gave the furniture students permission to create the furnishings for the building, a project that qualified as a "first" for the Community College System;[3] and approved a 10 percent increase in the cost of the proposed Health-Science building to $793,000.[4]

Construction projects during this era were managed by George B. Rottman, the Guilford County School's building consultant, subject to the approval of GTI's Long Range Building Committee. The Trustees were so determined to build the Health Science building to create a suitable facility for the dental programs they hoped to absorb from the MDTA that they devised a whole set of strategies in case they failed to get federal funding.[5] Out of desperation, they contemplated designing optional bids so they could award either a contract to build a "shell" structure or a whole building, depending on the availability of financing. However, by June 11, 1968, they had decided to advertise the Health Science building as a complete building using only state and local funds.

From this era forward, the Trustees' determination and in some cases, infatuation, with building projects form one of the most historical institutional aspects of GTCC's history. It is a seminal example of the phenomena associated with the creation of institutional settings. At the same time the Trustees were scrapping to pay for Health Science, they started planning another classroom building. This 22,000-square-foot, two-story structure designated Building #5 (now Gerrald Hall) to fill the footprint then occupied by the west wing of the administration building with classrooms and commercial arts laboratories.[6] As originally presented, a part of this project included the construction of an access road, a perimeter road, and additional parking. President Medlin's mission to improve the campus food service and create lounge areas in the newly remodeled areas of Furniture Hall where most of the Institute's classrooms were located emerged as a smaller project in progress.[7]

In March 1968, the stark reality of the price of this bold building scheme convinced the Board to discuss their facility needs with Dale Montgomery, Chairman of the Guilford County Commissioners and the county manager. They were concerned that, if they committed all of their county and state construction funds to build the Health Science building, they would be unable to match future federal grants. Montgomery endorsed the Health Science building and assured the Trustees that the commissioners would, within reason, favorably address the Institute's future needs. This was the incentive the Board needed to quickly initiate the construction process.[8]

Beyond the new construction considered at GTI in Jamestown, the Board expanded its services in Greensboro and High Point by utilizing existing facilities. Some of the MDTA programs and a "downtown" learning lab were installed in Central Junior High School on Spring Street in Greensboro ,and the William Penn School in High Point was remodeled as an expansion site for a cosmetology course. This precedent for establishing programs in preexisting buildings followed a strategy imposed in 1958 when the county commissioners installed the GIEC in the old TB hospital in Jamestown. As community colleges proliferated across the United States, the need for space and the lack of construction money made the acquisition of preexisting, often dilapidated, buildings an institutional practice.[9]

Program Update

GTCC was created during the early decades of the international Cold War and the American Civil Rights struggle. Assassins killed Dr. Martin Luther King, Jr. and Robert Kennedy in 1968. Three hundred North Carolina A & T State University students reacted quickly to news of Dr. King's death on the evening of April 4 when their march into downtown Greensboro prompted Mayor Carson Bain to request the mobilization of National Guard units, setting the stage for months of unrest.[10] There is no evidence indicating that this event affected students and classes at GTI. The US lost its 10,000th aircraft in Vietnam; the Viet Cong launched its TET offensive in Saigon and besieged Hue and Khe San. By year's end the U.S. death toll in Vietnam had passed 30,000. On the political scenes, Richard Nixon and George Wallace declared their presidential candidacy, and Nixon prevailed.

While the Board pursued its extensive building program, President Medlin proceeded to reorganize the curriculum to enable new students to start their course work at the beginning of each quarter, as opposed to beginning only in the fall quarter. The rapidly expanding curriculum now offered non-technical courses including Public Speaking, American Literature and Advertising. The Institute would soon add a high school program to grant a diploma issued by the county's three school systems as opposed to offering a "high school equivalency" certificate. Health Science programs were a major priority as the Institute awaited approval to acquire the Dental Hygiene program from the MDTA.[11]

The instructional programs directed by Richard Waldroup in March 1968, were divided into five primary areas; the enrollment indicated a significant improvement over 1967.

Student Enrollment 1968

Curriculum	
Technical	307
Vocational	214
Total Curriculum	521
General Adult, Basic Adult, High School	1,342
Manpower Development Training	175
Industrial Services (Occupational Extension)	153
Miscellaneous (High School Students)	13
Total Enrollment	**2,204**

The 2,204 total represented an increase of 29 percent over winter 1967 and 27.5 percent over fall 1967. The top five two-year technical programs with numbers of students enrolled included Business Administration, 72; Electronics Technology, 47; Drafting and Design, 43; Civil Technology, 35; and Commercial Art, 2. The top five one-year Vocational programs included Auto Mechanics, 42; Air Conditioning and Refrigeration, 31; Nursing, 28; Welding, 27; and Machinist, 25. Classes were scheduled at nearly three dozen off campus sites including the Sandy Ridge and McLeansville prison farms, and nearly two dozen courses were in various developmental stages during the winter 1967 quarter.[12] Further proof of GTI's improving image is reflected in the fall quarter 1968 enrollment report Medlin submitted to the Board: 2,009 students represented a 32 percent increase over fall 1967.[13]

Student Enrollment 1968

High School Programs	281
Extension	456
Adult Basic Education	287
Occupational Extension	141
MDTA	128
Curriculum Day	504
Curriculum Evening	212
Total Enrollment	2,009

The steady increases encouraged the president to forecast a 1967 fall enrollment of 2,800. In April 1968, the technical-vocational division was divided into nine departments with 31 full-time instructors, plus an unnamed number of part-time instructors, teaching 110 courses in 21 programs.

Roger Sharrock directed the General Adult Division that included all the high school programs, non-occupational programs, Adult Basic Education, and the Learning Laboratory. Since fall 1967, this division had conducted 71 classes for approximately 1,218 students. The occupational extension programs in the relatively new Industrial Services Department, headed by Jerry Owens, provided training at the semi-skilled, skilled, technician, and supervisory levels was currently operating 17 programs involving 234 students. Howard Hicks, destined for a long and productive career at GTI, directed the school's federally funded MDTA programs in conjunction with the Employment Security Commission.

GTI aggressively pursued partnerships with business and industry to train employees. Some of the major initiatives included a cooperative program with Bell Telephone Laboratories and a commitment by textile makers to sponsor 50–60 students per year in the Knit-Fix program that had jump started the

Guilford Industrial Education Center in 1958. President Medlin was determined to revitalize furniture technology, an original offering that had declined, by inviting Broyhill Furniture executives to discuss the successful program they sponsored at Caldwell Technical Institute in Lenoir. GTI was additionally poised to partner with the National Tool and Die Association in a federally funded program to train 20 entry level machine operators for the industry.[14]

Adult Basic Education Survey: April 1968

Basic Skills would eventually become a major part of GTI's service, but the program had a long way to grow in 1968. When asked what GTI was doing through facilities and programs to provide basic elementary education to the county's uneducated adults, Medlin could only report that the school "is now meeting the demands of those expressing interest, but not operating to the fullest extent possible."[15] In February 1968, the Department of Adult Education began offering classes for adults wishing to complete their course work and earn high school diplomas. Classes were conducted at Greensboro Grimsley Senior High, High Point Central High, Northeast Guilford High, Northwest Guilford High, Central Junior High in Greensboro, and William Penn High School in High Point.

Medlin's determination to strengthen service to educationally, economically, and socially disadvantaged adults was based on a survey conducted from October 1966 to April 1968. Of a total of 875 individuals who participated in Adult Education programs at GTI, 83 percent, or 725, were students in the basic education division and the remaining 150 in teacher-directed high school equivalency programs. The students ranged in age from 18 to 72 with the majority aged 30 to 52; their education level ranged from those with little or no school to those with less than an eighth grade education; many could not write their names and the majority were female heads of households.

The survey was formulated to reveal factors related to employment conditions, changing welfare status, community participation, political behavior, increased economic skills, and the changing educational motivations and aspirations of the participants.

The survey further indicated that 112 adults received certificates indicating completion of an 8th grade education, improvement of basic skills, and program participation. Fourteen of these completed the GED, one enrolled in a community college, one in a technical institute, one in a four-year college, and one passed a Civil Service Examination; 508 students reported positive changes and experiences from the Adult Basic Education program.[16]

Survey Results	725 responses
Employment as a Result of Schooling	41
Positions from custodial to manufacturing	
Inspired to continue their education through vocational, job training, and high school programs	47
Discontinued welfare checks — expressed desire to get jobs that would provide more money	14
Registered to vote	64
Joined Civic or Community organizations	49
Learned to read	41
Subscribed to newspapers or magazines	35
Visited a library for first time	23

Clearly under Medlin's leadership, GTI had rebounded from the disastrous 1966–67 malaise and was rapidly becoming a major educational force in Guilford County.[17] These positive figures inspired the Board to stress the need for even more basic education courses at school locations at night and during the summer months. Percy Sears suggested soliciting manufacturers as a strategy to identify prospective students.[18]

Dr. Luther Reece Medlin

President Luther Medlin was awarded an honorary Doctorate of Humanities by his alma mater, High Point College (now University), on May 19, 1968. The tribute was deserved given Medlin's exceptional background of civic service, including the presidency of Civitan International and a career highlighted by an enormous contribution of educational innovations. High Point College President Dr. Wendell Patton, Jr. lauded Medlin's outstanding contributions to society and his demonstrated leadership in maintaining GTI's unique mission. As a former GTI Trustee, Patton championed the technical mission of the Institute[19]

Student Activities and Honors

Scholastically active GTI students participated in the 41st annual Phi Rho Pi National Forensic Tournament in Miami. Founded in 1928, the society recognized the achievement of junior college students who had earned distinction in several forms of public speaking and promoted interest and excellence in public speaking. John Davis won second place competing against 400 colleagues representing 57 junior colleges in 27 states. In addition, Georgia Bikas, Patsy Daniel, Nancy Williams, and Ann Woodyard of Greensboro; William Gansman and Grace Kirkman of High Point; and Cynthia Rushing Veach of Spencer were recognized in *Who's Who in American Junior Colleges*.[20]

Financial Aid and the GTCC Foundation

Financial aid from various sources had been available for GTI students beginning with the establishment of the Guilford Industrial Education Center. Loans were provided by the Department of Community Colleges while qualified veterans could receive direct assistance from the VA. The agency also assisted dependents of deceased or disabled veterans, in addition to financing vocational work-study programs. Local scholarships for nursing students were established by the Moses H. Cone Women's Auxiliary and the Altrusa Club of High Point. The Sternberger Foundation Scholarships provided assistance for students in health-related courses as did the Guilford County Medical Association, the Junior Woman's Club of Greensboro, and the Wesley Long Hospital Auxiliary. Additional federal assistance became available in 1968 from the National Defense Student Loan Program, the Educational Opportunity Grant Program, and the College Work-Study Program. A number of scholarships, financed by a wide variety of benefactors, were offered on an individual basis. These individual grants were distributed by the Guilford Technical Institute Foundation, which had reported a balance of less than $1,800 in January 1968.[21]

Project 100

August 1968 ranks as one of Guilford Technical Institute's more significant public months. Greensboro Mayor Carson Bain proclaimed August 13 Greensboro Day on the Jamestown campus. The tribute recognized "Project 100," Dr. Medlin's initiative to convince 100 Gate City citizens and an additional 100 from High Point to each adopt a student for enrollment in GTI's educational programs. The program was designed to identify high school graduates or other youth not currently enrolled in an educational institution or employed in a full-time job, and to enroll each of them at GTI under the guidance of a "big brother or sister."

Once the mentors had recruited students, they were committed to advise those students during their term of study. With their background in business and industry, the mentors were aware of the critical shortage of trained manpower and shared the county's growing concern for training youth for productive citizenship. These men and women were charged with promoting public relations, recruiting, financial aid, counseling, and follow-up conferences with their adopted "little brothers and sisters." The project reportedly elicited a satisfactory and successful response while demonstrating the value of community action in promoting education.[22]

A Presidential Inauguration

Dr. Luther Reece Medlin was inaugurated as the second president of Guilford Technical Institute at the Greensboro War Memorial Auditorium on Sunday afternoon, August 18, 1968. The inaugural address was delivered by Dr. Felix Robb, Director of the Southern Association of Colleges and Schools. Jerry Owens chaired the Inauguration Committee with the assistance of Mary Breeze, Sylvia Eidam, Lynwood English, Magie Fishburne, Alwayne McClure and Kenneth Vaughn. Dr. Medlin concluded his first year at GTI by dedicating the new Library-Classroom-Administrative building, later Business Careers, on August 22, 1968. The evening ribbon cutting ceremony was followed by a tour of the 22,000-square-foot facility built at a cost of $361,496. This first of GTI's new facilities, extending from the 1966 expansion program, housed the library, the central administrative offices, the Business Education Department, and general classrooms. As an aside to the relocation of the library, the school spent $212 for books in July 1968.[23]

Summary

In December 1968, the Council on Dental Education of the American Dental Association extended their provisional accreditation of the Dental Assistant Program and the Dental Hygiene Program.[24] The Health Science building (1969) was in the approval stage and a classroom-laboratory building (1971) in the planning process as 1968 drew to a close.[25] Engineers were working to improve access to the campus by paving an eastern entry that would parallel the Southern Railway tracks to connect with a campus road adjacent to Machinery Hall. As he reviewed the Institute's budget, Medlin noted that he had operated the school for just over $1.0 million in 1968 ($1,030,316) and could expect $100,000 more in 1969 ($1,135,590). He now exuded a far different view of GTI's promise than his former perception of "a small and somewhat insignificant operation."

Meanwhile, along the Pacific Rim, Communist North Korea finally released the crewmen of the USS Pueblo after holding them captive for 11 brutal months. On a more positive note, the technological innovations emanating from the U.S. space program that would spark GTI's future in the latter decades of the 20th century nurtured the dramatic space voyage of Apollo 8. For a brief moment in time Americans were distracted from the darkness of the horror in Vietnam by our first glimpse at the dark side of the moon. Guilford Technical Institute bade its "dark side" experience of 1966–67 farewell and moved upward and onward on the shoulders of Luther Medlin.[26]

Chapter 12

Accreditation and Expansion

My first objective was to expand the curriculum offerings and gain for them full accreditation.

Luther R. Medlin, 1978[1]

The SACS Experience

Southern Association of Colleges and Schools accreditation solidified 1969's ranking as a defining year in the Institution's early history, an achievement that inspired the Board to commend Dr. Luther Medlin for the tremendous progress made by his administration. His predecessor, Herbert F. Marco, had initiated the chronological process in September 1966 when he hosted SACS representative Dr. David T. Kelly.[2] Marco accelerated the exercise in early 1967 by launching the required comprehensive self-study of the Institute's programs, policies, services, and facilities. The process remained on hold following Marco's resignation in June 1967 until President Medlin's reorganization proceeded to a point in August 1968 when the school was institutionally prepared to renew the drill with a defining document.

GTI's staff and faculty produced a "Statement of Purpose": a basic institutional "mission statement" that outlined the school's responsibility to Guilford County, defined the Community College System's "open door policy," explained the specifics of a "technical institute," and affirmed GTI's educational objectives to its various constituencies. The Board responded to this organizational platform by appointing Trustees Frank Starling, Percy Sears, Vance Chavis, and John Thompson to serve as an accreditation committee to support the SACS process. Illustrative of the attitudinal change in response to Dr. Medlin's leadership was Trustee John Thompson's observation that "more progress had been made at GTI in the last 10 months than had taken place in the last three years."[3]

Gaston College president Woodrow B. Sugg chaired the 24-member committee appointed by the Department of Community Colleges that visited Jamestown to establish the validity of the Institutional self study, identify its strengths and weaknesses, and suggest upgrades to assure SACS approval. The delegation's four committees investigated every aspect of GTI's institutional purposes and operations including student services, instructional programs, organization, administration, financial management, resources, and physical facilities.

The visitors' final report listed more that 140 observable limitations and recommendations needed to strengthen GTI's organization and performance. While the delegates believed that more time should have been devoted to the self-study, they found the Institute thinly staffed with inexperienced employees responsible for critical areas of operation. Personnel issues were exacerbated in an era when the school lacked sufficient control over the funding provided by Guilford County to pay its employees on a bi-monthly basis. Hiring and retention were problematic at GTI where applicants complained that a month was "too long between paychecks." Despite a compendium of suggestions for improvement, the report was generally favorable, and to their credit, the visitors sympathetically recognized the many challenges facing GTI's faculty and staff:

> It is evident that a great deal of progress has been made in the over all development of Guilford Technical Institute. Being aware of some of the past history of the Institution, the Committee feels that substantial progress is being made. A quality educational program is being provided for the citizens of the community. A great deal of improvement is still needed in many areas, but time, money, space, and leadership are beginning to prevail.[4]

Finally in May 1969 a SACS Evaluation Committee chaired by F. M. Fortenberry, director of the Junior College Division of the Mississippi Department of Education, visited GTI to conduct its official review of the institutional self-study. According to Dr. Medlin, the team found the staff and faculty qualified and the maturity level of the students impressive.[5] Years of hard work paid off handsomely when President Medlin's administrative assistant, Nelson Wallace, and dean of instruction, Richard Waldroup, had the pleasure of attending the SACS annual meeting in Dallas on December 3, 1969, to hear the formal accreditation announcement.[6]

This academic anointing inspired GTI Trustee and Guilford County Commissioner Percy Sears to revive the controversial name change issue by suggesting that GTI become GIT, the Guilford Institute of Technology. According to Sears, and as a matter of record, the Trustees had sought to get the Institute accredited without being called a college; and having succeeded, they planned to ask the State Department of Public Instruction to approve the name change before the 1970–71 school year. There is no record that the Board formally considered changing the Institution's name. Sears' euphoria aside, the students were the real winners in the lengthy struggle for accreditation, which facilitated the future transfer of their hard-earned credits.[7]

Board of Trustees

The Board experienced changes in leadership during 1969 that fostered long range implications for the Institution. High Point furniture executive John T. Davis, Jr. replaced Frank Starling as Board Chair on July 1. Starling's admirable record included exemplary leadership in the aftermath of the Rochelle-Marco debacle, the establishment of an exceptional business approach to governing the Institute and the recruitment of Luther Medlin as GTI's second president. Processes and policies instituted during Starling's chairmanship restored GTI's fiscal and administrative credibility to the satisfaction of the State Board of Education, the Department of Community Colleges, and most importantly the Southern Association of Colleges and Schools (SACS).

Davis, first appointed by Governor Dan Moore on September 15, 1965, brought a wealth of knowledge to his new position. His tenure as Board Chair would prosper on the strength of his personality and business acumen and the close personal and business relationship he forged with his colleague Percy Sears. Davis Hall, a major classroom building on the Jamestown campus, honors this former chair who served on the Board until December 1, 1981.

Another historic GTI moment occurred on July 10, 1969, when GTI's founding Trustee and former Board Chair Zalph Rochelle announced his resignation. Rochelle's relationship with the Institute extended from the genesis of the idea shared with Dean B. Pruette, Bruce Roberts, and others that established an industrial training school in a rented building on English Street in High Point, the venture that matured into the Guilford Industrial Education Center in 1958. Rochelle had been a member of the Center's first Advisory Board before becoming chairman when a Board of Trustees replaced the GIEC Advisory Committee in 1963.

Rochelle, who had joined the Tomlinson Furniture Corporation in High Point as Personnel Manager in 1935, was promoted to field sales manager in 1969. This new assignment required him to travel across the country three out of four weeks per month, ultimately forcing his resignation from the Board.

More than two years had passed since his public fight with President Marco to prevent GTI from becoming a "comprehensive community college." He had not attended a Board meeting for nearly 18 months since concluding the struggle that cost Marco his job and left his Board chairmanship bruised by a State Board of Education Task Force report and a damaging series of newspaper articles.

The Board accepted Rochelle's resignation with "regret and appreciation for his meritorious service." He told the *High Point Enterprise* that he was pleased with Dr. Medlin's work and complimented the President for building an image of promise and dignity.[8] Health problems forced Rochelle into early retirement a few months later, but his indomitable spirit survived until his death on February 8, 1987. High Point Mayor Judith P. Mendenhall eulogized the GTI founder as "unique and one of a kind, a real special person who loved life and High Point." Rochelle Road, a major artery stretching through the heart of the Jamestown Campus, commemorates his exceptional service to the Institution.[9]

Curriculum Update 1969–70

Under Medlin's tutelage, GTI began to extend its services. Learning laboratories, available to virtually every citizen, opened at Central School in Greensboro and the William Penn School in High Point in early 1969 and later that year the Institute was approved to administer the General Educational Development test (GED). Tuition in 1969 was $2.50 per credit hour for in-state residents with a maximum charge of $32.00 per quarter. Out-of-state students paid two-and-a-half times the in-state rate. Three consecutive quarters of 11 weeks each constituted the academic year for two-year technical curricula while one-year curricula were scheduled on a four quarter basis.

GTI implemented a two-year Aviation Management Technology program in the 1969 fall quarter and by November 1970 the State Board of Education had approved a two-year program in Avionics and a one-year program in Airframe and Power Plant Mechanics. Dr. Medlin reported that an accrediting team from the Council on Dental Education of the American Dental Association had granted "provisional accreditation" to the Dental Hygiene Program and unqualified accreditation to the Dental Assisting Program. Marguerite Guinn reported to GTI on August 13, 1969, to establish the Registered Nursing Program that welcomed its first students for the fall 1970 quarter as did the two-year Data Processing Program for an Applied Science Degree.[10]

Facilities and Finances

Funding has been a major Institutional challenge since the inception of the Guilford Industrial Education Center. To appreciate the trials and tribulations inherent in their governance, one must first understand how the 58 constituent units of the Community College System are financed. Trustees comprising the boards are appointed by the governor and by local governing entities including county commissioners and boards of education. Operational funding is provided by the county, the state, the federal government, and infrequent bond referendums subject to the whims of commissioners, the real property tax rate, and the prevailing economy. Aggressive institutions like GTCC continually apply for grants from a variety of governmental and private philanthropic sources.

The argument can be made that the Institution was financially encumbered from the moment the GIEC was relegated to the grossly decrepit hospital facilities, undulating topography, and geological challenges physically truncating the Jamestown campus. Early decisions to replace aging buildings without considering the implications of long-range program and enrollment growth are questionable in spite of the so-called 1969 master plan. The Institution historically encountered similar real estate, physical, and logistical problems while attempting to procure and maintain serviceable facilities in High Point and Greensboro. Many of these problems weakened the Institution's well-founded intentions to more adequately serve these population centers into the first decade of the twenty-first century.

Beyond the physical expansion needs he addressed at Jamestown in 1969, Medlin desperately sought funding for the Institute's extension programs, the High School Diploma Program, GED, and Industrial Extension Programs. When the state allotted GTI only about $66,000 of the $130,000 needed to pursue these initiatives, the beleaguered president asked the state to decide, "to whom shall we say yes, and to whom shall we say no," and lamented "breaking the school's commitment to youth, adults, and our public school friends." In this instance, the state advised Medlin to ask the county commissioners to fund the extension programs on a month-to-month basis until state funds became available.[11]

The Jamestown campus building program stumbled when the low bid for the technical laboratory exceeded preliminary cost estimates and funding by more than $100,000. While the Board asked the county to cover the shortfall until the expected federal funding was received, the anxiety surrounding these funding challenges has remained unrelenting for GTI's chief administrators, who have been fiscally challenged to manipulate various pools of money to minimally operate the Institution. An early example is the $3,000 that was transferred from the Cosmetology savings account in 1969 as a stop-gap measure to furnish the new Health-Science building.[12]

The President and his Board were consistently concerned about the education and welfare of the students, many of whom, then as now, had to balance their school schedules with work and family responsibilities. When Medlin informed the Trustees that an emergency fund to help financially stressed students was urgently needed, they transferred $1,000 from the often-targeted Cosmetology account to the GTI Foundation. Loans from this fund for deserving students could be repaid at a low interest rate.[13]

Five buildings comprised the Jamestown Campus in 1969 including "Old Main," a lingering sanatorium relic choked with classrooms and business offices. Commercial Art studios and classrooms filled its East Wing while Practical Nursing, Adult Education, Extension Services, and the Learning Lab occupied the soon to be razed West Wing. The new Library Building, stacked with 7,000 technical and scientific volumes, housed administrative offices and the Business Technology Curricula. Air conditioning, automotive, machine tooling, welding, sheet metal, metallurgy, and an engineering drafting lab were based in Machinery Hall. Furniture Hall housed a variety of programs including the two-year Furniture Manufacturing Technician curriculum, Upholstery, Sewing, Woodworking, a machinery shop, Cosmetology, and labs for Drafting, Electronics, Physics, and Chemistry. The student lounge, the bookstore, classrooms, and faculty offices maximized additional space in the building. Dental Hygiene and Dental Assisting were located in the Health-Science Hall. This 31,990-square-foot structure occupied in October 1969 and built for $685,951, (less than $22 per square foot), excluding equipment, was formally dedicated on April 19, 1970.[14]

Marketing and Public Relations

The Institute launched an aggressive recruiting campaign to attract traditional students by inviting groups of high school seniors to visit the Jamestown campus in spring 1969. President Medlin welcomed the young guests to a program that included an orientation by members of the staff and student leaders and a tour of the campus facilities. The visitations soon became an annual recruiting strategy. Seven hundred and six students from 12 high schools visited in 1970 and 833 seniors participated in the 1971 visitation as the program contributed significantly to GTI's growing enrollment.[15]

Dr. Medlin expanded his publicity campaign in 1969 beyond civic club speeches and the open houses he and Helen graciously hosted for various segments of the community. A thirty-minute color documentary film produced in association with Forsyth Technical Institute for WSJS-TV (now WXII-TV) was telecast on June 22, 1969. An April 13, 1969, headline proclaiming "People, Program, Plant—All in Progress March at Guilford Technical" introduced a laudatory article accompanying a GTI advertisement in the *Greensboro Daily News*. The article touted the school's 35 percent increase in enrollment, major faculty and curricula additions, its building program, and student accomplishments. The puff-piece may have been written to complement the advertisement, but it was a far more positive portrait of GTI than had appeared in recent years.[16]

GTI launched the fall 1969 marketing campaign with a colorful brochure and information centers in downtown High Point and Greensboro. Qualified personnel explained the Institute's programs, and counselors guided prospective students through the enrollment process. These off-site centers complemented the information-admission center on the Jamestown campus. Medlin's multifaceted strategy represented the Institution's first comprehensive marketing campaign. With the assistance of Alderman Studios in High Point, WGHP-TV (Now FOXNEWS), and WFMYTV, Channel 2, Norman Faircloth, Chairman of the GTI Art Department, reinforced the recruiting initiative in 1970 by producing a 60-second film commercial to advertise his program. Medlin additionally promoted the Institute by appearing on WFMY-TV's "Good Morning Show." [17] These promotional initiatives had a significant impact on enrollment for the fall quarter 1969. (See chart on page 130.)

The school's first record shattering registration occurred in the 1970 fall quarter when the nursing program, approved by the state for 40 students, received more than 90 applications. The deluge prompted Trustee Percy Sears to question whether GTI might be allowed to increase its enrollment of nursing students if the county consented to fund additional instructors.[18]

Campus Amenities

Food service was the "hot" topic at the first Board meeting in February 1970 when Trustees learned that the Institute had contracted with Ketner's Food Service of Salisbury to answer what was described as a "dire need for hot food" by providing lunches on a ninety day trial basis. The arrangement with Ketner's was short lived, but other measures were later implemented as pressures to provide food service for faculty, staff, and students persisted, like the ubiquitous parking problem, into the twenty-first century. GTI's beautiful but quaintly isolated Jamestown campus created issues with security, water, and sewage. The Board addressed the security issue by improving the lighting in

1969 Enrollment Report

Curriculum		
Vocational		
Air Conditioning and Refrigeration	41	
Automotive Mechanic	35	
Building Trades Drafting	14	
Cosmetology	61	
Dental Assistant	27	
Industrial Maintenance	8	
Machinist Trade	30	
Mechanical Drafting	20	
Practical Nurse	47	
Radio and TV Servicing	10	
Upholstery	25	
Welding	27	
Technical		
Accounting	10	
Architectural Technology	41	
Aviation Management	9	
Business Administration	89	
Chemical	7	
Civil Engineering	23	
Commercial Art	93	
Dental Hygiene	41	
Electronics	54	
Mechanical Drafting and Design	25	
Secretarial	47	
Evening Enrollment	**276**	
Day Enrollment	**535**	
Total Curriculum Enrollment		**811**
Adult Education (High School) and General Adult		**1,828**
Adult Basic Education		**326**
Occupational Extension		
Summer Quarter		**294**
Fall Quarter		**317**
Proposed		496
MDTA (Two Classes — other underway)		**145**
***Guided Studies**		145
Grand Total		**4,217**

*Reflected in other totals**

**Enrollment Report, BOT, Oct. 8, 1969; Jan. 14, 1971.

the campus parking lots and boosting the water pressure by hooking up to a Greensboro water line and forwarding the sewage to Jamestown.[19]

After meeting in area motel dining rooms for more than a decade, the Board finally consented to convene on the Jamestown campus at their November 13, 1969, session. The Trustees enjoyed coffee and donuts at their first meeting in the Library Board room at 8:00 A.M. on December 11, 1969. They returned on February 12, 1970, without recording an official change of meeting place in the minutes. It may have been a propitious decision considering that parking problems on the Jamestown Campus provoked the first "Policy on Parking" debate at the March 12, 1970, Board session.

Congestion and the reluctance of some students to use student parking areas sparked the discussion, but access for emergency vehicles to the major buildings was a logistical challenge. While a few Trustees were concerned that a parking policy might displease some students, the Institute's first parking policy fined first offenders a dollar and second offenders $2.50; a third offense resulted in the loss of the parking permit. Similar fines were charged for not displaying a parking permit, while offenders who chose to park after their permit had been revoked were fined $10.[20]

Transfer Contracts

Trustee Sidney Low reopened the issue of transferring credits to four-year institutions at the April 1970 Board meeting. Dr. Medlin reported that he had surveyed all the four-year institutions in North Carolina and a sampling from adjacent states. Fifty-four replies revealed a wide variance in policy with only two institutions responding with an unqualified "Yes, while few offered clear cut acceptance without penalty to the transferring student."[21] For once, the Board made a concerted attempt to solve this issue by sending a special subcommittee to counsel with Department of Community Colleges director Dr. I. E. Ready. Dr. Medlin met with the Joint Transfer Committee of the Board of Higher Education, where he specifically broached ways to transfer credits without immediately converting to community college status.

Rochelle and Marco were gone, but the issue of transfer credits that had divided them still had an impact on GTI's students. Comprehensive community college status would have granted students the opportunity to transfer credits, but that was not going to happen. Foregoing the arguments that had roiled the school and the county in 1967, Ready suggested that GTI consider contractual agreements with four-year institutions that would establish college parallel courses on the Jamestown campus to assure transferable credits. Ready plowed old ground when he reiterated the confounding circumstances that defined community colleges and technical institutes and penalized technical students:

> The most obvious step is to get authorization to add the college transfer program. This requires a local study to document the need and approval of the State Board of Education, the Governor, and the Advisory Budget Commission. Fiscally, it also requires appropriations from the General Assembly to provide the State support of the new program.
>
> In addition, a favorable vote by the people of the county authorizing a tax levy to provide local support for a community college is required. If the proposed constitutional amendment passes, this last requirement may be eliminated. This step would insure transfer credit for college transfer programs but would not help in the case of technical programs.
>
> As a technical institute, the Act under which we operate makes it possible for you to make a contract with a public or private four year institution to grant extension college credit for at least part of an Associate in General Education degree program.
>
> Even this, however, does not help technical program students. The Joint Committee on the Transfer Student and individual institutions are beginning to recognize the need that you have recognized for technical students to have left open additional rungs on the educational ladder. We are interested in and working on this so long as the requirements set **are on top of our** programs and **do not** subvert the primary purpose of our technology level courses.
>
> We do not want our programs to have to change and just become the first two years of a four year program. The University of North Carolina at Charlotte and Appalachian State University have programs in certain technology areas. Others are interested. Some others accept credit on a validation basis where the courses in question are similar to courses offered in the senior institution. It is clear that some progress is being made, but it is a slow process.[22]

Charles Bucher, Educational Director for the Department of Community Colleges, explicitly defined for the Board how contractual agreements operated between technical institutes and four-year institutions. The first example was piloted in 1967 between Tri-County Technical Institute and Western Carolina College (now University). By 1970 approximately sixteen technical institutes either had an annual contract that enabled a student to transfer four quarters of college parallel credit to a four-year institution or were working on one.

Some 208 full-time equivalent students were participating in this program statewide in May 1970. The State funded the first year of the program for up to one full-time instructor or an equivalent of 22 students, for a total allotment of $11,136, plus some money for supplies and travel. The approximate allocation for one teaching unit was $11,700. After the first year, the program was expected to become self-supporting with the tuition identical to that of a technical student.[23]

This contractual process would allow GTI to select applicants for the program and assign English and mathematics instructors from existing staff. The Institute would also provide remedial assistance since its instructors were considered more effective in delivering this instruction. The senior college would assign a representative to supervise the program through visits to the technical institute several times each quarter. The Board then authorized Dr. Medlin to discuss contractual arrangements with UNCG Chancellor James Ferguson and Guilford College President Grimsley Hobbs.[24]

Summary: 1969–1970

A determined Luther Medlin set GTI's right foot forward at the beginning of the 1970s to strengthen the Institution's credibility and to increase the capabilities of its staff and faculty. An aggressive building program materialized to supplant the decaying relics of the sanatorium era with modern laboratories and classrooms. Medlin had surveyed and then responded to the needs of the various communities the Institute served and extended GTI's outreach to Greensboro and High Point. He concluded the rigorous accrediting process and willingly alleviated the dilemma of the technical institute dead end by contracting with four-year institutions to accept credit for courses taught at GTI. As the fiscal 1969–70 year ended, a substantial increase in the summer enrollment prompted him to forecast an enrollment of 1,000 full-time students for the fall 1970 quarter as compared to 800 in 1969. Guilford County had become the beneficiary of Luther Medlin's decades of educational experience, but the unspoken question that unnerved his Board was how long would he stay the course?[25]

GTI Enrollment 1969–70

FTE: 1,247

Unduplicated headcount: 6,780

Budget: $1,393,582

Campus Notes

Mr. E. William Land, Chief of Apollo Space Planning, addressed the audience attending GTI's commencement on Friday night, August 21, 1970. For the first time in the school's history, some 150 adults were awarded high school diplomas. The *1970 Whispering Pines*, edited by Linda Miller, was dedicated to Alwayne McClure, the tireless educator who would occupy a number of administrative posts at the Institute. The annual saluted the Black Student Union for striving to stimulate the love of learning and the expression of creative ability. The Harlequins Drama Club was recognized for producing "The Gift of the Magi" and a group of students formed the Dental Hygienist Association to promote care of the teeth and gums. It was a banner year for SGA President David Chambers and his fellow faculty honor colleagues Cynthia Edge, Wayne Gibbs, Sharon Penley, Tony Martinez, Linda Miller and Linwood O'Neal.

Chapter 13

Medlin's First Five Years: 1967–1972

The stockholders of any business deserve a report on the progress, problems and operational success of their enterprise. At Guilford Technical Institute, students represent our prized product. You, the good people of Guilford County, are our stockholders.[1]

Luther E. Medlin, 1972

Flying High!

Luther Medlin bought an airplane to get GTI's aviation program off the ground and challenged the Art Department to decal it in the school colors. He attributed GTI's recent remarkable growth to a Board endowed with vision and high purpose and an administration and faculty committed to insuring quality in all their endeavors. As is the case with governance at most community colleges, the president's relationship with a politically appointed board is directly related to the growth and success of the Institution, not to mention the length of one's tenure. Much of Medlin's success is attributable to the support of Board Chair John T. Davis, Jr. and his close friend, the indefatigable Trustee and Guilford County Commissioner Percy Sears.[2]

Medlin's administration profited from his extremely valuable personal and professional relationship with his spouse, Helen; the companionable educator and elementary principal. She joined her husband to sweep and scrub the filthy classrooms that shocked them when they arrived on the Jamestown campus. She planned the public receptions they hosted at their campus residence, allowed her mate to crunch her toes at student dances, and graciously awaited his return from numerous speaking engagements, and civic assemblies. Luther Medlin's open and gracious demeanor and his formidable, but non-threatening, studious presence captured the resourceful confidence of

135

the Guilford County Commissioners, the State Board of Education, and the Department of Community Colleges. In the process of elevating GTI's reputation, he created an ongoing relationship with members of the General Assembly, and the business, governmental, and educational leaders of Guilford County that has seldom wavered through successive administrations since 1967. His presidency raised the bar in futuristic planning to the degree that the Institution's growth continues to reflect a cohesive pattern of fiscal, physical, and academic expansion.[3]

GTI's operating expenses increased steadily from $1,030,316 to $2,317,717 during Medlin's first five years, 1967–72.[4] Then as now, state and federal funds are allocated for instructional salaries, materials, and equipment, while Guilford County underwrites the physical operations and provides salary supplements. GTI benefited from federal funding provided by the Manpower Training and Development Act (MDTA, 1962), the Vocational Education Act (1963–68), the Higher Education Facilities Act (HEFA, 1963) and the Economic Opportunity Act (1964). By 1972, the Institute's annual $1,583,767 payroll was contributing significantly to Guilford County's economy.[5]

Facilities, Finance and the 1971 Bond Referendum

Beyond the rigors of maintaining their own viable professions, GTI's Trustees audited a myriad of financial details and facilities projects. They wrestled with construction and maintenance issues and coped with the ecological, geological, and topographical challenges unique to the Jamestown campus. They debated the installation of water, sewer, and energy infrastructure while arranging access and parking across a park-like campus. From non-compacting soil to insect-infested pines, stubborn rocks, and medical rubbish, they sought to superimpose a modern campus in the footprints of the decaying sanatorium they had inherited.

Anticipating GTI's inclusion in a 1971 bond referendum, building committee Chair James Williams projected five-year capital needs of $5,231,000 including $4,586,000 for four new buildings, $380,000 for parking areas, $185,000 for landscaping plus $80,000 for demolition and maintenance.[6] President Medlin's February 17, 1971, letter to Guilford County Manager John Witherspoon defined the Institute's construction priorities topped by a proposed new library as he prepared his Board and the county commissioners for the formal request for a bond issue he presented on March 10, 1971.

Emphasizing the shortfalls in library service created by an enrollment spike that surpassed the facility's capability to support student needs, Medlin reminded his audience that accreditation was directly linked to facilities, staffing, and the number of books in the library. In 1971, GTI was required to provide 16.71 library books per full-time student, but only 5.8 were available. Since this building also housed the entire business administration curriculum and the Institution's administrative offices, there was no room for additional library shelving, study carrels, or tables and chairs. The library was so taxed for seating space that students often had to sit on the floor, on the stairs, or stand. Medlin proposed a 25,000-square-foot library to duplicate the exterior design of the adjacent Technical Laboratory Building and save 40-50 percent of the architect's fee. In addition to the library-student center, his ambitious plan included an administration building and a materials resources center; he further advocated razing the remaining sanatorium buildings and constructing new roads and parking lots. [7]

The County Commissioners whittled GTI's wish list to $3 million and set the referendum for June 8, 1971.[8] Determined to secure voter approval, the Board transferred $4,000 in surplus funds from the fluid Furniture and Cosmetology accounts to finance a promotional campaign focusing on 19 ambitious projects. The strategies included a speaker's bureau, a voter registration drive, a slide presentation, a ten-minute film, and staff participation on the local TV talk shows.[9] The brochures, handbills, and newspaper feature stories that fleshed out the campaign were reinforced with a variety of merchandise, match books, bumper stickers, lapel buttons and posters.[10]

The importance of bond issues to GTCC can not be underestimated since they directly finance priority capital construction projects. In 1971, 13,128 (71%) of those voting on the GTI bond voted yes and 5,252 (29%) no. Notably, those opposed to the issue were mostly white Democratic females.[11] The issue eventually funded two major projects, a Learning Resources Center and a Campus Center.[12] Expansion during this period was not confined to new construction; in late 1971 GTI completed negotiations to expand its operations in Greensboro by lease-purchasing the Guilford College Downtown Division building on Washington Street for $961,000.[13]

The building committee was broadly engaged with planning, design, and construction projects. The five new buildings standing on the Jamestown campus in 1972 reflected a predictable escalation in construction costs and design sophistication; Machinery Hall (1957) $113,511; Furniture Hall (1965) $263,000; the Library-Classroom Building (1968) $361,496, and Health-Science (1969) $685,952. The 25,425-square-foot Technical Laboratories building (1971) $760,133 was formally dedicated on April 25, 1971, to celebrate the beginning of Occupational Education Week.[14] It housed Civil Engineering Technology, Commercial Art and Advertising Design, Architectural Technology, Data Processing, and Mechanical Drafting.[15]

Enrollment and Programs

The Trustees were aggressively committed to establishing a premiere aviation program at the Greensboro-High Point Airport, now PTIA, but the process demanded time and negotiations.[16] GTI eventually leased a 13,000-square-foot hangar in November 1972; meanwhile, Medlin bought a military version of the Cessna 310 (U3A), officially registered as N-10-GT, that enabled the Institute to lower training costs and increase enrollment. Second-year aviation students were ecstatic to have access to GTI's hourly $40 rate for the twin-engine craft as an alternative to paying commercial rates ranging from $45 to $100 per hour. While the Art Department relished its assignment to embellish the aircraft in the school colors, the Board scrambled to upgrade the Cessna to an advanced multi engine instrument trainer at a cost of $18,526.67.[17]

A record 18,126 students participated in GTI's instructional programs during the 1971–72 academic year when the maximum tuition was $32 per quarter. Two-year technical programs leading to the Associate in Applied Science Degree were available in thirteen subject areas. The Institute offered eleven one-year vocational programs and provided an additional eleven in evening certificate programs. The Adult Education Division offered basic education, a high school diploma program in association with the county's three public school systems, and general enrichment (continuing education) courses for certain skill and hobby enthusiasts. Many programs currently provided through GTCC's Business and Industry Division were Occupational Extension programs in the early 1970s. The bitter 1967 controversy over college transfer credits was a distant memory in February 1971 when GTI introduced four-year college level courses in English and history carrying college credit. The University of North Carolina at Greensboro (UNCG) managed the courses taught by UNCG instructors.[18]

A few weeks later, the *Greensboro Record* speculated that GTI could become a community college within the next five years. President Medlin fueled the prediction by intimating that "if GTI is to continue serving the total needs of this community, we will have to provide liberal arts instruction equivalent to the first two years of college work."[19] At that time, Dr. Charles R. Holloman, associate director and business manager of the State Department of Community Colleges, estimated that it would cost the state $92,502 if GTI were to immediately convert to a community college. Medlin cited low tuition and the open door admission policy as incentives for local students to take college prep courses at GTI. According to the president, a liberal arts curriculum would not harm the Institute's technical programs, but there is no evidence that the Board reopened discussions on the topic and the conversion issue languished for eleven more years.[20]

Marketing

A concerted drive to boost GTI's profile and strengthen its recruiting strategy commenced with a major advertising campaign utilizing radio, newspapers, and direct mail to promote the 1970 fall quarter schedule. Five commercials airing on six local radio stations were complemented by a series of week-long advertisements in the county's four newspapers and a tabloid distributed to 75,000 Guilford County residents. During this period individual courses numbered in the hundreds and 35 teaching stations were located throughout the county. *Greensboro Record* reporter Richard Benton's six-article series (March 1–6, 1971) earned him a commendation from the Board and a job as GTI's Director of Information Services beginning in 1972. GTI additionally received a large measure of pro bono support from WFMY-TV, the Triad CBS affiliate, in the form of public service announcements and interviews on "The Good Morning Show."[21]

Model Cities Child Care Program: 1971–72

GTCC's extensive history in early childhood daycare-education unfolded in April 1971 when the Comprehensive Community Child Care Agency of High Point, Inc., asked GTI to administer the multi-faceted Model Cities Child Care Program, one of more than two dozen projects operating under the auspices of the Model City Commission. The Board initially refused the proposal when Dr. Medlin introduced it on April 27, 1971, then tentatively reversed its decision by a narrow 5–4 vote on May 13, 1971. The reversal indicates the probability of intense behind the scenes negotiations to ease dissension and a possible Greensboro-High Point split on the project. Gilbarco President Sidney Low of Greensboro was the major dissenter; George Covington of High Point and Vance Chavis of Greensboro, the major proponents; Chairman Davis, from High Point abstained. The initial negative reaction extended from the belief by some Trustees that early childhood daycare-education was a dramatic departure from GTI's mission to provide technical and vocational education to adults.[22]

C. Roger Bell, Acting Director of the Comprehensive Community Child Care Agency (Fore-See), argued that child care was compatible with the Department of Community Colleges' philosophy that its units should seek involvement in community service projects. Bell envisioned child care as "a feeder for other departments and programs at GTI" while suggesting that "demonstration programs could be developed for use as laboratories for the training of students in a completely new curriculum area (Child Care Specialist, degree)." In his vision, the 1971 legislation creating the Child Care Licensing System in North Carolina would stimulate a huge demand for special and technical training in the field.

Proponents were attracted to his proposal because it could be implemented without state and county budgetary funds through a partnership with the Department of Social Services. DSS funded the program to the tune of $421,005 through the "Fore-See Agency" (CCCC-Comprehensive Community Child Care) by utilizing Title IV A funds and the High Point City Demonstration Agency. Since the funding procedure was identical to that supporting GTI's Manpower Training and Development Act programs and the EOA funds supporting basic education, administering the program was not a dramatic departure for GTI's administrators. The Board reconsidered their tentative approval of the program on September 9, 1971, and, following supportive remarks by High Point Trustees George Covington and John Davis, unanimously approved a one-year contract to administer the program.[23]

The first phase of the multi-faceted program was projected to serve 230 developmental daycare recipients, ages infant to four, and 60 developmentally challenged children. The Fore-See Agency division of GTI was fully staffed by April 1972 and serving 144 children in five High Point day care centers by May and 37 children at the Kindergarten for the Handicapped located at Forrest Hills Calvary Church. The four active Model Cities Programs in October 1972 included the Comprehensive Community Child Care Agency, Comprehensive Manpower Services, the Developmental Day Care program, and Developmental Day Care for the Handicapped. [24]

Criminal Justice Program

Under the Adult Education banner in 1965, GTI initiated a series of Community Services programs, basically the core of the present Public Service Technologies Division. They included Apprenticeship Training, Fire Service,

Fire Science, Law Enforcement, and Health Services.[25] In addition to basic law enforcement, the Institute provided training in specialized areas including breathalyzer, vascar, radar, narcotics investigation, general criminal investigation, civil process, and firearms. A two-year associate degree in Law Enforcement Education was approved and set to begin in September 1972 when the Institute attempted to win a $150,000 construction grant from the Piedmont Triad Criminal Justice Planning Unit. GTI targeted this money and matching grants to build a Law Enforcement Education and Training Center at the High Point Police Academy location gifted to the Institute by the City of High Point. The decision not to award the grant to GTI did not deter the Institute from implementing its degree program in the fall 1972 quarter.[26]

Faculty and Staff 1971–72

Medlin praised GTI's "highly selective process for appointing exceptionally credentialed faculty and staff," for increasing the quantity and quality of the Institute's master teachers and administrators from 85 in 1967 to 172 in 1972. Board members sought opportunities to enhance employee morale by recognizing exceptional faculty and staff. On April 13, 1972, A. P. "Al" Lochra, Dean of Student Services, and colleagues Sylvia Clayton and Phil Tate were commended for developing a recruiting program that attracted more than 1,000 high school students to the campus.

Dean of Instruction Richard E. Waldroup was praised for five years of excellent service and strong leadership when he resigned to become the Chief Administrative Officer of Charleston, South Carolina's Technical Education Center (Trident Technical College).[27]

Personnel Statistics		
Degree	67–68	72–73
Doctors	1	6
Masters	23	47
Bachelors	17	38
Craftsmen	21	34
Clerical	15	36
Others	8	11
Total	85	172*

*PAR, 1972.

Student Activities

GTI celebrated its first *Homecoming* January 24–28, 1972. *The Whispering Pines Yearbook* Jeanne Bailes of the Commercial Art Department presented to the Board on July 13, 1972, praised the school for offering "Quality education at the lowest possible cost." Ralph Deathridge presided over the SGA and Marty Hedrick won the President's Medal. The instructional gallery of photos included some of the Institute's most renowned instructors, Doris Simone and Wanda Russell, Secretarial Science; Kenneth Vaughn, Accounting; Lynwood English, Business Administration; Dr. Lyle Pepino, Associate Dean of Curriculum Programs; and Howard Hicks, Associate Dean of Curriculum Programs.[28]

The extra curricular activities documented in the yearbook are reminiscent of student life on any junior college campus of the era where the camaraderie is highlighted by a Halloween dance at the Shrine Club. The annual "I am An American Day" springtime observance at High Point Lake was described as "a healthy mixture of fun, fellowship, serious thought and reflection" at which the Embryonic Stage drama club presented an outdoor rendition of "Hair." Students, faculty, and staff were back at the Shrine Club just east of the school for their Christmas Theater dance highlighted by the Embryonic Stage's "heel-kicking" presentation of "Partridge in a Pear Tree." The year's homecoming queen and court included representatives from GTI's various programs.

The SGA sponsored "Coffee House" gatherings and presented musical programs for the Monday activities hour. Cheerleaders Sandy Gulledge, Diane Cline, Terry Sutker, Susan Pipan, and Margie Anderson boosted the Guilford Tech Hornets basketball team to a third place finish in the nine-team Community College conference. Roy Tharington and David Hodgin won All Conference honors thanks to support from teammates Butch Burton, Steve Causey, Gary and Kelvin Johnson, Fred Townsend, Harvey McGirt and Danny Bunn. The 13 clubs and organizations active on the Jamestown Campus were obviously popular. Scholarships were available for needy students, and in 1972 the Sigmund Sternberger Foundation, now the Tannenbaum-Sternberger Foundation, gifted GTI with $15,745.00 to provide an annual Nursing Scholarship Fund of $1,600 based on need for Guilford County residents enrolled in the Nursing Program. GTI provided $6,382 in scholarships during the 1971–72 academic year.[29]

Summary

In summarizing GTI's impressive growth during the first five years of his presidency, Luther Medlin recalled that when he began his tenure in 1967, the

Institute was at the bottom of the list of North Carolina's 56 technical institutes and community colleges. By 1972, it was ranked second and the largest of the technical institutes and its service to Guilford County was admirable:

> Our programs have literally trained thousands of people for better jobs. Additional thousands have received a new lease on life, a second chance. GTI has accepted students when no other school would. They have come from the jails and the prison camps, from the public schools and college dropout rolls, and from other circumstances under which the door of opportunity had been shut in their faces. GTI has taken the functional illiterate and made him educationally functional. It has taken many without funds and enabled them to prepare for worthy and productive employment and useful citizenship.[30]

GTI's future rested on its ability to fund facilities and programs for an ever increasing enrollment. Medlin foresaw a refinement of the curriculum, a need to increase faculty and guarantee transfer credits to more students. The past was prologue for this visionary CEO who anticipated constructing three more buildings: a health careers facility, a classroom building, and a second technical laboratories building. GTI's unduplicated curriculum enrollment numbered 2,493 at the end of the 1971–72 academic year with its president committed to serving three more years to the great relief of his broad constituency of supporters throughout Guilford County.

Operating Funds Expenditures				
	State	**County**	**Federal**	**Total**
1967–68	$541,644	$123,565	$365,107	$1,030,316
1971–72	$1,660,274	$391,300	$266,143	$2,317,717*

*PAR, 72.

Chapter 14

Projection 75: Progress and Challenge

The Arab members of OPEC triggered an international energy crisis in October 1973 (The Arab Oil Embargo) by halting petroleum shipments to the U.S. and its Western European allies in retaliation for their support of Israel during the Yom Kippur War.

The Energy Crisis of 1973

GTI was challenged to pursue orderly growth and development while coping with the issues and restrictions generated by a national crisis in energy resources that shackled the U.S. in late 1973. Thermostats were seasonally adjusted and lighting was monitored to conserve energy during the 14-hour educational day. Space was maximized to conserve fuel, prompting President Medlin to proclaim that "no institute in our state squeezes more out of the cost of facilities than GTI." The school exceeded all groups of institutions in both classroom and laboratory use with classrooms registering 16.9 hours per week and laboratories 21.1 hours. The broadly successful conservation program resulted in a 20 percent savings for 1973 over the 1972 operating costs.[1]

Enrollment Rollercoaster

By discouraging many students from commuting, the energy crisis precipitated a significant statewide enrollment drop among educational institutions during the 1973–74 academic year. The enrollment at North Carolina's community colleges and technical institutes plummeted from 431,174 (1972–73) to 400,220 (1973–74). GTI's total headcount slumped from 19,658 to 16,809 while the Adult Enrichment enrollment withered from 7,863 to 2,239. In an ironic twist, considering Jamestown's suburban location, the grand total FTE actually increased by 254 to 3,226. Energy crisis aside, GTI attracted more than four times as many students in 1973–74 as in 1967–68 and the availability of more gasoline indicated a recovering trend for 1974–75.[2]

An avid proponent of marketing, Medlin instigated the publication and distribution of an annual tabloid by the High Point and Greensboro newspapers that reached 200,000 readers in Guilford County. His aggressive promotional ventures were most significant during the summer of 1973 when GTI's staff and faculty appeared on 35 segments of the award winning "School Days" segment on WFMY-TV's "Good Morning Show" and on a series of local radio interviews (WCOG).[3]

The marketing strategy probably aided the Institute's ability to weather the energy crisis by delivering for 1973 the largest summer registration in the school's history. Curriculum growth grew 37.9 percent while extension enrollment drifted upward a modest 7.4 percent.[4] The 1974 figures posted spring quarter curriculum growth up 8.4 percent, to 1,701, with a 4.1 percent increase in continuing education, 6,236.[5] The summer 1974 quarter marked a historical increase for this specific period to 1,485 (25.5 percent) in curriculum and 8,360 (9.4 percent) in continuing education.[6] The rush to GTI resulted in a 19 percent (2,604) growth in curriculum for the 1974 fall quarter, a 40 percent (8,020) growth in continuing education, plus an enrollment of 3,400 students at the Greensboro Division.[7] The curriculum headcount grew from 2,722 (1972–73) to 3,447 (1973–75) and 4,556 (1974–75). The total enrollment reached 23,492 during Medlin's administration when the faculty and staff increased from 29 to more than 200 in 1975.[8]

Facilities Expansion

GTI had progressively developed as a loose network of four campuses and instructional centers by the end of the 1972–73 fiscal year, and Dr. Medlin envisioned even greater growth and expansion by 1975. The Jamestown campus thrived as the heart of the Institution where ground was broken for the $3.24 million Campus Center/ Learning Resource Center in January 1973. This complex was initially scheduled for completion by fall 1974. However, Mother Nature intervened to deter the builder's best intentions as "construction" continued to be the "infinite cross" that tormented GTCC's boards throughout the Institution's first fifty years as this excerpt from a committee report indicates:

> The report of the Building Committee is more nearly a weather report this month. It has snowed, sleeted and rained. The thunder roared and the lightening flashed. The rains descended and the floods came. As if this was

not enough from the clouds, the grading crew broke a six inch water main and flooded the building site from below as well. Be that as it was, however, our general contractor lost only five days in February due to the weather. They have been real busy moving the mud around on the site.[9]

The building committee minutes reflect periods of dissension over architects, engineering, and design. At one point during the planning stage for the Learning Resources Center (LRC) and the Medlin Campus Center, Trustees Frank Starling and Percy Sears clashed over the retention or dismissal of architect Hyatt Hammond, whom Starling charged, in Sears' absence, had been "nitpicked to death." Hammond was actually fired and rehired in a matter of days.[10] As the Institution matured, construction issues occupied more and more of the Board's time second only to the issue of transfer credits. Late 1973 found the Trustees planning yet another classroom building for Jamestown, and by the spring of 1975 the million dollar-plus Health Careers facility was in the design stage.[11]

Program Expansion

Beyond the furious construction activity at the Jamestown campus, major improvements in educational services were delivered in Greensboro, in High Point and at the regional airport's growing aviation center. Prior to building the T. H. Davis Aviation Center, "Hangar 3" provided more than 13,000 square feet for the Aviation Management Technology program including three classrooms, study areas, and administrative space.

The purchase of the former Guilford College Downtown Campus locked in a central location for GTI's Greensboro division in a nearly 48,000-square-foot building at 501 West Washington Street. The division operated its Manpower Development Training Center in the old Ingram Motor Company building in the 300 block of South Elm Street and sponsored classrooms in churches, recreation centers, housing projects and schools throughout the county.[12]

Classes in High Point, previously taught at the William Penn School, were transferred to a 5,300-square-foot area on the first floor of the Arcade Building at 329 North Main Street. Bolstered by the establishment of a Fundamentals Learning Laboratory, this facility became GTI's High Point division.[13]

GTI's faculty and staff begin developing the ubiquitous institutional self-study that would prepare them for an April 29–May 2 visit by the SACS accrediting team when they returned to work from the 1972 Christmas–New Year 1973 break. By year's end, the Institute and its programs had been reaccredited by SACS, the State Department of Community Colleges, the State Board of Nursing, and the Council on Dental Education of the American Dental Association.[14]

A new department of instruction was created when Child Care Worker was added to the curriculum during the 1972–73 academic year. This one-year vocational study program was designed to eventually lead to a two-year Associate in Applied Science Degree as a Child Care Specialist. [15]

Transfer Credit

Transfer credit was a persistent point of contention during the Medlin presidency. While GTI's instructional programs were accredited by the same agencies that accredited programs at four-year institutions, some colleges and universities still refused to accept credits earned at GTI and similar technical institutes. Traditional admission standards presented a major challenge for those ambitious and deserving students who wanted to continue their education at a higher level. One issue was faculty who were not appropriately credentialed; another was 3-quarter hour classes versus 3-semester hour classes. Some higher education administrators considered the Community College System a threat to existing four-year institutions. Another powerful group feared, like GTI co-founder Zalph Rochelle, that transfer curricula would erode the values of vocational and technical education.

The inability to transfer credits was a major problem for those students who were, for a variety of reasons, forced to remain in GTI's service area. Included were those who could not afford rising tuition at the four-year level and the many who needed to work while learning but could not fit into the traditional residential experience then offered by the typical college or university. Finally were those who had been rejected, or were disqualified by grades or test scores from entering a four-year liberal arts program.[16] President Medlin made it clear in 1973, 10 years before the Institute became a comprehensive community college. that "any new direction for GTI should include an open and easy flow of students to four- or five-year institutions where they can accomplish their educational goals." By the time of his retirement in 1975, dozens of four-year institutions across the nation were considering transfer credits from GTI students in more than 20 programs, but a bona fide college transfer program was almost a decade away.[17]

Continuing Education Debacle: The Poodle Problem

The *High Point Enterprise* profiled GTI's continuing education program in several articles on May 20, 1973, in response to a new law passed by the General Assembly. The measure specified that state funds could no longer be used for non-credit "recreational and avocational courses at community colleges and technical institutes,"[18] thereby excluding enrichment courses including poodle grooming, cake decorating, and floral designing. Bargain basement continuing education courses that cost $3.00 for 33 hours of classroom instruction were projected to increase to more than $14.00 a course.

The Department of Community College's policy manual stated that all recreational and avocational courses should be self supporting, but administering that policy was a matter for the individual institutions. The administrative problems associated with collecting fees from students attending classes at dozens of locations prompted GTI's Director of Continuing Education, Dr. Harold J. Fegan, to observe "Since GTI operates classes from one end of the county to the other, collection efforts would use up a lot of gasoline and time." Noting "the fine line between vocational and avocational courses," N.J. "Larry" Owens, Jr., GTI's Vice President for Instruction, suggested that many of these "hobby courses" could possibly develop into money making projects.[19]

GTI and the General Assembly

GTCC's attempt to maintain a positive relationship with lawmakers at every government level dates from the initial funding measure Ed Kemp sponsored in the General Assembly to establish the Guilford Industrial Education Center in 1958. The Institution's various boards have unanimously appreciated and cultivated the favor of the legislative bodies that fund the College. The College depends on federal funds and the generosity of the Guilford County Board of Commissioners, but the state provides the greatest portion of GTCC's current operating budget including salaries, library books, equipment, supplies, travel, postage, and other necessities; capital funding is an entirely different proposition.

Prior to 1973, the General Assembly had appropriated only token amounts for capital construction projects, but two new bills enacted that year provided $25.5 million in construction funds. GTI's growth in full-time equivalent (FTE) student enrollment and the community support it received in terms of local funds for capital construction, including $3 million in the 1971 bond issue, entitled the Institute to more than one million of the system's $25.5 million appropriation. This appropriation was destined to help build the Health Careers Building at a time when the need for trained personnel in this field was rapidly expanding.

Dr. Medlin expressed his appreciation for the "respect and recognition shown to GTI by our Guilford County Delegation to the General Assembly, and the splendid cooperation we have received from our Board of County Commissioners," adding that, "it no longer requires a selling job, or a high-pressure program to get all these people at various levels of government to understand what we are doing and why we are pursuing so diligently."[20]

Program Update: 1973–1974

By 1974 GTI was offering 19 Associate Degree programs, 12 Vocational Diploma programs, and more than a dozen Evening Curriculum programs, some of which duplicated the Associate Degree offerings, plus a wide variety of Continuing Education programs.[21] The Learning Resource Center (LRC) initiated innovative programs in three major areas during the 1973–74 academic year. Satellite LRC's were established at the High Point and Greensboro divisions and a new library collection was installed at Greensboro where complete LRC services, including audiovisual materials and learning laboratories, became available. The Jamestown campus LRC initiated a peer tutorial program where academically challenged students were tutored by students who demonstrated the proper proficiency in their respective disciplines. Beverly Folks coordinated the program, which served 27 students in January 1974. The LRC staff and faculty members also designed a series of self-instructional mini-courses that were offered for credit during the 1974 summer quarter.[22]

Student Life

The cryptic, truncated history of GTCC gleaned from board and committee meetings in no way, at least in the early decades, captures the collegiate spirit of this unique Institution. A glimpse of this essential culture from the Institute's 1972–73 annual *Whispering Pines* portrays the activities and interests of "a real live and kicking college-age student who comes with needs to be met and finds a ready response by faculty and staff in the joint pursuit of his educational goals."[23]

Photos of the SGA's traditional "I Am an American Day" observance introduce the 1974 *Whispering Pines* with its memories of games, seminars, speakers, picnic lunches, and rain. The North Carolina writer-photographer team of Nancy and Bruce Roberts highlighted the LRC's observance of National Library Week. Norman Faircloth's Commercial Art Department was extensively involved in Festival III sponsored by Greensboro and Guilford

Fall 1973–74 Student Body		
Male	60.9%	1,329
White	80.8%	1,763
Work Full Time	54.2%	1,182
Work Part Time	19%	415
Unemployed	26.8%	585
Daytime Programs	58.1%	1,267
Evening Programs	41.9%	915
Technical Programs	67.1%	
Vocational Programs	27%	
General Education	5%	
Total Curriculum Headcount		**3,447***

*PAR, 1974–75.

County, and the department's annual Commercial Art Exhibit Open House enticed more than 300 friends to view and buy student art.

Greg Mercer won GTI's golf tournament with a score of 77 while the Green Hornets basketball squad won eight and lost seven compiling a 4–4 conference record. The team defeated Durham Tech 83–82 to notch a homecoming victory before homecoming queen, nursing student Vickie Martin. Butch Vance presided over the 1973–74 SGA and a 4.0 earned Wayne McNairy the Outstanding Technical Student Award; the President's Medal was awarded to Phi Beta Lamba president Sarah Andrews.

The Criminal Justice program debuted to prepare students in the legal, philosophical, technical, and practical aspects of law enforcement. Cosmetology Department Chair Claude Culp utilized new audio visual equipment to train his students. Aviation Department head W. B. Johnson and Automotive chief T. L. Breedlove incorporated team teaching into their curricula.[24] The 1975 *Whispering Pines* highlighted the increasing integration of technology into Dental Science and Health Occupations. J. D. Rhyne began teaching GTI's new Fire Science curriculum in the 1974 fall quarter while Martha Hickey assumed the Guided Studies chair.

Marie Aldridge presided over the 1974–75 SGA. Harry Boody, the recipient of GTCC's first Distinguished Alumni Award in 2004, was elected president of his freshman class and Gary Gray won first place in the GTI golf tournament. One of the more exciting moments occurred at 12:30 P.M. on Monday, June 16, 1975, when the GTI tennis court opened on the Jamestown campus.

The $50,000 facility succumbed to a later building boom and is now part of the parking lot at the rear of the Sears Applied Technology Center.

The Consummate Educator Announces His Retirement

Luther Medlin announced his retirement on August 1, 1974, and set the official date for June 30, 1975. He had been considering the move for two years, but timing the decision for an effortless exit had been difficult, if not impossible:

> My hope has been that things would level off making an easy exit for me and an easier entrance for my successor. This has not happened and it appears unlikely in the foreseeable future. I do not expect our growth pattern to change, nor do I expect us to curtail the development and expansion of our campus as additional facilities become necessary to serve the needs of our students.[25]

Aware that Medlin's presidency had begun during a "low" period in the Institute's history when enrollment had declined to about 700, the Trustees thanked him for engineering a "turnaround" in the wake of the Institute's public humiliation resulting from fiscal and administrative failures. He assured the citizens of Guilford County that GTI was in "excellent condition in terms of administration, faculty and students." Medlin continued:

> The potential of this school is the greatest in the entire system as acknowledged by all who know the state's Community College System. The school's finances, although not abundant, are adequate for our needs.[26]

The Trustees moved quickly to insure that Medlin's contributions were suitably recognized by naming the new campus center for him on "Luther Medlin Day," Sunday, June 29, 1975.[27]

Luther Medlin's Heritage

Medlin's leadership did not go unappreciated by his peers who elected him to chair the North Carolina Association of Public Community College Presidents in 1973–74. His professionalism, as defined by leadership skills and administrative integrity, combined accessibility, the courage to listen, an appreciation for people, a love of education, and a gritty determination, saved Guilford Technical Institute in its moment of peril. Medlin halted its dissolution at the Institution's most vulnerable point in 1967 and rebuilt the county's confidence in its mission. He departed believing that his decision to leave the exceptional program he had created at Walter Hines Page Senior High School in Greensboro to accept the challenge at GTI had been the correct decision:

> An additional source of gratification lies in the fact that GTI now has the prestige that an educational venture of this sort must have if it is to serve the constituency. I truly believe that Guilford Technical Institute has the respect of the educational community that surrounds it as it operates in a cluster of colleges and educational institutions of various sizes and kinds. I know that GTI has the respect of 57 member institutions within the North Carolina Community College System, of which GTI is one of the largest schools.[28]

Medlin's tenure encompassed the replacement of dilapidated sanatorium buildings with Business Careers, Gerald Hall, the Learning Resources Center, and the Medlin Campus Center. He established campuses in High Point, Greensboro, and the Aviation program at PTIA. His operational achievements are exceptionally significant; at his departure, the budget totaled more than $4.8 million; the LRC housed more than 26,000 volumes and welcomed an average of 445 visitors daily. The school's enrollment was projected to exceeded 25,000 in 1975–76 and soar past 37,000 by 1979–80.[29]

Luther Medlin had compiled an impressive record of service, but he was not allowed to go quietly into retirement. By virtue of Joint Resolution 77, the North Carolina General Assembly honored him as "a dedicated and proven public servant in North Carolina Education." In 1975, he was named Greensboro's "Outstanding Civic Leader" for decades of community service, including a stint as president of Civitan International (1957), and recognition in *Who's Who in America* and *Who's Who in American Education*.

Medlin's relationship with the Institution continued into the GTCC era when he was awarded an Honorary Associate in Arts degree at the August 1984 graduation. The presentation, occurring one year before a GTCC student was eligible to receive this first-ever AA degree, marked the end of Medlin's long struggle to institute a strong college transfer program. He continued to serve the Institution as president of the GTCC Foundation until his naming as Foundation Director Emeritus on March 17, 1992. Mertys Bell, former Dean of the Learning Resource Center, reminisced about Medlin's personal impact on the campus morale:

> Dr. Medlin was so easy-going, warm, and cordial with a good sense of humor. He was so participative. He was aware of everything that was going on, from student activities to everything by the faculty and staff. He was right there—always, and was supportive of innovations.[30]

Dr. Luther Reece Medlin, characterized by former GTCC Dean of Student Services Dr. Albert "Al" Lochra, as a "master educator, very gracious, and flawless in his words," died at the age of 92 on Thursday, January 6, 2000.[31]

Student Profile	1972–73		1973–74	
Male	1,006	58.16%	1,329	60.9%
Female	767	41.84%	853	39.1%
White	1,464	79.87%	1,763	80.8%
Nonwhite	369	20.13%	419	19.2%

Employed	1972–73		1973–74	
Full-time	833	45.44%	1,182	54.2%
Part-time	430	23.46%	415	19.0%
Unemployed	570	3l.10%	585	26.8%

Unduplicated Head Count Enrollment		
	1972–73	1973–74
General Education	115	203
Two-Year Technical	1,723	2,288
One-Year Vocational	884	956
Total Curriculum	2,722	3,447
Occupational Extension	6,378	9,287
Adult Education	2,313	2,330
Adult Enrichment	7,863	2,239
Grant Total FTE	2,972	3,226
Headcount Total	19,658	16,809*

*These figures are directly attributable to the 1973–74 gasoline shortage that prevented many students from attending GTI and other technical institutes across the state. State enrollment declined from 431,174 (1972–73) to 400,220 (1973–74).

Dr. Woodrow B. Sugg
President GTI 1975–1977

Dr. H. James Owen
President GTI 1977–1979

The GTI Green Hornets played their first game in the fall of 1968.

Cheered on by GTI's inaugural cheerleading squad.

Section IV

The Sugg and Owen Administrations
1975–1978

Chapter 15

Quest and Crisis: Joy and Anxiety

We were not funded for adequate growth, but we are not crying. We're trying to cut every corner we can, but we don't want to sacrifice quality.

Dr. Woodrow Sugg, August 7, 1975

Dr. Woodrow B. Sugg

A commendable educational dossier accompanied 56-year-old "Woody" Sugg to GTI: a B.A. in Education from Atlantic Christian (now Barton College); an M.A. in School Administration from UNC-Chapel Hill; and an Ed.D in Education from The University of Florida plus post-doctoral studies at Duke and Columbia. The Pinetops, North Carolina, native had served as a public school teacher, principal, and superintendent of the Gastonia City School System, and as president of Gaston College. He had worked for the Ford Foundation and directed the Comprehensive School Improvement Project for the N.C. Department of Public Instruction. Having chaired the legislative committee for the Presidents' Association of the N.C. Community College System, Sugg was acutely aware that the budgeting process and legislative bias placed this system at a funding disadvantage.[1]

A veteran of the funding wars during his presidency at Gaston College, Sugg had pirouetted between skimpy state financing and budget slashing reversions to maintain a viable Institution; while that experience did not make his job any easier in Guilford County, it fueled his determination not to cap GTI's enrollment even when confronted by immense pressure:

I received a letter from the state that said we will have to cut the budget by 3 percent. This will be approximately $100,000. That's enough money to pay the salaries of five or six new teachers. If the people knock on our doors, we may not be able to serve them all. We want the population to know we are operating under some near handicaps.[2]

Funding GTI emerged as Woody Sugg's greatest presidential challenge, but his awareness that the Guilford County Commissioners were historically committed to the Institute and that the Board was consistently supportive enabled him to maintain his optimism and commend his staff for serving 500 students over budget.[3] He stepped diplomatically across the "community college conversion" issue at his first news conference by telling reporters that GTI's Board wanted to see the school continue as a technical institute with an emphasis on "the world of work" rather than move toward community college status:

Of course the Board of Trustees has the final authority in this matter, but I plan to talk with them about it. I hope the Board will keep its options open as it seeks to serve the people of this area. Vocational instruction and a liberal arts curriculum can be compatible. Quality is the most important criterion. Gaston College started as a two-year liberal arts college.

I want this Institution to serve the needs of the people. We want GTI to be what the community sees it as, a community educational institution. In order to do this we need a staff that is willing to take risks, try new approaches and listen to the people. The staff needs to turn to the community and the community needs to turn to us.

If the other schools in the area satisfy the first two years of college, we don't need to move in that direction. GTI has a unique responsibility to have a large continuing education program and to offer vocational and technical training. We want to increasingly become a fine technical institute.[4]

Sugg shared this vision with his staff and faculty at the opening of the 1975 fall quarter when he stressed the privilege of serving:

a new and unique kind of institution of higher education whose successes would depend on our understanding of the opportunities before us and our commitment to work together to achieve the goals which can, and will be so very satisfying to the multitudes of people who come through these doors, and to the community at large.[5]

He reminded his audience of the Institute's commitment to broad democratic principles by quoting John Gardner's observation that "the demand to educate everyone up to the level of his ability and the demand for excellence in education are not incompatible." Sugg continued:

There may be excellent plumbers and incompetent plumbers, excellent philosophers and incompetent philosophers. An excellent plumber is infinitely more admirable that an incompetent philosopher. The society which scorns excellence in plumbing because plumbing is a humble activity and tolerates shoddiness in philosophy because it is an exalted activity will have neither good plumbing nor good philosophy. Neither its pipes nor its theories will hold water.

Sugg outlined his vision for GTI with a series of goals and objectives:

- To help prepare people well for entry into the vocational trades contiguous to this community, with the knowledge, skills, attitudes and values which will provide them a chance for reasonable success and satisfaction.
- Prepare technicians for industry, business, and a multitude of service occupations which exist today and in the days ahead.
- To help people—young and the not so young—to compensate for the lack of adequacy in previous education by providing meaningful opportunities and experiences to bridge the gaps between where they are and where they choose to be.
- To upgrade people to better compete in the world of work and to help them more nearly realize their full potential.
- To guide and counsel people to accept responsibility for their own destinies and to place them in touch with the human and physical resources which will help them move ahead in life.
- To add satisfaction and joy to living by helping people to adapt to the world around them, to the changing times and to the evolutions in life itself, and
- To provide opportunities and learning environments in which learning and education can be optimized with what has been said as a background.[6]

Sugg offered an additional 16 opportunities to improve the quality and value of the Institution, its staff, and faculty. Targets ranged from enhancing the institutional life, to utilizing the school's diversity of talent, pursuing effective teaching, learning skills and methods, staff development, and continuing the commitment to the open door policy that welcomed all the citizens of Guilford County.[7]

The Controversial Presidential Residence

Woody Sugg's journey to Jamestown was not without controversy. Since his acceptance of the presidency at a salary of $48,000 was contingent on the Board's commitment to build a new presidential residence, the Trustees submitted a funding proposal to the Guilford County Commissioners almost at the moment of his hiring.[8] Commissioner Richard Maxwell strongly objected to the projected $70,000 cost and the precedent-setting justification to build a residence for a county employee. Commission Chair Gaston Faison supported GTI Board Chair John T. Davis's explanation that a new house was needed to replace the deteriorating residence lingering from the sanatorium period, but delayed official approval until the next commissioners' meeting.[9]

The projected four bedroom residence, featuring a living room and den with fireplaces, and a dining room for entertaining, was completed in 1976 at a cost of $79,253 including $70,000 from the county and the remainder from GTI funds. The Sugg family's move to the new home tolled the demolition of the previous residence located a mere 22 steps from the new Medlin Campus Center (MCC). The old home site was eventually turned into an open campus area through which a sidewalk connected the MCC with the nearly completed Health Careers Building.[10]

The Budget Crisis of 1975–76

Sugg's tenure coincided with the 1975 fall quarter, when GTI recorded an enrollment of 3,627 students, a 34 percent increase in day and evening curriculum classes, with continuing education up 12 percent to 9,020. 12,647 students were taking one or more courses, but the increase in staff earned by the previous year's enrollment was killed by legislative budget cuts. Faced with one of the most fiscally perplexing periods in the school's 18-year history, Sugg commended his staff and faculty for handling the enrollment increase with few additional teachers and support personnel. He and his administrators transitioned to a crisis mode to serve an escalating enrollment with an increasingly restrictive budget. What "Woody" Sugg characterized as the "joys and anxieties" of operating one of the county's most progressive educational institutions incited him to educate the school's constituency about the budget process in his 1975–76 annual report.[11]

The Financial Dilemma and the State Budget

The budgeting scenario deserves repetition since it structured financial crises into the ongoing governance of the Community College System. Then, as now, GTI and its sister institutions depended for fiscal sustenance on budget sources established by the North Carolina Community College Act of 1963. This partnership between the state and individual county governments assigned the major responsibility for building and maintaining the necessary facilities for school operations to county governments. The state funded administrative and instructional salaries, and paid for instructional equipment. Approximately 80 per cent of GTI's annual operating budget, including the tuition paid to the state by GTI students, was funded by the state with the remaining 20 per cent appropriated by the Guilford County Commissioners. The few available federal dollars provided financial aid to students through general assistance and to special students in nursing, criminal justice, and similar curricula.

GTI's growth and fiscal stability were throttled by a predetermined series of formulas based on full-time student enrollment (FTE) for the previous year. Sugg's anxiety increased exponentially as the funding process began with the General Assembly's appropriation of a lump sum education budget to the State Board of Education. He could only watch, and wait, and consult with Guilford County's legislative delegation as the State Board applied designated formulas to determine budget allocations to the Department of Public Instruction and the Department of Community Colleges.[12]

State funding for community colleges is determined by the average annual FTE students enrolled during the previous 12 months. To qualify as an FTE when GTI operated on the quarter system, a student had to attend classes for a total of 16 contact hours per week during an 11-week period for a total of 176 contact hours per quarter, or 704 contact hours per academic year. While the students who enrolled for a full class load generally qualified as a full FTE in themselves, those who enrolled for a partial class load had to be grouped with other part-time students to comprise a full FTE for budgeting purposes.

The state funding process began with budget officials consulting GTI's enrollment records for a 12-month period, in this case the 1974–75 academic year, to determine the 1975–76 state allocation. They found 23,492 students enrolled in both curriculum (credit) and continuing education (non-credit) programs during that period. Since the majority of those students did not enroll for a full schedule of 16 contact hours per week, the formula reduced the total headcount translated to 4,189 FTE students. This figure, when applied to various formulas established by the State Board of Education, determined GTI's allocation for teaching positions, clerical and support positions, and state financed budget items including employee benefits, equipment, and travel.[13]

The Guilford County Budget Process

GTI's staff developed the county budget by determining the actual and anticipated needs in physical plant operation and construction as defined by

General Statute 115-A. They surveyed the school's needs and created the necessary justifications in early March. Requests for renovations and repairs, housekeeping and maintenance positions, and supplies were reviewed along with utility costs, rents, salary increases for county-paid employees, and new construction projects. Dr. Sugg and the Board reviewed the staff proposals before meeting with the Guilford County Budget Director. This official's clear understanding of the budget is key to a successful appropriation. Following the formal adoption of the package by the GTI Board, the Trustees and the County Budget Director present the request to the Guilford County Commissioners. Following a public hearing, the commissioners adopt GTI's budget for the fiscal year July 1–June 30.

Where Did the Money Go?

Nearly 80 per cent ($2,672,373) of GTI's 1975–76 state operating budget ($3,327,918) was disbursed in salaries primarily spent by GTI employees in Guilford County. The remaining 20 percent paid for supplies and materials, employee benefits, printing and binding, travel, advertising, postage, books, and equipment repairs. Nearly 40 percent ($299,475) of the county budget ($744,866) was disbursed in salaries for GTI's county-paid employees and primarily spent in Guilford County. The county additionally paid $207,348 for water, fuel, and electricity, and $72,394 for repairs to facilities and various expenditures covering employee benefits, plant operation, rent, and insurance. The major 1975–76 disbursement under the Construction/ Capital Outlay allocations to GTI of just over $1.0 million helped build a new Health Careers Building on the Jamestown campus and pay for improvements to grounds and facilities.[14]

The Budget Versus the Economy

GTI's total headcount enrollment for the (1974–75) academic year totaled 20,608 students, a 22.6 per cent increase over the 1973–74 academic year and equaled 3,641 FTE. According to the State Board of Education's budgeting formula for technical institutes and community colleges, GTI's 1975–76 state allocation traditionally would have provided funds for 17½ new teaching positions plus additional dollars for supplies and equipment. Tragically, the Institute's earned state allocation for 1975–76 was never funded. The General Assembly's allocation to the Department of Community Colleges was slashed in a budget-stretching year stifling the operations of each of the 57 institutions in the system. [15]

Woody Sugg initially saw GTI lose 14½ of an earned 17½ new teaching positions critical to serving a student enrollment that had already increased 22.6 per cent over the previous year, and would jump an additional 13.9 per cent in the fall quarter. Before he could exhale, a second budget reduction erased the remaining three new teaching positions. Faced with the challenge of a significant enrollment increase, GTI was forced to operate the 1975–76 academic and fiscal year with virtually no new state funds to broaden and expand services. Smaller classes were combined or eliminated as the school struggled to serve 6,683 additional headcount students. More desks were added to classrooms, student laboratory loads were increased, instructional and staff positions were frozen, and GTI employees did not receive cost-of-living increases. Travel expenditures were restricted, and the Institute and its students did without needed, but not essential, instructional equipment and supplies. GTI's basketball team was an immediate victim of the budget crisis, but as Sugg recalled, the games were poorly attended and failed to capture any revenue.[16]

Between a Rock and a Hard Place

GTI's 1975–76 county budget represented a significant increase over the previous year; this increase was needed for utility rate hikes and the cost of operating the new Medlin Campus Center and the LRC. Since many other county-funded agencies were also requesting budget increases, GTI's request was reduced from $939,445 to $811,692 and administrators were instructed to spend even less. Federal funds from the Comprehensive Employment Training Act (CETA) were used to hire a number of unemployed workers to serve in maintenance and to work as technicians, secretaries, and low and medium level supervisors. The CETA dollars saved the day, and campus-wide efforts to conserve electricity and other county-financed items enabled the school to spend only $744,866 for the 1975–76 fiscal year—well within the $811,692 approved budget.[17]

Sugg and his staff tightened their fiscal belt to operate with a reduced 1975–76 budget as part of a state-wide effort to assist the legislature to survive within the anticipated income figures. They did so expecting an improvement in the economic picture and a restoration of full funding for the 1976–77 year. That did not happen. For the second year in a row, and the only two years in GTI's early history, the school was not fully funded. On July 1, 1976, GTI was instructed to reduce its earned state allocation by $718,000 (16.3%) leaving it to operate on 83.7 percent of its earned budget, a near-crippling cut on the wave of a significant enrollment increase. Few citizens beyond the Institute could grasp the effect of these debilitating cuts on staff and faculty morale. Ironically, shops, laboratories, and classrooms were mandated to operate with greater student-teacher ratios and equipment budgets restricted at a technical Institute where the quality of the education depended on state-of-the-art equipment.[18]

Board Activity: 1975–76

One of the most historically significant political pirouettes on the Board occurred when Republican Governor James E. Holshouser, Jr. appointed Percy Sears to the Board for an eight year term to expire June 1983, after the county commissioners did not reappoint him following the end of his term on June 30, 1975. Sears replaced John W. Thompson Jr., a former gubernatorial appointee not reappointed by Holshouser, who was subsequently reappointed jointly by the Guilford County, Greensboro, and High Point School Board, for an eight year term expiring June 30, 1983. Sears ability to manipulate his political associations enabled him to continue to nurture the technical institute which represented a major part of his life. He would ride that partisan horse as long as possible.[19] Mrs. Lois Snitzer, a gubernatorial appointee, and GTI's first female Board member, resigned in December 1975 when her family left the state. Governor Holshouser subsequently appointed Mrs. Joanne Bowie of Greensboro, a formidable Republican, to fill Snitzer's unexpired term until June 30, 1981.[20]

With GTI's administration, staff, and faculty determined to persevere regardless of full funding, the Institute's complex operational growth encouraged the Board to create additional sub-committees to attend to pyramidal increases in policy, finance, and personnel issues. Modeled on the long-standing Building committee, a Personnel Committee was organized to align the Institute's various personnel policies with state directives while an "Ad Hoc" Finance Committee was initially created to develop the 1976–77 county budget. The Board additionally moved to make the bookstore a self-supporting profit center by reducing inventory, increasing profitability, and assigning its operation to the Business Office headed by Dr. Ray Lane, the new Vice President for Business Affairs.[21]

The Building Program: 1975–76

The Trustees were committed to expanding facilities and services in Greensboro when President Sugg made it one of his top priorities. The former downtown location of Sears, Roebuck and Company on the northwest corner of Eugene Street and West Friendly Avenue had piqued their interest following the retailers' move to the suburban Friendly Shopping Center. While $750,000 in state funds were available, the cost of repairing and adapting the structure proved to exceed what the Board considered reasonable and the project was dropped.[22]

The Board unanimously approved a proposal to name the Technical-Laboratories Building (1971) in honor of Coswell "Cos" Ellis Gerrald. Gerrald chaired the Architectural Technology Department from 1968 until his death on July 11, 1975, and was instrumental in designing the Tech-Lab facility. He additionally served on the Faculty Council's founding committee as its first chairman (1970–71).[23]

Faith, Confidence, and the Future

The dichotomy President Sugg faced in fiscally managing GTI while endeavoring to train a workforce for Guilford County goes to the heart of North Carolina's fiscal integrity. The institutions comprising the Community College System had consistently proved invaluable in preparing a new workforce for emerging technologies, but the up-front investment that could have prominently elevated the system was not forthcoming.[24] Budget crisis aside, "Woody" Sugg could not ignore pressing needs including elevators to serve handicapped students in three multi-level buildings, 500 additional parking spaces on the Jamestown campus, plus new facilities for four curriculum programs, and facilities to implement an imminent series of health and safety programs. The Greensboro Division struggled with inadequate parking as well as the lack of shop and lab facilities, while a new teaching center was needed in High Point.[25]

Sugg did not falter in the search for new programs as he observed the average age of students increasing and employed workers enrolling for additional training. Their ranks included middle-aged females who needed counseling and assistance in preparation for the world of work and a substantial number of low-income earners who were buying into the promise that GTI's training could provide a bigger paycheck and greater opportunities; then, there were the aging and retired individuals who came seeking challenging, invigorating diversions in continuing education programs.

The difficult budget years did not dim Sugg's optimism for the future of GTI though he clearly realized that a high level of support from the state was necessary to insure the instructional responsibility in the state-county partnership. Only strong support from the state could insure the development of needed programs and staff them with professional administrators and instructors who had academic preparation and practical work experience. He assured the citizens of Guilford County that:

> We will complete this year and begin the next with a faith and confidence that our funding agencies both state and local, and our community as a whole, will rally and support this Institution in its sincere efforts to be of even greater service to the people of Guilford County.[26]

Luther Medlin had succeeded in growing the Institute while maintaining a non-controversial profile; Woody Sugg, through no fault of his own and much to his displeasure, emerged as a lightning rod for the media.[27]

Campus Notes

Seemingly impervious to the Institute's fiscal struggle to survive, the vitality of student life on the Jamestown campus flourished. The tremendous success of GTI's first Spring Festival on May 9, 1976, prompted the Board to formally praise those responsible for planning and promoting the event: Ray Moody, Director of Student and Alumni Activities; Richard Benton, Director of Information Services; Greg Mabe, president of the SGA; and art instructor, Jeanne Bailes. Talented students marketed their creative work during the festival and applied the proceeds to the cost of their education.

GTI's annual reflected a new level of imagistic sophistication with the artistic quality of its color and black and white photographs presented as a "photo essay of GTI and Guilford County." The contributions of Loretta Hethcox, Kathy Clinard, Jay Slaughter, Ed Potts, Molly Barker, Jane Goodman, and Henry McClendon are notably striking.

President Sugg commended GTI's student newspaper "Tech Talk," edited by Matthew Thekkekandam, for its positive tone and varied articles.

The "Mighty Majors" played for the semiformal Homecoming Dance" on February 14, 1976, at the Royal Villa Hotel in Greensboro; the cover charge was $2.00![28]

GTI was designated A National Bicentennial Campus to celebrate the 200th Anniversary of the United States of America in 1976. Machinist students designed and manufactured special Bicentennial Medallions from pewter for sale by the Institutes' Bicentennial Committee chaired by Mertys W. Bell. A Bicentennial Park was created between the Learning Resource Center and Gerald Hall to serve as a commons area for students.

Chapter 16

Transition: Sugg to Owens and Owen

> I would like to think that my most significant contribution over the past
> two and a half years was one of encouraging cooperation and involve-
> ment between faculty, staff, students, Trustees and advisory committees.

> Dr. W. B. Sugg, October 27, 1977

The Presidential Salary Controversy

Woody Sugg did not stick around in 1978 to celebrate GTI's 20th year of
service to Guilford County. He retired on December 31, 1977, his tenure untainted by a upcoming springtime salary flap that attracted media coverage
and triggered repercussions in the General Assembly. Sugg awakened one
April morning to find his picture and salary ($41,159) splashed across the
Guilford County media. The furor over presidential salaries in the Community College System erupted with a newspaper report listing the salary of
Wake Technical College president Robert LeMay, Jr. at $44,042. The fact that
LeMay's salary was second only to that of Central Piedmont's president
($45,029), raised Mecklenburg State Senator Craig Lawing's concern with
purported high salaries, entertainment and automobile allowances, country
club memberships, and other fringe benefits and prompted his demand for
a legislative investigation.

> I want to know what these cats are making. Some might be making as
> much as $75,000 a year if you take everything into consideration. LeMay's
> salary is within $1,000 of what my man (Central Piedmont Community
> College, Charlotte) makes and LeMay's school is no where near as large
> as my man who has 20,000 students.[1]

Gaston Faison, Chairman of the Guilford County Commissioners defended Sugg's contract noting that, "a man of Dr. Sugg's caliber cannot be paid too much." Sugg's salary was computed from a formula that accounted for the school's size, the president's education, and his professional resume. A doctorate, combined with over 30 years experience in educational administration, qualified Sugg for $31,051 from state funds and $10,108 from the county budget. Realistically, the county commissioners could pay GTI's CEO whatever pleased them.[2] When pressed to comment, Sugg confidently defended his salary.

> I certainly hope we are not overpaid. We are open out here (Jamestown) from 8 am to 11 pm. I live on campus and work many nights. As president of a community college, you have to be both a superintendent and a principal. You oversee the operation and of the school, but you also deal directly with students about their problems.[3]

The State Board of Education assessed the salaries of presidents twice in March 1978 and authorized the dispensation of appropriate credit for administrative experience in determining their remuneration. The SBE requested a comprehensive study of the salary schedule of presidents and suggested that further changes in the present salary pattern should be delayed until that study was completed.[4] Woody Sugg was far more concerned with meeting Federal Guidelines to equalize GTI's pay scale between males and females and African-Americans and whites than with the statewide controversy surrounding presidential salaries.[5]

His salary became a moot point after he tendered his resignation to the Board (October 27, 1977).[6] Retirement before age 60 had been his long term goal, and he and his wife were currently building a new home in Raleigh. Sugg, who had purposely worked without a contract, had warned the Trustees when he resigned that it might be impossible for him to stay on the job until June 30, 1978. He subsequently decided to leave on December 31, 1977.[7] According to Chairman John Davis, the Board was aware from the moment of Sugg's employment that he planned to stay only for three to five years and that he had been an "excellent president for GTI."[8]

Questioned about the lingering possibility of community college status for GTI, the departing president reiterated his original position; "I felt all along that we needed to spend our time doing what we're doing in the best way possible." He did suggest that the Trustees might need to consider community college status in the future;

> I think that as this Institution has grown and matured, the time is now at hand to review the status and reconsider the wisdom of community

college programs added to, not replacing, our present services. And I believe this matter will have to be considered at some time in the future.[9]

The State of the Institution: 1976–77

In his valedictory "Report to the People," Sugg noted that expense appropriations from state tax dollars had increased at the rate of 13 per cent from $3,360,694 (1974–75) to $3,377,115 (1975–76). While expense appropriations from local tax dollars had steadily increased from $652,267 (1974–75) to $903,602 (1976–77), the retiring president pointed out that the new dollars merely paced the rising costs for instruction, utilities, supplies, and the operation of the new Williams Health Careers Building. GTI's enrollment had remained basically flat during a period when it generally declined across the Community College System. The unduplicated headcount for the second largest institution in the Community College System in 1976–77 (23,458) was actually 34 less than 1975–76 (23,492) prompting Sugg to blame the stalemate on the lack of funding for new ventures.[10]

The bright side to the budget shortfall and the stable enrollment was that it provided administrators time to evaluate the staff and faculty for upcoming re-accreditation examinations and to review GTI's role in the community. In 1977, the Institute's 230 full-time staff operated from 10 major structures comprising 335,000 square feet of space; the average student was 26; male and female enrollment was about equal, and minority enrollment was nearly 22 percent. Sixty percent of the curriculum students were employed either full- or part-time and most resided in Guilford County.[11]

Adult Education

GTI spearheaded adult education in Guilford County for the approximately 75,000 adults who had not graduated high school, about half of whom had less than an eighth grade education.[12] The Institute offered an Adult Basic Education Program (grades 1–8) and an Adult High School Diploma Program (grades 9–12) as well as administering the GED (General Education Development) for the State Board of Education. After 11 years, GTI's Adult Basic Education program had become one of the largest in the state including, in addition to academic instruction, consumer education, government and law, and personal problem-solving. More than 15,700 individuals had enrolled since

1966 with 6,200 of them learning how to read and write for the first time. The Adult High School Diploma Program's day and evening classes had graduated around 1,700 students since 1967; more than 2,000 adults had received GED certificates since 1969.

GTI's Human Resources Development (HRD) Program helped the chronically unemployed and underemployed to sharpen their focus on career objectives and complete the necessary education and training to meet their goals. Six-hundred-eighty-three clients, many of them welfare recipients, had completed the program since its inception in 1971 and were working, or receiving additional education in preparation for employment. Indicative of its significant value to Guilford County's economy, the HRD Program (1976) recorded an "earnback index" of $7.31 for every $1.00 in funding.[13]

Curriculum Programs

In 1977 when more than half of the area's graduating high school seniors chose not to attend a college or university, GTI was teaching 37 curriculum day programs including 11 classified as one-year vocational studies leading to diplomas; 26 were classified as two-year technical studies leading to associate degrees in applied science. Studies leading to certificates or associate degrees were also offered during the evening. In addition to academic preparation, GTI offered personal counseling from pre-admission through job placement assistance following graduation. The 3,557 students who enrolled for the 1977 fall quarter represented an increase of 51 over the previous year.[14]

A Guided Studies Program, the precursor of Developmental Education, was available to day and evening students who needed additional preparation in reading, mathematics, language skills, or basic study habits. Developmental Education presently (2008) offers reading, English grammar and composition, and math. Pre-curriculum courses are also available in reading and English for students who speak English as a foreign language. The department became a division in 2006 when Dr. Nawachi Tafari was named the inaugural chair.[15]

Continuing Education

Continuing Education Programs for adults represented the largest area of service to the people of Guilford County in 1977 enrolling 8,000 to 12,000 students quarterly in short-term, inexpensive courses. Clients could select from several hundred personal enrichment offerings and attend classes at various times for a period of 11 weeks. Popular programs during the late 1970s included Gourmet Cooking, Knitting and Crocheting, Ceramics, Home Maintenance and Repairs, Tole Painting, Lawn Care, Transactional Analysis, Personal Income Tax Preparation, Painting and Wallpapering, Bricklaying, Floral Design, Upholstery, Ham Radio, Furniture Construction, Drapery Making, Stocks and Securities, and Macramé. Continuing education classes were taught on the Jamestown, Greensboro, and High Point campuses, and in churches, community centers, schools, and housing projects. Then, as now, continuing education instructors with keen interests and knowledge in particular subject areas were employed on a part-time basis and taught more as a service rather than for the money.[16]

Service to Industry: Advisory Committees

Francis White was the personnel manager for Myrtle Desk Company in High Point in 1977, and while he was neither on the staff nor payroll at GTI, White and similar executives played a major role in curriculum development. White chaired GTI's Industrial Management Advisory Committee as one of 180 representatives of business and industry voluntarily serving on 27 Advisory Committees for curriculum programs. He and his colleagues helped GTI administrators align instructional programs with employment demands. Their relationship with the Institute meant then, as now, when more than 600 advisors are involved on curriculum advisory committees, that GTI graduates have a higher probability of finding and keeping local employment.

The advisory committee concept was first employed by the Guilford County Commissioners in 1957–58 to study the feasibility of organizing the Guilford Industrial Education Center. A second advisory committee functioned as the GIEC's policy-making board until the Center became Guilford Technical Institute in 1963 and a Board of Trustees was constituted.[17] GTCC's working relationship with business and industry is managed today by the Business and Industry Division, successor to 1977's Occupational Extension Programs. The early staff monitored and assessed the changes in technology and legislation that generated an educational need for area businesses and industries. They worked with plant managers, human resource managers, administrators, and others to plan and implement educational programs determined by the specific need of each business or industry. Courses could be as simple as first aid instruction, an update of OSHA regulations, or represent more complex needs, such as a special class in structural steel drafting or instruction in heavy equipment maintenance. Some classes like "knitter-fixer" involved on-the-job training and were taught in-plant for the convenience of employees and employers at a cost of $5.00 per student.

Occupational Extension

During the 1976–77 academic year, OE offered programs in Management Development, Upholstery, Industrial Power Sewing, and Special Operator Training for the Handicapped, Nursing Assistant, and a RN Refresher course plus apprenticeship classes in Building Trades, Heavy Equipment Maintenance, and Sheet Metal. Seminars were conducted for Public Utilities, the Southern Furniture Market Association, Housing Authorities, and the N.C. Tire Dealers Association; miscellaneous classes were offered in Welding, Blueprint Reading, Data Entry, Credit Union Management, Traffic and Transportation Management, and Structural Steel Drafting. In addition to Wastewater Treatment, Pesticide Control, Executive Housekeeper Certification, Secretarial Refresher, First Aid, and Medical Assisting, Food Service instruction was provided for prison and public school personnel[18]

GTI Board Activities: 1977

The Board, chaired by John T. Davis, Jr., learned about one of GTCC's most innovative and historically significant programs at its January 1977 session when Executive Vice President, Dr. N. J. Owens, Jr., unveiled the concept of "live construction," a project involving students in the Air Conditioning and Heating, Carpentry and Cabinetmaking, and Electrical Installation and Maintenance curricula. The opportunity for students to construct a house for the purpose of a "hands-on" educational experience was endorsed by the Home Builders Association of Greensboro-High Point and the curricula's various advisory committees. The Trustees set in motion another major long-range program authorizing in April 1977 the formation of the non-profit GHG Corporation to buy a lot and manage the construction of a 1,550-square-foot house.[19]

Searching for a New President

We'll take our time to pick the individual that we think is best for the job. I think we have been very successful with Luther Medlin and Woody, and I hope we can keep up the high standard of leadership we had in them."[20]

Percy Sears, December 1977

By January 1978, the search for Woody Sugg's replacement as president of GTI was eliciting applications "from all over the country" according to search committee chair Percy Sears. In the interim, Dr. N. J. "Jerry" Owens, GTI's executive vice president and a presidential applicant, had assumed the interim presidency. The Wilmington, N.C., native had joined the Institute in 1968 as director of occupational extension responsible for evening, special and continuing education programs. The search committee preferred a North Carolinian for GTI's next president, but that was not a condition for employment.[21] The Trustees soon realized that members of the Institute's staff and faculty were interested in contributing to the presidential selection process. The disclosure that opinions varied on the question of who should participate in the selection was discussed at the January 19, 1978, Board meeting when Sears reported that a letter had been mailed to all GTI personnel seeking suggestions and/or recommendations for a presidential candidate.

GTI legal counsel Fred Hamlet questioned the legality of Faculty Council Chair Janet O'Brien's request to permit a representative of the Faculty Association to serve on the search committee. His argument turned on the problem of allowing individuals who were not Board members to sit on the search committee given that the Board of Trustees had the sole authority to choose the next president. Though a motion to add additional members to the six member search committee was soundly defeated, the committee agreed to invite representatives of the Faculty Association, administrators, and students to discuss the qualifications and traits appropriate for the Institute's next president. During that era, State Board of Education Chairman Dr. David Bruton was urging community college Trustees to take "special steps to insure that qualified women and minorities were considered for top leadership positions at the state's community colleges and technical institutes." None of the 57 schools in the system employed a minority president at that time.[22]

By April 27, 1978, the Board's presidential search committee had narrowed the candidate field from 169 to two: Dr. H. James "Jim" Owen, Jr., of Jacksonville, Florida, and GTI executive vice president Dr. N. J. "Jerry" Owens, Jr. Members were split three times on the candidates, both of whom were capable, before they voted unanimously to offer the presidency to Dr. Harold James Owen, Jr., a veteran of 14 years of service in Georgia and Florida community colleges. Owen was officially approved on May 1, 1978, but the transitional drama did not end there.[23]

On May 24, 1978, before the new president took office, Jerry Owens resigned his $30,000 a year position to preside over Kings College, a two-year Raleigh business school, a move he described as "the logical next step in his professional development." A few years later, having accepted a position with the State Department of Community Colleges, he was joined at the system office by his former competitor from GTI, Dr. Jim Owen.[24] The Board may have chosen to bypass Jerry Owens for the presidency, but his legacy is solidly embodied in some of GTCC's most prestigious programs including aviation, nursing, and early childcare.[25]

"Dr. Jim's" Challenge

From a budgeting standpoint, Jim Owen's fiscal management challenges were defined in a period when belt-tightening was the rule of the day. The institutional operating budget had been slashed from $1,091,000 to $1,025,000 and the capital outlay budget trimmed from $350,000, to $250,000 to comply with the wishes of the Guilford County Commissioners. The cut eliminated the purchase of land adjacent to the Jamestown campus, landscaping, repairs to buildings, and renovations intended to eliminate barriers to handicapped persons.[26]

"Dr. Jim," as the new president was affectionately known, had his work cut out for him. Beyond the ubiquitous issues of budgeting, enrollment, and accreditation, Owen would confront affirmative action and integration in a region where the public schools had only recently fully integrated and where the civil rights struggle was still smoldering. There were ongoing questions about program duplication, cooperation with the county's three public school districts, facilities, and services that framed the next twenty months as a major learning experience.

Campus Notes

The destruction of what the Board's Building Committee described as the "gate house adjacent to the historic Iddings House" was recommended in January 1977.[27] However, Trustees Percy Sears and Robert "Bob" Landreth defended the historic significance of the 1920's era structure and the motion to raze it was quashed. Architect Harry Barton designed the gazebo as a bus stop shelter for visitors and employees at the TB sanatorium. GTCC's foremost symbol heralds the Foundation and is prominently featured in various college publications and campus prints. GTCC instructor Shelley Lutzweiler championed the historical significance and preservation of the Gazebo and the Iddings House.[28]

A fire on Friday, November 18, 1977, gutted the x-ray darkroom in the Dental Science building slightly injuring one worker and causing $10,000 in damage. Seven fire trucks and 26 firemen from four stations answered the 2:53 pm alarm. The freak accident occurred when a solvent used to strip the finish from cabinets ignited when steel wool used in the cleaning process triggered an arc from an uncovered switch box. Dry powder prevented the blaze from spreading.[29]

Tech Talk reported that more than 5,000 people attended "Festival '78" on May 7, planned and produced by second-year commercial arts students as a part of their grades. Debbie Godfrey's review of *The Betsy*, Harold Robbins' intriguing novel about the auto industry appeared in the May 15, 1978, edition of *Tech Talk*. Adjacent to Debbie's review was a story about her personal battle to break the bonds of addiction and discover a new life at GTI thanks to the Drug Action Council.[30]

Chapter 17

The Owen Presidency: 1978–80

> The big thing I've got to do is relate the Institution to its several communities, but keep my hand on the pulse of the internal operations and not forget there are librarians, counselors, teachers, and students. I prepare myself. I come to work early and stay late.
>
> Dr. Jim Owen, May 1978[1]

"The Workhorse"[2]

Forty-year-old Harold James Owen, Jr., a Brookline, Massachusetts, native with undergraduate and graduate degrees from the State University of New York and a doctorate in education from the University of Georgia came to GTI from Florida Junior College where he had most recently served as vice president of campus operations. Owen's wide ranging responsibilities at FJC included occupational, vocational-technical and adult continuing education, learning resources, student development, records and registration, programs and budgets on the school's four main and 200 off-campus locations. His professional resume included a stint as executive secretary of the Southern Association of Colleges and Schools (SACS).

Owen left an operation annually budgeted at $27.5 million, supporting 18,000 FTE students plus 1,000 full-time and 1,400 part-time personnel, to manage GTI's state-county budget one eighth that size (nearly $4.7 million in 1976–77) and a staff and faculty fewer than 250. He agreed to work for an annual salary of about $33,000, including a county supplement, plus fringe benefits including a house, paid utility bills, and a car.[3] Owen was committed to improving literacy in a state with 750,000 illiterate adults, about ten percent of whom lived in Guilford County.

We're touching so many people—on the order of 23,000 students a year. When you can make an impact on reducing the number of illiterates, when you can make an impact on having an adult achieve a high school diploma, that's (increasing) the quality of life. Our job is to educate adults, whether they need to learn to read, or keep their house from falling in, or to improve their skills.[4]

Dedicated to building "a partnership between Institution and community," Owen had no intention of veering from GTI's stated goals and objectives, meaning that he did not plan to broach the community college conversion issue. Noting that, "it would not be appropriate to attempt to duplicate what is offered at other institutions in Guilford County," he made it clear he was not interested in elevating GTI to community college status. [5]

Affirmative Action and Desegregation

The most controversial challenge confronting GTI's new CEO (1978) was the dissatisfaction that motivated some community college and technical institute leaders to favor rescinding the federally approved desegregation plan for the 57 member system. Owen responded to the issue by clearly stating that he was "committed to equal access and equal opportunity in community colleges."[6] As a matter of fact, affirmative action was a major strategic planning initiative at GTI. The desegregation of the public higher education system in North Carolina was a work in progress when the Owen presidency unfolded relatively late in the civil rights struggle. "The Revised North Carolina State Plan for the Further Elimination of Racial Duality in the Public Higher Education Systems, Phase II: 1978–1983" (August 15, 1978) focused on disestablishing the structure of the dual system by desegregating student enrollment, faculty, administrative staffs, non-academic personnel, and governing boards.[7] During this crucial period of change, the North Carolina Community College System was without a female president until the State Board of Education approved Dr. Neill McLeod's appointment as president of Martin Community College in Williamston effective May 14, 1979.[8]

GTI's first Affirmative Action plan emerged from an Institutional self-study examining compliance with Department of Health Education and Welfare regulations. The eventual plan was designed by Alwayne McClure, GTI's Personnel/Compliance officer, and Wanda Daughtry, Chairperson of the Affirmative Action Committee. Morris W. Johnson, Director of Affirmative Action for the Department of Community Colleges, commended GTI for developing what he described as "one of the more detailed and logically arranged plans his office had received." Compliments aside, in September 1979, GTI was ordered to readdress the program from the narrow perspective of "black" employment as opposed to the more general collective term "minority" employment. SACS also asked for an evaluation of the degree requirements of faculty and administrators.[9]

Capital Needs: The 1979 Bond Referendum

The Guilford County Commissioners began hearing the requests in September 1978 that would enable them to compile a five-year capital needs' program to comprise a bond issue for the November 6, 1979 election. President Owen asked for $9.9 million to finance physical improvements at GTI locations in Greensboro, High Point, and Jamestown. The school needed funds for construction, real estate purchases, renovations and modifications to comply with handicap-access specifications. Owen identified $2.1 million for a new building in Greensboro (1980); $1.5 million for a classroom building in High Point (1981), and $1.9 million for a shop-laboratory building designated for the Jamestown campus by 1982.[10]

In July 1979, Percy Sears informed his fellow Board members that the county manager had not decided how the bond funds would be allotted. Sears presumed the guideline would be based on "GTI's Capital Program for 1979–84," which designated $3.5 million for building and handicapped renovations, repairs, land, and $1.5 million for a building in High Point. When it initially appeared that GTI would get only $2.5 million, the Board unanimously approved a recommendation by the Building and Grounds committee (Facilities and Finance) to ask the county manager to restore funding for the Greensboro building to the bond issue. The Board did not want to ask money for a building in High Point without including a request for a similar structure in Greensboro. Trustee John Thompson argued that GTI could sell a $4.5 million issue as easily as $2.5 million since the Institute was listed on a separate ballot. This is another example of how the Board bonded to maintain its integrity by balancing services to its largest communities.[11]

The five-issue $40 million bond referendum Guilford County Commissioners eventually approved for the November 6, 1979, election included $2,500,000 for GTI; $32,500,000 for public schools; $3,045,000 for county buildings; $1,155,000 for solid waste disposal, and $800,000 for the sheltered workshop. The Support Committee formed to promote the issue marketed the referendum with the slogan "Great Guilford." T-shirts promoted the five issues in the referendum with the slogan, "Do It Five Times on November 6."[12]

An inexpensive brochure highlighted the Institute's 21-year record of providing essential educational services to residents beyond the scope of the county's three public school systems and six post-secondary institutions of higher learning. By 1978, approximately 26,000 individuals had received low-cost, quality instruction; but additional funds were needed to support construction costs, maintenance, and operation of facilities. The message emphasized that continually increasing demands on the rapidly growing Institution could no longer be met with existing funding. Classrooms and laboratories needed redesigning to accommodate new instructional programs; existing buildings and parking facilities required renovations and repairs; additional priorities included new facilities and additions to existing buildings and real estate for future expansion.[13]

GTI's Student Government Association sponsored voter registration drives. When Advisory Committee members were invited to the Jamestown campus and asked to promote the bond issue, Percy Sears asked each Board member to contribute $100 to the promotion package. The GTI bonds passed, but not with the same support the Institute received in 1971.

Year	# Voting	Yes	Percentage	No	Percentage
1971	18,480	13,128	71%	5,352	29%
1979	30,976	16,771	54%	14,205	46%

Registered Voters in County in 1979:	146,312
Total Voting:	36,646
Turn Out:	25%

GTI's 54 percent approval rate in 1979, compared to 71 percent in 1971, did not resonate as an overwhelming endorsement for the Institution. The cultural statistics, indicating a considerable lack of support by white female and male democrats, raised more questions about GTI's credibility when coupled with the fact that 5,670 (15 percent) of the voters voted neither for nor against the GTI bond. Significantly, too, the 1979 voter turnout totaled 25 percent of the registered voters in the county in an election that occurred three days after the Nazi-Klan shootout in Greensboro. This social tragedy, one of the most traumatic civil rights events of the 20th century to affect Guilford County, immediately separated whites and blacks in the city and presumably throughout the county. This incident could have dramatically affected voter psychology.[14]

Further evaluation of the voting indicates that the predominant numbers of "no" votes came from precincts throughout the county where, based on income and opportunity, voters had to most to gain from GTI and should have provided its greatest support. The narrow "pass" margin in this election should have sent a clear message to GTI's Board that the Institute's image and mission thirsted for a strong marketing campaign. What went wrong? It is the author's editorial opinion, based on observations as a working journalist during this era, that GTI's county-wide credibility had not fully recovered from the press expose that shrouded the era over a decade earlier. Lack of confidence in the Institute and the absence of consistent leadership may have been additionally exacerbated by perceptions of instability based on Woody Sugg's brief stopover and the Owens to Owen transition. Historians have yet to analyze fully the history of Guilford County 1960–80, but the record of events includes incidents in which the overwhelmingly conservative residents did not react positively to change. It is also probable in GTI's case that, given its mission, far too many citizens did not take the Institution seriously unless they desperately needed its services and programs to survive moments of personal and corporate crisis.[15]

GTI Board Action

The 1979 Board debated numerous expansion projects in Greensboro particularly focusing on properties in the 400 and 500 blocks of West Market Street stretching to West Washington Street. Interest centered for a time on the old YMCA building at 517 West Market until the Board decided to renovate a structure at 449 West Market.[16] They also considered the Christian and Missionary Alliance Church at the corner of Sycamore and Edgeworth and purchased the "Parker property" at 418 West Washington Street, for $47,000. At the same time they were scouting expansion in downtown Greensboro, Board members were investigating land and buildings to grow the High Point division.[17]

The Board named Jamestown campus roads for Dr. M. D. Bonner, former Director of the Guilford County TB Sanatorium, and Zalph Rochelle, a GTI founder and former Board Chair. Montgomery Circle honored former Guilford County Commission Chairman, Dale Montgomery; the Williams Health Careers building, recognizing the service of Trustee James L. "Jimmy" Williams, was dedicated on Thursday, June 14, 1979.[18] The Board faced a major problem in mid 1979 with the departure of gubernatorial appointee and Board Chair John T. Davis, Jr. Davis' appointment expired on June 30, 1979, and he had asked not to be reappointed. The nominating committee, chaired by Daniel Fouts, recommended that it would be in the Board's best interest to ask the Governor to reappoint Davis. However, the Board and the nominating committee recognized that given the timing, if a Governor's appointment was not available, other means might be found to secure a seat on the Board for Davis. Excusing himself due to obligations at his law firm, Fouts solved the dilemma by tendering his own resignation. The Guilford County commissioners appointed Davis to fill Fouts' unexpired term until 1985 enabling Davis to accept another term as chairman, though his service ended with his resignation on December 1, 1981.[19]

GHG "Live" Construction

The 1,502-square-foot house students built on Halifax Court in High Point's Foxwood Meadows subdivision for $40,783, sold for $49,500. As the "live" project flourished, the Board commended Carpentry Instructor R. P. Hughes for his leadership and approved a second house for the Beechcroft subdivision in Greensboro. GTI Trustee Frank York, president of the Home Builders Association of Greensboro-High Point, noted that the successful program was attracting local contractors to the merits of GTI's students and that one contractor had offered to employ the entire class.[20]

Enrollment Figures

The 1979 fall quarter enrollment equaled 3,670 curriculum students, 55 more than the previous fall, but FTE funding was problematic since it was subject to legislative whims. In 1978–79 the overall Community College System was funded on 119,000 FTE students and in 1979–80 at 112,000 FTE after the legislature reduced the over-all funding by approximately 7,000 FTE. While the system as a whole declined in FTE, GTI's portion of the FTE funding bounded from 4,609 annual FTE to 5,582, a 21 percent increase over 1977–78. 25,981 unduplicated headcount students were enrolled in curriculum and continuing education programs during 1978–79.[21]

The Children's Center

On March 15, 1979, the Board established the GTI Children's Center to provide high quality child care to the children of students, staff, and community families. Director Doris Martin and her staff welcomed 50 children when the center opened on May 1.[22] The facility additionally provided curriculum students in Child Care, Teacher Associate, and Nursing programs with opportunities to observe children and professional teaching models and participate directly in the day-care setting. This exceptional program was based on proven child care developmental concepts incorporating the educational philosophies of Maria Montessori and John Dewey. The center was founded on the premise that children learn and thrive in an environment in which there is an opportunity for them to manipulate real objects and materials, and in which the program grows out of their interests and abilities. Based on the applications of theories by psychologists Jean Piaget and Erik Erikson, the center's program was strengthened by embracing the hypothesis that teacher-child relationships can significantly influence the development of young children and that every attempt shall be made to minimize disruptions in the formation of trust relationships between teacher and child.

The center provided daily lunches and morning and afternoon snacks in accordance with the Type A Standards of the North Carolina School Food Service Program. The meal was served family style to promote good eating habits and assure proper nutrition. The center staff was committed to creating a setting reflecting the qualities found in a nurturing and positively stimulating home environment. Parents were welcomed and encouraged to participate in the program. The Children's Center operated Monday–Friday, from 7:30 A.M. to 5:30 P.M., and remained open during the inclement weather closings of the main campus except when extreme weather conditions prevailed. An open door policy enabled children to enroll regardless of their families' race, religion, or economic status. Handicapped children were and still are accepted in compliance with Public Law 94-142. Children between the ages of six weeks and five years (or until they enter public school) may be enrolled at the center. The children are grouped according to age following group size and child-staff ratios determined by the Department of Social Services Board of North Carolina. Tuition rates for the Children's Center in 1979 included a nonrefundable registration fee of $15 plus $40 per week for children two and younger and $35 per week for children three and older. Tuition assistance was available through the Department of Social Services for a family who met the stated income requirements.[23]

"Dr. Jim" Bolts

On January 17, 1980, twenty months into his tenure as GTI's fourth president, Jim Owen submitted his resignation to the Board. The move did not surprise the Trustees who were aware of rumors concerning his imminent departure. When they reportedly questioned him about the gossip during a December executive session, he answered that he preferred not to comment and the subject was dropped. His resignation was courteously accepted with "regrets and best wishes" from the Trustees. Owen resigned to become the state vice president for program services in the Department of Community Colleges at a salary of approximately $42,000, about $2,000 more than he was paid at GTI. He told reporters the position would "give him a direct hand in guiding programs" at the state's community colleges and technical institutes in Dr. Larry Blake's new administration.

> I've done work in the last six years with a number of state boards for community colleges. It's something I've always been interested in. With the advent of a new state board for community colleges in North Carolina this opportunity was very exciting.[24]

The presidential search committed chaired by Frank York included Percy Sears, Odell Johnson, and Robert Landreth. A special interim executive committee headed by Board Chair John Davis included Dr. Roy Lane, vice president for financial affairs; Dr. Harold Fegan, vice president for instructional affairs, was named to provide administrative leadership during the search.[25]

During his 20 months at GTI, Owen worked to expand the school's cooperation with business and industry to determine the county's future employment needs. He presided over the opening of the Children's Center and the inauguration of a medical assisting program. As he noted in remarks recorded during GTCC's 40th Anniversary celebration in 1998, Owen was disappointed with the state's lack of recognition for the Community College System. Capital funding for the system had waned in the late 1970s and was in a general state of decline relative to backing for public schools and the university system.[26]

One of the most contentious campus issues Owen confronted during his tenure at GTI was the question of faculty schedules. Guided by their business instincts, which emphasized the 40-hour work week, Board members labored throughout 1979 to document the "Proposed Policies and Procedures of Guilford Technical Institute." Academicians are traditionally possessive when it comes to allocating their time, but GTI's Board preferred a more structured system. One of Owen's last duties was to inform the faculty that they must schedule class, lab, or office hours five days a week.[27]

Revamping the Community College System: The Mills-Holt Bill

Jim Owen was professionally attracted to a new challenge within the North Carolina Department of Community Colleges, which had welcomed a new president and would soon function under a new order of authority. Dr. Larry J. Blake of Fraser Valley College in Chilliwack, British Columbia, had emerged from an acrimonious political struggle to win the presidency of the reorganized system. The finalists in that showdown included former North Carolina Governor Robert W. Scott and Dr. Eugene Speller, an African-American community college president from Chicago. Scott's failure to get a strong endorsement from his former political ally Governor James B. Hunt bitterly disappointed Scott's powerful associates, but Blake's credentials as a professional educator eventually convinced the State Board of Education that he was the choice. After wrangling for the same salary his previous job paid, Blake assumed his new post on July 1, 1979.[28]

Another major political issue somewhat eclipsed by the bleating struggle for the system presidency, but probably more important in the long run, was the decision by a 12-member commission appointed to change the way the Community College System was managed. Three alternatives considered by the panel included (1) leaving the system under the State Board of Education, (2) placing it under the University of North Carolina Board of Governors, or (3) organizing a new and independent Board of Trustees. The Mills-Holt Bill passed by both chambers of the General Assembly on June 7, 1979, created a 19 member Board of Community Colleges and Technical Institutes to assume control of the system in January 1981. Blake used the 18-month transitional period from the State Board to the new panel to evaluate his organization and the objectives of the Community College System and assemble his administrative team. During this process, he reunited former GTI administrators Jim Owen and Jerry Owens.[29]

Seeding a Salary Controversy

In Guilford County for the second time in three years, a GTI presidential search committee had narrowed its choice to two candidates; Dr. Ronald W. McCarter, president of Southeastern Community College in Whiteville, N.C., and Dr. Raymond J. Needham, president of Linn-Benton Community College in Albany, Oregon. The media informed the public that, as in the case of former president Jim Owen, the Board had rejected requests by Mary Breeze, president of GTI's faculty-staff association and Patricia Bray, president of the SGA, to participate in the presidential selection process. Trustee Frank York, who headed the search committee, was quoted as saying that the requests were not considered by the Board "because a state law empowers the Trustees of community colleges and technical schools to elect presidents." However, as reporter

Blanche Alston pointed out, "The law places no restrictions on the means they (boards) may use: Presidents may be elected 'under such conditions as the Trustees may fix' subject to the approval of the State Board of Education."[30]

The job officially became Needham's on June 18, 1980, when McCarter excused himself "because the Board had been unable to meet his conditions," an impasse apparently involving "timing and personal matters and the relationship between the Board and president in governing the school."[31] Needham's employment was a rigorous process for the Board's executive committee, who reportedly convened six times after he initially declined, because the salary offered was less than he would make at Linn-Benton. When the Trustees found a way to raise the additional cash to hire Needham, the funding strategy created a flood of public criticism which was not in the Institution's best interest.

Campus Notes

The opportunity to arrive safely on the Jamestown campus increased measurably when a traffic light was installed at the intersection of Vickery Chapel and High Point roads in March 1979.[32]

Thermostats were raised across the campus during the prevailing energy crisis to adhere to the new federal requirement to maintain the temperature at 78 degrees. The Board also considered a four-day work week as an energy-saving strategy.[33]

On June 18, 1979, the staff discovered that thieves had stolen approximately $1,500 in cash and checks from the Institute, but there is no evidence that the culprit was eventually apprehended.

Following renovations, the Board raised the rent on the historic Iddings House from $120 a month to $150 and cautioned future tenants, who were generally GTI maintenance personnel, not to drive nails into the wood walls, which should neither be papered nor painted.

A volleyball court was laid in the plaza at the side of the Dental Science Building and a basketball court was constructed just beyond the front entrance to the Medlin Campus Center.[34]

Adria Zimmerman presided over the SGA during the 1977 academic year when a five-year survey of 20 GTI-SGA officers revealed a variety of interesting statistics.

Most SGA members worked part-time and some full-time during the evening hours; none had experienced any leadership experience before attending GTI; seven were married and had at least one child. Two carried more than 12 credit hours. Those surveyed represented a cross section of programs.[35]

More than 19 student clubs were active at GTI in 1977, though the number had diminished to 15 by 1979. The Black Student Union boosted the holiday 1977 spirit with food and gifts for Sadie Johnson and her 10 children, who lived on Rugby Street in Greensboro.

Parking on the Jamestown campus continued as the major campus challenge with four cars involved in a fender bender on September 21, 1977.

Wayne Vestal supervised GTI's Greensboro Division in 1978 when Criminal Justice was the sole curriculum program offered at 501 West Washington Street. In addition to continuing education classes, Greensboro's Adult High School, GED prep classes, and Occupational Extension courses attracted more than 2,000 students per week.[36]

Thomas Heffernan, an internationally published poet, was named Visiting Artist for the 1978–79 academic year.[37]

Dr. Harold Fegan, who had served as Dean of Continuing Education for seven years, was named Vice President for Institutional Affairs on October 1, 1978; Dr. Lowell Speight assumed Fegan's former position on February 20, 1979.

Dr. Raymond J. Needham
President GTI-GTCC 1980–1990

Frank W. York
Chair, GTCC Trustees 1982–1984

J. William McGwinn, Jr.
Chair GTCC Trustees 1984–1987

Dr. Stuart B. Fountain
Chair GTCC Trustees 1987–1992

191

Section V

The Needham Decade
1981–1990

Chapter 18

Restoration and Reorganization

I am going to be the person who manages the school. I will work hard with the Board, though I will work very closely with the staff and the community to fulfill the needs.[1]

Ray Needham

Needham's Salary Controversy

Ray Needham's $50,000 salary represented the state contribution of $32,160 plus the county supplement of $10,108 with the remainder provided, according to the *Greensboro Record*, "from a private fund, made up of donors whose identities were not disclosed."[2] The Board arranged the salary and benefits package in executive session. According to Frank York, who chaired the presidential selection committee, "It came about because the donors wanted it that way."[3] Ray Lane, GTI's Vice President for Financial Affairs, said the private fund, which would be audited by the state, amounted to about $12,000, including pledges that had not been paid, though some press accounts listed $20,000.[4]

Needham, who evidently believed that he could work with a historically strong Board, won the salary he sought plus a house and car; but, as he and the Board soon discovered, the salary issue did not disappear.[5] The president-elect, who would officially become GTI's president on July 28, 1980, stopped over at the Jamestown campus on his way home from a conference in Washington, D.C., and held an "informal news conference." Predictably, two of the first questions he fielded dealt with the on-going question of comprehensive community college status for GTI and the presumably private contributions to his salary. The first question was answered in a snap; the second elicited a longer explanation from the Board. Needham characterized GTI as "a complementing Institution" to the area's four-year colleges: "If there's no need for liberal arts, then the community college shouldn't be doing it."[6] Years later in a videotaped interview, he revealed that he had indeed shared his vision of the advantages of a comprehensive community college with the Board and discussed the opportunities transfer programs would provide for the students.[7]

Regarding his $50,000 salary, $8,000 more than his predecessor was paid and presumably comparable to what he would have collected at Linn-Benton Community College, Needham told reporters "there were no strings attached", adding, "the money isn't my major purpose" even though he had reportedly turned down the job twice because the salary did not match his Oregon contract.[8] Remuneration for public sector employees is a perpetually contentious issue in Guilford County. Salaries are legally public information and the media salivates over opportunities to report them. The negotiations over Needham's salary became public when the Guilford County commissioners balked at increasing their annual allotment to help the College meet his salary request. Their decision propelled the GTI Board, led by Percy Sears, on a treasure hunt for private dollars. Woody Sugg's hiring had been publicly tainted by a question of subsidized housing, an argument that distracted citizens from the promise of his tenure; now, ethical questions about Needham's salary foreshadowed his presidency. The *Greensboro Daily News* responded to the controversy with an editorial entitled "The Price of Excellence" and demanded a full disclosure of the contributors:

> Frankly, it is discomforting to know that a public official in such a high visibility job is receiving private money even though the arrangement is temporary and completely within the rules, according to state community college officials.[9]

The editorialist asked for contributors' names and numbers and suggested that the College and commissioners subsidize more of Needham's salary in the next·GTI budget. The State Board of Education was encouraged to adjust the salary scale to make North Carolina community colleges and technical institutes more competitive in the job market. The editorial's point was fiscally sharpened; the Trustees were encouraged to be sure they could afford the president they hired.[10] Ten days later, the editor again broached the subject in "GTI's Secret Fund", noting that Trustees were attempting to raise $20,000 from private sources to supplement Needham's salary for four years. The author demanded that the State Board "flatly prohibit the use of outside, private funds to supplement a chief executive's salary," adding, "If salary levels are inadequate to attract candidates of Dr. Needham's caliber, then, let salaries be raised."[11]

This furor, which may seem petty by highly inflated contemporary pay standards, raged over the promise of a president who, according to the chair of the GTI search committee, "agreed to stay at GTI for a minimum of a year or two."[12] Why did the Board spend so much time, effort and money on Needham for such a tenuous commitment? Perhaps they were pressured by the fact that GTI had been without a president for almost six months and faculty and staff morale was sinking.[13] From the beginning of his tenure, Ray Needham was challenged more by the fiscal challenge threatening GTI than the public debate over his salary package. On June 18, 1980, the day his appointment was announced, GTI Trustees voted to approve an operating budget for 1980–81 of $1,209,768, $80,232 less than the $1,290,000 they had requested from county commissioners. The cut was significant considering that the commissioner's allocation represented about 20 percent of the school's annual budget. Ray Lane, vice president of financial affairs, admitted that "this is going to be a tight year for us but we are going to live within the budget."[14]

The Builder

I'm a builder, but I'm not going to fix something that doesn't need fixing.[15]

Ray Needham

Needham was further challenged to improve GTI programs in High Point and Greensboro, a situation he addressed during his June 1980 news conference by stressing the importance of "tailor-making a program to fit the needs of the community."[16] He was specifically hired to align the Institute's vocational and technical training with the industries comprising the nation's 26th largest manufacturing region. The Trustees hired Needham because they believed "he would do a better job of discovering the needs of the community and preparing students to fit those job needs than the school has done in the past."[17] When the *High Point Enterprise* questioned Needham about the High Point facility, he frankly admitted that "he had a hard time finding the building and a harder time finding the school in the (basement of) the North Main Street Arcade building." Needham stressed that "continuing education should be close to the people and the facilities should be inviting." He did not encounter that atmosphere in the subterranean Arcade location where some typewriters appeared to be 50 years old.[18]

High Point residents noted an immediate improvement in transportation when the city's municipal bus service (HiTran) initiated service to the Jamestown campus. Five roundtrips a day from the High Point terminal through several stops in the city on the route to GTI Jamestown transported students to early morning classes and home again at the end of the class day. The service was funded 100 percent by the Urban Mass Transit Administration and the NCDOT. Thirty five riders were using the service shortly after its implementation.[19]

While 50-year-old Dr. Raymond John Needham's June 1980 press conference attracted more attention and controversy than he or the Board would have preferred, it was not until July 31 that Chairman John T. Davis, Jr. officially introduced GTI's fifth president to the Trustees. The Bellingham, Washington, native's credentials included a B.S. in Agricultural Education and M.Ed. in Educational Administration-Sociology from Washington State University, and a Ph.D. in Vocational Education Administration from Colorado State University.[20] Needham officially began his presidency by succinctly outlining his immediate goals: (1) to acquaint himself with faculty and staff, the Guilford County community, and with business and industry within the school's service area; (2) to review GTI's proposed policies and procedures and share his concerns with the Board's personnel and policy committee; (3) to make "minor changes" within the present organizational structure and set staff goals and objectives for the 1980–81 school year.[21]

Needham's administration began on one extremely positive note when the Board approved a 10 percent cost-of-living salary increase for the staff; however, he delayed an additional 3.53 percent earmarked for merit raises until the school completed a salary study. It addressed the situations of staff members whose remuneration was significantly low and that of those eligible for additional formula points to make their salaries more comparable with business, education, government, and industry. The staff eventually received increases averaging 13.9 percent when the contracts were issued in mid September 1980.[22]

The new president proceeded immediately to establish institutional goals, developing an ambitious five-year plan for 1981–86. His 23 objectives resembled an institutional self-study, encompassing College operations, initiatives, practices, policies, programs, and objectives, some of which would prove controversial. The Board accepted his recommendation to establish only two standing committees for 1980–81: Buildings, Grounds, and Finance, chaired by Percy Sears and Personnel, Policy, and Curriculum, chaired by Frank York.[23] He reorganized the administrative lines of authority to have eleven people reporting to him compared to five for his predecessors. This organizational shuffle purportedly enabled him to get a better "feel" for the Institute's operations and time to evaluate subordinates' job performances. The *Greensboro Daily News* reported that "many GTI employees said the school was drifting administratively before Needham was hired," adding, "critics complained that some of the 12 Trustees became too much involved in day-to-day operations of the school."[24] Needham had a considerable serving of brittle issues on his plate and did not complete his administrative reorganization until August 1, 1981.[25]

SBI Probes Total GTI Class Time

I told the Board that I am going to find out as much as I can (about the probe) and I'm going to be taking some official action on it as quickly as I can get sufficient background.[26]

Ray Needham

Needham was "surprised" to learn about a State Bureau of Investigation investigation of the continuing education section of the Criminal Justice program.[27] The Board reportedly briefed him on the case in executive session with the Trustees on July 31, 1980. Determined to have an open relationship with the press, Needham assured reporters that he would immediately look into "how much money had been misappropriated, how many people might be involved, and whether the alleged irregularities stretched beyond the program that was located at the downtown Greensboro center." Dr. Ray Lane, a member of the interim management committee, was quoted as saying, "The SBI was out here (Jamestown) yesterday looking at records. They have not officially met with us (GTI administrators) to give us any information."[28]

In a story headlined "GTI Head Tightens Justice Management," the *Greensboro Daily News* reported that one aspect of Needham's aforementioned staff organization was that it "would provide closer supervision of GTI's troubled criminal justice department by assigning one dean, rather than two to supervise the department." The article further revealed that Needham had suspended three employees, two instructors and a secretary on August 5 pending the outcome of the probe into the alleged misuse of state funds. More than 41,559 student hours were allegedly incorrectly reported during school sessions between 1978 and 1980.

According to sources close to the investigation, investigators are looking into the possibility that department officials set up fake classes. Classes must have a minimum number of students for instructors to be paid with state funds.[29]

Three employees of GTI's Criminal Justice Department were indicted on October 7, 1980, by a Guilford County Grand Jury on charges of embezzlement and false pretenses. They were eventually found guilty, sentenced to suspended prison terms, and ordered to pay fines and/or restitution. GTI returned $40,241 from the 1980–81 state budget to satisfy the Criminal Justice FTE audit exceptions.[30]

The Overtime Issue

Needham quickly discovered that his policy of openness with the media was a two-way street. It is great to have the media in your corner when the atmosphere is positive, but when circumstances sour, negative stories linger interminably. Personnel issues are the media's meat and potatoes and Needham's attempt to change the workweek hours and overtime policy at GTI incited a rash of emotionally charged stories. It appears that the overtime issue may have been indirectly linked to the indictment of GTI employees in the Criminal Justice case.[31]

Conceding the issue's contentiousness, Needham felt compelled to address a situation whereby some employees were working 37 and a half hours per week and others 40. Overtime pay, as opposed to compensatory time off, was an additional concern with the president favoring overtime. As previously noted, the Board had been reviewing personnel polices and procedures issues since September 1979, but the proposed changes were tabled when the initial study triggered a petition from professional non-faculty employees. Custodians, groundskeepers, and maintenance employees worked 40 hours a week while the clerical staff worked 37 and a half.[32]

Needham's initiative inflamed the emotions of some GTI employees who were reportedly motivated to "fight attempts to increase their work week from 37 and a half to 40 hours, especially if the increase wasn't covered by a pay hike." Frank York, who chaired the Board committee on personnel, policy, and curriculum, attributed the dual system to a formerly "liberal" GTI administration. State law allowed the Trustees in the Community College System to set policies on work hours and benefits, but policies varied widely from institution to institution. The law also allowed GTI the option of compensating overtime work with either pay or compensatory time off; Needham preferred to pay the employees.[33] Currently, (2008) overtime hours, normally earned by classified employees, are compensated through a time-off plan managed through an overtime bank. In emergency situations, the President or Vice President can authorize pay for overtime work. Professional (i.e., exempt) employees are salaried.[34]

Administrative Reorganization

Needham's initial decision in August 1980 to have eleven people reporting directly to him instead of the customary five eventually provided the "feel" he desired to have for the Institute's operations and the time to evaluate his subordinates' job performances. By January 1981 he was planning to hire two new vice presidents and establish new titles for two current administrators to strengthen planning, budgeting, and standards. Two former vice presidents lost their titles when Harold Fegan, Vice President for Instructional Affairs, was named Dean of Business and Industry, and Ray Lane, the Chief Financial Officer, became the Assistant to the President for Business Affairs.[35] Dr. Nicolas Gennett, formerly of Miami-Dade Community College, was hired as Vice President for Student Development and Instructional Support.

In a decision that proved to have historical implications for the Institution's future, Dr. Donald W. Cameron, Vice President of Academic Affairs at Spartanburg Technical College, was appointed to occupy an identical position at GTI. For the Robbins, North Carolina, native and his wife Jayne, it marked a prestigious return to the Old North State. While the position and his responsibilities were similar, the promotion to GTI brought Cameron to a school three times larger than Spartanburg Tech.[36]

Enrollment Update

Needham's decade began with 4,247 curriculum students enrolled for the 1980 fall quarter, a 19 percent increase, compared with 3,556 the previous September and more than 20,000 people in continuing education and extension courses.[37] While there were notable fluctuations during the decade 1970–80, GTI's total FTE enrollment had increased 150 percent; minority enrollment improved from 20.1 percent to 23.7, and the percentage of females jumped from 41.8 percent to 50.7. At the end of the Institution's first year (1958–59) eleven full-time and ten part-time instructors were teaching 593 students in six vocational programs. By 1980–81, 114 full-time and 118 part-time instructors were providing training for over 4,000 students in fifty vocational and technical programs. An additional 297 part-time instructors were teaching over 30,000 people in continuing education and extension courses.[38]

Community Service and Expansion

Needham moved quickly to more closely align GTI with its various constituencies by establishing a greater emphasis on support for the United Way campaigns in Greensboro and High Point through the payroll deduction process. The Institutional initiative to improve programs in High Point received a tremendous boost in May 1981 when the Board bought the former Chrysler dealership at 901 South Main Street. This new High Point Center opened in October 1981 with 27,000 square feet including three acres, two buildings, and 300 lighted parking spaces.

Internal renovations at the Greensboro Center provided additional space for students, faculty, and staff. At Jamestown, the Medlin Campus Center was renovated to add 3,000 square feet on the second floor to facilitate student access to the Business Office and Student Services and two new parking areas were paved to provide 100 additional spaces.

For their 1980–81 "live" project, the GHG Corporation decided to build a field house for Southwest Guilford High School.

In 1981, 634 adults received their high school equivalency diplomas after passing the GED exam in the LRC testing center. The Job Placement Office was reorganized to focus on job development and the Institute's ongoing efforts to serve disadvantaged, handicapped and unprepared persons through the new Developmental Education and Special Programs area expanded to serve approximately 3,500 people during fiscal 1982.

Packaging Machinery Servicing, a one of a kind program in the Southeast, attracted an expanding enrollment on the strength of more than a half-million dollars in donated equipment and supplies.[39]

GTI Foundation Reorganized

Dr. Needham recognized the Foundation as a promising source of revenue for equipment purposes and began working with Dr. Edward Duffy, GTI's Director of Research, Planning, and Development, to develop a system to actively seek money from business and industry to support the school's technical needs. The reorganization expanded the Board of Directors to 30 members serving two-year terms and limited the number of Trustees who could become members. An ad hoc Board committee was charged to offer 15 names for nomination to the Foundation Board and executive and finance committees were organized to promote the Foundation's mission.[40]

Summary: 1980–81

Mr. John R. Foster, a founding member of the GTI Board, and one of the schools greatest supporters, died Thursday, February 19, 1981. Mr. Foster was initially appointed by the Guilford County School Board on September 3, 1963, for a term of six years to expire on June 30, 1969. He was subsequently reappointed for an eight year term to expire June 30, 1977, and another 8-year term to expire June 30, 1985. One of the state's foremost African-American educators, Dr. Katie G. Dorsett, was appointed to replace Mr. Foster and served until she resigned in 1993 to accept a position in Governor Jim Hunt's first administration cabinet.[41]

President Needham closed the book on his first year with his staff reorganized and much of the detritus that had greeted him sorted out. New administrators had been hired and others reassigned. A variety of new policies and procedures had been approved, but there were formidable challenges in the offing; notably, the approval of transfer credits for technical and general education students and the initial steps toward the ubiquitous self-study process that marked SACS (Southern Association of Colleges and Schools) re-accreditation.

The argument for community college status for the third largest school in the state's Community College System lingered on the horizon. From an historical standpoint, his most important accomplishment was the hiring of his successor, Don Cameron, who began his tenure at GTI managing the Institute's curriculum programs. The one or two years Needham promised the Board became a decade wrought with frustration, investigation, debate, and historical educational progress for the Institution that ultimately became Guilford Technical Community College. In his first year, Needham spent a huge amount of time strengthening the Institution's foundational mission to support Guilford County as its number one workforce preparer. He thoroughly intended to build an institution that would teach citizens the skills to get better jobs, develop courses to help people upgrade themselves, encourage women to enter non-traditional courses, and create an awareness of vocational opportunities among the young.[42]

Chapter 19

GTCC: A Brittle Battle

The original idea of the technical institutes across the state was, as their name implies, to give technical training to those who are not interested in going to a liberal arts college. As a former governor I have been concerned with the trend to make these institutions colleges. This, in my opinion, should not be done unless there is definite need for additional opportunities for institutions of higher learning.

Former Governor Dan Moore, 1982[1]

A Long, Brittle Battle

By 1981 when President Needham implemented the strategy to achieve community college status for GTI, the school had been offering transfer level courses for five years. The Associate Degree in General Education had been in place since 1976, but most students were aware that senior institutions traditionally refused to accept credits from this program with the result that only six had graduated with the degree. The survey of 372 schools in the Southern Association of Colleges and Schools requested by former GTI President Jim Owens revealed that "by and large, general education credits earned at technical schools were not transferable and that only two of the six senior institutions in GTI's area accepted any of these credits."[2]

Transfer options for GTI students were Needham's objective from the beginning of his presidency and he was clearly aware of the articulation challenges with local institutions. He understood that GTI's mission should remain focused on vocational-technical training, but he was determined to see that students had the privilege to transfer general education credits to four-year institutions. His initial move toward elevating GTI to a comprehensive community college included upgrading the arts and sciences department to an institutional division directed by a full-time administrator. Dr. Vern Loland, Ph. D., whose credentials included 15 years of community college experience in Washington State, was charged to strengthen the designated transfer courses with qualified faculty possessing at least a master's degree in the teaching discipline.[3]

Assisted by the Educational Services Management Corporation, GTI conducted its first comprehensive community impact study in the spring of 1981. The objective, in line with President Needham's mandate to discover the area's employment needs and better prepare students to fill those jobs, was to chart the level of awareness relevant to GTI's programs and services and to measure the Institute's success in meeting its stated goals and objectives. The research sampled public and business interests about institutional issues including the possible conversion to community college status and the creation of a transfer program linking the school to senior institutions.

The survey was sent to employers, civic leaders, GTI students and alumni, high school students and counselors, and the general public. The response rate was highest, 60–95 percent among GTI students and high school students and counselors; and disconcertingly, lowest among employers, with only 83 out of 496 responding for a 17 percent return. 8,399 surveys were distributed and 2,948 (35%) returned by the general population at the rate of only 23 percent. The survey inspired Needham and his staff to formulate new strategies to gain the attention of business, industry, and the general population. The student surveys indicated that 96 percent of the respondents believed that GTI students should be able to transfer credit; while 81 percent believed they should have the opportunity to transfer all eligible GTI courses to four-year institutions.[4]

The Trustees endorsed the addition of a college transfer program for technical and general education students on November 19, 1981, enabling GTI administrators to actively pursue the transfer credit option during the 1981–82 academic year.[5] The strategic public relations campaign they drafted included a briefing for Guilford County commissioners and a brochure detailing the advantages of community college status. GTI promised to emphasize vocational and technical education, assuring the community that the specialized programs of neighboring colleges and universities would not be duplicated and that conversion would not require immediate additional financing. The message further emphasized that Guilford County students would no longer have to travel across county lines to attend one of the area community colleges which offered transfer options.[6]

GTI's road to community college status remained littered with objections from the county's four private college presidents who appeared before the Guilford County Schools Board of Education on Tuesday, January 19, 1982. This visible show of concerted opposition from Greensboro, Guilford, Bennett, and High Point Colleges argued that transforming GTI into a comprehensive community college would duplicate liberal arts courses offered at their institutions and cost the taxpayers dearly. Needham countered that the cost to tax payers would be minimal. In making the case that GTI students needed a guarantee that their credits would transfer should they decide to further their education, he cited GTI's "traditional" emphasis on technical education:

> We do have a commitment to vocational and technical education, and that will not change. I have a personal commitment. I was a vocational agricultural teacher, and I taught both welding and mechanics. All we want to do is provide transfer options to our students.[7]

He probably should have added, "GTI students are not second class students;" that was the insinuation many observers were drawing from the ongoing debate regardless of one private college president's disclaimer that, "It's not a matter of elite schools versus the little man, it's a matter of avoiding duplicated services with escalating costs", estimated to approach $330,000 to $3,750,000 per year."[8] Beyond the arguments posed by private colleges, GTI also needed the often grudging approval of the county's three school boards. For example, the Guilford County School Board debated the issue for an hour before delaying its eventual decision by a 4–3 margin, hardly a strong endorsement.[9]

The *High Point Enterprise* ruminated over the college transfer debate posting GTI's claim "that if it could just change its name, all sorts of good things would occur," against the private college argument that "the benefits of becoming a community college are being greatly oversold and the move could hurt private schools in Guilford County."[10] Another major factor affecting GTI's future, in addition to the inability to transfer credits, was the unequal funding formula for community colleges and technical institutes. The *Enterprise* editorialist supported the private college fear of competition, but suggested that the State should consider more equitable funding for technical institutes. The social culture of this educational argument is worth noting since the principals in this debate, the institutional CEOs, were pillars of the community and exceptionally credible administrators. Excepting High Point College (now University), the institutions, including both branches of the university system and three private colleges, were in Greensboro where GTI had neither an attractive facility, a signature program attracting wide public interest, nor an exemplary public reputation.[11]

Community College Status: Round One

GTI's Community College Application requesting the addition of college transfer courses was presented to the State Board of Community Colleges on March 11, 1982.[12] As defined in the formal letter to Board Chair Carl Horn, Jr., GTI requested permission to add the two-year college transfer or parallel program to its curriculum offerings, according to North Carolina Administrative Code, 4C.0105(C). GTI assured the Board that the resulting two tier delivery system would continue to emphasize technical and vocational education. Technical graduates would be prepared for immediate employment while the transfer program would provide students the option to continue their education at some future time. With the transfer option in place, two levels of course offerings would be available in general education. Technical students interested in continuing their education could enroll in transfer English; curriculum students not interested in that option would choose applied English. In addition, this proposal would enable unprepared or under prepared high school graduates to benefit from remedial programs before progressing to a four-year institution. While the transfer option provided "strong" basic general education courses to support the Associate Arts or Science degree, GTI promised not to offer specialized pre-professional curricula. It was an exercise in futility. At the end of the day, the State Board of Community Colleges denied GTI's request for community college status.[13]

"The Public Be Damned: A Question of Loyalty"[14]

Guilford Technical Institute's extended battle to achieve community college status is extensively documented in at least three dissertations, the comprehensive study by Lin Fain and Steven Brooks, and numerous newspaper articles.[15] The bottom line is that the issue of GTI's request became highly politicized at various governmental and institutional levels. While the application was, to some degree, endorsed by Guilford County's three school systems and the county commissioners, the approval was not unanimous in either case. As Fain and Brooks note, this was the first time a request for community college status had been made in a county with two public universities (UNCG and NC A&T) and four private colleges. The State Board of Community Colleges summarily refused GTI's March 11, 1982, request for community college status when pressured by "concentrated opposition"[16] from private colleges in addition to the Council for Higher Education of the Western North Carolina Conference of the United Methodist Church. Former Governor Dan Moore, who had spoken on the occasion of GTI's elevation to a technical institute from an industrial education center, stated his opposition in a letter to Guilford County Commissioner Paul Clapp:

> The original idea of the technical institutes across the state was, as their name implies, to give technical training to those who are not interested in going to a liberal arts college. As a former governor I have been concerned with the trend to make these institutions colleges. This, in my opinion, should not be done unless there is definite need for additional opportunities for institutions of higher learning.[17]

The seminal perception of the technical institute mission was a quarter-century old when Dan Moore mailed his letter; furthermore, GTI was bracketed by community colleges, including Rockingham and Davidson, that offered transfer credits to Guilford County students who drove across the county lines to get them. Realistically, the time had long since passed for considering a technical degree as a terminal degree, but from a competitive standpoint, the argument presented by Ralph M. Byers, executive secretary for the NC Center for Independent Higher Education, had a modicum of validity in its warning to the State Board of Community Colleges.

> If that request (GTI's) is approved, there will absolutely be no grounds for disallowing any other technical institute from becoming a community college and we'll have 58 community colleges. We just don't think that's the way the state ought to be going.[18]

The State Board encouraged GTI to pursue individual transfer agreements with area schools, but Needham returned from Raleigh geared to reload for another major offensive. At the April 1982 Board session, he reported his intention to meet with area senior institution presidents to discuss a transfer agreement for GTI's students in general education classes. Trustee Percy Sears chimed in with a recommendation that GTI's Board meet with the UNCG and NC A&T State University Boards.[19] As the year progressed, transfer agreement requests were presented to High Point College, Greensboro College, Bennett College, NC A&T, UNCG, Guilford College, Winston Salem State, UNC-Chapel Hill, and NC State University; however, the original objections continued to block the road to community college status and ignore Needham's pledge to control the transfer program.

> After GTI becomes Guilford Technical Community College, there is no intention of changing its major priority of vocational and technical education. We are committed to limit our transfer offerings to 8 percent of our full-time equivalent student population. Placing this limitation on the program may well deny some interested and qualified students a

choice. But to maintain our top priority of vocational and technical education, we feel it is important to impose this limit on ourselves.[20]

Needham reiterated that GTI could add a college transfer program "without
its costing a lot of money." He noted that the school had been continually upgrading the faculty and did not anticipate a major expense in hiring and concluded by restating the value of a transfer option for students.[21] Opponents consistently argued every salient point with Needham excepting the *moral and just
right* to allow GTI's students a "choice" in being able to transfer credits should
they consider moving beyond GTI to a four-year institution. Fain and Brooks
(1983) noted that "more than 2,000 technical institute graduates had transferred
into public and private institutions in North Carolina in the past two years."[22]
Obviously, senior institutions preferred to accept transfers on an individual basis.

Community College Status: Round 2

At the beginning of the 1982 fall quarter Dr. Vernon Loland, GTI's Dean of
Arts and Sciences, admitted that the school did not have a single transfer
agreement in place. The response to GTI's transfer requests had been slower
than anticipated; of the nine schools contacted only Guilford College appeared
close to adopting the contentious "blanket" agreement. The other colleges and
universities had either denied the request, ignored it completely, were still
studying the issue, or preferred to continue accepting transfer credits on an
individual basis. The duplication of liberal arts courses at taxpayer expense
was an immovable barrier.[23]

Needham did not wait for the daily mail or a call from his peers; by December, he had formulated a new strategy targeted toward the State Board's
January 13, 1983, meeting at Wake Technical College. He was determined to
ask for the name change; but, to soothe the private colleges and state officials,
he vowed that GTI would limit its general education enrollment to eight percent of its full-time equivalent students and not ask for additional funding.
Meanwhile, some courses, primarily English, were revised to make them more
transfer compatible and subject hours were increased to make them equivalent
to semester hour courses at other institutions. Concessions aside, GTI was again
headed to Raleigh without the support of Guilford County's private colleges.[24]

The State Board reconsidered and then authorized by a 9–4 vote GTI's request to establish a college transfer program on January 13, 1983, subject to
the approval of the Advisory Budget Commission. But, a crafty politician spun
another hoop for Needham to jump through. Convincing the ABC was a formidable challenge. On a more positive note, the State Board's reconsideration

was aided by letters of support from newly elected Guilford County Commissioner Dorothy "Dot" Kearns, Dr. Gerald B. James, the president of Rockingham Community College; and Dr. William Moran, Chancellor of UNCG. Moran indicated that "a failure to have community college status severely limited the transferability of courses to nearby four-year colleges in spite of GTI's qualified faculty, its integrated curricula, and its quality standards."[25] Needham had won a battle, but he still needed to convince the Advisory Budget Commission and Governor James B. Hunt, Jr. that community college status for GTI was a positive move.

Needham believed he had Hunt's support, but the Advisory Budget Commission was a volatile political entity and their eventual vote ranks as one of the most crassly political maneuvers in North Carolina's educational history. Before rolling out that drama, it is important to note that the State Board members voting against GTI's request bought into the argument that approval would prompt the state's 34 other technical institutes to seek community college status. They contended that setting a precedent in GTI's case would unleash an avalanche of requests that would drain funds from vocational and technical programs and ultimately cost the taxpayers multiple millions.[26]

Two weeks later, on January 28, 1983, it appeared that GTI's request for community college status had been jeopardized by one of the state's most powerful politicians, Senator Kenneth Royall, chairman of the Advisory Budget Commission. Denying the commission and the governor an opportunity to act, Royal removed the request from his Board's agenda and forwarded it to the General Assembly, where it could have landed in the Joint House-Senate Appropriations Committee. While the Guilford County delegation unanimously supported the request, they could not assure its approval.

Royall was presumably influenced by GTI enrollment projections that could have required more funding by the 1984–85 academic year; this in light of the fact that Needham had projected only a three percent enrollment increase because he did not have the money available to expand the enrollment beyond that number. One editorialist characterized Royall's "reversal" as "a disturbing development since he patently ignored the Guilford delegation and GTI officials by ripping the request off his commission's agenda and sending it to the General Assembly."[27]

> Regardless of the intent of Senator Royall, it appears that GTI must now convince lawmakers of the legitimacy of its case. If so, the county's legislative delegation, particularly its chairman, Rep. Mary Seymour, must do the convincing. Governor Hunt, who says he supports the switch, should also give some evidence of it.

If the Royall reversal is more than just a power play, the merits of the GTI position should prevail. If the senator and his allies are intent on killing the measure, it will take some heavy politicking to get it to the governor's desk. What a way to run an educational system.[28]

When questioned by a reporter, the Durham County democrat said he doubted that the General Assembly would approve GTI's request in view of the financial implications objected to by dissenting members of the State Board.[29] The drama then skips from winter to spring 1983 when Senator Royall again reversed himself, by calling a meeting of the Advisory Budget Commission and adding GTI's proposal for community college status to the agenda. Following discussion, the vote on the issue resulted in a tie and the setting thickened with political intrigue. It appeared that, for better or worse politically, Royall would have to cast the tie-breaker; then Senator Conrad Duncan, a Rockingham County democrat, perhaps envisioning a future political opportunity, changed his vote in favor of GTI; the issue passed and Royall was off the hook. On June 9, 1983, Governor Hunt approved Guilford Technical Institute's conversion to Guilford Technical Community College. In its 25th year the seventeen-year-old struggle for community college status was resolved. GTI's Trustees unanimously approved the new name and submitted it for approval to the State Board of Community Colleges.[30]

Epilogue to a College Transfer Program

It can be argued that simply because neighboring community colleges had transfer options that attracted Guilford County students, GTI's request for a similar program should have prevailed above politics. The opposition from the county's revered private institutions, threatened by competition and confronted by lower enrollments and rising costs, is understandable, but as the succeeding years indicate, this perceived threat spurred those institutions and the universities to develop new programs, ratchet-up their marketing and fund raising and create new educational opportunities for adults. For these reasons, as Ray Needham pointed out when asked if a college transfer program would compete with private colleges and universities, GTI's elevation to a community college was an educational boon to all of Guilford County's citizens.[31]

> It may actually be a feeder into the college and university system. The average age of the student attending Guilford Technical Community College (1983) is 28. That factor, plus the (self-imposed) limitation should actually work favorably for other schools.[32]

In its 50th anniversary year the greatest recipients of transfer students from GTCC are UNCG and NC A&T State University. Beyond the time consuming transfer credit issue struggle (1980–83), GTI's administrators maintained the school on a positive, progressive path. New data processing systems were instituted to enhance registration services and a Career Center opened in the Learning Resource Center on the Jamestown Campus. The newly refurbished High Point Center, as the facility was known at that time, was officially dedicated on November 14, 1982.

A downturn in the economy during this era affected GTI, but failed to distract its leaders from their educational mission. When funding for 1982–83 was cut five percent forcing the school to transfer $200,000 into a contingency fund, Dr. Needham instituted a hiring freeze that affected all positions regardless of their funding source. The economy was also blamed for lagging enrollment in the carpentry and auto mechanics programs, and the school explored grant funds to assist the unemployed in Guilford County.[33]

The design plans for Davis Hall were approved, even though by January 1983 the projected cost had risen from $1.4 million to $1,589,451.[34] HVAC, Electronics, Welding, Industrial Maintenance, Civil Engineering, and Building Maintenance would occupy the first level with Data Processing/Computer Science on the second floor and classrooms on the third.[35] GTI Vice President for Academic Affairs, Don Cameron, began developing the Technical Scholars Program, the genesis of the immensely successful Tech-Prep Program in Electronics and Engineering. Approximately 30 scholarships were envisioned by 16 companies employing technicians in the electrical, mechanical and computer fields. However, the economic situation would delay implementation of this program at least until fall 1984.[36]

Administrators noted in 1983 that the 25-year-old Upholstery Program, one of GTI's first, was still one of the strongest vocational programs in the curriculum. Preliminary studies were well underway to create another signature program in Culinary Technology. Its Ad Hoc Advisory Committee held its first meeting on January 20, 1983, and Dr. Stuart Fountain, Chairman of the Board's Curriculum Committee, recommended that the program point toward serving Guilford County's convention needs.[37] At the Greensboro Center, Mike Taylor operated 32 classrooms and labs with 17 full-time personnel. The Center also housed the Continuing Education staff, personnel from HRD, CETA, Adult Basic Education, and the Dropout Assessment Program. Enrollment at the Greensboro Center for the 1983 fall quarter totaled 3,285.[38]

The Silver Anniversary

GTI celebrated its 25th anniversary during Spring Fest '83 Sunday, May 15, 1983. Special guest Virginia Bangiola commemorated the occasion by slicing a six-tiered 36-inch square cake big enough to serve 2,000 guests. The former commercial art student had been GTI's first and only graduate on May 22, 1966, and the initial recipient of an Associate in Applied Science degree. The New Jersey homemaker, who had relocated with her family to High Point, recalled that when she came to GTI seeking something to do in her spare time, she registered for art classes. More than 30 thousand people, or 10 percent of Guilford County's population, were enrolled in at least one course at the Institution during its 25th anniversary year.[39]

The sole surviving evidence of the structures that once comprised the TB sanatorium that occupied GTCC's future Jamestown Campus for 32 years from 1923 to 1955 was the brick, ivy-draped gazebo along the Greensboro High Point Road. The former bus stop for sanatorium residents and employees had been designated for restoration and rededication. The undulating, tree-shrouded campus was likewise soon to be rededicated as Guilford Technical Community College. It was the greatest moment in President Needham's career. As the *Jamestown News* recorded, community college status, and its meaning for Guilford County, rested in the eloquent persistence and tenacious courage of this highly committed chief executive who fought a persistent, uphill, politically tainted battle for three tough years.[40]

Chapter 20

GTCC: 1983–85: The Early Years

In that Guilford Technical Community College was granted community college status July 1 (1983) following many years of effort, I feel it is difficult to leave my commitment to students, the staff and the community here in Guilford County. I feel that it is important that I remain to help GTCC develop into a comprehensive community college that is truly committed to vocational and technical education as we promised our local citizens, businesses, and industries.

Ray Needham[1]

July 1, 1983

"GTCC: Guilford Technical Community College, may I help you?" Callers were immediately informed that the former technical institute was officially a comprehensive community college. Visitors were greeted by a huge banner draped across the Medlin Campus Center foyer that proclaimed "*Happiness is GTCC*." President Needham's staff promptly ordered new stationery, seals, logos, business cards, and signage from the NC Department of Transportation as the fiscal year 1983–84 dawned across Guilford County. A major educational issue had been decided in Guilford County, but the big campus question concerned the future of the battling CEO who had finally won the struggle for comprehensive community college status; how long would Dr. Ray Needham remain at the helm?

Needham's Persistent Oregon Connection

The leadership skills of Ray Needham that had attracted GTI's Trustees in 1980 remained a strong memory among his admirers in the Pacific Northwest and there were indications in 1983 that they wanted him back. A few weeks after GTCC became an official reality, the local media surprised Needham one morning by announcing that he was one of three candidates for the presidency of Chemeketa Community College in Salem, Oregon. Chemeketa's enrollment was similar to GTCC's and the school was near Linn-Benton Community College in Albany, Oregon, where Needham had presided for ten years before coming to GTI. Many of Chemeketa's staff formerly worked for Needham and his wife had served as the president's assistant. Needham owned a home two miles from the Chemeketa campus and his son attended school in the region.

Friends had supposedly nominated him for the position even though he had reportedly declined to go to Oregon for an interview. He later revealed that he had expressed an interest in the job before GTCC attained community college status. Reports linking Needham to Chemeketa persisted until late September 1983 when he formally asked that his name be withdrawn from consideration. Needham, who was earning about $55,000 at GTCC, said salary was not a factor in his decision. On this occasion GTCC Trustee Percy Sears correctly told a reporter that he believed Needham would stay at GTCC, but the west coast connections would continue to ring the presidential phone during the remainder of his tenure in Guilford County.[2]

NCCCS: A Change at the Top

I'm pleased with the confidence that's been placed in me. I'm pleased that I can share in this system's future growth.

Robert W. Scott, March 1983[3]

Had Needham returned to Oregon, he would have been the second community college administrator to fly west in 1983. Larry J. Blake, who left Oregon to preside over the North Carolina Community College System from 1979 to 1983, returned as president of the Oregon Institute of Technology in March 1983. On March 1, 1983, the State Board of Community Colleges elected former North Carolina Governor Robert W. Scott to the presidency of the North Carolina Community College System. Scott, who lost the post to Blake during their bitter struggle to succeed Dr. Ben E. Fountain, Jr., had finally grasped his long-denied political prize.[4] The selection of Scott, as opposed to the well-respected professional educator Dr. Johnas "Jeff" Hockaday, was presumably based on Scott's "commendable political reputation and his working relationship with the General Assembly." Hockaday, president of Central Carolina Technical College in Sanford, soon solaced his ambition by accepting the presidency of the Virginia Community College System. [5]

The 1983–84 Academic Year

Needham's prediction that 300–400 students would register for GTCC's college transfer program in the fall of 1983 did not materialize. While he had promised to limit the enrollment of transfer students to eight percent of the school's full-time equivalency enrollment, which means he could have accepted 638 based on the 1982 FTE of 7,982,[6] only 20 were accepted; approximately 150 who expressed an interest in the program were enrolled in Guided Studies and General Education courses.[7]

At the beginning of the GTCC era in 1983, the 86-acre Jamestown Campus featured classrooms and administrative offices in contemporarily designed buildings and more were on the way. Two new paved parking areas accommodated another 100 cars and construction was underway on the future Davis Hall. The shift to community college status and the addition of a college transfer program was accompanied by an expansive series of growth initiatives in programs, staff, and facilities during the 1984–85 academic year. On January 1, 1984, GTCC became a member of the Greater Greensboro Consortium. This group of seven colleges and universities agreed to provide open access to students who wished to register for courses at institutions other than the one in which they were matriculating. The semester before GTCC joined the consortium, fall 1983, found 392 students cross-registered for 570 courses at Bennett College, Greensboro College, Guilford College, High Point College, NC A& T State University, and UNCG.[8]

The Machining Technology curriculum responded to an expansion in the metal working trades while Packaging Machinery, the only program of its kind in the southeast, burst strongly from the gate thanks to a half million dollar donation in equipment and supplies. The Carpentry Department developed a Cabinet Making Certificate program while its non-profit spin-off, the GHG, Greensboro-High Point-Guilford, Corporation, continued its house building projects.

The staff at GTCC's High Point Center, Sandra Sarantos, Rob Everett, Norma Glasener, and Nancy Craven operated from new offices at 901 South Main Street. Programs continued to expand with more than 1,838 students attending 119 non-credit classes at dozens of locations across the city. 77 curriculum credit students were enrolled in typing and accounting and 60 in the automotive curriculum. 114 students attended GED classes at the Alma Desk Company, Thomas Built Buses, Davis Furniture Industries, Slane Hosiery and Thayer Coggin while 48 students were enrolled in a GED TV Series.[9]

The Guilford County commissioners funded the Culinary Arts Program for the 1983–84 winter quarter and spent $100,000 to locate it in three renovated rooms in the Service Careers Building; they did so with the stipulation that the quality of food provided to the Children's Center would not decline.[10] To complement the conversion to community college, an Arts and Sciences Division replaced what was then known as the Associate of General Education Program.[11] The tuition for the 1983 fall quarter increased from $3.25 to $4.25 per quarter-hour and registration fees for occupational and academic courses jumped from $8 to $10. President Needham reported that the fall quarter FTE enrollment figures showed a four to five percent increase over 1982 while the unduplicated headcount for curriculum reflected a 21.5 percent increase from 1982.[12]

Sports: Wellness and Physical Education

According to Dr. Cameron (2005), funding for physical education programs in the Community College System and at GTCC has been a historically negative issue. However, history did not stand in the Board's path when they approved a new athletic program in 2006 by instituting men's basketball and women's volleyball teams. GTCC's early sports teams floundered on a lack of funding, work barriers to student participation, and attendance at games, but the possibility of a college transfer program in the early 1980s spurred administrators and faculty to consider adding intramural and intercollegiate sports. Tennis, volleyball and basketball courts were added to the Jamestown campus and the student government launched a few successful, though limited, activities.[13]

The college transfer program convinced the Board to build a wellness center with unallocated capital funds on the Jamestown campus. It opened on March 7, 1985, with Nautilus equipment, free weights, treadmills, stationary cycles, space for aerobics, a general classroom, three offices, shower, and locker facilities. Deborah M. Allison, Department Chair of Physical Education/Health, joined the College in August 1983 to plan the wellness program. The Board approved a wellness education philosophy statement on September 1983 that introduced Guilford County's citizens to a series of lifelong health initiatives. Some 15 years later in 1998 a proposal to establish a YMCA on GTCC property answered the desperate need for more facilities and encouraged the aforementioned development of a competitive intercollegiate athletic program.[14]

Electronics and Transportation

During 1983 the Board investigated the feasibility of locating a three-building, $4 million Electronics/Transportation Complex on the eastern edge of the campus. Originally designed by William F. Freeman and Associates, this facility was projected to consolidate curriculum programs in transportation, electronics, and related program course work in applied sciences. President Needham was dismayed when the General Assembly approved only $1.8 million in June 1984 and suggested the College ask for the remainder in 1985.[15] The good news was that the complex could be built in segments; construction on the first phase, housing classrooms and shops for courses in auto mechanics, diesel and heavy equipment mechanics, electronics, and air frame and power mechanics could have started by February 1985, but for a major communication problem.[16]

At its December 13, 1984, session, a motion to ask Guilford County for $689,000 to develop the site and prepare the infrastructure for the complex incited what one newspaper described as "a heated debate and an hour-long executive session before the proposal was sent back to the administration for more work." Trustee Percy Sears argued that building the aviation and automotive/diesel building first and excluding the electronics facility might be interpreted to mean that GTCC's support for the program was waning;

> Everybody in the state is asking for electronics. We can't make it fly on its own. It needs to be a part of the package with the aviation program.
>
> I don't know why we're in such a hurry to go to the county when we don't have the entire package put together. We need to know more. We need to put everything together all at once.[17]

President Needham and Board Chair J. William McGuinn, Jr. argued that the site needed to be prepared regardless of the number of buildings and that GTCC should submit its request to the county at once. When Sears asked if GTCC needed to purchase additional land, presumably for the site, the Board adjourned into executive session. They emerged having decided to present the plan to the county commissioners as a three-building package; a commitment that, reportedly, had not been cleared with the full Board. A mollified Percy Sears motioned successfully to ask the Guilford County Commissioners for $830,190 across a three-year period to develop the site for the complex. The money would pay for water and sewer lines, roads, parking lots, curbs and gutters, erosion control, grading and landscaping[18]

The GTCC Foundation

Following the Foundation Board's reorganization in the fall of 1982, Dr. Needham and its members began an extended series of breakfast meetings with

business and industry CEOs. The response was excellent and the meetings continued as Needham prodded the Foundation to raise additional money to meet
certain college needs. In September 1983 the College employed Charlotte based
Ketcham, Inc., to survey a cross section of top potential donors in Guilford
County to determine their knowledge about the College and discover if they
believed GTCC could successfully stage a $2 million campaign to provide for
faculty enrichment, student aid, equipment, and new programs. Personal, con-
fidential interviews were conducted with 52 individuals whose support and potential involvement in the proposed fund raiser would be decisive.

The reputation of the College and its administration not withstanding, negative factors surrounding the transition to community college status, recent
large-scale capital fund campaigns within the county coupled with the lack of
identifiable contributors for a $2,000,000 campaign, convinced Ketcham to
recommend that GTCC reduce its expectations to a goal of $1,000,000 based
on the possibility of a $150,000 top gift. The firm suggested postponing the
campaign until 1985 to allow GTCC time to market its new image and educational objectives.[19]

Needham strengthened the Foundation in late 1984 by hiring Jim Halstead
as a direct report to serve as the Director of Development and the Foundation.[20]

Faculty Honors: 1983–84

Social Science Instructor, Dr. Carol Schmid, was named a Fulbright
Summer Scholar and assigned to a program in Germany. Commercial
Art Instructor, Ralph Calhoun, received a full scholarship from the
Reynolda House Museum of American Arts that included a trip to New
York.[21]

Making the Difference: The 1984–85 Academic Year

The Community College Funding Conundrum

Innocent observers of community college funding procedures are often
puzzled by the complicated processes and formulas that questionably maintain the state's major workforce preparedness institutions. For example
GTCC's institutional 1984–85 budget of $17,844,243 included an operational
budget of $15,581,157 and a capital budget of $2,263,086. The capital budget
included $1.8 million in State funds and a $436,086 contribution from the
county.[22] The State provided operational funds of $11,211,835 with the county

contributing $1,988,995. Grant and special funds provided an additional $2,380,327. These auxiliary funds included bookstore and vending profits, grants from Federal agencies and private foundations, and gifts and pledges to the Foundation. As discussed, these dollars are critically important given that State funds are allocated to community colleges on a formula basis, essentially in proportion to student enrollment.[23]

The keystone to this tentative process rests on the method chosen by the State to calculate full-time equivalent students. By comparison, during this era, 176 class hours equaled one FTE. In 1983–84, GTCC's FTE enrollment was 6,366 which the State funded at a rate of $1,716 per FTE. Two decades later in 2005–06, 512 curriculum hours equaled one FTE or 16 credit hours times 48 hours net for each class and the funding rate was $4,231.97 per FTE.[24] By its nature, the funding formula favors the one and two-year curriculum programs leading to a degree or diploma.

Extension enrollment, continuing education, short-term occupational programs or classes, and other non-degree programs and classes are funded at a lower level. Another peculiar and limiting aspect of State funding involves its time cycle. Funding is on a delayed basis meaning that 1984–85 FTE enrollment would not be funded until the following budget year. This payment-in-arrears-policy forces the Institution to bear all start-up expenses for a new program and to maintain the program for a full year before any State funds are received.

The allocation of County funds is simple and timely; GTCC makes an annual request to the County Commissioners for funds to meet maintenance and operational expenses. The commissioners generously and promptly respond to the request and allocate funds accordingly. There is no formula and no required categories for funding. The GTCC Board approves budgets for all funds and a final integrated budget is submitted to the State Board of Community Colleges.[25]

Davis Hall Dedicated

More than two hundred students, faculty, and staff gathered for the ribbon-cutting ceremony at Davis Hall on Thursday, March 22, 1984. The 28,237-square-foot building, designed by the firm of Allred and Mercer and built by M & M Builders honored John T. Davis Jr. for his 16 years on the Board and his ten-year chairmanship of the panel. As he unveiled a portrait of Davis to hang prominently in the new arts and sciences facility, Dr. Needham acknowledged contributions of the High Point furniture executive as "an outstanding Board member who served in the crucial years of GTCC." Vice President Don Cameron added that "John Davis cares about human beings and believes everyone deserves an opportunity."[26]

A $6.9 Million Drive to GTCC Jamestown?

The energy crisis that emerged as a permanent fixture in world society in the early 1970s consistently escalated the commuting costs of Jamestown students. A 1984 survey by GTCC's Civil Engineering Technology Department gauged the average student's mileage at 320 miles a week times 22 cents per mile, the national average at that time. At this rate, the student spent $774 per quarter on car expenses compared to $170 per quarter for books and tuition. The cost of gas in that era comprised only 20 percent of total auto expenses, while depreciation and time-value of money accounted for around 50 percent. The study ultimately determined that GTCC's 1984 students paid $132,000 per week to drive to Jamestown at an annual cost of $6.9 million.[27]

Greensboro Center Expands to Price School

The J. C. Price School Complex at 400 West Whittington Street opened in November 1984 and remained a major home to many GTCC programs until purchased by Greensboro College in 2005. Price marked a major expansion for the College in Greensboro, but once again its programs were installed in an aging facility in a nearly inaccessible location. Price housed the Business and Industry Institute, the Human Resources Development Program, Criminal Justice, Fire Science, Upholstery, Liberal Arts courses, and Continuing Education. A Small Business Assistance Center was located at 449 West Market Street.[28]

Salary Issues

GTCC's student newspaper, "The Guilford Technician" (May 22, 1984), reported preliminary results from a controversial survey administered to faculty and staff separately as a follow up to an October 1983 evaluation. Questions about the on-campus morale climate yielded dismal results: excellent 0, good 4, fair 18, poor 30, very poor 8, and not applicable 2. A second question requesting an evaluation of the individual's personal morale indicated excellent 6; good 15; fair 14; very poor 10, and not applicable 1. The computerized survey included a "morale" portion and a "service" component and in its final form would presumably reflect opinions from faculty and staff. The 161 responses from approximately 300 employees included 62 from approximately 120 faculty.[29]

An intensive reading of the Board minutes extending from the GIEC in 1958, indicates that the Trustees were historically aware of salary needs and inequities and instigated measures to improve the fiscal needs of the Institution's employees when possible. During this particular era, the Board approved the selection and hiring of a consulting firm to conduct a salary study and recommend a classification system for all employees, except faculty, and managers. The administration also considered establishing a merit pay system not to exceed $9,000.[30] At its August 23, 1984, meeting the Board unanimously approved a salary increase averaging 14 percent for permanent GTCC administrative, faculty/support, and classified employees retroactive to July 1, 1984. The Board further approved an expenditure of funds from state, county and special funds to support the pay increase.[31]

Dr. Needham informed the Board on March 14, 1985, that a salary review of classified (hourly employees) had been completed and that recommendations would be implemented within the next 90 days. A comparison of faculty and professional (exempt) staff salaries with those of the three local public school systems indicated that on average GTCC salaries were $2,389 less than those paid to public school personnel.[32] Salaries for North Carolina's public school and community college teachers were abysmally low and below average into the first decade of the twenty-first century. Community college faculty salaries are more comparable to public school than university salaries because of differing funding formulas. Following this particular study, GTCC employees requested that the Board consider asking the County Commissioners to supplement the salaries of GTCC employees. More than two and a half years passed before a county supplement was approved for qualified employees effective December 1987.[33]

According to the Southern Regional Education Board, N.C. community college faculty earned $36,809 for 2001–02 compared to a SREB average of $42,736. Relative to other states, N.C. Community College faculty salaries rank near the bottom. GTCC conducts periodic salary surveys to determine its competitive relationship to other institutions, businesses and industries and is presently fulfilling recommendations recommended by the Mercer Study in 2003–04.

Program Update: 1984–85[34]

Significant changes occurred in all areas of instructional programs during 1984–85 as GTCC succeeded in establishing transfer agreements with four-year colleges and universities. Students could transfer credits to senior institutions after earning the Associate in Arts or the Associate in Science degree. The Dental Assisting Program and the Dental Hygiene Program received full five-year accreditations and the Emergency Medical Science Department conducted a self-study in preparation for accreditation by the American Association of Medical Assistants. Ninety percent of GTCC's Registered Nurses passed their State Boards as did 100 percent of the Licensed Practical Nurse's including one who tallied a perfect score.

Vocational programs experienced moderate but continued growth during 1984–85 due in part to the addition of the Aviation Airframe and Power Mechanics program. The Carpentry and Cabinetmaking program and its spin-off GHG Corporation built and sold a house in Greensboro. Automotive Technology began offering a two-year associate degree while the Machinist program used a $40,000 grant from the State to purchase a CNC Bridgeport Milling Machine and a Bridgeport Ezy-Cam computer.

The College introduced The Business and Industry Institute of GTCC at the J. C. Price Campus. The forerunner of today's Business and Industry Services created four on-the-job training operations to meet the needs of Guilford County's business, industry, and public safety organizations. The Occupational mission provided short-term extension training for business and industry. Special programs included Cooperative Skills Training and Small Business Assistance. Criminal Justice Extension, EMT, and Fire Science Extension filled the Public Safety category with a strong slate of curriculum programs: Automotive Body Repair, Criminal Justice, Electronics Servicing, Fire Protection Technology and Upholstery.

That year, 1984–85, the Guided Studies Department, the present Developmental Education Division, and the Learning Center strengthened the academic skills of 2,500 GTCC students by providing basic skills instruction in reading, English, and mathematics for adults preparing for curriculum programs. Some 1,200 students enrolled in self-instructional courses for elective credit through the Learning Center, received additional academic assistance through the Peer Tutorial Program and the Microcomputer Lab. The GTCC Jamestown library, formerly a component of the Learning Resource Center, was named for its retiring Dean on *Mertys W. Bell Day*, June 27, 1984.[35] The library participated in a COM-CAT project with ten other community colleges to convert its holdings to machine-readable form thereby enabling all GTCC campuses to have a master catalog of the library's collection.

GED testing was extended to the High Point Center in the spring of 1985 when GEDs completed in Jamestown and Greensboro increased from 510 in 1983 to 563 in 1984. The Career Planning and Placement Center (CPPC) placed more than 700 students in jobs during 1984–85, while serving 1,548 students and prospective applicants; more than 417 students were tested and 603 students were provided direct career counseling services. The Cooperative Education Program placed 200 students in training-related jobs, targeting 232 more for placement during the 85–86 school year.

The Technical Scholars Program premiered in the 1984 fall quarter by awarding 13 technical scholarships in three curriculum areas: Mechanical Drafting and Design, Industrial Management, and Electronics Engineering Technology. Eight companies sponsored the scholarships which paid for books, tuition, and fees, in addition to providing curriculum work-related job experience.

Student Aid and Services

The Financial Aid office assisted approximately 1,100 students with a variety of packages while the Veteran's Assistance Officer served more than 300 veterans and others qualified for veteran's benefits. The Admissions Office corresponded with more than 12,000 potential curriculum students and processed more than 5,000 applications for admittance. The Educational Assistance and Counseling Center assisted approximately 10,000 clients; the Special Services staff helped more than 50 handicapped and 150 disadvantaged clients, and the testing Center administered approximately 3,000 placement tests to prospective students.

1984–85 Profile

A May 1984 survey revealed that 236 companies in the Triad employed one or more GTCC graduates as GTCC continued to expand its offerings with 140 full-time and 400 part-time instructors. [36] More than 50 percent of the 2,164 extension and adult basic education classes held throughout Guilford County during the 1984–85 academic year were taught at off campus locations. Full-time enrollment at GTCC increased by 246 students in the fall of 1984 to 4,939 while Continuing Education enrollment held steady at 12,000. A national decrease in community college enrollment during this period was attributed to falling unemployment rates, but GTCC's numbers were exceptionally impressive. (see next page)[37]

GTCC's employment totaled 831 — 335 permanent and 496 temporary or part-time employees; the latter mainly taught continuing education classes throughout Guilford County. The total payroll exceeding $9 million represented a significant contribution to the growth of the Guilford County economy. However, GTCC and the economy were seldom synchronized. In March 1985, Needham outlined an emergency strategy to balance yet another tenuous budget by instituting a hiring freeze; travel and supply budgets were subject to review; procedures were instituted to cancel classes with fewer than 12 students, classes were combined when feasible, and proposed new classes were delayed.[38]

By the end of the 1984–85 academic year, President Needham was confident that GTCC was beginning to "make a difference" in Guilford County, but formidable challenges continued: the pursuit of transfer options with four-year institutions, the implementation of competency based teaching and learning, and a program for working adults who would like credit for life and work experience. GTCC's lingering challenges included constructing the Transportation Electronics Complex and the ongoing commitment to economic development with its inestimable challenges.[39] The question of administrative leadership was a consistent concern and with it the tone of the Trustees and the question of low long Ray Needham would contentedly retain the presidency.

Enrollment Figures*

College Transfer	593
General Education	919
Technical	5,820
Vocational	1,122
Curriculum Total	**8,454**
Adult Basic Education	**2,479**
Occupational Extension	6,343
Avocational/Practical Skills	3,413
General Academic	7,024
Extension Programs	**16,780**
Adult High School/GED	**2,952**
Total Enrollment	**30,665**

*"GTCC 1984–85 Annual Report;" This data includes estimates for the Spring Quarter 1985.

Chapter 21

1985–89: Strategies for Excellence

North Carolina has more than 835,000 adults over age 25 who have not completed the eighth grade. An additional 700,000 have not finished high school. The state dropout rate is rising and now exceeds 27,000 per year.

Bob Scott, Former Governor
President of the N.C. Community College System, 1986[1]

The GTCC Foundation Endowment Fund Campaign: 1985–90

GTCC's modern emergence dates from 1985 when several initiatives at the Board and Foundation level inspired new directions for institutional growth as an internationally recognized community college. The GTCC Foundation, managed by marketing and development director Jim Halstead (1985–87),[2] named job retraining and specialty training as its goals when it launched a one million dollar fund raising drive on March 27, 1985. The projected five-year campaign marked the first full-scale solicitation of private funds in the College's 27-year history. The venture premiered with approximately $100,000 raised in a multi-year silent campaign among corporate leaders including a $60,000 gift from Guilford Mills, one of the county's largest textile manufacturers.

Foundation President Paul Stephanz positioned the campaign to increase the community's awareness of GTCC as the county's "best-kept secret," and to serve as a harmonious strategy to bridge the lack of civic trust that periodically divided the High Point and Greensboro leadership.[3] By late 1987, $603,263.54 had been raised when the Foundation appropriated $20,000 to support 10 innovative faculty and staff projects designed to enhance instruction and student services. GTCC alumnus Harry Boody, President of Guaranteed Energy Efficient Systems, Inc., presented the Foundation a check to kick off its first Annual Fund Campaign.[4]

The Foundation's Board of Directors presided over by David L. Hilder (1987–88) included business and community leaders who promoted the College and solicited gifts to enhance its many programs and services. By July 31, 1989, under the leadership of Park R. Davidson, the Foundation's assets totaled $626,328.19. The earnings financed a portion of the start-up costs for the Customer Service Technology program, provided for drop-in child care service for needy students, and funded professional development for instructional support personnel.[5]

Strategies for Excellence

GTCC's second public awareness offensive emerged on July 9–10, 1985, when eighteen College employees led by President Needham and Trustees William F. "Bill" McGuinn, Jr. and Frank York, convened the Sixth Annual Campus Planning Session to plot the Institutions' future direction. The five-year plan they created with twelve fundamental initiatives strengthened and grew the College into today's internationally recognized Institution.

1. Marketing: Increase GTCC's market penetration in the college service area.

2. Quality: Ensure the quality of instructional programs through the development of competencies for each program.

3. Unity: Promote better understanding among campuses through improved communication.

4. Productivity/Efficiency: Achieve measurable increases through the use of resources.

5. Budgeting: Develop a process that accommodates fluctuations in fiscal resources and needs.

6. Professional Development: Increase and promote professional development for faculty and staff.

7. Salary: Achieve salary parity with comparable jobs in Guilford County for faculty and staff.

8. Retention: Develop and implement a system to define and measure retention.

9. Part-time employees: Develop an institutional plan for the recruitment, selection, and monitoring of part-time employees.

10. Career Development and Job Placement: Develop a recruitment effort from a career planning and job placement perspective to encourage enrollment in high demand, low enrollment programs.

11. External Funding: Develop a system for Institutional involvement in securing external funding, inclusive of grants, based on Institutional priorities.

12. Student Activities: Examine alternative plans for providing students on the Greensboro-High Point Campuses with student activities and establish a system for providing those activities; the system should include student involvement.

These initiatives were historically reviewed, revitalized and refined throughout the Needham administration and remained as fundamental goals for the administration of his successor, Dr. Don Cameron. Cameron participated in this landmark Camp Caraway planning session that also included long time GTCC administrator Dr. Edward M. Knight, Dean of Enrollment Services.[6]

An Institutional Overview: 1985–86

GTCC's 1985–86 total institutional budget of $20,838,166 included $3,378,897 in capital funds to construct the first phase of the Transportation Electronics Complex that would house six major instructional programs on the Jamestown campus. The College employed 343 people in permanent positions with approximately 445 teaching part-time in curriculum, continuing education, and special interest programs. Using the standard projection that each dollar expended was re-spent threefold, the $11,000,000 faculty and staff payroll in 1985 increased Guilford County's economy by more than $33,000,000.[7]

Program Summary: 1985–86

By 1985 GTCC had earned a reputation for providing relevant education and training for business and industry in Guilford County. For the first time, the school is remarkably defined by exceptional statistics representing a dramatic increase in programs, students, services, faculty, and staff. Thirty-four career programs led to an Associate in Applied Science Degree; students could select from 20 one-year vocational diploma programs, or pursue certification in 18 study areas.

The multi-campus Institution was the third largest two-year public community college in the state and its institutional goals, synchronized with the technology revolution, were visible in every program. Competency-Based Education (CBE), an instructional technique focusing on the specific skills and tasks GTCC graduates needed for entry-level employment, was implemented in the fall of 1986. This innovation earned the College recognition as a leader in establishing this revolutionary method of instruction.[8]

New approaches to experiencing business and industrial working environments helped the faculty upgrade their teaching skills by participating in two highly successful programs. Return-To-Industry (1985) enabled instructors to reacquaint themselves with new equipment and processes. Food Services Instructor Brenda Greenwood worked with the Marriott and Radisson Hotels; Lynwood English, Department Chair, Business Administration, worked in a computer store; EMS instructor Bruce Shaw signed on as a paramedic with the Guilford County EMS; Early Childhood instructor Anna Cunningham experienced daily activities in a primary school and a day care center.[9]

Numbers of faculty and staff participated in a DACUM (Developing a Curriculum) process, the intensely creative exercise where expert facilitators direct a panel of business and industry specialists through brainstorming to detail and organize the competencies and skills necessary to perform a particular job. DACUM conclusions continue to guide curricula development and revision procedures.[10]

The Technical Education Division partnered with business and industry to design three new curriculum programs. Computer Office Automation Technology attracted 1,055 students to micro computing classes in 1985–86. The Customer Service Technology program emerged from the educational incentive package American Express, Inc. received when the financial giant moved to Guilford County. [11] This combination of business and computer courses, plus 13 new consumer service technology courses, predictably led to jobs paying around $15,000; a Small Business Management Entrepreneurial Development program followed in the spring of 1987.

The Arts and Sciences Division revised its Business Computer Programming curriculum to include microcomputer courses; offered a series of special classes in Child Care Education to help employees comply with new state requirements, and increased its list of transfer agreements with four-year colleges and universities in the state.[12]

In 1986, the Business and Industry Services staff instituted a two-year weekend training program for assistants in all of North Carolina's 500 chiropractic offices. North Carolina pioneered this unique program for the nation's community colleges and GTCC served as the sole training site. Ten weekends of classes at the J. C. Price facility and thorough examinations prepared first-year students for certification as Chiropractic Assistants; those who opted for a second year of training were certified as Chiropractic Nurses.[13]

The Vocational Education Division welcomed FAA certification for the Power Plant Mechanics Option of the Aviation Maintenance Technology Curriculum. Packaging Machinery Servicing was recognized by a national publication for its commitment to success through a strong advisory committee, the support of educational administrators, and enthusiastic, dedicated instructors. When the Packaging program succumbed to the technological revolution, its Jamestown Campus facility was renovated to house Welding Technology in the fall of 2006.[14]

GTCC's Occupational Extension and Cooperative Skills programs enrolled 2,026 students in 167 courses in 53 companies in 1985–86. New and Expanding Industry Training (NEIT) designed programs for five companies and trained a total of 585 persons for jobs in those industries. The Small Business Assistance Center enrolled 1,025 students in 42 courses and made more than 9,800 contacts with the public through course offerings, telephone communications, and personal counseling. The Public Safety Department conducted 41 Fire Science courses with 1,093 students, 30 Police Science courses with 596 students, and 13 Emergency Medical Technician courses with 371 students.[15]

Outstanding programs countered illiteracy, apathy, and unemployment. The General Education Development (GED) program; the Adult High School Diploma Program (AHS) and the Adult Basic Education (ABE) programs served 2,364 adults in 1985–86. The Human Resources Development (HRD) program helped participants escape the welfare rolls and secure productive employment and the Job Training and Partnership Act (JPTA) provided job training and employment opportunities for economically disadvantaged, unemployed, or underemployed individuals.[16]

California Dreaming: Needham Stays Home

President Needham resolved his second summons to the far west on June 18, 1986, by informing his staff and faculty that he had declined the presidency of Glendale Community College in Los Angeles, California. His letter acknowledged "special circumstances in my life which have led to me to reassess my future as President of Guilford Technical Community College," and thanked his staff and faculty for hosting two Board members from Glendale who had visited the campus.[17]

Enrollment 1985–86: 31,553

The 1985–86 total enrollment (unduplicated headcount) for curriculum increased 4.5 % to 8,833 as compared to 8,454 in 1984–85.

Enrollment by Program

College Transfer (CT)	916
General Education (GE)	284
Technical (T)	1,541
Vocational (V)	1,092
Adult Basic Education (ABE)	2,534
Avocational/Practical Skills (A/PS)	3,481
General Academic (GA)	7,186
Adult High School/General Education (AHS/GED)	3,020
Total Enrollment	**31,553**

The increase in enrollment was attributed to (1) the addition of Computer Office Automation Technology (fall 1985); (2) the college transfer option for part-time, special credit students and (3) the number of recent high school graduates opting to attend GTCC. According to a 1985 community college study, 620,000 students (124,899 FTE) were enrolled in the N.C. Community College System's 58 institutions. [18]

Student Profile: 1985–86*	
25 yrs of age or older	50%
Employed full- or part-time	91%
Enrolled full-time	35%
Married	53%
Minorities	21%
Guilford County Resident	86%

*GTCC: 1985–86; "Community College Study, Sept. 11, 1985," in BOT, Oct. 11, 1985.

GTCC: 1986–89: Addressing the Literacy Gap

In 1986, America's leaders began focusing on the challenge to educate people with less than an eighth grade education and those who could not read or write. The 1980 census indicated that 34,547 of Guilford County's 186,981 adults 25 and older had not finished the eighth grade and that an additional 34,161 had not finished high school. The statewide figures were similarly staggering; more than 835,000 adults over age 25 had not completed the eighth grade plus an additional 700,000 had not finished high school. With the state drop-out rate exceeding 27,000 annually, GTCC aggressively sought to expand adult education classes into business and industrial sites, shopping centers, and churches.[19]

The GTCC Literacy Education Program continued to expand through the end of the decade serving approximately 3,500 students in 1987–88 and 3,800 in 1988–89. Literacy classes thrived in churches, schools, governmental agencies, and service organizations and at 18 workplace locations in Guilford County. The 518 GED (General Educational Development) graduates in 1987–88 and 576 in 1988–89 were joined by 165 Adult High School graduates in 1987–88 and 150 in 1988–89.[20]

Women in the Workforce

GTCC instructors Carol Schmid and JoAnn Buck were inspired by the fact that for the first time in history (1986), American women professionals outnumbered male professionals by 29,000. Buoyed by a Ford Foundation Grant that funded their research into the changing roles of women and men, they wrote a textbook and created a course on the topic for fall 1987. The changing faces and figures in the workplace were additionally reflected in the vocational programs that trained machinists, auto mechanics, carpenters, and packaging machinery technicians. Programs that traditionally enrolled students named Mike, Jim, Rick, and Joe registered Daisy, Millie, Dawn, and Jean. GTCC marketed the message that uncommon jobs offered good salaries and rewarding careers. Fortuitously, a 1987 grant enabled the school to provide job training opportunities for 35 females in the skilled trades.[21]

The decline of the American family in this milieu portrayed a major social upheaval as the divorce rate tripled between 1960 and 1982 before leveling off at around 50 percent. By 1986, North Carolina ranked ninth in the nation with 608 divorces out of every 1,000 marriages and eighth in the nation with women in the work force (53.7%). Leveraged against these statistics is the historical fact that living standards for women customarily drop about 30 percent in the years following divorce.[22] The odds seemed stacked against single mothers who wanted to improve their situation by enrolling at GTCC. They labored to carve out time to go to school and find the cash for groceries and child care.

The child care factor was a major deterrent to women starting or returning to GTCC until a $40,000 state vocational child care grant funded a drop-in center on the Jamestown campus. The program accepted the children ages 2–5 of vocational and technical students based on their mother's needs. The children were supportively enrolled in a licensed educational program while their mothers benefited from a parent education program that ideally improved their opportunities.[23]

Business and Industry Services: 1987–89

> Our impact on Guilford County's economy can be measured in many ways, but one of the most notable has taken place through our services to business and industry. For example in the past three years, GTCC has trained more than 6,500 new employees for newly created jobs in Guilford County.
>
> GTCC President Ray Needham, 1989[24]

GTCC's training services (1986–89) during this surging era of industrial growth in Guilford County supported an approximate total payroll of $85 million involving 16 new companies. The Business and Industry Services Center managed by Ben Gray, Al Lochra, Karin Pettit, and George Anderson provided highly experienced occupational training professionals to help business and industry executives analyze training needs; counsel and orient management on training options; design custom training programs; provide the most qualified instructors available; and schedule and conduct the necessary training. The Center conducted more than 475 customized and general training programs for area employers in 1987–88 establishing the College as a major player in recruiting high profile companies: Levolor, Sears, Karastan-Bigelow, Proctor and Gamble, and Konica.[25]

GTCC Goes International

When Konica Manufacturing decided to move to Guilford County, GTCC was asked to help train its workforce. To facilitate this initiative, Business and Industry Services Director Karin Pettit, President Needham, and Vice President Don Cameron visited the company's Japanese operations (July 1987) to get a first-hand look at their production processes. Ron Abernathy, Director of Administration for Konica, later noted that GTCC's cooperation and enthusiasm helped convince the corporation to build a plant in Guilford County and join a GTCC client list that included Proctor & Gamble and American Express.[26]

Putting the Piedmont Back to Work: Part I

An ongoing workforce preparedness mission GTCC eagerly accepted, and one that intensified into the twenty-first century, was the charge to rescue displaced and laid-off workers. Hundreds of employees became a merger statistic when Liberty Life Insurance Company (Greenville, South Carolina) bought Greensboro based Southern Life Insurance Company. Workers with years of clerical experience were suddenly unemployed. When shock gave way to anger and reality, many realized that their skills were out-of-date for today's job market. GTCC's George Anderson and Brenda Brown (Employment Security Commission) designed an intensive nine-week training program that emphasized current office technology and customer service. This program, a forerunner of "Quick Jobs with a Future," (February 2004) joined a growing list of examples of how GTCC has consistently identified the county's educational needs and worked with agencies to respond decisively to those needs.[27]

Transportation Systems Technology

Luther Bell, a member of the DACUM panel that developed the curriculum for GTCC's Air Traffic Control program, the only one in North Carolina, joined GTCC after retirement to serve as the new program's first instructor in the fall of 1987.[28] By this time, the Aviation Maintenance Program had doubled in size to meet student and employer needs. Trustee Percy Sears closely monitored the program to determine its permanent location. At one time it was slated to move from the regional airport to the new Transportation/Electronics Complex at Jamestown, but by late 1987 Sears had convinced the Board to keep the programs at PTI and hire an architect to design new facilities.[29]

Construction began on GTCC's new aviation school, the eventual T.H. Davis Aviation Center, in 1989 on a 7.5-acre tract at the southwestern corner of PTI. A state grant of $1.7 million and $800,000 from a county bond issue financed the 37,000-square-foot building. The facility included a 12,000-

square-foot hangar in addition to laboratories, offices, classrooms, and a library. Pilot training, airport management, and air traffic control courses formerly taught at Jamestown were transferred to the new campus.[30]

The Transportation/Electronics Complex at the eastern edge of the Jamestown Campus formally opened on May 1, 1988, to house five programs: Automotive Technology, Diesel Vehicle Maintenance, Electronics Technology, Computer Office Automation Technology, and Customer Service Technology. The passage of the community college bond issue on November 8, 1988, added $1,800,000 in county funds to the $1,700,000 allocated by the State. This financed the addition of an Auto Body Repair Building to the complex.[31]

To reinforce its marketing pitch that "a Ford product is serviced by a college student," the auto maker launched its Automotive Student Service Technology Education Training Program (ASSET) by naming GTCC its sole site in North Carolina. The first graduates were recognized in a special ceremony on the Jamestown Campus in spring 1989. Today's ASSET students earn an associate degree in auto technology and receive paid work experience in Ford, Lincoln, or Mercury dealerships. The ASSET program was assigned to the new transportation electronics complex on January 4, 1989, where GM's ASEP (Automotive Service Educational Program) was operating.[32]

Technical Division

In 1989, the Technical Division prepared students for paraprofessional positions in Allied Health, Engineering, Computers, and Business by awarding the Associate of Applied Science degree. The division's Customer Service Technology Program tied for first place as the exemplary community college instructional program in the nation for 1988–89 winning over 600 programs nominated by 1,300 community colleges.[33] Three area hospitals, Moses H. Cone Memorial, Wesley Long, and High Point Memorial provided laboratory facilities and funded the first year of the Surgical Technology Program in the fall of 1989.[34]

Arts and Sciences Division

GTCC continued to broaden its College Transfer/General Education offerings to better serve students with foreign languages, fine arts, a broader range of sciences, and social sciences. A drama class, the precursor of today's Pre-

Major Drama Program directed by Dr. William R. Lewis, produced its first show, "Vanities." Business Computer Programming developed a one year certificate program. Physical fitness opportunities in the Wellness Center were expanded through cycling, water aerobics, a walk/jog/run course, and a computerized lifestyle assessment program for students.[35]

Community Service: Continuing Education

GTCC continued to offer an extensive selection of non-credit courses to develop and satisfy personal interests. The High Point Campus instituted a program of mini-grants in the spring of 1989 and worked with community agencies and individuals to offer a variety of unique events, lectures, and concerts. Diverse offerings included "Student Success and Parenting," co-sponsored with the High Point Affiliate of the National Black Child Development Institute; "Dealing With the Problems of Mentally Ill Family Members," co-sponsored with the High Point Mental Health Association; a phonics workshop designed for parents and educators on using the technique to improve the reading skills of children and adults. In 1987–89, the Greensboro Campus conducted approximately 100 community service classes per quarter, plus a variety of seminars and lectures; the High Point Campus served 5,315 community service students, not including those served through the mini-grant program.[36]

Teaching hundreds of extension classes and thousands of students was a major administrative challenge in the late 1980's. Criticism from state auditors concerning the quality, attendance, and content of avocational courses offered in nursing and rest homes was addressed the moment the College was informed of discrepancies. The auditors admitted that the quality of courses taught in elderly care facilities was not unique to GTCC. Part of the problem lay with the mission of the Community College System to be "all things to all people." GTCC asked the State to decide where the dividing line lay between legitimate educational courses and social activities for senior citizens.[37]

But the College moved quickly to reinforce its credibility. Employees who mismanaged the extension courses they were hired to teach were promptly disciplined and measures were adopted to reduce the possibility of fraud in the continuing education program. The Board studied the challenges incurred in conducting immured classes in rest homes, nursing homes, prisons, sheltered workshops, and adult day care centers during their fall 1987 work session. These programs are now consistently and minutely monitored by an in-house auditor as well as the state.[38]

Institutional Profile: 1985–89

Comparisons are provided here to illustrate how the succeeding years reveal major changes in the demographic pattern of GTCC's students.

Student Profile		
	1985–86	**2003–04**
Student Age		
14–24 yrs		57%
25–34 yrs		24%
35–44 yrs	Over 50%	12%
45 +		7%
Employed	91%	62%
Female	53%	56%
Minority	21%	40%

The state's third largest two-year public community college had grown from 50 students in 1958 to 34,864 in 1988–89. The facilities had expanded from a store front in High Point and a campus in Jamestown to three locations in Greensboro and one in High Point. Instruction was available at over 200 locations throughout Guilford County.[39]

Needham Says 'No' to Seattle Community College

I've talked with them, but I really am not interested in the position. They contacted me partly because I am from that area. I interviewed with them, but I plan to stay here with GTCC.

Ray Needham, President[40]

Ray Needham had been GTCC's president for almost nine years in March 1989 when he was named as one of six finalists considered for the chancellorship of Seattle Community College. The unrelenting pleas to return to the west continued until he finally received one from Tacoma Community College. After a decade of superior leadership and achievement, this call from the institution nearest his Washington State home signaled his departure from GTCC. The Institution had enjoyed an exceptional period of growth and stability during his lengthy administration and while it may not have been transparently apparent to the citizens of Guilford County who depended on GTCC, Needham's prime successor was his Executive Vice President Don Cameron.[41]

Campus Notes

Groundskeeper David Schlosser won the 1987 President's Award for Innovation and Service. The SGA office complex at Jamestown was named in honor of the late Raymond W. Moody, GTCC's Student Activities and Alumni Affairs Officer, for 12 years of professional service (July 1974–January 1987).[42]

The Small Business Assistance Center directed by Gary Dent received the Small Business Advocate of the Year Award in 1989. More than two decades later, the Center continues to have a widespread impact on Guilford County by assisting people who want to learn how to start their own business or develop an existing business.[43]

On May 18, 1988, President Raymond Needham officially inducted 108 students into GTCC's Alpha Pi Alpha Chapter of Phi Theta Kappa. The National Honor Society for two-year colleges was founded in 1918 and modeled after Phi Beta Kappa to recognize and encourage scholarship, leadership, and service among associate degree students. The society's first officers were President, Carl Stewart; Vice President, Phyllis Clabough; Recording Secretary, Vickie Hill; Public Relations Secretary, Lone Anderson; and Treasurer, Jennifer Walton. The first Honor Society Committee appointed by Faculty Association President Peggy Teague included JoAnn Buck, Janet Boyd, Mildred Mallard, and Wid Painter.

The Inauguration of President Donald W. Cameron, Tuesday, October 8, 1991. Standing, from the left—Dr. Stuart Fountain, Chair, GTCC Board of Trustees; President Cameron; Jayne Cameron; and the Honorable Robert Scott, President, North Carolina System of Community Colleges.

President Donald W. Cameron, 1991 to present

James F. Morgan
Chair Trustees, 1995–1998

J. Patrick Danahy
Chair Trustees, 2001–2004

David S. Miller
Chair Trustees, 2004–2007

Shirley M. Frye
Chair Trustees, 2007 to present

Section VI

The Entrepreneurial Presidency of Donald W. Cameron
1991–

Chapter 22

1990–91:
The Needham-Cameron Transition

I would like to stay there until I retire — about 20 years from now. We had always wanted someday to go back to Puget Sound.

Ray Needham, May 1, 1990[1]

Building GTCC for the 21st Century

GTCC's 21st century image emerged dramatically during the first six months of 1990 on the strength of two major documents: a ten-year plan in February 1990 to construct eight new buildings on the Jamestown campus and a "Vision for the 90's" document in May 1990.[2] Ironically, a third incident, the May 1, 1990, announcement of Ray Needham's resignation, and the prolonged selection of his interim successor introduced one of the most provocative institutional scenarios in GTCC's history.

Needham applauded the construction proposal: "Ten years ago," he said, "we had about 3,000 day students on campus ... this fall we have 7,200 and the campus is not much larger." He qualified the ambitious building program, courageously approved without a financing plan, by noting that "We have just identified our needs. We'll have to work on financing in the future."[3] As is often the case with long range planning, the facilities scheme changed as the decade progressed and needs were reassessed.

The eight buildings and two centers envisioned in 1990 included an advanced technology facility for computer related programs (the eventual Percy T. Sears Applied Technology Building); a communications building providing expansion space for English and Guided Studies and broader offerings of basic and advanced communication skills;[4] a building containing financial and facilities operations thereby opening additional administrative space in the Medlin Campus Center; a building housing food service and additional service programs (Service Careers) that would also provide a large assembly area, conference rooms for the College and the community and space to expand the child care and cosmetology programs.

The mix included a building consolidating GTCC's public safety programs on the Jamestown Campus with a complementary complex that would include an obstacle course, a driving course, track and drill tower (Public Safety Field Service Training Facility). Additional construction projects included an activity and wellness center for trade shows, large banquets, graduation, job fairs, and physical education plus a science building housing astronomy, geology and general applied science programs.[5]

The proposals, including business centers for Greensboro and High Point, encouraged the Board to ask the county commissioners to authorize an $18.5 million GTCC bond referendum for the November 1990 election.[6] Buoyed by this grandiose scheme, the College appeared headed for a period of tremendous physical expansion when President Needham resigned to accept the presidency of Tacoma Community College in Washington State.[7] His announcement preceded by two weeks (May 15) the presentation of the second major document in GTCC's modern history, "Vision for the 90's."

This futuristic set of initiatives aggressively challenged the College to fulfill the expectations of many more students and satisfy the needs of the county's employers. It called for expanding programs, increasing classroom space, and providing more sophisticated support services to students. This expansion of instructional programs and student services, projected to cost $24.5 million for buildings, site development and equipment, completed the rationale for the anticipated bond issue.

Instructional programs identified for expansion included Computer Literacy and Advanced Technology, Basic Skills and Advanced Communication, Service, Health and Business/Trade Careers, Public Safety Training, and programs in Literacy and Occupational Extension. Targets in the Student Services area focused on Child Care, Counseling and Academic Advising, Financial Aid and Job Placement. The official resolution asking the county commissioners for an $18.5 million bond issue to partially fund these services was approved by the GTCC Board in July 1990 as Needham packed for his departure from Jamestown.[8]

Needham's Legacy

My ten years here at GTCC have been interesting and exciting ones. I have found the faculty and staff at GTCC to be very committed to students and learning. Also, the faculty, staff, and community have made me very welcome in Guilford County, and I have gained a new appreciation for southern hospitality. As a result, it was a difficult decision to return to Washington when this position became available. Most of my family lives in the Tacoma-Seattle area, and I will be going home.[9]

Ray Needham, May 1, 1990

It was never a secret that Ray Needham was highly respected in the Pacific Northwest and that he dearly loved his native region; for those reasons, it was probably a gift to Guilford County that he remained at GTCC for ten years. Board Chair Dr. Stuart Fountain was clearly aware of Needham's emotional attachment to his homeland and sad to see him leave: "We regret that Dr. Needham has taken this move; we wish him well in his new position, but we realize that this has been a lifelong dream of his."[10] Needham, who was consistently gracious about his relationship with the Board during and after his tenure at GTCC, actually accepted a pay cut from a smaller institution to return home. The presidency of Tacoma Community College paid in the low $90,000s as compared with the nearly $100,000 he was earning in Guilford County where GTCC's 7,000 full-time enrollment and 23,000 part-timers eclipsed TCC's 5,000 FTE.[11]

Needham's greatest achievement was clearly the tenacious leadership strategy he exercised to win community college status for GTI in 1983. His legacy included 19 new programs; Air Traffic Control, Computer Office Automation Technology, Customer Service Technology, and Packaging Machinery Servicing were introduced during his tenure. The number of students in degree programs doubled and the enrollment of high school students attending GTCC grew from nearly 7 percent in 1980 to around 24 percent in 1990.[12]

Enrollment in credit courses increased 57 percent from 2,687 in 1979–80 to 4,207 in 1988–89 while enrollment in all courses increased 27 percent from 25,187 to 32,089. The High Point campus underwent a major expansion, two locations were added in Greensboro, and a new aviation facility at PTI opened a few months after Needham's departure. Six of the 15 buildings on the Jamestown campus were constructed during his administration with the total value of the school's buildings increasing from $9.1 million in 1980 to $31 million.[13]

Needham departed on a positive fiscal note by breaking even on expenditures following a $200,000 state reduction in the budget. The fiscal and FTE audits (1989–90) were the best of his presidency, and Barbara Kazazes was commended for reversing the major auditing problems that previously and consistently forced the College to return money to the state. An award of $35,000 from the General Assembly enabled GTCC to create an institutional research office directed by Lowell Speight. Food service, long a thorn in Needham's tenure, appeared to have improved with a reversion to in-house service directed by Food Service Director Joyce Anderson Hill.[14]

A highlight of Needham's last Board meeting on June 21, 1990, was a demonstration of TRACS, GTCC's new telephone registration and communication system. TRACS was implemented two days later thanks to the leadership skills of Dr. Ed Knight, Dean of Enrollment Management, Comptroller Rae Marie Smith, and Director of Computer Services Angus Small, the third member of the team described as "the genius, sparkplug, and heart" of the system. The launch of this revolutionary registration system owes its success to Knight's commitment to computerize student records and Smith's devotion to financial management. By August, TRACS had registered 1,564 of 2,800 students for the 1990 fall quarter.[15]

Ray Needham left with thanks from a grateful faculty for supporting the need for a county supplement. As one editorialist commented, "Ray Needham has cultivated a friendly, outgoing style that served him well in dealing with GTCC's diverse constituencies. He leaves his institution a much better place than when he arrived, and for that Guilfordians can be grateful."[16] Needham was an early advocate of succession planning at the community college level. Vice presidents Delores Parker and Don Cameron would prove invaluable during the brief presidential transition. When Needham hired Parker in 1989 the former Dean of Student Development at NCA&T State University became the first female vice president in GTCC's history.[17]

The organizational chart indicates that while Needham supervised facilities, development, and business affairs, and Parker managed student development and institutional support, executive vice president Cameron was the team heavyweight supervising every educational program the College offered plus the Learning Resource Center and the High Point and Greensboro campuses. Cameron's athletic energy, voracious appetite for work, complimented by an innate understanding of organizational leadership and nine years of on-the-job experience, prepared him for his appointment as interim president and launched his campaign for the presidency.[18]

Years later, Needham acknowledged that he had enjoyed a close personal and professional relationship with Cameron, the "team-player for whom he had enormous respect." From the moment he hired Cameron, he believed the Moore County native could one day lead GTCC, but his executive vice president would have to earn the promotion by negotiating a challenging process crowded with nearly a hundred candidates.[19] Board Chair Stuart Fountain made it clear in May 1990 when Cameron was named interim president, that the College would probably not choose a permanent successor until the spring or summer of 1991.[20] The Board demonstrated its commitment to a major search by hiring James "Jim" Tatum, a past president of the Association of Community College Trustees (ACCT), and a veteran of 40 similar searches, to find a president representing the qualities Fountain demanded:

> We think that the Community College System is moving into a new era in which we have got to confront the need for a highly skilled trained employee to participate in the kind of industry in this area in the 21st century. We need to have a dynamic individual who can lead us into the 21st century.[21]

The 1990 presidential search became the most democratic in the Institution's history. Ignoring its historical reputation for disdaining outside input, the Board welcomed participation by Trustees, faculty, staff, the Classified Employee Association, Student Government Association, the GTCC Foundation and members of the Guilford County community. The winner of the coveted post as head of North Carolina's third largest community college would be challenged to implement the projected ten-year construction plan and the "Vision for the 90's" initiatives.[22]

The Interim Presidency of Donald W. Cameron: August 1990–91

Board Chair Dr. Stuart Fountain officially welcomed the Institution's interim president to his new appointment on July 19, 1990.[23] For the vigorous administrator who first saw the light of day in Greensboro, North Carolina, and grew up in the small Moore County town of Robbins, the temporary assignment became the springboard to an illustrious future. After graduating from Elise High School in 1961, the student-athlete packed his baseball gear and headed to Wingate Junior College (now University) in Wingate, N. C. to earn an Associate in Arts degree in 1963. He traveled back across the state to take a B.S. at Atlantic Christian College (now Barton College) in 1965 followed by a Master of Arts in Teaching from the University of North Carolina at Chapel Hill in 1970. Cameron received his doctorate in Education from Nova University (1977) and completed post graduate studies at Harvard University's Institute for Educational Management in 1987.

Don Cameron began his professional career as a history teacher and head football and baseball coach at Union Pines High School in Cameron, North Carolina (1965–70). He joined Campbell College as an admissions officer in 1970, headed the New Hope Boy's Home in Sanford, North Carolina (1971), and launched his community college career by directing the continuing education program for Dr. Jeff Hockaday at Central Carolina Technical College in Sanford from 1972 to 1977. Cameron's career path then turned southwest to Spartanburg Technical College, South Carolina, where he served as Vice President for Academic Affairs from 1977 to 1981. Cameron and his wife, the former Jayne Evelyn Boyd of Charlotte, moved to Guilford County with their children Douglas and Suzanne, when Ray Needham lured the 38-year-old administrator to Jamestown in August 1981 to serve in the newly created position of vice president for academic affairs.[24]

Cameron recognized that his path to the presidency possibly rested on the successful promotion of the forthcoming $18.5 million bond issue the Board resolved to pursue on July 19, 1990. He quickly warmed to the task of creating a textbook strategy designed to win this and future referendums by organizing a "Vision for the 90's" Bond Steering Committee. Co-chaired by Trustees Stuart Fountain and Charlie Greene, its members included additional Board members, citizens, key staff, student representatives, and a consultant from the Winston Salem-based public relations firm Horn and Stronach.[25]

The components of the committee's plan, supported by the GTCC marketing department, included a "speaker's bureau" that booked more than 40 venues; printed 26,000 brochures; purchased 18 billboards; bought newsprint, radio and TV advertising, arranged conferences with newspaper editorial staffs and scheduled TV interviews. The steering committee met weekly to assess their progress toward raising more than $45,000 from private and corporate sources to finance the drive.

Campaign literature extolled GTCC's mission and its achievements; 37,000 citizens, or 1 in 9 residents of Guilford County, were enrolled in at least one course at the College. The Institution had experienced a 40 percent growth during the past three years with an instructional schedule that extended from 7:30 A.M. until 10 P.M. One-hundred-year-old art student Estelle Eaton, Eastern Guilford High School Tech Prep student Brain Graves, and freelance illustrator Chuck Kirby of High Point, were just a few of the students appearing in press stories. Respected business reporter Jack Schism labeled the GTCC bond a "super bargain for the area."[26]

The referendum was overwhelmingly approved on November 6, 1990; it was projected to cost Guilford County taxpayers about one cent for every $100 of assessed property value for the next ten years. Cameron breathed a sigh of relief, knowing that the Board could not ignore the obvious evidence of his leadership in the victorious election that assured the College and its interim leader a major role in workforce preparedness and economic development in Guilford County.[27]

College Tech Prep

Cameron's interim tenure intensified productively when he partnered with the Guilford County Schools and area business and industry to finance and implement College Tech Prep. This innovative program was designed to meet the needs of high school students who were not four-year college bound. Participants could enroll in career-related technical courses in addition to mathematics, science, and English. This plan permitted them to pursue career goals while meeting college course requirements. Following the completion of four credits in a career/technical sequence, completers had multiple options to pursue two or four-year college degree programs or adult apprenticeship programs.[28]

Tech Prep associate degree programs were approved with Guilford County's three school systems on April 23, 1992. Each system promised to prepare at least 85 percent of their high school students with either a Tech Prep or a College Prep program of study and to work with GTCC to guide the continuing development and implementation of a Tech Prep associate degree program. "These students, thus prepared, will be equipped to enter, without remediation, post-secondary education and to enter the work force with technological skills appropriate to the majority of the new jobs then available."[29] Dr. Cameron's support and that of Percy Sears, convinced the Guilford County Commissioners to provide $900,000 to fund Tech Prep.[30]

GTCC's Sixth President: Dr. Donald W. Cameron

Forty-seven-year-old Don Cameron rose above over 100 applicants to become GTCC's sixth president on February 7, 1991, when he signed a three-year contract to lead the College at an annual salary of $75,624. The fact that Cameron is gifted with innumerable attributes is historically documented in the ensuing record of his service, awards, and recognitions; foremost among these values is the quality of his character, his unimpeachable integrity, a scholarly, research oriented approach to conceptual planning; a fierce loyalty to those he admires; and political astuteness. These qualities are consistently evident in his approach to various boards of governance and particularly to his Trustees whom he consistently acknowledges as his partners in developing the College.[31]

The consensual approval of his Board is central to Cameron's leadership of the College as a partnership and a principle he acknowledged in accepting the presidency: "Together we will develop the future goals and objectives for GTCC. Together, we will provide the direction for this college to become a 'flagship' institution." Cameron was distinctly aware that a successful administration also needed the partnership and support of faculty and staff. This "team player" and former athletic coach Ray Needham hired was well-schooled in cohesive collaboration:

> I am proud that I will be working with such a first class faculty and staff who strive for excellence above all else. We are privileged to have here at GTCC a faculty and staff who believe in the individual worth of all students. I look forward to serving the 30,000 plus individuals who take classes with us every year. They are the reason we are here and we should never lose sight of that.[32]

The Trustees had selected a serious, centered educator committed to outcomes-oriented education, a process that focuses on learning rather than teaching, and measured outcomes. As a continuous improvement strategy, it helped measure accountability and competency and formed the basis for the "GTCC Guaranteed Degree" Cameron instituted in 1994.[33]

George Fouts: The First Term 1991–94

One of the first executives Cameron added to his management team prior to his official installation was introduced to the Board as GTCC's new vice president of administrative services on June 27, 1991. Forty-three-year-old George Fouts, a Thomasville native, who had served as interim president at Maryland Technical College and Roanoke Chowan Community College, came to GTCC fresh from a stint as assistant to former Governor Robert W. Scott, president of the North Carolina Community College System and coordinator of the Commission on the Future of the North Carolina Community College System.

Fouts launched his community college career in 1973 as an instructor at Western Piedmont Community College, where he eventually rose to executive vice president. His greatest contribution to GTCC, beyond his exceptional administrative wisdom and analytical political acumen, was his successful leadership in the GTCC bond referendums of 2000 and 2004 that raised $72 million for the College.

Fouts' highly productive administrative career was built on an almost innate understanding of the Community College System, and the political and social fabric in which it is embedded. His understanding of the monstrously complicated system of rules, regulations, statutes, and processes that define the General Assembly's petulant distribution of the state's largess is immediately apparent in the GTCC Board archives. Clean, crisp financial reports reflect his mentoring of Rae Marie Smith, the comptroller who would succeed him as Vice President of Administrative Services when he became GTCC's Executive Vice President, but that is getting ahead of the story.

Even though his first official day on the job was still a few weeks away when he met the Board on June 27, 1991, Fouts delivered a uniquely perceptive report on the status of budget deliberations in the legislature. The Trustees quickly learned that his financial analyses were models of clarity and preciseness conditioned as they were by his knowledge of state and county funding processes, which, at least in the case of the state, were consistently unpredictable and annually subject to reversions. The state budget seldom arrived minus a built-in reversion clause, best described as a case of "giving with one hand while taking away with the other."

Conversely, the funding provided by the Guilford County Commissioners generally and graciously matched expectations due to planning and communication between the College and the county. Perhaps it is best to characterize the financial status of a community college as a perpetual contingency operation dominated by a series of frustratingly unpredictable variables including the economy, enrollment, emergencies, fluctuating labor costs, and unpredictable revenue streams. It was perhaps providential that George Fouts' experience as an avid fisherman and a cunning observer of natures incongruous currents, prepared him to monitor with great skill the College's cash flow during a huge budget shortfall in 1994.[34]

The Installation of Dr. Donald W. Cameron
October 8, 1991

Dr. Stuart Fountain, Chairman of GTCC's Board of Trustees, presided and proclaimed the tremendous promise of a Cameron administration when he told an audience of more than 300 gathered on the plaza before the Learning Resource Center on the Jamestown Campus: "We were looking for a diamond, wherever it may be found, even if it was in our own backyard, and it was."

This is an historic day in the life and history of Guilford Technical Community College as we announce our new president, a new administration and a new beginning for the College. Our sixth president of GTCC is Dr. Donald W. Cameron, who had handled so well the difficult task of being an administrator in tight fiscal circumstances. He has done this with fairness, openness and firmness. He has earned the respect of everyone.[35]

"There is Nothing Permanent Except Change"

The Honorable Robert Scott, President of the North Carolina Community College System, challenged the new chief executive "to maintain credibility rather than seek credit, to exhibit honesty rather than honors, to espouse truth rather than rhetoric, and to stand firm in your convictions rather than compromise your principles.[36] President Cameron followed his recognition of the official party by acknowledging one of the Institution's most popular students, Mrs. Estelle Eaton, who attended GTCC in 1990 at the age of 100, and related her experience to the culture and the mission of the College.

During his address, Cameron positioned GTCC as a complementary companion to Guilford County's two major state universities and four private colleges. He pledged to maintain the mission of a comprehensive community college by emphasizing a commitment to occupational education and training as part of the economic development of the county and the state. His experience had prepared him to confront the unpredictable shifts in corporate power and production during the last decade of the 20th century that would forever alter the business and industrial face of Guilford County and exacerbate a desperate rush toward a new level of technological training and retraining to survive the vagaries of an unruly global economy.

Last year, GTCC had 37 different countries represented on our campuses. In Greensboro, some 46 foreign firms have local sites, and another 25 foreign owned businesses operate in High Point. The International Furniture Market in High Point (next week) will bring visitors from over 50 foreign countries. These statistics are more than just passing notes of interest for those of us at GTCC. If we are to continue serving the needs of the community, we must examine how our community is changing. We must also examine our educational programs to determine what changes are necessary in order to appropriately respond to the cultural differences in our community.

Cameron chose his installation to assail the ritualistic process of institutional under-funding that had historically, and tragically, prohibited the Community College System from reaching anywhere near its potential as an agent of workforce preparedness. Noting that he shared the community college leadership's "frustration with the lack of additional funding to support the recommendations made by the Commission on the Future of the North Carolina Community College System," he confessed that he was out of patience; "GTCC is not waiting on additional funding to respond to the vision of the Commission's report or to the goals set forth by the State Board in response to that report. In truth, we cannot wait." The new president emphasized the value of partnering with school systems, colleges, universities, and business and industry, a philosophy that benchmarked his educational philosophy and the goal of his administration. Cameron pledged that GTCC would break from tradition to experiment with fresh approaches and new methodologies; he cited distance learning and the applications of fiber optics to deliver a wider range of instruction. Turning again to the necessity for funding beyond the state, he pledged to devote increased attention to the GTCC Foundation, a promise that emerged as the Legacy Campaign in 2004. He further promised to operate an accountable, quality community college with standards second to none.

President Cameron was distinctly aware that no one person could direct GTCC to a successful future, but he was confident that his team of over 400 full-time employees was sufficiently energized to launch the Institution into the twenty-first century. He concluded:

> GTCC is blessed with a truly outstanding faculty and staff. It is a great professional honor to have been asked to serve as president of a college with such a distinguished group of professionals. And I do not just mean that they have sound credentials, which they do; but in addition to that, they are committed, loyal, and believe in serving students. Our theme at GTCC is that "We're not here just to make a living; we're here to make a difference." Those words are not just a credo on a wall somewhere; they are lived out everyday in some way in scenarios large and small on our campuses.[37]

The Cameron presidency began with the state's third largest community college operating from three campus locations in Guilford County serving 11,000 degree-seeking students and around 27,000 non credit students in 58 programs, but enrollment and programs did not mean that GTCC and its sister institutions were solving the state's employment problems. Statewide projections in 1990 revealed 10,474 annual job openings in food preparation and services; 2,992 openings for nursing assistants; 2,089 in law enforcement, 1,620 in heavy equipment operation; 1,567 in carpentry; 880 in general woodworking; 789 in banking and finance; 574 in automotive technology; and 362 in machine tool technology.

The greatest cultural challenge Don Cameron faced in Guilford County was coping with a huge population of "hands people" who found security in menial, manual labor and with many parents and students who failed to see that a set of technical, vocational, and occupational skills could lead to a rewarding career.

While he may not have noted it on that significant day, one of his greatest challenges was the same one that Luther Medlin confronted in 1967, selling the College to Greensboro's leadership. In time, he would mount a campaign to force every resident to "*Imagine Guilford County without GTCC.*"

Chapter 23

1991–94
Beginning to Make a Difference

GTCC is a quality outfit. It's known throughout the system and it's known outside the state. You're moving ahead; you're alive and you're vibrant and I commend you for it.

The Honorable Robert W. Scott
President of the North Carolina Community College System[1]

The View from Third Floor Medlin Campus Center: 1991–92

The Board was particularly active during 1991–92 as the new president began considering a variety of special initiatives. The issue of a semester system was revived and ultimately approved by the community college presidents and the State Board in April 1992. Internal studies moved to complete and implement a new compensation plan for GTCC employees by July 1, 1993. Planning began for a projected statewide bond issue that promised construction money for GTCC in spring 1992, and the three Guilford County public school systems approved the College Tech Prep program supported by a $900,000 grant from the county commissioners.[2]

The new administration (1991) introduced nine special projects dialed into a five-year plan designed to change the College; (1) a multi-year strategy to meet the next ten-year SACS accreditation in 1994; (2) the implementation of the Kellogg ACCLAIM project; (3) a building plan based on the 1990 bond funds; (4) an employee compensation plan; (5) distance learning; (6) a semester system to facilitate transferring credits; (7) planning for global and cultural diversity;[3] (8) building the Foundation; and (9) pursuing organizational effectiveness through the Total Quality Management process (TQM).[4] These projects were complimented by eight goals in an era when the professional development of GTCC employees was directly linked to creating a culture based on skill, efficiency, respect, and quality:

1. To provide accessible and comprehensive instructional programs committed to excellence in teaching and successful student achievement.

2. To provide comprehensive services to assist students and employees in their development.

3. To enhance institutional effectiveness through planning, research, and resource development.

4. To provide leadership thereby encouraging communication, innovation, productivity, and accountability.

5. To provide and maintain a physical environment, including facilities and equipment, conducive to student learning.

6. To increase awareness of the College by promoting its programs and services.

7. To provide an environment that attracts, retains, develops, and rewards employees.

8. To provide opportunities for the College and the community to interact in educational, civic, social, economic, and multi-cultural activities.[5]

Cameron's determination to train the county's workforce more effectively by reforming workforce preparedness stemmed from the electorate's overwhelming approval of that $18.5 million bond package in November 1990. He would be true to the bond issue that helped make him president by reimbursing the voters.[6] Beyond creating a productive future for high school students through College Tech Prep, he wanted to provide more convenience for citizens enrolling in a variety of educational opportunities by developing innovative approaches to training. Flexible class scheduling and distance learning would soon open the College to the community as never before, but the initiatives fueled by the omnipresent SACS self study would also enhance the leadership qualities of faculty and staff, reward them with better pay and benefits, and prepare them to confront the burgeoning immigration onslaught.[7]

Cameron was committed to creating partnerships with divergent groups including his Board, county commissioners, legislators, and the immensely powerful, often charismatic individuals and groups of industrialists, businessmen, and public educators who dominated the county and its major cities,

High Point and Greensboro. Beneath the positive points in his inaugural address boiled a deep seated consternation with what he perceived as GTCC's mostly unfilled promise to provide the best technical-skills training available, a perception aggravated by the often frustrating experience of supervising a wide variety of programs.

Cameron's determination to "do it (skills-training and workforce preparedness) right and by the book" would distinguish his administration. As a matter of fact, his "gritty determination" to raise public awareness about GTCC emerged as a specific personal challenge for an imaginative, innovative administrator who fed on the pulse of his Institution. The major problem he confronted from an institutional point of view was that of the stereotypical community college surrounded by six established liberal arts institutions within a 15-mile radius. With GTCC lost in this historical batter, Cameron knew he had to get out of his office and adopt a more public role to sell the College and his embryonic workforce preparedness vision to the community. Reinforced by his "Mr. Inside," Executive Vice President George Fouts, Cameron assumed a "Mr. Outside" persona and charged into the county, the state, the nation, and the world. It would take him about two years to define his vision for the College and establish himself as Guilford County's workforce planning czar.[8]

1991–92: A Multi Campus College

The Cameron administration managed three major campuses located in Jamestown, Greensboro, and High Point, serving more than 35,000 students with 45 two-year associate degree programs, 20 one-year occupational diploma programs, and certifications in over 40 areas. Beyond Jamestown, High Point, and Greensboro, students could enroll in courses at more than 300 locations throughout the county.[9]

GTCC: Greensboro

The dispersed, but substantially thriving, Greensboro facilities included the J. C. Price Complex, off East Lee Street, a classroom building at 501 West Washington Street, and the Small Business Assistance Center on Yanceyville Street. Price offered an average of 339 curriculum and continuing education classes per quarter serving 5,815 students, including classes at approximately 42 off-campus sites. 3,896 students were enrolled in 280 community services classes in 1991–92.[10] The GTCC Washington Street facility operated 279 classes (134 occupational extension and 145 community service) enrolling 4,427 students. Curriculum classes averaged 61 and students numbered around 889 per quarter to study accounting, business, computers, English, guided studies, history, psychology, sociology, speech, math, office technology, and political science.[11]

The GTCC Aviation Center: 1991–92

This facility, comprising 36,000 square feet of classroom and labs plus a 12,000-square-foot hangar, was formally dedicated at the southwest corner of the Piedmont Triad International Airport in March 1991. Students pursued the Associate in Applied Science in Career Pilot/Management and the AAS in Aircraft Maintenance Technology. Optional continuing education courses were available in flight simulator training, FAA Oral and Practicals, avionics, non-destructive testing and composite materials repair. The facility provided students opportunities for restoration projects including a Piper Cub in 1991 and a vintage 1954 Super Cub the following year. 125 students were enrolled in Aviation Management Technology and about 175 in the Career Pilot/Management and 51 students graduated with associate degrees in August 1992.[12]

GTCC: High Point

The 901 South Main Street campus experienced steady growth in 1991–92, adding the Customer Service Technology Program, a Weekend College, the Small Business Assistance Center, Business and Industry Training Services, and the Upholstery Program relocated from Jamestown. These additions doubled the campus curriculum enrollment from fall 1991 to fall 1992. High Point excelled in GTCC's literacy initiative, graduating nearly 350 high school completers in 1991–92. An amazing 4,446 students took at least one class in Adult Basic Education (ABE), Adult High School (AHS), and General Education Development (GED) at GTCC with 1,467 served from High Point and 2,979 from Greensboro and surrounding communities. While the figures were impressive, the challenge was immense: 70,000 citizens needed to upgrade their literacy skills.[13]

High School Graduates	192
GED Graduates	562
Curriculum Matriculations	192

GTCC: Jamestown

GTCC celebrated a first time articulation agreement with UNCG in the fall of 1992 in Accounting, Business Administration, Early Childhood Specialist, and Nursing. The Jamestown Campus expanded its evening offerings, hired an assistant to the vice president to coordinate the program, and enrolled 2,531 (34%) of the curriculum students in fall 1991. Fifty-two of sixty curriculum programs were offered during the evening including seven college transfer and general education programs plus 31 technical and 14 vocational programs.[14]

1991–92: Educational Support Services

The Counseling Center averaged serving 1,475 students per month including 129 with disabilities. Pell Grant recipients increased from 441 to 600 in a year. The Student Government Association (SGA) sponsored a leadership retreat for 60 students, faculty, and staff at the Betsy-Jeff Penn 4-H Center in Reidsville and funded approximately 30 clubs. The student newspaper, *GTCC Gazette*, won Best Writing and Best Overall at the N.C. Comprehensive Community College Student Government Association Conference that spring.[15]

Business and Industry Services: 1991–92

GTCC's unrelenting commitment to increase services in this spectrum enrolled 3,150 in occupational extension classes, Focused Industrial Training (FIT), and apprenticeship classes. The Small Business Assistance Center counseled 326 individual small business owners, conducted 272 small business sessions, and provided occupational extension courses to an additional 36 companies. The SBAC began offering services at GTCC High Point and moved its main location in Greensboro to the Center for Entrepreneurship on Yanceyville Street. While these numbers indicate that some of GTCC's core responsibilities were working in the best interests of certain segments of the community, Cameron was determined to find ways to better serve the high tech and service industries that were replacing the declining textile and tobacco industries.[16]

Student Enrollment Data

	1990–91*	1991–1992**
Curriculum	10,806	10,882
Male	48.4%	51%
Female	51.6%	49%
Extension	25,098	25,666
Male	46.6%	51%
Female	53.4%	49%
Ethnicity		
White	77.1%	78%
African-American	18.3%	19%
Other	4.6%	3%

* N. C. Dept of Community Colleges, July 7, 1991.

** Ibid.

GTCC Student Ambassadors

The GTCC Foundation's first student ambassadors were selected in the spring of 1992 during the administration of Chairman B. G. Tweedy. That year they represented the College at more than 40 functions. Chosen for their communication skills, academic standing, and leadership qualities, the inaugural class included Luann Hubbard, Medical Assisting; Patsy Johnson, College Transfer; Steven Koger, Commercial Art; Jon Lagergren, Business Computer Programming; Tara McGuire, College Transfer, and Gail Smith, Paralegal Technology. Generally, eight Ambassadors are selected annually to assist faculty, staff and students during special events and are compensated with scholarships valued in 1999 at $650 a semester.[17]

ACCLAIM:
Creating a More Viable Community College Mission

Technical courses provided the "central theme" in Don Cameron's vision of a 21st century model of GTCC, but he was consistently rebuffed by outdated courses, obstinate faculty, students lacking the basic skills to satisfy hi-tech employers, and a shortage of modern equipment to train those students. It was obvious that faculty and staff needed additional training and indoctrination if they were to launch GTCC on a new era of workforce preparedness. The presidential strategy to elevate GTCC to a more productive level of service to the citizens of Guilford County began with his drive to have the College designated as a demonstration model for the ACCLAIM program, North Carolina State University's Academy for Community College Leadership Advancement, Innovation and Modeling in January 1992.[18]

This three-year Community College Leadership Program was funded by a W.K. Kellogg Foundation Grant and designed to strengthen and broaden the mission and role of 114 community colleges in the Carolinas, Virginia, and Maryland. GTCC was one of eight institutions designated as "models" to develop and implement educational strategies that would "make community colleges the catalyst for changing communities." Cameron was intent on transforming his institution into a major catalyst for economic development by training a cadre of change-agents and charging them to investigate the community's needs. ACCLAIM empowered the College to serve as a learning laboratory for leadership development for administrators, faculty and Trustees.

Fifteen GTCC faculty and staff participated in the first ACCLAIM Institute in October 1992.[19] The participants, including GTCC employees and community leaders from High Point and Greensboro, conducted a major study that identified workforce preparedness as an issue critical to Guilford County. This was one of the research instruments that would later link Cameron in an innovative partnership with Jerry Weast, the founding superintendent of the newly merged Guilford County Schools.[20] The ACCLAIM survey was subsequently merged with a chamber of commerce revelation that the greatest detriment to economic success in Guilford County was the lack of skilled workers. Cameron was progressively accumulating all the documentation he needed to create a modern workforce preparedness model for Guilford County, a topic further pursued in the following chapters.[21]

Campus Highlights 1991–92

GTCC centenarian and star scholar Estelle Eaton's story led the local TV news programs when the College presented its oldest student a custom-made three-foot-tall birthday cake ablaze with 102 candles during the September 5, 1992, College opening. Preschoolers from the GTCC children's center sang "Happy Birthday" as cameras from area newspapers flashed and TV crews videotaped the celebration. At the age of 93, the retired college teacher and administrator originally registered for oil painting classes at the Greensboro Washington Street Campus; nine years later she still enjoyed taking classes, writing poetry, and reading the works of Dr. Norman Vincent Peale.[22]

GTCC instructor Ken Vaughn was a finalist for the State Board of Community Colleges/First Union National Bank Award for Excellence in Teaching. Bobbie Van Dusen, a 1988 finalist, and Vaughn were honored by the Board for their instructional creativity.[23]

Statewide Bond Referendum: 1993

Department of Community Colleges President Robert W. Scott laid the ground work for one of the most significant educational bond referendums in North Carolina's history when he visited all 58 colleges late in 1992. At the December 17, 1992, GTCC Board session, he explained the legislative strategies that had been developed in response to legislative criticism that the system was consistently shortchanged on funding because it wasn't proactive. The positive responses from a legislative survey the Department subsequently conducted encouraged the system to request $311 million in a statewide bond referendum for capital construction.

One of the community college's strongest promotional points was the huge disparity between university and community college funding; out of every dollar spent for education from pre-school to graduate programs in the universities, the Community College System received a mere 7.9 cents. Scott's modest projection for an increase to 10 cents appeared almost pathetic based as it was on the premise that, if the system could get at least 10 cents from every dollar appropriated, it could at best escape its 50th ranking among states and move to 48th or 49th.[24] President Cameron, the Board, and the College devoted an enormous amount of time and energy to promoting the 1993 referendum beginning with an intensive letter writing campaign.

"Operation 10,000 Letters"

North Carolinians for Community Colleges, an organization based in Winston Salem, in association with the Department of Community Colleges, launched "Operation 10,000 Letters" in February 1993. The campaign was designed to inform legislators about community college needs and promote the statewide bond referendum. The first of three rounds of letters were mailed on March 1, 1993. Dr. Cameron implored Trustees, students, Advisory Board members, alumni, and associations to write legislators soliciting support for the system and specifically for GTCC. With enrollment in the state then approaching 750,000 and one out of six citizens enrolled in a program or course, community colleges were already issuing one out of five diplomas awarded in North Carolina. In addition, enrollment was expected to increase 21 percent within three years; more than 30 percent of the state's high school seniors were forecast to attend a community college.[25]

A Day in the Legislature

Nearly all of GTCC's Board members attended this event sponsored by the State Board of Community Colleges and North Carolinians for Community Colleges on Thursday, May 27, 1993. Thanks to this tremendous grassroots promotional campaign built on letters and handshakes, for the first time in the 30-year history of the system North Carolinians approved $250 million in construction funds for the state's 58 community colleges. The vote of confidence accompanied the recognition that many colleges, including GTCC, were at capacity.

GTCC earmarked its $7.7 million share to construct the 105,000-square-foot Applied Technologies Building, which would house state-of-the art classrooms and a gigantic 250-microcomputer lab; additional facilities included a 250-seat auditorium, training rooms for business and community groups, computer demonstration labs, a Computer Integrated Manufacturing Lab, three different Local Area Networks, and an Office Technology lab simulating a functioning office. Future construction, proposed as a part of the 1990 ten-year building plan, would utilize $9.1 million from that year's successful Guilford County bond referendum to construct a Service Careers Building and a Public Safety Building. The College would use another $2 million in county bond money to expand the Medlin Campus Center in 1994.[26]

Distance Learning

Distance learning, originating in marvelous strands of fiber optics, empowered GTCC to provide instruction from a specially equipped lab on the Jamestown campus to several locations in the county. The enormous transmission capacity of fiber optics enabled teachers and students to see others and communicate simultaneously. This revolutionary educational tool was installed in classrooms on the Jamestown, High Point, Greensboro, and Aviation

Center campuses at a start-up cost of $200,000; money the College hoped to recoup through savings on buildings and instructional costs.[27]

Total Quality Management (TQM)

President Cameron's determination to strengthen the College's ability to solve the escalating technological and social challenges of the 21st century made powerful training programs like Total Quality Management available to every employee. W. Edwards Deming created TQM after World War II to improve the production quality of goods and services. Most Americans did not take the concept seriously until the Japanese adopted it to resurrect their economy and dominate world markets by 1980. TQM principles applied to educational reform enabled institutions to redefine their roles, purposes, and responsibilities and train their leadership to address the attitudes and beliefs of staff and faculty to improve schools as a way of life.[28]

GPAC: Government Performance Audit Commission

The powerful emergence of Japanese business and industry and its effect on the United States economy also forced business, industry, and government to review their longtime practices. North Carolina's controversial 1993 Government Performance Audit Commission Study (GPAC) was the nation's first legislatively driven efficiency study of state government. The 27 member commission chaired by Daniel T. Blue, Speaker of the N.C. House, and Senator Marc Basnight, President Pro Tempore of the N.C. Senate, devoted 22 of the commission's 350 recommendations to community college governance.

GTCC's Board supported one recommendation that would have placed a moratorium on establishing new colleges and satellite campuses until the State Board of Community Colleges created a restructuring plan. The Trustees refused to support three others which would have significantly weakened community college boards; one would have empowered the State Board to "appoint" rather than to merely "approve" the presidents of community colleges; a second would have eliminated school board Trustee appointments; and a third would have authorized the State Board to review GTCC's programs with a goal of eliminating those programs considered unproductive, duplicative, unnecessary, and/or weak. The GPAC found that the Community College System was an excellent investment and valuable resource for economic development but was "chronically underfunded."[29]

1993: Guilford County School Systems Merge

The major historic event that exerted a positive influence on workforce preparedness reform in Guilford County and set the stage for a strong partnership between GTCC and the public school system occurred when the county's three systems merged in 1993 to form the Guilford County Schools. As journalist Ned Cline points out in his study of the workforce preparedness model developed in Guilford County, the merger cleared the way for Dr. Cameron to end four years of frustration resulting from his inability to get three vastly different public school systems to stop competing and start cooperating to confront the social, economic, and political changes threatening the area's past industrial successes.[30] He quickly bonded with Dr. Jerry Weast, the founding superintendent of the new system, who promised the GTCC Board that the Guilford County Schools would focus on enhancing technical teaching standards to prepare a new workforce in partnership with GTCC.[31]

Not waiting for industry and community attitudes to change, GTCC quickly upgraded its Tech Prep marketing by publishing a curriculum guide detailing courses of study for technically minded high school students.[32] Hosting a series of seminars, luncheons, and workshops for business and industry, and public school administrators, counselors, and teachers, the College introduced the Tech Prep concept by mailing information letters to the parents of 4,500 rising ninth graders. The Tech Prep Associate Degree program was revised in 1993 when the State Board of Education and the State Board of Community Colleges required local boards to approve and develop the program statewide.[33]

By developing a Youth Apprenticeship Program that successfully enrolled 23 students at companies including Dow Coming, Burckhardt America, Kerns Construction, TRW, L&O Body Shop, and Tri-Mac Electric, the College additionally promoted co-op education. This academic program enabled students to combine formal academic study with periods of practical work experience in business, industry, government, and service organizations. Thirty-two courses of study provided opportunities for students who compiled 13,538 working hours at 57 companies.

At the end of 1993, the Board was considering implementing a Physical Therapy Assistants program and studying the viability of adding Commercial Heating and Air Conditioning, a Veterinary Assistants Program, International Business, and Environmental Technology.

Don Cameron's broad offensive to reform GTCC, by positioning the College as an institution committed to workforce preparedness, was built in part on the Institution's ability to attract and implement innovative programs including ACCLAIM and TQM. The College became the Quality Center for the

N.C. Department of Community Colleges in April 1994 winning a three-year, $270,000 grant to establish the Carolina Quality Consortium (CQC). But, GTCC's greatest achievement in the mid 1990s remained the workforce preparedness initiative as defined by Tech Prep and the partnership with the newly merged Guilford County Schools.[34]

Chapter 24

1993–94
The Tech Prep Partnership

If our students receive the degree and go to work in a company at an entry-level position, then they need to be able to perform the tasks for the company. If they cannot perform, then we need to reexamine our curriculum.[1]

President Don Cameron

School-to-Work

The history of Don Cameron's mission (1993) to reform workforce preparedness in Guilford County with GCS superintendent Jerry Weast was documented by journalist Ned Cline (1998) in an unpublished paper and by Cameron and George M. Fouts in "Reforming Workforce Preparedness," in *The Leadership Dialogues: Community College Case Studies to Consider* (2004).[2] An in-depth historical analysis of this phenomenal initiative developed from private conversations and public partnerships remains to challenge future historians. One aspect of this provocative topic is that certain stratagems formulated in private discussions between Weast and Cameron were never explicitly recorded. Reliable records are equally vague on the topic with only a single reference to Tech Prep in the 1994 GTCC Board minutes, a crucial year in the partnership's developmental process.[3]

Whatever form a future investigation ultimately pursues, it cannot be presented in isolation from the social and educational history of Guilford County. In many respects workforce preparedness reforms in the 1990s were spawned by politics and school integration as much as by industrial needs for skilled employees and the changing industrial landscape.[4] The merger of the county's three public school systems inevitably demanded that white leaders become more socially conscious of the plight of the African American students and the poor whites they had previously hired, irrespective of their education, to fill menial labor positions in their plants.[5]

Don Cameron was arguably an expert analyst when it came to identifying Guilford County's strengths and weaknesses. He had been intently studying its industrial climate since arriving at Jamestown in 1981. By the late 1980s, he was distinctly aware that the county's traditional industrial giants, locally owned textile and furniture companies, were being absorbed by national and international conglomerates. Nontraditional clusters representing manufacturing, financial, and service industries were beginning to locate in the region. He was also aware that GTCC and her sister institutions were seriously failing to keep up, or cope with the tectonic industrial shifts impacting the state and its various regions.[6]

A lesser reform-minded administrator would have found the institutional morass at GTCC insurmountable, muddled by outdated courses, some faculty opposed to change, students lacking the basic education to succeed at the college level, and a shortage of equipment to train skilled workers, but Cameron persevered. By 1993–94, when Guilford County's 650 square miles harbored a population of 375,000 and a workforce of around 187,000 employed at 8,700 companies, GTCC had implemented continuous improvement leadership projects through ACCLAIM, TQM and CQC,[7]

Cameron's initial attempt to sell the public schools on the Tech Prep concept was hampered by the politics and personalities of the county's three premerger public school systems. Two of them were blatantly visionless, stubbornly ignoring the need to prepare the area's future workforce, a conclusion confirmed by an analysis of the movement of the county's high school graduates to GTCC. Fouts and Cameron argue, and most astute local observers would agree, that the chief mission of the three previous systems, in keeping with the vision of the wealthy and educationally elite School Board members prior to merger, was to prepare high school graduates for matriculation at four-year colleges. There was little focus, except in traditional terms, on vocational education, or preparation for technical careers.[8]

Not only had the systems lagged embarrassingly in integrating, but their timid leaders, preferring power to vision, fought merger relentlessly. Ironically, many of the same businessmen with a sizeable stake in the county's future economy, who complained about the public school's failure to prepare workers for their industries, fought to protect their institutional fiefdoms in Greensboro, High Point, and Guilford County from merger.[9]

Therefore, Guilford was one of the last North Carolina counties to merge its public school systems (K–12). The controversial 1993 process was accomplished through legislative mandate as opposed to a referendum. The unification, some 40 years after Brown versus Board of Education (1954), was shaded by an embedded hatred of integration. Merger actually stalled for a time the white middle-upper class flight from Greensboro and High Point school districts to the historically less integrated county schools. At the same time, the process forced the citizens of Guilford County to participate in a joint project for the second time in the region's history; the first being the countywide initiative to establish the Guilford Industrial Education Center.

College Tech Prep blossomed on the premise that high school graduates who did not intend to go to a four-year college took less rigorous vocational education courses and graduated unprepared for a technically oriented job market. Comparatively, Tech Prep helps high school teachers guide those students into more challenging technical courses and, ideally, to further training at a community college. Cameron and his Board had long expressed concern that a smaller percentage of local high school graduates enrolled at their local community college than did so in other North Carolina counties. While community leaders and industrialists often praised GTCC's technical and vocational programs, they also wondered if some of those programs needed to be revised or even deleted in favor of new programs created to respond to changing employment patterns.[10]

Merger convinced a few discontented industrialists to wonder if the newly consolidated school system, lead by a superintendent without historical ties to the region, might be amenable to instituting a bona fide program of technical preparation. These machinists confronted Jerry Weast with their concern at the same time he was discussing the topic privately with Don Cameron. Cameron was getting an earful from his own Board and several members of the new Guilford County Board of Education. Phenomenally, the concept of Tech Prep originated as the result of a number of dialogues occurring simultaneously in different venues, but the scope of the project was immense.[11]

Merger challenged Cameron to partner with a large (65,000 students; 8,000 employees; 14 high schools) public school system in a coordinated effort to improve workforce skills to cope with a rapidly changing economy. Because so many business leaders, chamber of commerce officials, and economic development leaders were involved in the daily life of GTCC, several as Trustees or members of the Foundation Board, and hundreds on the College's program advisory committees, Cameron felt that it was his job to develop an action plan.[12]

Given that GTCC had been criticized for presumably not graduating enough students with the proper skills to meet the present and future needs of area companies, Cameron had to rethink GTCC's position in the community before he launched his vision of workforce preparedness reform, a process that brought him face-to-face with GTCC's lack of image and respect.[13] By its nature, GTCC, unlike the covey of liberal arts institutions that smothered it, seemed only important to workers who really needed it to survive at crucial times in their productive lives, or dropouts at odds with the discipline and structure of public schools.

GTCC's students included the impoverished who could not leave the area, employees needing to upgrade their skills, service personnel needing certification, a variety of health care trainees, the physically and mentally impaired, dropouts, illiterates, and miscreants. The Institution that positioned itself as an "open door—all things to all people school" lacked widespread respect and educational focus as it wallowed in the vortex of industrial change.

These and other factors motivated Cameron to press his ideas for a possible joint Tech Prep initiative with GCS Superintendent Jerry Weast, himself a community college graduate. The partnership that emerged from their relationship was created in the trust of their bonding.[14] With strong support from Chamber of Commerce officials, Cameron and Weast launched a study of workforce preparedness issues in Guilford County. They assigned key staff members to the process and contracted with an outside marketing firm to analyze workforce issues. Cameron, who had frequently spoken in public about his views, felt that an impartial observer was needed to confirm, deny, or refine the positions he had already taken. The ensuing workforce preparedness assessment, which included more than 700 people in focus groups and telephone interviews, was one of the most comprehensive ever done in the county. Employers, chamber of commerce officials, managers of employment agencies, and high school graduates contributed their thoughts to the process.

The results indicated that the quality of local job applicants was low and that potential workers were deficient in "soft, or employability skills": responsibility, ethics, teamwork, problem solving, listening, and technical abilities. The survey further revealed that the county needed a better overall educational system and that a holistic approach involving business, parents, and the community was paramount to reform and change in the workplace. The study recommended a promotional campaign to publicize the survey results, incentives to create more participation by local businesses to enhance workforce preparedness, a plan to provide more cooperative education programs and jobs, and a concerted effort to help students get internships, apprenticeships, and shadowing experiences.[15]

Cameron, Weast, and their key staff worked with their Boards and principal business leaders to develop short- and long-term strategies to respond to the survey's recommendations. They developed a comprehensive plan under the umbrella-like Partnership for Guilford County Workforce Preparedness to form a Workforce Investment Council and created ten program-specific business councils. The comprehensive Tech-Prep program they implemented in all of the Guilford County public schools began with a career-awareness curriculum in the elementary schools, a career-exploration program in the middle schools, and a career-preparation focus in the high schools.

Tech Prep became a reality when GTCC and the Guilford County Schools signed a joint program agreement (1993–94). The College introduced business, industry, public school administrators, counselors, and teachers to the concept through a recommended series of seminars, luncheons and workshops. GTCC wrote 4,500 rising ninth graders to explain the program's concept, advantages, and expected outcomes. The Tech Prep Curriculum Manual designed by the College to help high school students choose their courses was eventually adopted as a model by the Community College System office.[16]

"School to Work" became an on going initiative. College Tech Prep inspired the development of a Youth Apprenticeship Program (1993–94) that began with 23 students working for six companies. Cooperative Education emerged as another school-to-work opportunity. This academic program enabled students to combine formal study with periods of practical work experience in business, government, and service organizations. Thirty-two courses of study enabled students to work with 57 local employers and compile a total 13,538 hours in valuable on-the-job experience.[17].

By 2003 the percentage of Guilford County high school graduates enrolling at GTCC had increased substantially since 2000 when 10 Tech Prep scholarships were awarded to 85 awarded in 2003. The 160 students enrolled in GTCC's cooperative education programs in 1999 were exceeded by 313 in 2003. CTP proved that many of the educational initiatives that define the entrepreneurial value of community colleges germinate from shifts in consumer interest and industrial production. They are created, mature to productivity and disappear, but more than a decade later the Tech Prep partnership lives and thrives.[18]

The following chapters will track Tech Prep through changes in the leadership of the Guilford County Schools and a major restructuring of Greensboro's leadership group. Meanwhile, those models of consistency, the High Point Partners and the High Point Chamber of Commerce, continue their commitment to a program that focuses on education and work force issues. In succeeding years, Cameron and GCS Superintendent Jerry Weast's successor Dr. Terry Grier, continued developing workforce training models for the 21st century by establishing the first Middle College at GTCC Jamestown where it was eventually reinforced by North Carolina Governor Mike Easley's "Learn and Earn" Program."[19]

NCIH: The North Carolina Information Highway

A multitude of continuous improvement projects propelled GTCC through 1993–94. The "GTCC Guaranteed Degree" assured students and employers that the College was committed to excellence; faculty and staff participated in the *Carolina Quality Consortium* (CCQ) while work force preparedness reforms were instituted through *School to Work* and *College Tech Prep*. Beyond these internal and external initiatives, the College continued its metamorphosis into the age of technology by linking with the North Carolina Information Highway, a major initiative of Governor Jim Hunt. By the fall 1994 quarter, at a cost of $115,000, the College had coupled a Jamestown Learning Resource Center (LRC) classroom with Greensboro's Washington Street Campus. Course offerings included Early Childhood Education, Real Estate, and Advanced Literature. The High Point Campus and Aviation Center were linked in January 1995.[20]

SACS Reaccredidation: 1993–94

Once again it was time for the ten-year oversight process crucial to sustaining GTCC's institutional credibility. Conducted by the Southern Association of Colleges and Schools (SACS), this massive evaluation certifies the College to issue financial aid for students and veterans and validates classes and credits for transfer. The lengthy procedure began in 1992 with the formation of a self study team composed of a ten member steering committee and subcommittees to evaluate GTCC's strengths and weaknesses. This visiting panel met with a cross section of the faculty and staff March 21–24, 1994, to determine if the College satisfied the accreditation criteria. They responded with 21 recommendations for improvement and, while GTCC was officially reaccredited in December 1994, President Cameron was less than pleased with the lengthy list of recommendations. Ten years later (2002) when the process began again, his demand that the GTCC team hold the recommendations to single digits resulted in a lone recommendation.[21]

The Carolina Quality Consortium: April 1994

CQC was a system wide initiative designed to expand and strengthen the implementation of continuous improvement concepts and practices in community colleges through collaboration and cooperation. As one of the "lead institutions," GTCC developed and conducted "train-the-trainer" programs that taught employees at each institution how to lead quality initiatives like "Building Quality Together." This GTCC project trained nearly every college employee to identify areas for improvement, provide research solutions, and implement change. The goal was to insure that the College piloted and instituted new measures to become more responsive to its customers. CQC was a Don Cameron strategy to streamline thinking and programming by forcing employees to rethink and recast their job to insure that the budding Tech Prep partnership with community leaders and the newly merged Guilford County Public School System was exceptionally productive.[22]

The GTCC Guaranteed Degree

The "GTCC College Graduate Guarantee" was another Cameron initiative, albeit a borrowed one, in what may have been one of his most creative years (1994). He was sold on the quality of instruction at GTCC to the extent that he decided to guarantee the value of a degree and to *personally* reimburse the College to retrain any student who returned to collect on the promise. The guarantee states: *GTCC graduates can perform in an entry level position directly related to their field of study; if graduates cannot perform that entry-level work, GTCC will retrain them during an additional tuition-free 10 hours at no cost to the employer.*

In order for the graduate to receive free training, the employer must (1) certify in writing that the employee is deficient in skills; (2) specify that deficiency within six months of employment, and (3) develop a written educational plan for retraining. GTCC joined Sandhills Community College as the second community college in the state to guarantee its graduates. As late as 2006, only two companies had returned their employees for retraining.[23]

State Budget Crisis: 1994–95

GTCC's determination to reform workforce preparedness and build on its 1993–94 institutional successes was seriously imperiled by what Vice President of Administration Services George Fouts termed as the "tightest state budget for fiscal 1994–95 that GTCC has faced in some time, maybe ever."[24] While the threat posed major challenges to GTCC's mission, the strategy devised to cope with the crisis serves as an excellent example of Fouts' management and leadership which had involved more faculty and staff than ever before in the budgeting process. Had he and his staff not cut approximately $228,000 in non-instructional costs, the College would have been forced to engage in a reduction-in-force by June 30, 1994.

The insightful administrator argued that the steady growth of college transfer enrollment during the past decade, coupled with the resulting budgetary increases that flowed to the College through the FTE operating formula, had masked some existing budgetary problems that only emerged when the FTE cushion disappeared. By June 16, 1994, Fouts and comptroller Rae Marie Smith, who would later succeed to Vice President, Administrative Services, conducted 29 budget review sessions in an effort to cover a $610,000 budget shortfall due in part to a loss of around 186 FTE (full-time equivalency students). They identified $400,000 in cuts that could be instituted without reducing the workforce, or affecting teaching and learning, and were devising a balanced budget to include a contingency. Dr. Cameron approved Fouts' recommendation to freeze all vacant or vacated positions, excepting critical instructional positions, and review requests for conversion of part-time or term positions to full-time and new positions.

Fouts knew that the long-term solution to the crisis involved rebuilding the FTE through recruiting and retention while monitoring the wide range of financial variables that impacted the Institution, but he had to first successfully navigate the College through the huge budget reduction without significantly affecting the classrooms, labs, shops and clinics that trained Guilford County's workforce. The tremendous changes in North Carolina's economy encountered in the mid 1990s would prevail through 2004–05 forcing the Institution to rely more than ever on its Foundation for critical support. [25]

GTCC Foundation: 1993–94

The Foundation approved $19,912 to fund a variety of projects; training for adjunct faculty in the physical science department, software and instructional materials for the job placement office, the development of a marketing package and data base for the High Point campus, the provision of staff development and resource materials on global diversity, professional development for part-time instructors in continuing education, financial aid for students in the Workers at Risk Program, seed money to publish an Association of Classified Employees' cookbook, the sale of which would raise money for an endowed scholarship. The Foundation additionally funded instructional supplies for the Substance Abuse Counselor Certification Program, supported GTCC's first Diversity Day and a weekend retreat for part-time instructors on the Greensboro campus.[26]

Campus Notes

Faculty members publishing books included Shanna Chastain, *Aerobics: A Guide for Participants*; Grace Ellis. *Textures: Strategies for Reading and Writing*; Carol Schmid, *Conflict and Consensus in Switzerland*; Dick Statham, *Experiments in Electricity*; and Sabrina Woodberry, *Economics: A Study of Markets*.[27]

The Aviation Maintenance Technology and Aviation Management technology programs at PTIA enrolled an average of 82 students per quarter as the demand for graduates exceeded the supply.

Greensboro's Price and Washington Street campuses averaged 305 Curriculum and Continuing Education classes and 4,542 students per campus per quarter. Courses were also available at 50 locations in the area. GTCC sponsored Real Estate Continuing Education Courses (1993–94) and contracted with the Guilford County Schools to offer effective teacher training, teacher performance appraisal, and mentor support training.

Small Business Assistance Centers in Greensboro and High Point provided counseling, training, and technical assistance through 98 educational programs. The centers worked with 1,398 clients and generated almost 23,000 hours of training.

GTCC High Point's 32 curriculum classes averaged 136 students per quarter; 40 literacy classes instructed 650 students and 155 continuing education classes enrolled 1,220 to 1,700 students per quarter.

3,991 students enrolled in at least one Basic Skills Class: 1,317 in High Point and 2,674 in Greensboro and the surrounding area. 142 students graduated from the Adult High School, 365 were awarded their GED and 116 students moved into curriculum programs.[28]

58-year-old "Chuck" Hayes who dropped out of high school in the 10th grade decided to earn his diploma after building Guilford Mills Inc., a Greensboro textile manufacturer, into a Fortune 500 company. Hayes presented the commencement address to more than 700 GTCC graduates when he received his diploma in August 1994. Hayes, who served on the GTCC Foundation Board and as a member of the UNCG Board of Trustees (1980–91, chairman 1983–89), died Sunday, July 21, 2002, in Myrtle Beach South Carolina and is remembered as one of GTCC's most ardent supporters.[29]

1993–94 Employment Data

Full Time	382
Part Time	20
Male	151
Female	231
Whites	284
African Americans	89
Native Americans	2
Hispanics	2
Asian/Pacific Islanders	55

1993–94 Student Enrollment Data

Curriculum Students	
Total	**10,755**
College Transfer	2,167
General Education	1,673
Technical	5,964
Vocational	951
Gender	
Female (52%)	5,578
Male (48%)	5,177
Race	
White (75%)	8,024
African American (22%)	2,415
Other (3%)	316
Residence	
Guilford County (74%)	7,984
Other NC Counties (24%)	2,579
Out-of-state (2%)	192
Attendance	
Day (70%)	7,437
Evening (30%)	3,318

1993–94 Student Enrollment Data (continued)

Extension Students	
Total	**22,055***
Literacy	4,143
Community Service	4,479
Occupational Extension	12,247
New & Expanding Industry	928
Human Resources Development	242
Self Supporting	1,038

GTCC Student Success

- 100% of nursing graduates passed the state nursing exam.
- 100% of dental hygiene graduates passed state and national exams.
- 100% of dental assisting graduates were placed in jobs within three weeks of graduation.
- 100% of law enforcement graduates passed the state exam
- Aviation program graduates passed 99.7 percent of the multi-part FAA Air Frame and Power Plants License exam.[30]

President Cameron and Mrs. Percy H. Sears, widow of the former Trustee Percy H. Sears, at the dedication of the Fountain on the Plaza at the front of Sears Applied Technologies Center, August 28, 2003.

Chapter 25

1995–96:
Rethinking Education

It's not just money that's needed. We all know that you can't solve anything by throwing money at it; you have to follow your dollars and get involved, too.

Marshall White Jr., President
CIBA Chemicals Division

Percy Sears: 1963–1995

1995 was a pivotal year for GTCC. The Board approved the College Tech Prep Partnership and planned the Public Safety complex and a Service Careers facility that evolved into the Koury Hospitality Center. Percy Sears, who chaired the Board's Facilities and Finance committee, concluded his spectacularly productive 31-year, ten-month reign on the Board on June 30, 1995. "I don't know of anybody who has done any more for this institution than Percy Sears," said Chairman James F. "Jim" Morgan in recognizing Sears's service. On October 19, 1995, the Board officially named the Percy H. Sears Applied Technology Center in his honor. This monument to one of the most intensely involved Trustees in GTCC's history would play a dynamic role in the education of the first Tech Prep students to matriculate at GTCC.[1]

GTCC's Problem Teens

The community college systems' mission in North Carolina is to serve adult students. These students are, number one, not adults, and number two, not behaving as adults.

Kitty Montgomery, Dean
GTCC High Point[2]

Amidst the positive advances in construction projects and workforce preparedness issues (1995), one of the Board's major distractions concerned a
challenge some of its sister institutions were successfully avoiding by refusing
to accept 16- to 17-year-olds. In GTCC's case, some of these students were accused of creating havoc on the Greensboro and High Point campuses. GTCC
administrators reported that:

> The problem had worsened in recent years because the Gillespie Educa-
> tion Center in Greensboro, the last alternative school to operate in Guil-
> ford County and a holdover from the former Greensboro Public Schools,
> had closed in 1992, and because judges routinely offered offenders the
> option of going to jail or attending classes at GTCC.[3]

Forsyth Technical Community College and Davidson County Community
College did not accept this age group in their Adult High School and GED
programs and similar institutions had instituted measures to cope with the
situation. The problem escalated on the High Point campus in the fall of 1994
when a dispute involving 21 teenagers, including 18 enrolled in GTCC's adult
high school program, spilled into the parking lot of a nearby restaurant where
one youth was reportedly badly beaten with a pool cue and another fired shots
into the air before police arrived. The problem was compounded by the fact
that administrators did not know if the students were high school dropouts,
or if they had been expelled for disciplinary reasons; either way, they were concerned that their unruly escapades were driving serious adult students from
the College.

It is unlikely that all of the 221 16- to 17-year-olds enrolled in the Adult
High School Program in 1994–95 were guilty of disruptive behavior. Instructor Frankie Lane, a future counselor, hoped that the College would not close
its doors to these students: "If we don't take them, what is going to happen between 16 and 18?"[4] Dr. Stuart Fountain, Chair of the Board's Curriculum
Committee and its Ad Hoc Committee discussed the issue with Guilford
County School administrators on January 5, 1995.[5] A few weeks later (January 23, 1995), an "Over-Sight Committee" including representatives of GTCC,
the Guilford County Schools, and the JPTA (Job Training Partnership Act) explored solutions with District Court Judge Lawrence McSwain.[6]

Dr. Karin Petit, GTCC Vice President for Continuing Education and Satellite Campuses, considered a number of options to alleviate the situation including (1) not admitting 16- to 17-year-olds from outside Guilford County;
(2) making these students wait six months instead of three after leaving the
public schools before allowing them to enroll; (3) admitting them only under
special conditions; i.e.: when a student has to work to support her/his family,

or is pregnant and (4) helping the Guilford County Schools and community agencies develop alternatives for this age group when they leave school for whatever reason.[7]

By law (2007), a high school student who is at least 16 years old can enroll in courses as a dual or concurrently enrolled student. Students who are 16 or 17 years old who have been suspended from a public or private secondary school for disciplinary reasons, or those who want to voluntarily enroll in Adult High School or GED classes must wait up to three months before they can be admitted to the College. Waivers associated with students enrolled in the three Guilford County Schools Early Middle College programs on GTCC campuses in Jamestown, High Point, and Greensboro (2007) enable students as young as 13 to enroll in college classes.[8] During 2005–06, 85 participants were enrolled in correctional programs and 164 participants had been referred to Basic Skills.[9]

College Tech Prep Update: February 16, 1995

Representatives of the Tech Prep Partnership updated the GTCC Board on the program's first 18 months when they attended the first Board session of 1995. Sylvia Anderson, the Guilford County Schools' Tech Prep specialist, discussed the graduation and post secondary educational requirements associated with the program. Dr. Sylvester McKay, GTCC Vice President for Curriculum and Instructional Technology, outlined the process that directed students into the two-year Associate Degree program and presumably into employment. Robert Mackey, co-owner-President of Burkhardt America, a maker of textile spinning machine parts, reviewed the industry apprenticeship dimension of CTP and thanked Superintendent Jerry Weast and President Cameron for instituting the program he and fellow machinists had suggested in 1993.[10]

School to Work — The CIBA Grant

GTCC was not operating in a vacuum when President Cameron launched his workforce preparedness initiative in 1991; economic drivers including the High Point and Greensboro Chambers of Commerce, the High Point Economic Development Corporation, the High Point Partners, and the Guilford County Economic Development Council were also primed to cope with the ongoing industrial production shift and the 21st century job market. Their mission to enhance teaching and learning was driven by statistics indicating that by 2000, 5 percent of the jobs would go to unskilled labor; 65 percent would be skilled; and 20 percent professional. "School to Work," the emerging system of educational and career development that threaded a career path through the elementary, middle, and high school curriculums, represented a major opportunity to train a new, empathetically skilled workforce. A program of this magnitude could only succeed if business and education partnered and that appeared to be happening in Guilford County thanks to a business leader who was an exemplary educational visionary.[11]

Dr. Marshall "Sonny" White, Jr., President of the CIBA Specialty Chemicals Division (High Point) and a future GTCC Executive Vice President, boosted the implementation of the School-To-Work program (February 1996) with a $136,000 grant from CIBA's Educational Foundation. The gift enabled GTCC and Guilford County Schools to incorporate work force preparedness skills and work-based learning into their current curriculums and tailor a three-year model to integrate new teaching skills and teamwork into the employability tests offered at the College. The grant additionally provided a professional development experience for 20 instructors (10 from GTCC, 10 from the public schools) to learn new strategies to teach employability in the workplace.[12]

The CIBA Grant was the catalyst that spurred overdue changes in teaching methods and skills training. Until that moment, virtually all college courses had been self-contained with little or no attempt to integrate one with the other. Soon, teachers were no longer working in isolation and students accepted the integrated courses as a collaborative effort to ensure employment! Dr. White was willing to help implement the changes in workplace training because the need existed and a cooperative effort was the only guarantee of success.

> This all just made good sense to us; the schools were working on the needs and we and other companies needed technically trained workers. GTCC had by far the best presentation on what needed to be done. We were willing to help, but now we've all got to keep the pressure on to insure continued success. We just wanted to help bring all the interested groups together.[13]

The CIBA grant further enabled GTCC to provide up to 45 scholarships for students in technical programs.[14] The College and the JobReady Partnership Council used an additional $220,000 grant from the national School-to-Work Opportunity Act (1994) to complete several emerging models of work force development and extend and adapt those models to other industry groups. By 1996, metal working and automotive servicing were in the advanced stages of implementing School-To-Work partnerships; the process-manufacturing and finance industries were in the intermediate development stage; and the health care, furniture, textiles, construction, and hospitality industries had expressed an interest in becoming involved in School-To-Work initiatives.[15]

The implementation grant mandated GTCC, the Guilford County Schools, and designated industries to partner in career development in the early grades where it provided intensive industry experiences for students from field trips and job shadowing to cooperative education and apprenticeships. The program was totally inclusive. Specially designed career development and work-based learning activities and components were suggested for students with disabilities, disadvantaged students, Native Americans, school dropouts, and other special populations.

General employability skills were integrated into the curriculum to change the classroom culture and measures were designed to evaluate a student's readiness to work. Finally, the partners were tasked to provide industry-based professional development for teachers, counselors, administrators, and workplace mentors to educate them to the necessity for change. School-to-Work was not a fly-by-night diversion and employability skills are continually emphasized in every program offered at GTCC. CIBA Specialty Chemicals also developed "GTCC and Workforce Preparedness: A GTCC Faculty Guide" that listed the 15 faculty members associated with the CIBA Cadre who created a model for the integration of "soft skills" into the curriculum.[16]

CLASS: Changing the Way GTCC Teaches

GTCC's vitality during the early years of the Cameron presidency can be monitored through a repetitive series of "continuous improvement concepts" that generated new teaching and learning initiatives; CLASS is a prominent example. When the College introduced Total Quality Management Training in 1994, some faculty questioned how TQM practices and concepts could be applied to the classroom. A committee of 12 instructors charged to answer that question titled the new instructional model they created CLASS (Continuous Learning Assures Student Success).[17]

CLASS was organized around (1) the concept of what a quality classroom should look like; (2) the development of teacher-learner teams utilizing learning styles and theories of multiple intelligences; and (3) improving instructional processes to make learning more active. CLASS advocated significantly decreasing lecture time to allow for increasing student involvement.

When Math instructor Jane Brandsma used her CLASS training to assign students to teams where they worked together on problems, presentations, homework, and tests, she saw a startling rise in grades and a major improvement in her retention rate. Brandsma initially found it difficult to change the way she taught and the team format required more work, but the improvement in student outcomes was worth the effort. While she reported that the students "looked at her like she was crazy," the results verified the value of this new "continuous improvement concept;" 85 percent of the students remained in class and the number of students making C or better increased 58 percent.[18]

Teaching Technicians to Write

GTCC's enviable record of successfully preparing students for work and life is built on Dr. Cameron's determination to achieve successful "outcomes." The CLASS model inspired English instructor Rita Gress to visit an automotive repair shop to research the amount and type of writing the job required of an automotive technician. Her field trip was a prerequisite to participating in a learning project with automotive instructor Rankin Barnes on ways to employ and improve the writing skills of automotive students. Gress's understanding of what was actually needed in the workplace contributed to the integration of academic and technical skills that assured the practical relevance of schooling.[19]

Business & Industry Services

You have an excellent community college in GTCC; they did a real nice job in helping us prepare employment training programs.
Tim Schira, HR Manager, Dana Corporation[20]

GTCC Business and Industry Services' director Bill Shore was thrilled by this endorsement from an automotive parts manufacturing company that had invested $27 million in Guilford County. The more than 150 training programs Shore's division provided to 90 companies (1995) improved the skills of nearly 5,000 area workers. Eleven new and expanding industries (NEIT) used the department's services to school nearly 1,200 people in cross training, in-plant problem solving, and pre-employment training and 95 percent of the department's programs were taught on-site.[21]

GTCC Foundation: 1994–96

Pam Hawley assumed the directorship of the GTCC Foundation (1994–95) and laid the groundwork for the Institution's first annual campaign. The initial $500,000 goal was destined to fund the College's most pressing needs including scholarships, equipment, grants, faculty training, and emergency loans. Hawley launched the campaign in August 1995 with a faculty and staff fund drive that surpassed its goal on the way to raising $511,151 by June 1996. The total number of donors contributing to the College increased 401 percent, from 171 to 686 including 468 first-time donors. The ensuing 1995–96 faculty and staff grants improved a basic skills classroom in High Point, added multimedia instructional equipment to the dental programs, funded the purchase of dental chairs and equipment for the Dental Hygiene and Dental Assisting programs, and financed a multimedia workstation for the library.[22]

Project Goal: The Cline Observatory

The first trained astronomer in the Community College System began teaching at GTCC under less than optimum conditions in the fall of 1990. Aaron Martin's first classroom was a physics lab and limited observing sessions were scheduled in selected parking lots. Students physically lugged the telescopes to their observing sites, but the risk of damage made it virtually impossible to use some of the delicate equipment. While they could occasionally use the Three College Observatory, a consortium facility owned by neighbor institutions, these limitations made it difficult for the students to gather data from direct sources.

Martin introduced his ambitious vision of an Observational Astronomy Laboratory (GOAL), to the Board on April 20, 1995. A committee formed to seek funding for the project included representatives from local colleges and universities, the public schools and scout troops. J. Donald Cline, a founding partner in Micro Computer Systems, represented the business sector. Cline, whose interest in astronomy dated from childhood when he built his own telescope, pledged $100,000 to the project and a gracious Board granted him full approval rights for the design of the building including the interior layout, excepting only the selection of the telescope and furnishings.[23] The Cline Observatory was dedicated on October 23, 1997. Under the guidance of founder Martin, whose family contributed significantly to its funding, and his successor astronomer Tom English, the Cline Observatory has continued to educate GTCC students and the community with a stimulating variety of research-oriented programs. The Friends of the Cline Observatory reinforced the Astronomy program measurably in 2006 when they dedicated a scale model Solar System Walk on the Jamestown Campus.[24]

Consortium Agreements

GTCC (1995–96) participated in a number of consortium agreements as it pursued creative ways to respond to the demands of its service area and neighboring community colleges. This regional innovation provided an alternative to duplicating programs and allowed the FTE to be prorated to institutions based on their contributions. The Emergency Medical Science agreement with Surry Community College obligated Surry to provide the instructional facilities, marketing, testing, and General Education courses for 40 percent of the FTE, while GTCC received 60 percent for providing the accredited program and its curriculum design, evaluation, faculty, and advising. Other agreements were arranged with Durham Technical Community College and Rockingham Community College.[25]

Enrollment: 1994–95

The fall quarter consistently reflected GTCC's largest enrollment totaling 6,607 (1994); 52.4 percent in technical education programs; 23.5 percent in the College Transfer program; 16.5 percent in General Education, and 7.6 percent in vocational education for a total FTE of 5,184. FTE was determined by dividing the number of student hours in a quarter by 176, the time a typical student would attend class, 16 hours a week for 11 weeks.

By comparison, the 1995 fall quarter enrollment (6,447) registered roughly identical percentages in Technical, College Transfer, General Education, and Vocational programs for a total 5,112 FTE. The College experienced slightly declining enrollments from 1992 until winter 1996, when enrollment appeared to stabilize.[26]

A ten-year comparison with the academic year 1985–86 indicates statistical changes in the enrollment pattern including the ratio of males to females and minority enrollment, which increased 7 percent from 21 percent to 28 percent (1994–95) and to 37 percent by 2006.[27]

Curriculum Students: 1994–95

Day	72.0%
Night	28.0%
Employed	75.0%
Female	52.5%
Male	47.5%
Guilford County	97.0%
Ages 18–24	51.0%
Ages 25–34	27.0%
45+	8%
Total Enrollment	**10,382**

Extension Students Served: 1994–95*

25 yrs of age or older	50%
Employed full- or part-time	91%
Enrolled full-time	35%
Married	53%
Minorities	21%
Guilford County Resident	86%
Basic Skills	3,554
Occupational Extension & Other	18,381
Male	51.6%
Female	48.4%
Total Enrollment	**21,935**

*PAR 1985–86; 1994–96, p. 12.

1995–96 GTCC Profile

GTCC served nearly 32,000 students annually on three campuses with total operating revenues of $29,261,249. Its 455 permanent full- and part-time employees, ranging from public safety officers to instructors, child care workers to administrators, and house-keepers to grounds-keepers, were 76 percent white, 22 percent African-American with other races numbering 2 percent. The gender breakdown revealed 58 percent female and 42 percent male employees. [28]

Summary

The persistent battle of the budgets did not deter President Cameron and his staff from the College mission. The individual success stories emanating from GTCC's Guided Studies program directed by Jane Stilling won the 1994 John Champaign Award presented to the outstanding developmental program in the nation by the National Association for Developmental Education (NADE).[29] For an institution that had survived a half million dollars in budget cuts in a three-year period and was destined to be featured in the *Wall Street Journal*, GTCC reigned as an exceptional model of fiscal management and programmatic integrity.[30]

While Guilford County (1995) was in the process of reforming education, more than 100 local executives listened as journalist Hedrick Smith discussed his best-selling book about the global changes in work place needs. *Rethinking America* offered insights on the changing complexion of job skills and the need to align school curriculums to match employment opportunities. Smith's thesis provoked the industrialists' interest in a broad range of apprenticeship programs and strategies to create new workplace skills, topics that Don Cameron and Jerry Weast were already busily planning and implementing.[31]

Campus Notes

GTCC became a multi-campus college when its Greensboro facilities qualified in recognition of services offered and students served. Dr. James Wingate, a former vice president of student development (1984–88), returned to the College (1996) to serve as campus Dean.[32]

The Upholstery program's mission changed dramatically in 1995 when furniture manufacturers again needed talented upholsterers. GTCC revamped the curriculum, hired a new instructor and began training people for specific industry jobs. A classroom designed as a plant floor assured a smooth transition to industry for students who completed the program.

GTCC High Point had historically offered certification courses for drug and alcohol abuse counselors that did not count toward a degree, but the increasing need for trained counselors, and requests from current counselors who wanted to earn a degree, led to the creation of a Drug and Alcohol Technology (Now Human Services Technology) program (1995). Credits earned in the two-year Associate Degree program count toward a four-year degree at High Point University and the University of North Carolina at Greensboro.[33]

Chapter 26

1996–97:
GTCC and the *WSJ*

It's nice to feel excited about what I'm doing. Students are excited. We have begun to make connections among the courses. Like the oatmeal commercial said: It's the right thing to do.

Dr. Carolyn Schneider, Chairperson[1]
Division of Arts and Sciences

Partnerships: "The Magic Wand"

President Cameron's campaign to forge partnerships with the education and corporate communities was "the right thing to do," but it was a geographically unrestricted project. Enthused by the letter of agreement he signed with VOLVO following a trip to Sweden (January 19–26, 1996), Cameron announced a collaboration with the car, truck, and bus giant to establish a faculty and student exchange program oriented toward technical careers and a diesel engine repair program.[2]

Twenty months later (September 24, 1997) he returned to Jamestown from a flight to Shenyang, China with two more international working agreements in his pocket. Located in northeastern China, Shenyang was a highly industrialized city and the country's fourth largest with a population of 6.8 million. GTCC and Shenyang University agreed in principle to exchange instructors on a regular basis, share information about educational issues and cooperatively assist North Carolina companies interested in pursuing business opportunities in China. Cameron signed a similar pact with a second Shenyang institution, the United Employees University Commerce College.[3]

Monetarily partnerships were more substantial when the Moses H. Cone Memorial Hospital (Moses Cone Health Systems, Inc.) granted GTCC

$100,000 grant to institute the Physical Therapy Assistant program; a similar grant from the Duke Power Company (Duke Energy) supported the Culinary Technology program destined for the forthcoming Koury Hospitality Center.[4]

PTCAM Apprenticeship Program

Since the presidential mission to make GTCC's curriculum relevant and integrated demanded a team approach, Cameron recruited Gerald Pumphrey (1996), the former director of Tech Prep for the N.C. Community College System, as GTCC's Director of Workforce Preparedness and Department Chair, Transportation. Pumphrey was charged to make sure that PTCAM, a metals-working cooperative apprenticeship program and the model for future cooperative programs, worked to the partnership's mutual satisfaction; he was also assigned to direct the College Tech Prep program.[5]

Guilford County School superintendent Jerry Weast partnered with Cameron to hire Eleanor Herndon to monitor the apprenticeship program's success.[6] By way of background, PTCAM, (Piedmont Triad Center for Advanced Manufacturing, 1993), was the first major career program for high school students that provided skills training the public schools and GTCC did not initially teach. It became the model for integrating technical training into high schools through apprenticeships in metal working combined with opportunities to enroll at GTCC for further training under the sponsorship of private companies. Pumphrey shared the concept of PTCAM and College Tech Prep with journalist Ned Cline.

> We felt the apprenticeship experience gave us the most control over quality because it was the most structured way of putting a student in the workplace. We gambled that if we did that and business leaders had a positive experience with students, then over time they would learn other things. Once you get a relationship between businesses and students, there is some excitement. It personalizes the experience. Having industries do the recruiting also showed the business representatives the students were unprepared for the message given, so businesses now want to get more involved at earlier grade levels.[7]

More than 200 guests provided testimony to PTCAM's importance when they attended a dinner recognizing 23 metal working apprentices in August 1996.[8] It was obvious to Pumphrey, whose administrative successes would lead to his promotion as the school's chief academic officer (Dean of Instruction, 1998),[9] that the concept of offering innovative programs below the 12th grade was connecting with students who needed direction to select a trade. Programs that steered them toward a practical education were particularly effective to those not planning to attend a four-year college. The model's structured introduction to the adult world of work earned the respect of N.C. Community College System president Martin Lancaster.

> It is a model for the rest of the state. I can't imagine one any better. A key to the success has been the relationship forged between Don Cameron and Jerry Weast. If you could wave a magic wand over the state and use Guilford County as the model, that would be great. A demonstration of what they have done is needed in all other community colleges. Guilford has just grasped the need for these kinds of programs more quickly than others."[10]

The workforce preparedness initiatives Cameron and Weast originated attracted a $3.1 million pledge from the Greensboro Development Corporation (GDC) in June 1996 to support apprenticeships and two years of full College Tech Prep scholarships.[11] By 1997 students were taking metal working courses at the Weaver Education Center in Greensboro and at High Point Central High School thanks in part to a $219,592 Job-Ready-School-to-Work grant (May 1997).[12] Late that same year, Dr. Cameron reported that 10 PTCAM metals program graduates were enrolled at universities, two at GTCC, and several were working outside their field.[13] By 2002, the machining industry's need for metal workers had declined and the PTCAM apprenticeships were phased out; GTCC, the Guilford County Schools, and the business community formed a Business Committee in Metals Manufacturing and began offering scholarships to high school graduates.[14]

College Tech Prep Update

This more broadly based school-to-work program prospered from its notoriety earning GTCC and its partners, the Guilford County Schools and the Greensboro Area Chamber of Commerce, the R.J. Reynolds Tech Prep Marketing Award (1997) for outstanding marketing and recruiting materials. GTCC was selected a Bellwether Award Finalist (1998) in Instructional Programs and Services for its "College Tech Prep Apprenticeships program." The Nine College Tech Prep Programs created in 1998 included Automotive Technology; Banking and Finance; Chemical Process Technology; Culinary and Food Service Technology; Electrical Trades; General Construction; Heating, Ventilating, and Air Conditioning; Heavy Equipment and Transport Technology; and Metals Manufacturing.[15]

Total enrollment in College Tech Prep courses in the Guilford County Schools by spring 1998 reached 1,160. At the same time, *85* students were working directly in youth apprenticeships, 502 in cooperative education and 245 in internships for a total of 832 in some form of work-based learning.[16] CTP continued to thrive (2000–06) under the direction of GTCC Workforce Preparedness Director Bill Eversole. Of the 472 tuition awards Eversole offered in 2005–06, 192 were accepted. The program is infinitely valuable to the county in terms of students served, FTE, Pell Grant monies accrued, and GTCC programs bolstered by this exemplary workforce preparedness initiative.[17]

October 1996: Cameron Says No to the Sunshine State

Don Cameron concluded his fifth year at the helm of GTCC (1996) with a series of accomplishments that significantly elevated his reputation locally, nationally, and internationally. In the midst of this educational success, he was called to head a prestigious Florida community college. It was an outstanding opportunity he wisely abandoned after it sparked a racially tainted debate in the Sunshine State.[18]

The turbulent flirtation with Florida Community College (FCCJ) in Jacksonville is not a memory Cameron relishes, given that the opportunity went further south than he could have imagined. At one point, he was inclined to make the move to a position for which he had been recruited without applying. It was obvious that some FCCJ officials wanted him because they offered a $50,000 increase beyond his $104,612 GTCC salary, but according to Cameron, this job wasn't just all about the money; "I told my family if we go down there, I want to be buried in Guilford County. They said, 'then why are we going?'"[19]

While Cameron pondered his future, to the consternation of his family and most of the business and industry leaders in Guilford County, controversy over his proposed hiring erupted in Jacksonville. After his approval by a 5–3 vote over two African-American candidates, the FCCJ Board Chair informed him that "his selection had raised concerns by many of the city's African-Americans." Cameron, who cherishes his commitment to diversity, was uncomfortable with the split and asked to personally present his case to those opposing his candidacy.

> My real purpose was to try to convince the other three dissenters to come back and vote unanimously; two Board members refused. At the time I was in negotiations (there) my Board here was talking with me; 'Don, why would you want to go to Jacksonville on 5–3 when you have a 12–0 here?' I believed that this college (GTCC) had a lot to offer and this was the best fit."[20]

Meanwhile, in Jacksonville, the private meeting FCCJ Chairman John Wiggins had arranged with Cameron to enable the opposition to express their concerns over his hiring, prompted another Board member Howard Kelley to charge that the selection process had been "tainted" and demand an investigation by Florida's Ethics Committee. More concerned than ever about the intensifying controversy over his selection, Cameron withdrew his name prior to engaging in contractual negotiations. "To the great relief and pleasure of local business and education leaders," he emerged from the political maelstrom to resume fleshing out his vision for GTCC.[21]

Cameron's decision to forego the presidency of the 10th largest community college in the U.S. was crucial to the future of workforce preparedness in Guilford County. It meant that he and Guilford County Schools' superintendent Jerry Weast could continue their partnership to prepare students for productive employment through course work, internships, and apprenticeships. These strategies were critical to economic development in a region transitioning from a manufacturing-based economy to one based on knowledge. Days after Cameron turned down the Florida job, GTCC made the front pages of the prestigious *Wall Street Journal*. [22]

The Wall Street Journal: Tuesday, November 26, 1996

I think that GTCC has finally reached a milestone, that we have demonstrated we are a major player in economic development in the county, and that we have been recognized as a leader.

President Don Cameron

WSJ reporter Fred R. Bleakley's "Ready to Work" article fortuitously elevated GTCC's national and international reputation. Elaborating on what he described as "the war between the states over economic development," Bleakley observed that, "while some states were relying on economic incentives like tax breaks to attract companies, community colleges were North Carolina's secret, but often successful job training weapon, to attract and keep manufacturing companies."

In Guilford County, halfway between Charlotte and Raleigh, Guilford Technical Community College turns out a steady supply of graduates in more than 50 fields while racing to update its curriculum and equipment as business needs change.

GTCC largely explains why the thriving county's per capital income has quintupled in 20 years to more than $22,000, why cutbacks in textile, furniture, and tobacco work forces have gone so smoothly and why the unemployment rate is only 3.5 percent. Non-agricultural employees in the county now total 253,000, up from 140,000 in the early 1970s.[23]

The author credits GTCC's partnerships with Japanese filmmaker Konica, the Dutch pharmaceutical company Banner Pharmacaps, Inc., and Convatec, a subsidiary of Bristol-Meyers Squibb, as examples of North Carolina's policy of offering free custom training in the specific skills needed by certain industries.

> To students, GTCC offers the prospect of a good job at a tuition cost of less than $1,000 a year for full-time students. That is why GTCC's three campuses are packed with 10,000 students each day. A walk around the main campus, a sylvan 100 acres in Jamestown, just outside Greensboro, is like a tour through a commercial website. One path leads past a new Applied Technology Center, which houses 800 computers. Another goes by a Transportation Complex, where a Volvo AB truck-making unit is funding a new diesel repair program and General Motors Corp. and Ford Motor Co. are relying on GTCC to train technicians in computer diagnosis of engine problems. Along the way are Dental Science and Business Career Buildings and signs pointing to Furniture Hall, Packaging Center and Machinery Hall."[24]

It was a "heady" moment for GTCC, but Cameron tempered the effusive commendation by attributing GTCC's success to industry research that convinced the College to redesign its instructional programs to graduate workers with the precise skills local industry needed. He credited GTCC's partnership with the Guilford County Schools and superintendent Jerry Weast as an additional factor in attracting the interest of the *WSJ*. Economic developers characterized the article as a "godsend," and local reporters observed that, "the Community College System is the key tool for luring industry, and the article seemed to validate the system's value."[25]

The *WSJ* article elicited tens of thousands of dollars in free publicity for the College. The superintendent of the Mobile, Alabama, school system visited Jamestown to discuss workforce preparedness and invited Cameron and Weast to discuss their partnership in his city; an additional invitation was forthcoming from Baton Rouge, Louisiana. Visitors from Connecticut toured the campus and queries arrived from Mexico; a New Yorker donated $2,000 to the College and requested information that would enable him to contribute to the Foundation.[26] The results of the Cameron-Weast partnership were immensely gratifying, but it would take teams of equally motivated administrators to insure that the initiatives they instigated were successful. The *Wall Street Journal* article capped a highly productive 1996 and set the cadence for a march toward the future.

GTCC's President's Leadership Seminar: March–April 1997

Don Cameron's ongoing commitment to elevating community college leadership, and his early inspiration for "succession planning," framed the seminar that succeeded ACCLAIM, the N.C. State University program that had runs its course. The inaugural seminar was moderated by Dr. Jonas F. "Jeff" Hockaday, Cameron's mentor at Central Carolina Technical College (Sanford), and a former president of the Virginia Community College System. Two of the twenty GTCC employees who participated in his first President's Leadership Seminar (March 31–April 4, 1997), discussed their experience with the Board; Sandie Kirkland, Director of MIS (Management Information Services), was excited to learn how GTCC operated at the local, state and national level. She enjoyed the opportunity to meet national leaders, community college presidents, and the chance to bond with her colleagues. GTCC Greensboro campus dean Bill Geter was impressed by the caliber of the speakers and the general quality of the program. [27]

The President's Leadership Seminar, produced at a cost of between $20–$25 thousand and sponsored by the GTCC Foundation, continued on an annual basis through 2000 when it became a biennial event. It is conducted in a highly desirable venue, the Grandover Resort in Greensboro. A major innovation was instituted in 2005 when GTCC's new Department of Organizational Development assigned volunteer PLS graduates to four major LEAD teams charged to pursue projects that would allow them to positively demonstrate their leadership skills to the advantage of the College. The precedent setting teams focused on the institutional initiatives; "Creating the Learning College", "Marketing/Branding," "Preparation of Tomorrow's Workforce" and "Achieving the Dream."

A Race to the Wire: Don Cameron's Bid for the NCCCS Presidency

The only job I would ever consider is the president of the Community College System."
GTCC President Don Cameron (1996)[28]

Eight months after saying no to Florida Community College, Cameron was one of three front runners gleaned from a pool of 60 applicants, for the Presidency of the North Carolina Community College System. The surprising vacancy occurred when Lloyd "Vic" Hackley resigned after less than two years on the job. Hackley had reportedly struggled in the limited role of president in a system where 58 colleges operate independently and the president has no say in personnel issues. His so-called "tense dealings" with legislators prodded the search committee to pick a candidate with "political finesse."[29]

This perceived need for a professional politician may have ultimately tilted the office toward former congressman (1987–95) Martin Lancaster, then assistant secretary of the Army for Civil Works (US Army Core of Engineers); the third finalist was Marvin Joyner, president of Central Carolina Community College. There is no denying that Cameron, basking in the aura of a national media blitz and his election to the Board of Directors of the American Association of Community Colleges (AACC),[30] was a strong candidate; search committee member Phil Kirk was quoted as saying; "workforce preparedness is probably the single biggest issue facing our system and (Cameron) is strong on that issue;" it should be noted that Cameron, never a political neophyte, was serving at the time as an advisor to the legislative committee of the State Board of Community Colleges.[31]

GTCC Board chairman James F. "Jim" Morgan, who had reportedly discouraged Cameron from taking the Jacksonville post, joined other Board members in supporting Cameron for the position while admitting that, "It would be a big loss to GTCC, but it's not like he is leaving the state." Guilford County Schools' superintendent Jerry Weast, Cameron's partner in their workforce preparedness initiative, suggested that Cameron's "hands on" management style would earn him nothing but frustration in the job that paid almost $150 thousand; "I've seen his eyes light up when he visits students in the workforce preparedness programs. The new role he's a finalist for is different. It's not as much as a practitioner; it's more political. I think he'd really miss being president (of GTCC)."[32]

> I head the largest engineering firm in the world (Army Corps of Engineers) and I am not an engineer. Now, I am going to lead an education system, but I am not an educator.
>
> Martin Lancaster, May 16, 1997[33]

The State Board of Community Colleges chose Martin Lancaster, the one finalist without educational experience, to preside over the North Carolina Community College System at a salary of $155,000. It was far from the worst day in Don Cameron's life, as a matter of fact, it may have been the best; at least that was the message conveyed by the 250 supporters who greeted him with a surprise party when he returned to Jamestown from Raleigh where he was invited to hear the announcement of Lancaster's appointment.

"I thought I had a good shot at it." Cameron was disappointed, but in the final analysis, he believed that the decision favored the candidate with the most political experience. Weast's perception that the system presidency would have made Cameron miserable was a reasonable assumption; he is his own man, a calculating, determined, focused visionary who knows how to navigate his ship, the courses to pursue, and where to dock. Don Cameron came home to Jamestown to stay on May 16, 1997, and, as the accomplishments of the next decade would prove, it was the best decision he could have made for himself, his family, the College, and the people of Guilford County.[34]

Implementing the Semester System: August 21, 1997

The semester calendar was instituted at GTCC 11 years after the Board restated the school's need for the scheduling system (1986) and 14 years (1983) after GTCC became a comprehensive community college. It allowed the College to conveniently schedule the classroom hours that had been compressed into an 11 week quarter with 5-hour classes into a 16 week semester with a three-hour per week format. Credits would no longer have to be translated from quarter hours to semester hours; they would simply transfer as they were recorded. The process trotted through the Community College System for two years allowing instructors time to incorporate new technology into their syllabi and align their courses with those of the four-year institutions. The semester system provided students greater options in selecting course work and more flexibility in transferring even as it reduced the internal and external expenses associated with the quarter system.[35]

GTCC High Point: JobLink Career Center

GTCC introduced a highly beneficial community service when it established a JobLink Career Center at GTCC High Point (October 1997). The one stop resource for job seekers offered placement and application assistance, coaching in resume writing, interviewing, job search training, and basic skills development. During its first year (1998), the center served an average of 7,090 clients per month and succeeded in placing an average of 125 clients per month in new jobs. The founding partnership included GTCC; the Department of Social Services; JTPA (Job Training and Placement Act), the Employment Security Commission, the Community Action Program, Vocational Rehabilitation and the Guilford County Schools.[36]

Summary

GTCC planned to celebrate its 40th anniversary in 1998 and launch initiatives that would propel the College to a brighter and more productive future

in the 21st century. Dr. Cameron would announce plans to establish the Larry
Gatlin School of Entertainment Technology; controversy would surround a
proposed 2000 bond issue for the College, but executive vice president George
Fouts would mobilize the community and the GTCC family and Guilford
County voters would once again resoundingly support GTCC at the polls. A
major economic downturn would mar the millennium, but the College would
respond with innovative programs like "Putting the Piedmont Back to Work"
and "Quick Jobs with a Future."[37]

Campus Notes[38]

The GTCC Board of Trustees presented the 1996 Teaching Innovation
Award to Mathematics instructor Jane Brandsma for applying cooperative learning techniques to her algebra course.

Dr. Linda Thomas-Glover, Department Chair for Physical Sciences,
won the 1997 Teaching Innovation Award for creating the Associate in
Applied Science Degree in Chemical Processing Technology.

Accounting instructor Merilyn Linney, a recipient of the 1997 GTCC
Excellence in Teaching Award, was a finalist for the North Carolina Community College Excellence in Teaching Award.

Vince Williams, Automotive Department Head and GM ASEP Coor-
dinator/Instructor for the General Motors Service Technology Group at
GTCC, won the "1997 National ASEP College Instructor Award of
Merit."

The Trustees busily broke ground in February for the 45,000-square-
foot Public Safety Building and hefted the shovels again in October to
scuff the soil for the 53,000-square-foot Koury Hospitality Center. The
Cline Observatory was completed thanks to $166,000 in grants and sci-
ence labs were renovated at a cost of $1.05 million. GTCC's 1996–97 total
operating revenues and expenditures totaled $32,768,549.[39]

The full-time staff and faculty numbered 448 including 192 full-time
instructors. The part-time instructional faculty totaled 339 of the school's
381 part-time employees.

Student Enrollment	
College Transfer	26.18%
General Education	14.12%
Technical	59.7%

Student Body	
Day Classes	73%
Night Classes	27%
Employed	77%
Female	52.6%
Male	47.4%
Minority	32.%

Curriculum Students By Age	
18–24	43%
25–34	32%
35–44	16%
45+	9%

Chapter 27

1958–98:
40 Years of Building Futures

I give you my commitment, and that of the Board of Trustees, that GTCC will continue its long tradition of providing the best educated workforce a community could ever want. I challenge each of you, faculty and staff, to continue this strong support. By working together, we will be able to meet the challenges of the next millennium.

President Don Cameron
Founders' Day, April 3, 1998

GTCC Anniversary Profile: 1998

The fourth largest of North Carolina's 58 community colleges launched its anniversary commemoration, "Forty Years of Building Futures," with a Charter Day Legislative Reception on April 3, 1998.[1] The celebration expanded during the fall semester when North Carolina Poet Laureate Fred Chappell (1997–2002) delivered a distinguished lecture series. Chaired by Shanna Chastain, Division Chair, ICET, "Showoff Saturday" (October 24, 1998) attracted hundreds to a variety of interactive demonstrations on the Jamestown campus.[2]

From an institutional perspective, the superior Board leadership that guided GTCC across the last three turbulent decades of the 20th century seldom wavered after the unfortunate public expose of the quarrel between the president and chairman of the Board in 1967. Board Chair James F. "Jim" Morgan (1995–98) and Charles A. "Charlie" Greene (1998–2001), who guided the Trustees during the era committed countless hours to approving institutional polices, programs and facilities. Respected leaders in their various Guilford County communities, they were the insightful navigators charged with transitioning the College through the social, political, and industrial challenges that accompanied the millennium.

Board Chair James F. "Jim" Morgan (1995–98), who assumed the chair from fellow High Pointer Charlie Greene (1992–95) is a prime example of the quality of leadership GTCC had profited from since the Institution was rejuvenated during the chairmanship of H. Frank Starling (1967–69). Morgan, who left the Board on June 30, 1998, after eight years, presided during the construction of the Sears Applied Technologies Center, the Public Safety building, the Cline Observatory, and the Koury Hospitality Center. He directed the acquisition of land for expanding the High Point campus, was closely involved in the workforce preparedness initiative, the implementation of College Tech Prep, the youth apprenticeship program and distance learning. Lt. Governor Dennis Wicker recognized Morgan's contributions to GTCC during the June 18, 1998, Board session.[3] Around 10,000 students enrolled in curriculum programs during GTCC's 40th year; 7,891, the largest contingent historically, registered for the fall 1998 semester and nearly 23 thousand others signed up for continuing education courses.[4] The full-time workforce of 448 included 192 faculty augmented by approximately 350 part-time instructors. Driven by nearly $2.5 million in partnerships and resources, GTCC was a major force in Guilford County's workforce preparedness initiative. These impressive figures contradicted troubling statistics in a year that saw the U.S. plummet from 31st to 49th in world literacy and state appropriations to community colleges decline by 32 percent as traditional funding sources diminished.[5]

The addition of 19 new programs in 1998 increased GTCC's offerings to more than 100 degree, certificate, and diploma programs. Some notable additions included Chemical Process Technology reinforced by a $125 thousand grant from Dow Corning,[6] Biotechnology, GIS/GPS Technologies, Human Resource Management, and Physical Therapy Assistant. It was a banner year for Continuing Education with an estimated 20 thousand students registering for more than 1,000 classes taught at GTCC campuses and locations throughout the county.[7]

Facilities: 1998

Without a financial obligation for the Institution, GTCC exchanged the J.C. Price Complex for the Washington Street facility.[8] The College dedicated its $4.5 million state-of-the-art Public Safety Building on June 18, 1998, and the facility hosted its first students that fall for the Criminal Justice programs, Emergency Medical Science, Fire Protection Technology, and Surgical Technology. The building increased GTCC's space on five campuses to approximately 800,000 square feet.[9]

Following the relocation of Guilford College Road to the east of the Jamestown campus, the College built a Fire Science Demonstration Building and a Public Safety Driving Track on a 16-acre training site.[10] The Board's Finance and Facilities committee began tentatively considering a Technical Education Center (April 1998) that would house most of the ICET(Industrial, Construction and Engineering Technologies) programs and eventually anchor the future GTCC Greensboro campus on East Wendover Avenue.[11]

Mary Perry Ragsdale Family YMCA

The Board approved a partnership with the Greater Greensboro YMCA (October 1998) to construct and operate a 50,000-square-foot facility on 17 acres of college property leased from GTCC at $1 per year for 50 years. This proposal reopened for Dr. Don Cameron, at least, the controversial community college approach to physical education programs and intercollegiate athletics foreshadowing the revival of men's and women's intercollegiate sports at GTCC in 2005–06. The College was invited to schedule curriculum physical education classes at the facility while the Y pledged to provide offices for faculty and reduced membership fees for College employees and students.[12]

N. C. Community College Faculty Association

Community college instructors founded the organization during their 1998 NCCC Instructors Conference in Greensboro. System president Martin Lancaster endorsed its goal to foster professionalism among community college faculty; he also believed it could play a major role in lobbying the General Assembly to increase faculty salaries. Instructors in the NCCCS were paid an average of $32,100 for nine months (1998) when the national average was $46,258; only South Dakota paid less. A year later, the NCCCFA took credit for the largest overall funding increase in the history of the NCCCS.[13] Four years later (2003–04), the General Assembly gave the University of North Carolina System 362 percent of what the Community College System received to train and teach 95 percent of the students attending college in the state.

1999–2000

The effusive collegiate and community spirit generated by the 40th anniversary commemoration framed another historically significant year. The Board briefly turned its attention to the possibility of establishing a charter high school before dismissing that proposition to lay the groundwork for a 2000 Guilford County bond referendum.[14] The Trustees considered the implications of the new millennium by exploring technical issues related to Y2K compliance that insured the integrity of computers and their data.[15] Grammy Award winning entertainer Larry Gatlin cut the ribbon dedicating the Koury Hospitality Center and President Cameron took the stage to introduce the Larry Gatlin School of Entertainment Technology. The College created its own law enforcement agency, partnered with High Point to promote their ambitious literacy initiative, and joined the Vision 2030 Project task force charged to guide the state into the twenty-first century.[16]

Lessons from Abroad: Youth Apprenticeship Programs

GTCC's various School-to-Work programs fostered a Youth Apprenticeship visit to Switzerland and Germany by a contingent of math and science instructors (March 6–13, 1999). After preparing for their excursion for more than two years through the sponsorship of CIBA Specialty Chemicals, Novartis, Stockhausen, Konica, and High Point Central High School, the panel lead by Dr. Carolyn Schneider, Division Chair Arts and Sciences, visited the Novartis Chemical Processing Apprenticeship Program in Basel, Switzerland. They observed machine tool apprentices plying their trade in Grenzach, Germany, and at a technical school in Metzingen, Germany, where apprentices worked in textiles, building maintenance, machine tooling, and automotive trades. In her report to the Board, Schneider noted that the apprentice systems they observed were strongly driven by industries that recruited the students, compensated them fairly, and provided them with meaningful work.

According to Schneider, the Swiss and German industrialists appeared far more focused than their U. S. counterparts. They manipulated their system to guide students toward a career instead of preparing them, through a laborious series of courses, to make a choice toward the end of their secondary education. Their approach to training, similar to the College Tech Prep elementary, middle, and high school strategy that introduced students to the world-of-work, was an integral part of European cultures that historically utilized apprenticeships to train the national workforce. The Swiss and Germans valued work of all kinds and expected students to form career decisions at an early age. Their education/training process was based on the premise that *people are a nation's main natural resource* and that their training/education is a long-term investment in the whole nation's well being.[17]

GTCC Public Safety Department

Following the enactment of N. C. General Statute 115-D-21.1, the Board established a Public Safety Department as the campus law enforcement agency (June 17, 1999). The department was empowered to employ campus police officers and coordinate with the county's various law enforcement agencies including the Guilford County Sheriff's Department and police departments in High Point, Greensboro, and at PTI.[18]

GTCC's first police officer Robert Storz retired in the summer of 1999 after transforming a security office with 8 employees (1991) into a department with 15 sworn officers. Jerry Clark, a 30-year veteran of the Guilford County Sheriff's Department and commander of the Jamestown office of the Sheriff's Department, succeeded Storz and began adjusting to student-focused enforcement.[19]

The Campus Police Department (2008) is staffed by twenty-two full-time personnel consisting of a chief, two sergeants, one corporal, an administrative assistant, and seventeen (17) officers. The department employs part-time, non-sworn security officers to augment the organization and provide relief on the weekends. Sworn personnel have the power to arrest and are certified by the N.C. Criminal Justice Education and Training Standards Commission within the Department of Justice. Officers in this full-service department enforce college, state, and federal regulations and can arrest violators for any offense committed on College property and on all roads that pass through, or are adjacent to any of the campuses. The GTCC campus crime rate is generally low with larceny of property the biggest problem.

Campus police supervise parking, traffic control and enforcement, the ticketing and towing of vehicles, building security, and serve as first responders to campus emergencies. The department keys buildings, issues keys, completes and files personal injury reports, provides motorist assistance, and oversees the issuance of temporary disability parking. Chief Clark serves on various committees in addition to his law enforcement duties.[20]

New Programs

Internet Technologies topped a list of new programs designed to prepare graduates for employment with organizations using computers to disseminate information. Telecommunications and Network Engineering Technology trained individuals for the telecommunications networking industry. The Hotel and Restaurant Management curriculum prepared students to understand and apply the administrative and practical skills needed for supervisory and managerial positions in hotels, motels, resorts, inns, restaurants, institutions, and clubs.

Industrial support for Chemical Process Technology contributed to the installation of a $300,000 laboratory on the J. C. Price campus in Greensboro. The shared-use facility was a joint effort with the Guilford County Schools, local industry, the Greensboro Area Chamber of Commerce, the High Point Chamber of Commerce, and the North Carolina Department of Labor. The project was funded by the Dow Corning Foundation; CIBA Specialty Chemicals; Novartis; Konica Manufacturing, USA; Deborah A. Overby, CTS; Stockhausen; Mother Murphy's Lab; Kao Specialties; Bonset America; Kay Chemicals (Ecolab, Inc.); Carolina Process Piping, Inc.; Procter & Gamble; ProChem Chemicals; Morflex; GTCC; and the Guilford County Schools.

The lab trained College Tech Prep students as lab technicians and process operators for the chemical/biotechnical industries. They learned analytical lab skills and how to operate chemical reactors, heat exchangers, various pumps and valves, filtration systems and distillation units, and to master safety and environmental protection procedures. Their training was enhanced by opportunities to work in cooperative studies with participating companies. The Chemical Process Technology program was one of eleven Career Pathways programs available to Guilford County students in 1998. By 2005–06 the program had fully incorporated BioWork into its Process Operations classes enabling students to work toward certification as a BioWork Process Technician.[21] GTCC ended its collaborative agreement on a Paralegal program with Surry Community College following approval to offer the curriculum (A25380) independently.[22]

Project Diploma

Literacy is an individual's ability to read, write and speak in English and compute and solve problems at levels of proficiency necessary to function on the job and in society, to achieve one's goals and develop one's knowledge and potential.

1991 National Literacy Act

This bold campaign, enriched by incentives and launched by High Point businessmen, encouraged high school dropouts to pursue a GED, or a high school diploma. 1990 census figures revealed that High Point contained fewer adult high school graduates than any other city of comparable size in N.C. According to the National Institute for Literacy, 21 percent of Guilford County's population and 25 percent of High Point's were in the lowest functioning category of literacy. GTCC Trustee and High Point businessman David Miller, who chaired the 78 member High Point Partners and the educationally oriented Non-Group, believed that the GED program was crucial to the city's future: "A less educated workforce makes existing companies less productive and therefore, less competitive."[23]

Project supporters set a goal of 6,000 GED/High School Diploma graduates by 2010 to move High Point from having 67 percent, the largest percent of high school dropouts in the state, to 88 percent. With Crescent Ford sponsoring a graduation drawing for a $25,000 Mustang convertible, GED attendance jumped from 190 students in December 1998 to 400 in 1999. Jody Germaine Byers pulled the winning number from the hat on June 9, 2000, and sped away from commencement in style.

Hurricane Floyd: September 16, 1999

The GTCC family responded to disastrous flooding triggered by Hurricane Floyd in Eastern North Carolina with a unique "Kiss the Pig Contest." The SGA event raised $11,050 and featured "an exchange" between the pig and GTCC Executive Vice President George Fouts; Fouts won the right to smooch the piglet by personally raising over $400. The GTCC community also donated 4,899 pounds of food and other items to flood victims. Thirty-five of Floyd's 57 deaths occurred in eastern North Carolina where rains of between 10 and 20 inches inundated thousands of acres, roads, and villages causing damages estimated at $3–$6 billion.[24]

Huskins Programs: August 25, 1999

The "Huskins Bill" (G. S. 115-D (20)) (1983, revised 2003) created what is described as "a powerful tool for improving articulation and increasing a student's college participation rate without blurring the distinctive roles of high schools and community colleges. It was designed to enrich the high school experience for selected students by making available college level academic, technical, and advanced vocational courses, not otherwise available to them. Basically, the system aligned certain college courses, in GTCC's case, with high school courses in Criminal Justice and Fire Technology.

The College established a high school Criminal Justice program in 1999 to help local law enforcement agencies recruit officers. Guilford County high school juniors and seniors were allowed to earn college credit toward an associate degree by taking criminal justice courses taught by GTCC instructors. The GTCC Foundation paid tuition and fees for students who elected to continue their studies in Criminal Justice at the College following their high school graduation. In addition to classroom study, students could participate in internships and job shadowing through local law enforcement agencies. The program was then a joint effort between police departments in Greensboro and High Point, the Guilford County Sheriff's Department, GTCC and the Guilford County Schools.[25]

Business & Industry Services: 1998–99[26]

B&I served more than 130 different clients and trained more than 9,500 employees in Guilford County through more than 700 different courses. Through the grant funded FIT (Focused Industrial Training) program, GTCC provided a wide variety of specialized training including Fiber to Fabric, Hazardous Materials Handling, CAD/CAM, and Metals Machining to 25 companies. The Occupational and In-Plant Training Program supplied customized training to 15 companies and 1,371 employees.

The Small Business Center offered seminars, workshops, counseling, a resource library, and referrals to owners and potential owners of small businesses. It created cooperative, working relationships throughout Guilford County cosponsoring programs with the Greensboro and High Point Public Libraries, the chambers of commerce, the Greensboro Merchants Association, High Point Convention & Visitors Bureau, and the Oak Hollow Mall. Significantly, the SBC conducted small business seminars for the steadily increasing Hispanic community.

B&I partnered (September 1999) with I/Tech, a Microsoft Certified Technical Education Center, to offer programs that certified computer service technicians, and the Microsoft Office User Specialist (MOUS) program that validated operators for Office 2000. More than 900 students opted for day, evening, and weekend classes taught at GTCC: High Point, and the T.H. Davis Aviation Center at PTIA.

The NEIT (New and Expanding Industry Training) program provided customized training assistance to support new, full-time positions created in the state of North Carolina. From 1958 to 1999, the state invested approximately $80 million to train more than 300,000 people for more than 3,200 new and expanding companies. NEIT programs administered by GTCC provided customized training for 16 new or expanding companies and 2,058 employees.[27]

Koury Hospitality Center Opening

Stephen Showfety, President and CFO of the Koury Corporation, presented a check for $500,000 to the GTCC Foundation to celebrate the dedication of the 54,000-square-foot, $6.16 million Hospitality Careers Center on October 15, 1999. This unrestricted gift was, at that time, the largest single contribution received by the College. The Trustees responded by naming the facility for Joseph S. Koury, the corporation's deceased founder. GTCC Board Chair Charlie Greene, CEO of Classic Galleries in High Point, also contributed furnishings to the center's Classic Gallery Parlor. Thomasville Furniture Industries and Davis Furniture also contributed to furnishing the facility.[28]

The Koury Hospitality Center was designed by Allen & Mercer Architects (High Point) to house Pre-Drama, Culinary Arts, and Hospitality Management programs. Its amenities include a 435-seat auditorium, a 100-seat fine arts theater, shops for scenery production and costumes, and dressing rooms. The culinary facilities comprise five separate kitchens, a garde manger room, bakery, a main dining room with 120 seats, a demonstration kitchen, and a 30-seat executive dining room. Extending from GTCC's efforts to develop a food preparation facility (1983) and establish a two-year Culinary Technology curriculum (1989), the facility profited from a major entrepreneurial partnership Dr. Cameron arranged with Duke Power Company (Duke Energy), Piedmont Natural Gas, and the Koury Corporation.[29] GTCC was the only college in the state operating a program accredited by the American Culinary Association when the center opened (1999). The community quickly embraced the culinary program's lunch service on Wednesdays and Thursdays for $6 and its Thursday dinner menu for $7.50. The drama and culinary programs often partner to offer a dinner theater experience. The center also embraces classrooms, meeting rooms, and facilities supporting the Hotel and Restaurant Management program.[30]

Guests attending the opening reception on October 15, 1999, were entertained by Grammy Award winning country music star Larry Gatlin. President Cameron capped the evening by formally announcing the development of the Larry Gatlin School of Entertainment Technology scheduled to welcome its first students in the fall of 2000.

Distance Learning

There's something magical about the face-to-face contact a student receives in the classroom. The challenge is learning how we can use the technology to make this type of learning just as magical.

Dr. Beverley Gass, 1999

Dr. Beverley Gass, GTCC's Dean of Learning Resources, received the "Order of the Long Leaf Pine" (1999) for serving as a member of the State Library Commission (1995–99) and working to advance learning through new technologies. Gass chaired the Commission's Committee on Inter-Library Cooperation and served as a charter member of N. C. Live to license the electronic data bases of libraries across the state. By century's end, Gass, who joined the College as a public service librarian (1973), had emerged as a key player in making GTCC a leader in Distance Learning. This powerful tool empowered students to complete college courses without traveling to a campus for traditional classes. Sixty-three online classes were offered for 1,025 students during the 1998–99 school year and 53 were scheduled for the 2000 spring semester. Students could select telecourses through Public Broadcasting, the public school system cable channels, via the information highway, or simply check out a VHS cassette.[31]

GTCC Foundation 1998–99

On May 6, 1999, the Foundation, chaired by James F. "Jim" Morgan, announced a goal to raise $750,000 during the following three years. It pursued external funding from local, state, and federal sources to support emerging institutional needs aligned with GTCC initiatives including curriculum integration, employability skills, faculty development, and distance education; targeted populations included English as a Second Language and English for Speakers of Other Languages (ESOL) students, Work First participants, technical students, and first-generation college applicants.[32]

Thomas H. Davis, founder and former Chairman of Piedmont Aviation, Inc., contributed more than $250,000 to fund student scholarships in the Aviation Technology program. The Board responded by naming GTCC's PTIA campus the T. H. Davis-GTCC Aviation Center.

The foundation received a grant worth more than $800,000 from IBM's "Partners in Education" program that provided an AS/400 computer and operating software to help teach AS/400 programming and e-commerce. The partnership with IBM, spearheaded by Sue Canter, enabled the College to upgrade its AS/400 system hardware every two years and retain a free five-year licensure period for the operating software.

Miller Brewing Company's unique scholarship program Tools for Success®, instituted at GTCC in 1998, provided $50,000 in tool sets to technical program graduates from a variety of programs.

A $38,000 Hillsdale Foundation grant financed astronomy workshops for Guilford County School science teachers, and opened the Cline Observatory to many groups, including school classes and scouts.

Summary

As the millennium approached, the proposed 2000 Guilford County Bond referendum was by far the most important issue challenging President Cameron and the Board. Meanwhile, the Trustees pondered the space GTCC would occupy should the county purchase the Carolina Circle Mall off Highway 29N north of Greensboro. GTCC was primed to occupy the entire Mall's so-called "little" stores excepting the space then occupied by Montgomery Ward, Belk, Dillard's and the Food Court.[33] President Cameron faced the reality that with the departure of GCS Superintendent Jerry Weast, he would soon have to forge a bond with a new, yet-unnamed Guilford County School superintendent. What Americans did not know, and what would steer early decisions in the new century, was the event that revealed that a handful of extremists could warp the world on its axis.

The English for Speakers of Other Languages (ESOL) program instituted in 1978 expanded dramatically. In October 1999, the College reported an 85 percent increase in ESOL students served since 1997.[34]

Campus Notes

Excepting Occupational Therapy, GTCC was offering nine of the top ten programs available at U. S. community colleges by 1999.[35]

1. Registered Nursing

2. Computer Tech/Information Systems

3. Electronic Technology/Electrical Engineering

4. Physical Therapy Assistants

5. Automotive

6. Law Enforcement

7. Computer Programming

Campus Notes continued

8. Dental Hygiene

9. Machinist/Machine tool technology

10. Occupational Therapy Assistants

GTCC's operating revenue for 1998–99 totaled $36,758,479 including $23,107,090 in state appropriations, $5,868,011 from Guilford County and the remainder from a variety of sources.

Curriculum Students: 1998–99	
Total Students	9,616
Employed	77%
Day Students	71%
Night Students	29%
Female Students	54%
Male Students	46%
Minority Students	35%
By Age	
18–24	42%
25–34	32%
35–44	16%
45 and over	10%
Student Enrollment	
Associate Degrees	67.5%
Certificates	7.3%
Diplomas	3.8%
Transfer	21.4%

Faculty and Staff: 1998–99	
Full-Time	445
Part-Time	565

Approximately 60 students and faculty from Dental Assisting and Dental Hygiene participated with the Guilford County Dental Society in a project to seal the teeth of 195 Guilford County second graders, to celebrate the 80th anniversary of North Carolina Dental Public Health.[36]

Nicole Arnold, AA Information Systems, and Shown Campagna, pre-chemistry, won the first North Carolina Community College Excellence Awards. Kristin Ljung, UNC Chapel Hill, and Nicole Arnold, High Point University, each received a $12,000 1998 Hites Family Community College Scholarship to transfer to a four-year institution. Lyung planned to study psychology and criminal justice while Arnold chose computer science.[37]

Maria W. Brown, Stephanie Davis, Karen S. Dean, Toby Hamilton, Barbara Kidd, Edith King, Kristin B. Ljung, Dana A. Lopez, Kelly McCall, Charles L. Miller, Angela M. Regan and Christy C. Routh were selected for the 1998 edition of *Who's Who Among American Junior Colleges.*

GTCC's Alpha Pi Alpha chapter of Phi Theta Kappa was designated a five-star chapter by the Honor Society's international office. The Culinary Arts Program was accredited by the American Culinary Federation Educational Institute Accrediting Commission.[38]

GTCC Trustee and future Board Chair (2004–07) David S. Miller was named 1999's "Citizen of the Year" by the High Point Chamber of Commerce while "North Carolina Business," a publication of The North Carolina Business and Industry Council {NCBIC) profiled current Board Chair Charles A. Greene.[39]

Historian Jeff Kinard, PhD. appeared as an extra in "The Patriot," a Revolutionary War epic, starring Mel Gibson. Filming on the $100 million film began September 7, 1999, near Rock Hill, South Carolina.[40]

The Children's Center received a Four Star rating (December 1999) after voluntarily serving as a trial center for the state's new daycare licensing system. The Children's Center staff included a director and 10 full-time trained caregivers serving 65 children.[41]

GTCC and the Guilford County Schools received three state and national awards in 1999 for College Tech Prep; the *Magna Award* recognizing programs that "raise the bar" on student achievement; the *Parnell Tech Prep Award* presented by the American Association of Community Colleges, and the *RJR Tech Prep/Associate Degree Award for Outstanding Overall College Tech Prep Reform Efforts* presented by the R.J. Reynolds Tobacco Company Foundation in cooperation with the North Carolina Community College System and North Carolina Public Schools.[42]

Chapter 28

2000:
GTCC at the Millennium

> I don't see it as a public necessity that we have to have that mall to do what we want to do in Guilford County. We're already using other alternatives.
> Skip Alston, Guilford County Commissioner[1]

> What better atmosphere could you have than to go in there with the water fountains going? You'd be under one big roof with air conditioning; we'd have conference rooms available, and you could make the area open to the community as well.
> Don Cameron, GTCC[2]

The Millennium Stage

It was time to fold GTCC into the 21st century, but as Don Cameron pondered his strategy near the dawn of the millennium, his concern focused on three major challenges: the questionable future of the College Tech Prep partnership following the departure of Guilford County Schools' superintendent Weast, the campaign to assure passage of a controversial local $25 million bond issue on May 2, 2000, and the impetus to convince those same voters to approve a statewide $3.1 billion Higher Education Bond on November 7. The latter issue would net GTCC $33 million, but the former was problematic given the plotting of the county commissioners.[3]

The local referendum had evolved into a political football after the Carolina Circle Mall (1976), "a well intended, though failed concept in development," emerged as a possible location for consolidating GTCC Greensboro's Washington Street and Price facilities.[4] Cameron and his Board were positively aligned on the desperate need to pass these referenda from the standpoint of locating, designing, and financing a variety of facilities, but many of the deci-

317

sions about GTCC's future presence in Greensboro rested with the Guilford County commissioners and Percy Sears was no longer around to run interference for his beloved institution.

The Carolina Circle Mauling Timeline

The Guilford County Commissioners voted 7–1 in executive session on August 4, 1999, to launch the legal process that would buy most of the declining mall in northeastern Greensboro. They planned to offer $5 million for 625,000 square feet of the 23-year-old facility excluding the space occupied by troubled retailer Montgomery Ward. Rumors of the mall's availability had quickly piqued the interest of several county agencies that were seeking more administrative space and Don Cameron was intrigued by the opportunity to partner with the county and consolidate the services GTCC offered at two aging Greensboro locations at the mall.[5]

Arguably, for the second time in its 40-year history, GTCC was precipitously close to inheriting a "huge dingy white elephant" that would questionably enhance the school's nondescript Greensboro image.[6] However, it is unlikely that those involved in this transaction would have compared the mall's possible acquisition with the opportunistic 1958 decision that relegated the Guilford Industrial Education Center to a derelict TB sanatarium.

Historically, community colleges, including GTCC, had converted "unconventional places," store fronts, abandoned shops, factories, and public schools into classrooms. But an accumulative forty years of makeshift campuses and the lack of signature programs in Greensboro had not, in Dr. Cameron's opinion, established a positive image of the College among The Gate City's business and civic leadership. Consolidating services at the Carolina Circle Mall provided an opportunity to properly showcase the College in facilities other than abandoned public schools, plus the mall would provide 100,000 more square feet than was currently available at the two Greensboro campuses.[7]

The groundwork (timeline) for the 2000 bond muddle is traceable to 1997 when GTCC's Board first asked the county commissioners to approve a $55 million issue to enhance the school's Greensboro facilities. Counseled to scale back their request to $35 million to forego the possibility of an unpopular tax increase, the Trustees reduced the request to $25 million when the mall's availability offered an opportunity to relocate the Washington Street and J. C. Price campuses and forego remodeling Price at a cost of $10 million.[8] The plan made perfect financial sense, but the purchase became problematic when Democrat Melvin "Skip" Alston, at this moment the sole dissenter among the eight commissioners, revealed that a private investor was interested in buying the property and that he (Alston) did not believe the facility was an essential investment for the county.

> I don't like the idea of the county, a public entity, competing against a private group and I don't like the idea of taking that (property) off the tax books. I don't see it as a public necessity that we have to have that mall to do what we want to do in Guilford County. We're already using other alternatives.[9]

About half of the mall's 700 thousand square feet was available for retail when its sale attracted entrepreneurial interests. The FreeMen Group of Greensboro and other investors reportedly offered $7 million based on a plan to transform the facility into an African-American-themed shopping center. At the same time, the Guilford County Department of Public Health and the Department of Social Services were considering moving their administrative offices to the mall contingent on the county purchase. Officials estimated the purchase price at $8.25 a square foot and renovation costs at around $8 a square foot during an era when construction costs ranged around $90 a square foot.[10]

GTCC planned to utilize approximately 200 thousand square feet for its adult high school and basic skills center and a selection of programs leading to associate degrees, diplomas, and certificates. The College would add a continuing education center; a library serving students and the community; a flexible new and expanding industry (NEIT) training center; a small-business center and community meeting spaces; 75 classrooms, 23 computer rooms, and a number of conference rooms would move to the facility. According to President Cameron, GTCC's Board and staff were excited about the idea.[11]

> The mall presents the best opportunity we have had in years to expand service to Greensboro. The College has explored a number of options over the last several years, but nothing has been very promising. This plan offers us a way to do so many things we have only dreamed about for Greensboro. It is tremendously exciting.[12]

Cameron perceptively reminded the commissioners that if they decided against buying the mall, GTCC would be forced to revisit its plan to upgrade the J.C. Price campus for a minimum of $10 million and request the reinstatement of the original $35 million bond issue. He reassured the commissioners that GTCC preferred the mall for a variety of reasons including the 100,000 more square feet of space than was currently available to the College in Greensboro. The total estimated cost to relocate GTCC and selected county offices to the facility ultimately totaled $19.35 million, including the $5 million property cost. Some speculated that renovation could approach $25 million creating the county's most expensive restoration to date.[13]

The specific cost to remodel 222,170 square feet for GTCC was pegged at $4.4 million. Cameron assured the commissioners that GTCC would pay for equipment and furnishings from its state operating budget, but the project was still a long shot and fading quickly. Good intentions aside, many commissioners were already shying from the deal by mid-November 1999 even though the county's 90-day option to purchase would not expire until December 17, 1999.[14]

Acts of Bondage!

The commissioners voted 7–4 to squash the purchase of the Mall on November 23, 1999. The tally would have been 6–5 had not Democrat Alston, who now supported the county's purchase, decided to vote with the opposition. This ploy bought him time to call for another vote when he was assured of a favorable majority. He was aware that two commissioners who opposed the purchase would miss the next commissioners meeting and, having voted with the majority in this case, he was privileged to ask for another vote which he could presumably win with a party-line tally. Believing that the deal had been too good to fail, a disappointed Don Cameron told the media that GTCC's Board would find an alternative to meet the school's needs.[15]

The next episode in this drama occurred on December 2, 1999, when the commissioners met to resolve the status of their three proposed bond issues, $200 million for the public schools, $10 million for parks and recreation and $25 million for GTCC. Before they could make a final decision, the GTCC Board, as promised, revived its original plan to spend $10 million to renovate the Price campus and asked the commissioners to reconsider a $35 million package.[16] This reversal reportedly confused the commissioners, to the consternation of GTCC Board Chair Charlie Greene, who restated the historical scenario surrounding the $10 million in a letter (December 14, 1999) to Guilford County Manager Roger Cotten.

Greene, who believed that the College and the commissioners had been in agreement during every step of the bond issue negotiation, wrote that he felt "GTCC was being cast (by the commissioners) as an agency that showed up at the last minute with another $10 million request." Not wishing to jeopardize any of the referendums on the ballot, Greene informed Cotten that, "the GTCC Trustees have unanimously decided to withdraw our request for reinstatement of the $10 million in bonds and ask that your bond resolution for GTCC be in the amount of $25 million."[17] Greene reminded Cotten that the GTCC Board "wants you and the commissioners to clearly understand that $25 million will not adequately address our identified facility needs."

Those needs, expressed in terms of $55 million recalled the original bond discussion in 1997 when, according to Greene, "the commissioners said that they could not support any bond referendum, but would be willing to consider one at a later date."[18] The GTCC Trustees inevitably revised their request out of historical respect for the generally unwavering support provided the institution by the Guilford County commissioners. GTCC could not consistently count on the General Assembly for adequate funding, but Guilford County had never failed its technical community college in the worst, or the best of times.

GTCC's $25 million proposal forced the College to cut $5 million for renovation and $5 million for technology improvements, but it included:
- $12 million for a new building for industrial and construction programs (ICET) on the Jamestown campus.
- $5 million for an expanded furniture center in High Point.
- $3 million for technology improvements.
- $5 million for a building with classrooms, offices, and a student lounge at the J. C. Price campus in Greensboro.

This original plan also included the property swap involving the West Washington Street campus owned by GTCC and the J.C. Price campus at 400 West Whittington Street owned by the Guilford County Schools.[19] Eventually the Technical Education building targeted for the Jamestown Campus would anchor GTCC's new Greeensboro campus on East Wendover and the expanded furniture center targeted for the High Point Campus became the $9.2 million Larry Gatlin School of Entertainment Technology. GTCC sold the J.C. Price Campus (circa 1922) to Greensboro College for $1.8 million in June 2003.[20]

The success of GTCC's controversial $25 million bond issue rested on the confidence of the Guilford County voters. Cameron charged his power forward, executive vice president George Fouts, to direct a promotional campaign designed to guarantee voter approval of the May 2, 2000, issue. Fouts, the acknowledged historical authority on the N.C. Community College System, energetically and optimistically seized the initiative. The Board paid fund-raising consultant Ralph Simpson and Associates of Winston Salem $15,000 to manage the campaign's $60,000 budget. Since the campaign could not be funded with state money, Board heavy-weights Pat Danahy and David Miller co-chaired a committee that solicited contributions from local businesses.[21] Aside from the bond issue and facing crucial needs, the Board asked the county commissioners to increase their appropriation by $5 million to pay for renovating the Price campus and create a design for the project in 2000–02.[22]

GTCC won crucial press endorsements for the bond issue on the record of its long term fiscal stewardship of public funds and the clear cut facts Board Chair Charlie Greene reiterated;

> There are no frills in the current plan to replace and add new classrooms and training facilities to GTCC campuses. It is a conservative approach that has been carefully and thoughtfully planned to take GTCC well into the new century.

Guilford County voters approved all three issues in the referendum with 63.9 percent favoring GTCC's $25 million request.[23]

2000 State Higher Education Bond Referendum

The Guilford County issue was dwarfed by this gigantic (November 2000) $3.1 million State Higher Education Bond Referendum that included $600 million for the consistently under funded Community College System and $2.5 billion for the university system. GTCC and its neighbors, N.C. A&T State University and UNCG, partnered to promote the issue's passage by 73 percent of the voting North Carolinians.[24] This generous endorsement guaranteed the three Guilford County institutions $347 million. The bulk of GTCC's $33 billion would add buildings to the school's campuses in Greensboro, High Point, Jamestown, and presumably to the PTI Aviation Center.[25] An elated Don Cameron told the Board that, during his 10 year tenure as president, the College had accrued $84.5 million from successful state and local bond referendums; funds that subsequently built or renovated 248,000 square feet of facilities.[26]

The overwhelming vote of confidence in November 2000 was, at least in the case of the Community College System, a sentimental endorsement for the contributions of 58 local institutions. Governed by politically appointed local boards and dependent on state and county funding, most had operated on a 50-year-long shoestring to train and retrain a workforce that virtually saved the State's faltering economy from total collapse as its traditional industries disappeared.

Those who lament the loss of North Carolina's textile and tobacco industries should realize that the majority of these historical enterprises thrived on and perpetuated the "hands-people-culture," that great mass of underprivileged, uneducated workers the community colleges welcomed through an open door to recreate a better educated, technically prepared workforce. The successful bond issues in 2000 would enable GTCC to focus on upgrading the skills of the "hands people" to create a more literate populace.

GTCC's "Vision for the 90's" had charged the College to aggressively prepare to fulfill the expectations of many more students in addition to meeting the training needs of the county's employers. The new programs and initiatives previously described attest to a Cameron-enforced entrepreneurial focus; they confirm the swell of energy and creativity as faculty and staff sought to establish the institution as Guilford County's number one economic development entity.[27]

> Economic Development is the only mission for community colleges today.
> Kathryn Baker Smith, GTCC
> Vice President for Institutional Effectiveness[28]

Reviewing the Mission: Changing the Focus

Kathryn Baker Smith, GTCC Vice President for Educational Support Services (2001–present), is one of the foremost authorities on the North Carolina Community College System. Her experience at the North Carolina Department of Community Colleges (1982–95) included a stint as the Associate Vice President for Planning and Research. Smith's dissertation, "The Role of the North Carolina Community Colleges in the Economic Development of the State's Communities," (1996) won the National Dissertation of the Year Award" presented by the Council of Universities and Colleges of the American Association of Community Colleges in 1997.

Smith, who joined GTCC as Executive Liaison to the President in 1995,[29] concluded in her complex study that North Carolina's investment in its Community College System was profitable "in terms of one of its major purposes— economic development." But, as she informed the community college Trustees in September 1999, that mission had dramatically broadened. Employers were demanding employee-training in "soft skills" including problem solving, teamwork, ethics, and responsibility. These warm, personal skills were vitally important to a state transitioning from an industrial to a technology economy. The rough and tumble authoritarian workplaces inhabited by the "hands people" were rapidly disappearing as technological change transformed workers for a new advanced series of productive enterprises. Smith advocated for "employability skills" to make community college training more profitable for the system's students and GTCC instructors were encouraged to weave lessons about teamwork, communications, ethics, and responsibility into their courses.[30]

Workforce Preparedness: A Review

The widespread apprenticeship initiatives of the 1990s acquainted more students with career possibilities at an earlier age with the result that more than 850 Guilford County students were actively engaged in workplace training through apprenticeships, internships, and cooperative learning during the 1997–98 academic year. These programs became valuable recruiting strategies for GTCC as the metals industry model (PTCAM) spread through other industries and programs at GTCC.

George Autry, president of the MDC Corporation, a labor-education think tank, credited Cameron and Weast for demonstrating "what community colleges can do with workplace preparedness because of good steady leadership." Local businesses led by CIBA Specialty Chemicals had responded by committing almost one million dollars to the apprenticeship programs.[31] One of Don Cameron's highest priorities at the millennium's dawn was to convince the Guilford County School's new superintendent (Terry Grier) to support the Tech Prep programs; his second goal was to launch the Larry Gatlin School of Entertainment Technology in the fall 2000 semester.[32]

The Larry Gatlin School of Entertainment Technology

I have always had a dream of a school of country music and Larry Gatlin might just be my chance, if I could share my dream with him. Larry is standing in Nido Quebin's home alone for about 30 seconds by himself and I said to my wife, 'now is my chance,' and she said, 'do not embarrass us tonight.'"

Don Cameron, President GTCC[33]

Don Cameron hitched Larry Gatlin's Grammy Award winning stardom to his dream of a school of country music at GTCC and the College gained a friend with international fame, a truckload of number one songs, a starring role on Broadway, and top billing in two feature films. By 1999, the immensely talented entertainer whose career blossomed at a Jaycee Talent Contest in Odessa, Texas, in 1959, and who abandoned law school for the Nashville country music scene in 1971, was looking for a major challenge. Cameron's idea of a "school of country music" piqued Gatlin's imagination, but the entertainer found the vision narrow and told him so with a curt; "I don't like country music." But Gatlin remained positive: "Let's call it the Larry Gatlin School of Entertainment!" Cameron acquiesced, "Larry, if we can use your name, we will call it anything you want to (call it)."[34]

The entertainer proceeded to lecture the College president on the broad structure of show business reminding him that entertainers need business managers, graphic designers, cosmetologists, writers, and a variety of other technical skills GTCC taught. Between the educational entrepreneur and the intellectual entertainer, the dream of a comprehensive School of Entertainment Technology etherized in the vagaries of a digital landscape. Research may not precisely reveal how many community college programs are attributable to presidential visions, but Don Cameron's dream of a school of country music materialized into an unparalleled success when more than 400 students registered for classes in its fourth year (2004).

"Build it and they will come."

Dr. Carolyn Schneider, Chair of GTCC's Arts and Sciences Division recalled her initial misgivings about the boss's vision: "I thought it was the dumbest idea I had ever heard," she exclaimed, and was promptly saddled with the task of designing a curriculum. Todd Dupree, an audio-visual technician in the Learning Resource Center and a professional show business "roadie," was recruited to partner with Schneider to formulate the technical curriculum. Schneider tempered her early doubts about the soundness of Cameron's dream when she realized that Entertainment Technology marked GTCC's first venture as an economic "driver" as opposed to its traditional role of "responder."

Community colleges historically react to their regions industrial and economic needs, but Schneider believes that, if GTCC had pursued that model, there would have been no ET program because there was no vocal demand for it in the area. As she explains; "We really did a *build it and they will come* on this project." Schneider and Dupree grounded their research by personally examining successful music programs at South Plains College in Levelland, Texas, and in the Dallas, Texas, Community College System. By the time Cameron assigned this author to market the program in February 2000, Schneider and Dupree were in the final stages of curriculum development. "I developed a brochure to promote the program, participated in recruiting missions to high schools and music venues, and arranged for media coverage."[35]

Some faculty and staff believed that, in promoting his dreams, Cameron was again "chasing rabbits," a strategy he self-consciously employed to explore new ideas. Some were concerned that money spent on Entertainment Technology would be better invested in established programs. Others were disappointed with Cameron's steely intention to install the program at the High Point Campus along a distressed ribbon of South Main Street. Call it what you may, a dream, a gamble, a dumb idea, the success of the program had ultimately depended on promotion, recruitment, student interest, and opportunities for internships and employment. If those of us involved in promoting the program missed anything, it was the phenomenal need by people of all ages to make and record music. ET succeeded by delivering effective, efficient, and economic engineering skills to a broad range of entrepreneurs who flocked to courses that credentialed them to design and install sound systems for churches, businesses, and other institutions and people highly motivated to build personal recording studios.

Guilford County was actually a fertile region for entertainment production with five local companies operating locally, nationally, and internationally. Executives and producers from these firms were recruited for the ET advisory committee as was Larry Gatlin's sister LaDonna and two Nashville area musicians, songwriter-performer Jana Stanfield, and Robin Crowe, guitarist and owner of the Dark Horse Recording Studio. Locally, WTQR personality "Big Paul" Franklin[36], the Piedmont Triad's top country DJ and Kay Saintsing, Executive Director of the North Carolina Association of Festivals, were joined by retired broadcasting executive Gene Bohi; Bill Daves, the local IATSE steward;[37] Cliff Miller, SE System Production Services; Thomas Gaffney, Managing Director of the North Carolina Shakespeare Festival in High Point; and area musicians, entertainers, and producers: Kristy Jackson, Claire Holley, Ashby Frank, Stephanie Wilson, Robert J. Grier, and Wally West plus music store owner Dave Osborne, and Ed Roberson of American Audio-Video.[38] The Greensboro Coliseum Complex offered a perfect venue for internships, part and full-time employment, as did major entertainment venues and coliseums in Winston Salem, Charlotte, Raleigh, and Myrtle Beach.[39]

Cameron's dream intensified in the summer of 2000 when he and I visited South Plains College in Levelland, Texas to counsel with the music faculty, study the facilities, check out the curriculum, funding, and enrollment and assure ourselves that this was truly the premiere music program that had so vividly impressed the GTCC delegation. A side trip to the Buddy Holly Museum in Lubbock influenced Cameron to incorporate an outdoor amphitheater into the design for the state-of-the-art facility destined for GTCC High Point.

And then, a natural miracle contributed to the actual development of the curriculum. A January 2000 snowstorm that closed the College gifted Schneider and Dupree with a respite from routine chores and time to write the Entertainment Technology curriculum (State Code A25190) for a two-year Associate of Applied Science Degree that prepares students for entry-level employment in the entertainment industry.[40] The program's four initial options included Sound Engineering, Concert Sound and Lighting, Management/Promotion, and Performance.

ET's permanent High Point facility was several years away when the first 80 students gathered on August 24, 2000, in remodeled studios in the basement of the Business Careers Building on the Jamestown campus. This positive response from students overshadowed the dire predictions of skeptics who expected fewer than two dozens applications. Built for around $250,000, the program's early facilities included two small recording studios, classrooms, and a tiny auditorium with a proscenium stage. Larry Gatlin lectured, entertained, and queried the inaugural class about their individual decisions to enroll in this innovative program. Nearly half of them amazed the Grammy Award winner when they responded that, "Entertainment Technology was their sole reason for attending GTCC." Their enthusiasm validated Cameron's dream and Gatlin's broadly conceived vision of a comprehensive school of entertainment. Founding father Todd Dupree and lead teacher T. J. Johnson introduced the students to the courses Schneider and Dupree had designed to prepare them for entry-level employment in a variety of show business venues. From that early beginning, students and instructors could only envision their future $9.2 million home in High Point.[41]

Summary

Two bond issues, the Larry Gatlin School of Entertainment Technology, High Point's GED initiative Project Diploma, and a variety of other high profile programs showered GTCC with mostly positive attention as the universe whirled into the millennium, but the horizon was littered with a perturbing array of challenges including national defense issues, literacy, tectonic economic shifts, and complicated partnerships. Amidst this notoriety, the indomitable Don Cameron would discover that despite a decade of personal and professional achievements including record setting enrollment and innovative new programs, his four-decade-old community college was not on the radar of some of Greensboro's movers and shakers.

Chapter 29

2001:
Creating, Changing, and Achieving

Cultural change in the workforce impacts extensively on the plant floor. This evolution extends beyond the Hispanic influx to include workers from Southeast Asia, India, Pakistan, and other nations across the globe.[1]

Cultural and Technological Transitions

The major future funding events of Y2K, the Carolina Circle Mall prelude to the successful May 2000 local bond referendum coupled with the November 2000 $3.1 billion higher education referendum taxed the resources of GTCC's Board, faculty, staff, and students. While the positive results were invigorating, President Cameron was seriously concerned about GTCC's corporate and community image. He questioned the school's ability to provide cutting-edge transformational training to the masses displaced by factory closings in the low-tech manufacturing sectors. Four of the region's industrial clusters—apparel, fabricated textiles, wood products, and tobacco—were declining at a rapid pace.[2]

Transition was the phantom label Cameron applied to a complex series of innovative countermeasures driving business and industry in the Piedmont Triad. Competition, cost controls, a diverse work force, and a global economy tormented Guilford County's CEOs. One out of four jobs was tied to manufacturing. Productivity was essential in a region that, having banked its prosperity on textiles and tobacco, was rapidly transitioning to a diverse manufacturing base. In Cameron's estimation, GTCC was poised to play a vital role in this technological transition by spearheading creative training and retraining to insure the Piedmont's economic health.

As evidence, he cited the skills taught by GTCC's Business & Industry Services faculty; leadership training, developing work teams, improving customer service, honing supervisory skills, skills for implementing statistical process control, problem-solving, geometric dimensioning and tolerancing, blueprint reading, and preventive maintenance. Cameron realized that cultural change in the work force affected the plant floor in an evolution that extended beyond Latinos to include Southeast Asians, Indians, Pakistanis, and workers from dozens of other nations.

English as a Second Language programs (ESOL) exemplified the school's leadership in work force preparedness. Participatory leadership, taught by GTCC's professionals, stretched the American vision of leadership from reforming one person at a time to training groups of leaders for the plant floor. The Work Keys Program, marketed by B&I, assessed production problems and created training programs to close production gaps and get the product through the factory and onto the loading dock.[3]

In 2000, B&I partnered with the N.C. Employment Security Commission to train hundreds of employees for entry level positions with United Healthcare of North Carolina and Uniprise. Day and evening pre-employment classes focused on the soft or employability skills including teamwork, problem solving, basic math, and reading for information. New training opportunities in occupational extension reflected the technology revolution by including Computer Classes in Spanish, BioWork Technician Training, Computer Software Training for Dreamweaver, Fireworks, and Visual Basic, Lean Manufacturing, and a cafeteria of career based technology certifications, recertifications, and prelicensing credentials.

Online courses were available for over 100 subjects in business, management, computers, and other areas through the Ed2Go program.[4] In one 12–month period, the Small Business Center provided over 350 clients with individual counseling sessions, trained more than 4,300 workers, and conducted 140 classes ranging from technology courses to basic record keeping and IRS e–filing tax workshops.[5] B&I profited from this historical record of service to the community, but struggled to keep up with the changes roiling the industrial landscape in Guilford County.

Vision 2030

The Vision 2030 project provided much of the impetus for Cameron's enthusiasm to upgrade technical training at GTCC. Governor Jim Hunt's "real–options" planning effort to strengthen the competitiveness of North Carolina's workforce and industrial power was implemented to take advantage of science and technology–driven economic development opportunities by inventorying the state's resources in these areas. The project extending from August 1999 to June 2000 was directed by The North Carolina Board of Science and Technology, the North Carolina Department of Commerce, and the North Carolina House and Senate Technology Committees.

Beginning on a regional basis, industry, education, and government leaders were charged to investigate the science and technology innovations that would drive the global economy over the next 30 years. Next, task forces, comprised of individuals representing the state's seven economic development partnership regions, were charged to create policies to keep the state's workforce and industry competitive in the new economy. Cameron learned the dramatic extent of the state's declining productivity when he attended Vision 2030's September 1999 kickoff. The numbers were shocking; North Carolina had lost 23,000 jobs in 1998 alone and approximately 27,000 in the first three quarters of 1999. The speed of change wrought by high speed telecommunications, and the need for skilled workers to operate high tech devices that could apply science and engineering to add value to products, was exerting unprecedented pressure on North Carolina's traditional manufacturing base. Economic survival hinged on the assets a particular region like the Piedmont Triad possessed to prosper in the 21st century economy.

Community colleges were crucial to restoring the state's ability to compete productively. GTCC and its sister institutions were charged to retrain workers displaced from traditional jobs to perform productively in the new economy. The model workforce development programs GTCC had successfully created in the 1990s were cited as examples to encourage business and education leaders to cooperate at a higher level and integrate strategy to further develop partnerships in Information Technology, Biotechnology, and high-tech manufacturing.

One of the most important concepts to materialize from Vision 2030 was the notion of "industry clusters." The strongest emerging technology cluster perceived in 2000 included chemicals and plastics.[6] Based on the research strength of Wake Forest University and the Wake Forest Medical Center, Biotechnology materialized as a major cluster. The region's community colleges were given notice to support this cluster by training lab technicians, but by 2006, Don Cameron was not convinced that Biotechnology was evolving on a broad scale in the Piedmont Triad.[7]

Realistically, in 2000, the most promising industrial model in the Piedmont Triad was transportation, shipping, and logistics employing around 30,000 workers. Extensive growth was predictable based on the arrival of Dell Computers in 2005; the future Fed Ex hub at PTI, and the proposed convergence of I-73–74 corridors with I-40–85.[8] These factors, enhanced by the growth of firms like New Breed Inc., made community college programs related to storing, shipping, tracking, and delivering goods a distinct possibility.

The opportunity to build a new campus in the midst of an evolving air and highway transportation hub set Don Cameron walking the wooded acres near PTIA in search of land.[9] The impetus to look ahead provided by Vision 2030 was not misplaced; the decline of traditional manufacturing clusters including apparel, fabricated textiles, wood and tobacco products, would soon dramatically affect employment in the region forcing GTCC and its sister community colleges into a partnership to "Put the Piedmont Back to Work."[10]

Fall 2000: Record Enrollment

Based on the 7,981 curriculum students, a 9 percent increase, registered for courses at GTCC in the fall 2000 and the 750,000 that signed up across the North Carolina Community College System, citizens appeared to be responding to the need for technological training to counter the disappearance of traditional industries. Community college enrollment historically increased when the economy soured, but GTCC's enrollment had risen at about six percent a year during the prosperous 1990s, with state funding at around $24 million (1999–2000). Administrators had to scramble that fall to park an additional 532 vehicles on the Jamestown campus. Faculty added additional seats to their classes and the College hired more instructors to accommodate the applicants.[11]

The opening of the Larry Gatlin School of Entertainment Technology showered the school with a cascade of positive publicity that Cameron banked on to change the public's stereotypical perception of a bland community college. At the same time, he recruited a phalanx of retired businessmen to enhance the image of the school with broader marketing initiatives and to generate a fund raising campaign to increase the wealth of the Foundation. Confidently believing GTCC could lead the way in reversing Guilford County's questionable industrial future, Cameron was surprised when the McKinsey Report, an economic study of the Greater Greensboro community, totally ignored GTCC.

The McKinsey Report

Sponsored by a consortium of Greensboro foundations, the McKinsey Report suggested that economically, Greensboro ranked slightly above average among its peers in the Southeast, but its researchers warned that an "undirected business-as-usual approach" would likely like lead to an erosion of the community's overall prosperity. Cameron was furious when he discovered that the researchers had overlooked GTCC in their sketchy review of Greensboro's higher education assets. While they cited the Center for Creative Leadership for its premiere leadership training program, North Carolina A & T State University for its engineering and business schools, and UNCG for its School of Education and Bryan School of Business, they ignored GTCC, the Institution that in the vision of its president was arguably the county's number one workforce preparedness educator and its major economic developer.

After Cameron called the oversights to the attention of Jim Melvin, CEO of the Joseph M. Bryan Foundation, and one of the report's major sponsors, Melvin graciously acknowledged the slight in a letter to GTCC Board Chair, Charlie Greene.

> We have quickly admitted to Don Cameron this serious flaw in the report and want you and your Board members to know there was no premeditated intent. It was just a serious error on our part. The McKinsey people, not being keenly aware of Greater Greensboro, did not include GTCC in their interview list and we failed to pick up on it.
>
> We want you to know that in everyone of our physical presentations since the report came out we have prominently mentioned that GTCC is one of our strongest assets and will serve as a major factor in our improving ourselves as we move forward.[12]

A major thesis of this study is that GTCC's lack of a positive physical presence and signature programs in Greensboro until 2004, coupled with an ongoing struggle to connect personally with the city's business community, was historically detrimental to the school's reception in the city. While this concept in no way diminishes the programs and services GTCC provided, it did not attract the sense of community ownership the College enjoyed in Jamestown and High Point. After 40 years, the best that could be intimated about the community college was that it belonged to amorphous *Greater Greensboro*, a vaguely defined geographical sphere of influence.

The new Wendover Avenue campus, anchored by the impressive Technical Education Center, elevated GTCC's presence when it opened in 2005, but McKinsey convinced Don Cameron to reposition and sharpen the school's corporate image. Within weeks he organized a marketing committee and contracted with McNeill Lehman, Inc. to research the school's reputation in Guilford County and prepare a marketing action plan. Their proposal would inspire a new branding and marketing initiative to encourage the public to "Imagine Guilford County without GTCC. "McKinsey" may have personally embarrassed Don Cameron but it was a wakeup call that did not go unanswered.

The Terry Grier Partnership

Cameron was determined not to allow the partnership with Guilford County Schools to falter after Superintendent Jerry Weast's departure and he quickly established a personal and professional partnership with Weast's successor Terry Grier. As aggressive as his controversial predecessor, Grier arrived towing a slate of successful programs behind him; but, the middle college program he had established in Tennessee was altogether different from the Tech Prep model Cameron and Weast had developed.

The middle college originated historically as a joint venture between City University and the New York City Board of Education. Designed to create a learning environment on a college campus, it essentially provided disengaged high school students with a fresh start. Cameron and Grier talked for almost a year before the superintendent was invited to discuss his "Middle College High School" with the GTCC Board at its fall 2000 retreat. By that time, the concept, described as a school for creative non-conformists who could not fit successfully into a traditional high school, had spread to 25 college campuses across the nation and was setting records for returning disengaged high school students to the educational process.

A visit to one of Grier's high profile middle colleges in Williamson County, Tennessee, convinced Cameron that the concept could work at GTCC. The first middle college in North Carolina was established at Jamestown in 2001; the Early Middle College of Entertainment Technology accepted its first students on the High Point campus in 2005; and a third Early Middle College opened on the GTCC Greensboro campus in the fall of 2006.[13] The concept evolved as one of Terry Grier's strongest strategies in his goal to lower the dropout rate in the Guilford County Schools. Each early middle college was designed to have an enrollment of around 125 students and stipulate a zero tolerance policy on behavior; as will be noted later, the GTCC early middle college initiative has been exceptionally successful.[14]

Groundbreaking for Fire Science

Try to imagine smoke so thick you can't see it before your face.

Dr. Stuart Fountain, Chair
Finance and Facilities Committee
GTCC Board of Trustees[15]

College Trustees, area law enforcement and fire safety officials cracked the clay to build a $2.2 million Fire Science Demonstration Building and Public Safety Driving Track on the Jamestown campus on Thursday, March 16, 2000.[16] The 16-acre training site's paved drive track and four-story "burn tower" equipped the Fire Science, Criminal Justice, and Emergency Medical Science programs with realistic sites to teach driving and rescue procedures. The tower's height allowed for spectacular ladder exercises and the roof could be chopped away to practice ventilation techniques enabling students to train for leadership roles in a variety of controlled environments. The paved drive track supported the heaviest fire apparatus and provided a practice site for low-speed pursuit and precision maneuvering exercises on an emergency situations course. At the official opening on September 6, 2002, Fire Protection Technology and Emergency Medical Science instructors dramatically rescued a "child" from a smoke-filled second-story room.[17]

"Smart Start" Substitute Program

GTCC's lengthy record as a high quality daycare provider through its Children's Center won a major grant of $494,000 from the Guilford County Partnership for Children (GCPC) to train a new cadre of day care workers. Completers of the Smart Start Substitute program replaced employed daycare workers who needed to return to school to earn the Early Childhood Credential required by the state for lead daycare teachers. In 1999, approximately 70 percent of Guilford County families were relying on child care facilities; almost that many—69 percent (20,746) of the children under age 5 were enrolled in state regulated daycare. Many daycare workers were not adequately qualified; their education level was low, as was the pay, and the turnover rate was high. The GCPC grant was designed to upgrade their child care skills by paying for 12 weeks or 240 hours of instruction including "hands-on" training at GTCC's Children's Center. The "Smart Start" program also granted the College $250,000 to renovate the center and provide professional development for a faculty reeling from its own problematic turnover.[18]

Highways to Success

GTCC introduced the "Highway to Success" job training program in March 2000 to help the unemployed and underemployed find fulfilling work. The 12 week program obviously appealed to people out of work, but it also helped those shackled in un-fulfilling, low paying jobs. The program provided training in human resources and occupational, basic and adult education skills. Each session was geared toward a specific career interest consisting of eight weeks of course work and a four week internship at a business. The program cost the general public $60, but it was free to participants in the Department of Social Services Work First Program and scholarships were available. Students could participate in four programs; Legal Office Specialist, Medical Office Specialist, Computer Office Specialist, and Financial Office Specialist. The first 42 graduates were certified in December 2000.[19]

Faculty in Training (FIT): Teaching Assistantship Program

GTCC formed one of its most productive partnerships with UNCG in 1999 when the institutions established the Teaching Assistantship Program. The first program of its kind in the state, now Faculty in Training (FIT), was actually spawned by competition among area colleges and universities for adjunct professors. English Department Chair JoAnn Buck helped create the program that offered graduate students, who had completed at least 18 hours of course work, the opportunity to explore teaching at a community college. Students are mentored by GTCC faculty and paid a competitive salary.[20] Ten trainees were participating in the program by 2006 and 30, representing 12 disciplines, had graduated as of May 10, 2005; as a result, 12 graduates were employed full or part-time by community colleges and seven FIT graduates were currently registered in Ph.D. programs at UNCG.[21]

GHG Construction, Inc.

The non-profit corporation (1988) that managed the Industrial Construction Engineering Technologies Division's "live" building projects had financed 18 homes by 2000 when administrators decided to make the program a collaborative effort. For the first time, residential carpentry, HVAC, and electrical students built a house from blueprints developed by their colleagues in architectural technology. The 2,350-square-foot, three-bedroom, two-and-a-half-bath home with garage in north High Point's Colony Park subdivision sold for $175,000. Veteran Carpentry Department Chair R. P. Hughes and Virginia Tunstall, associate professor of architecture, coordinated this inaugural collaborative venture. Profits from the sale of this and other properties were re-invested to purchase materials for the next project.[22]

At publication the residential carpentry class had built 23 homes, with one under construction in Greensboro, N.C. Additional projects completed included low income qualifier construction for High Point Housing Authority, a field house for Southwest Guilford High School, several construction projects for not-for-profit organizations and numerous storage and playhouse structures.

Project Diploma: June 9, 2000

GTCC student Jody Jermaine Byers discovered the value of working for a GED and showing up to collect his certificate when he won a brand new Ford Mustang ($25,000). Crescent Ford of High Point contributed this prize as part of the "Project Diploma" promotion sponsored by the High Point Partners, 102Jamz and GTCC. Byers' name was drawn at random from among the High Point GED and adult high school graduates actively participating in the graduation. 424 graduates were awarded either an Adult High School Diploma or their GED at the ceremony in the Millis Athletic and Convocation Center on the High Point University campus. This marked a 72 percent increase over the number of graduates receiving their diplomas in 1999; nearly 500 more graduated from the GTCC Greensboro programs.[23]

High Point Education Alliance

In the fall of 2000, Dr. Cameron assigned the author to liaison with administrators from UNCG and High Point University to develop a consortium that would offer 2 plus 2 cooperative programs at GTCC High Point. Ideally, the scheme would enable "place bound" students to move seamlessly into four-year degree programs at UNCG and High Point University. The idea was forwarded by the Non-Group, an association of High Point citizens who had bonded to promote and develop community wide education initiatives including "Project Diploma." The "Non-Group's" alliance concept emerged in an era when a number of colleges and universities were promoting outreach degree programs in the Piedmont Triad.

This specific idea, spearheaded by GTCC Trustee David S. Miller (Board Chair, 2004–07), was modeled after the Appalachian Learning Alliance that linked Appalachian State University with 9 regional community colleges. The project was tenuous from the beginning due to the various high profile priorities UNCG and HPU were pursuing at the time. Both institutions were experienced in presenting evening and off campus programs, but GTCC's campus in downtown High Point, just 15 miles from UNCG's main campus in Greensboro, and only a few miles from HPU's campus did not positively resonate for a variety of reasons.

There were questions about student interest, debates about whether to offer a variety of courses or programs, and subtle insinuations that a partnership with UNCG could possibly transition into a branch of the UNC System in High Point. Following a research project that assessed student interest and a $7,000 marketing campaign, the institutions sponsored a series of informational sessions on GTCC's High Point campus in May 2001. The inconclusive results from these sessions convinced the participating institutions to forego the project.

By December 2001, ongoing discussions with UNCG officials revived the project as a cooperative venture between UNCG and GTCC excluding HPU. The UNCG School of Environmental Sciences and the School of Education assigned one course each to the High Point campus in 2002, but enrollment was low and the project was discontinued.

The High Point Education Alliance was a noble project designed to offer an affordable four-year degree in downtown High Point for "place bound" students; the social work and education courses that were offered articulated with GTCC programs, but failed on the paucity of student support. What is important here is that GTCC and two neighboring universities positively responded to an invitation extended by a consortium of civic leaders determined to improve the literacy of their community.[24]

Youth Build USA

Grants from the High Point Housing Authority and UNCG created the Youth Build program from a national model in 1990 to train unemployed and undereducated young adults (18–24) in construction while they pursued their GED. This program was founded to harness the positive energy of low-income young people and motivate them to simultaneously rebuild their communities and their lives. Its components included counseling, peer support groups, extracurricular activities, job placement, leadership training, decision making and involvement in community issues. This particular program grew out of an effort by the High Point Housing Authority and UNCG's Center for Youth, Family, and Community Partnerships to alter the environment in High Point's blighted Macedonia neighborhood. High Point builder Bill Cochrane (Cochrane Construction Company) supported the program by offering his Hamilton Place project as an off campus laboratory experience for students enrolled in the program.[25]

During the period 2000–05, a total of 58 participants, 33 of whom graduated from the program, built 12 houses for low income families; almost 93 percent of those completing the program entered job training, employment, or higher education.[26]

Summary

The universally ballyhooed millennium introduced a rush of bond issues, construction projects, new programs, projects, and initiatives at GTCC. Research triggered by the controversial "McKinsey Report" would provide benchmarking opportunities to motivate the College through the first decade of the 21st century. The report had crystallized Don Cameron's worst fears by disclosing, what he interpreted, as a lack of appreciation and basic understanding of GTCC by Greensboro's civic and corporate leadership. It may have been, as Greensboro's champion Jim Melvin intimated, "an oversight on the part of the researchers," but as the decisions and events of the following years would prove, the McKinsey snub was the dart that prodded the elephant to move.

The phenomenal concept of the millennium, fraught with its plethora of historical, religious, and psychological implications, fostered an overabundance of dire predictions throughout the world, but beyond the wild and eerie speculation, the events of 2000 provided GTCC with an opportunity to revitalize its image on the stage that chaotic national and world events would subsequently alter in 2001.

Campus Notes

GTCC dedicated its remodeled nursing lab on the Jamestown Campus on November 16, 2000, thanks in part to a $100,000 grant from the Tannenbaum Foundation and $100,000 solicited in matching funds by Dr. Kathryn Baker Smith.

Biology Professor Dr. George H. Whitesides reaped an "outpouring of media attention" after his article detailing the possible extinction of a rare West African species, "Miss Waldron's Red Colobus Monkey," was published in the international journal *Conservation Biology*.[27]

GTCC partnered with Western Carolina University and three community colleges to offer a B.S. degree in Emergency Medical Technologies.

Chapter 30

1991–2001:
Don Cameron's First Decade

There are not too many two-year colleges featured on the front page of the *Wall Street Journal*. As I look back, I think of the faculty and staff we have assembled here at the College; they made it happen; not Don Cameron.[1]

Procreative Leadership

The man who really counts in the world is the doer, not the mere critic—the man who does the work, even if roughly and imperfectly, not the man who talks or writes about how it ought to be done.

Theodore Roosevelt, 1891

Don Cameron is a "doer," whose physically imposing presence is arguably his most powerful introductory attribute. He exemplifies Roosevelt's "man who does the work". His demeanor embodies a spirit of self assurance embedded in the steeliest blue-collar tradition inherent in the pine woods of the North Carolina sandhills and honed on the competitive athletic fields of his youth. If his presence epitomizes power, his often ambiguous, situational leadership style is formulated on an obsession with *getting the job done*. He leads by example and expects his faculty and staff to similarly respond beyond the limits of their personal expectations. He assigns jobs and gauges the results by what *he* could have done, or has done, in the same position. To those who have foolishly said to him, "I'll do whatever you want me to do," he is quick to warn, "If I have to tell you what to do, what do *I* need you for?"

As a reporter observed about the former baseball catcher, "from his crouch behind home plate, he adjusted the outfielders, shifted the infield, called the pitches. He was the backstop, and he relished it." [2] Don Cameron has Guilford

341

County's "back" as GTCC's number one economic development player, coach, and general manager. His leadership style is that of the idealistic, inspirational athletic director who is fiercely motivated to promote leadership through exaltation, expectation, and intimidation. He will exercise guilt and humor to get the job done. There is no doubting his power: GTCC is *his* college. Frankly, his leadership style dwarfs the frivolous outcomes of most leadership programs ranging from the pathetically clinical to the elementary "do it by the number" formulas to the ultra-executive "business models."

Some employees have observed that "Don Cameron never saw an initiative he didn't like;" others have visualized his ideas as "seeds flung randomly across the campus to live or die depending on who has the insight to nurture them." But when he reflected on the major achievements of his tenure during a 2001 celebration of his 20 years at GTCC and 10 as President, it was apparent that the workforce preparedness partnership models he had created with industrial, educational, and political entities were the exceptionally significant contributions that represented a brilliantly executed decade of maturation for the College and its president.[3] Most notable were the partnerships he forged with the Guilford County Schools, RF Micro Devices, Banner Pharmacaps, Dow Corning, and Degussa-Stockhausen.

During Don Cameron's first presidential decade (1991–2001), the College benefited from four successful bond referendums, two state and two local, totaling $84.5 million. The school added three new buildings, the Sears Applied Technology Center, the Koury Hospitality Center, and the Cline Observatory, and expanded the Medlin Campus Center. The GTCC Foundation, Inc., grew from $800,000 to $3.8 million. The College added numerous programs and the budget more than doubled.[4] Jim Melvin, president of the Joseph M. Bryan Foundation of Greater Greensboro, Inc., eloquently summarized Cameron's contributions to economic development and workforce preparedness.

> If you look at some of the significant industry finds that we have had, GTCC has been one of the strong selling points in providing employee training. That is obviously the front page of our resume as we go out and try to attract additional employees to this area. One (thing) that makes Don so effective is that he is so likeable and stays focused. He understands the mission of his Institution and he doesn't get off that particular track. The employment base is changing dramatically and he has kept GTCC on the cutting edge to provide the kind of training that the employers need.[5]

Cameron, a man of many moods and not immune to digression, acknowledges an imaginative tendency to soar away into experimental, innovative, futuristic tangents. He characterizes the fearless, self-confident aerialist who works "without a net" high above the arena. Self consciously, he disclaims these forays into the outer limits by forewarning his leadership team, "You may think I'm crazy, but what if … ?"

By 2001, Cameron's professional reputation as an executive who could execute was soaring locally, statewide, and nationally. His reputation earned him a gubernatorial appointment to a 30 member task force charged to develop a long range plan to improve the state's public schools. He was elected to a three-year term as a member of the President's Academy Executive Committee of the American Association of Community Colleges (AACC), but his major honor came when the North Carolina State Board of Community Colleges named him its first "President of the Year."[6]

Carolina Circle Mall Redux

The Guilford County Commissioners may have dismissed the Carolina Circle Mall, but Don Cameron remained intrigued by the derelict shopping center's possibility as a future GTCC campus.[7] In late January 2001 when Montgomery Ward, the mall's sole remaining anchor, filed for bankruptcy, a real estate agent contacted Cameron about purchasing the space. In discussions with Cameron, the four county commissioners who had originally opposed the county purchase indicated they would support his objective as did three commissioners who originally supported the buyout.

Their interest in locating some county offices at the facility rekindled, the commissioners approved GTCC's plan to buy the mall on February 1, 2001, with only one dissenting vote.[8] GTCC Trustees promptly authorized Cameron and Board Chair Charlie Greene to negotiate with proposed mall purchaser entrepreneur Don Linder about buying a part of the facility.[9] The College proposed to pay for the property with $6 million from the 2000 bond issue, contingent upon approval by the State Board of Community Colleges.[10]

Negotiations ceased when Linder decided to transform the entire 800,000-square-foot facility into a grandiose recreation and retail center operated by his Pyramids Wellness Centers. Noting that private ownership of the complex would generate tax revenue which would not happen if GTCC bought the facility, Linder reportedly intimated that he would like for the College to lease the upper level of the mall and buy the Montgomery Ward space.

Cameron spurned Linder's leasing proposal by noting that GTCC wanted to be an owner, not a tenant, stating for record that he wanted the entire mall and its 62 acres to create a campus atmosphere. Unless something unexpected stopped Linder from completing his deal, Cameron said GTCC would solve its spatial needs by building a 53,000-square-foot classroom facility on the J.C. Price Campus. GTCC at the mall would have been a tremendous investment for the county's tax payers and an economic boost to northeastern Greensboro and Guilford County. GTCC could have purchased and renovated the center for about $25 a square foot as opposed to paying $100 to $125 a square foot to build a new facility.[11]

By the end of March 2001, GTCC had three building projects on the books, totaling around $28 million: the proposed $9.25 million Entertainment Technology building in High Point; a $7 million classroom building on the J.C. Price Campus in Greensboro, and a new Technical Education Center at Jamestown. A few weeks later, in April 2001, the Guilford County Commissioners approved by a seven to three vote, GTCC's request for $350,000 to expand the Price campus by purchasing an adjacent 17 acres.[12] During this period of accelerated growth, the Board was also purchasing land to expand the High Point campus and financing parking facilities for the Koury Hospitality Center on the Jamestown campus.[13]

Imagine Guilford County Without GTCC

Responding to the McKinsey report, the College launched a new image campaign in January 2001. Convinced that the survey-snub was directly related to a general lack of knowledge about the Institution among CEOs and prominent citizens, Cameron contracted with the High Point public relations firm McNeill Lehman, Inc. (now McNeill Communications, Inc.), to compile the business community's opinion of GTCC's services and programs and develop an institutional marketing action plan. While Cameron's personality and professional reputation won the popular vote in the July 2001 survey of some 2,000 prosperous citizens with the wherewithal to support the GTCC Foundation, their understanding of the College was marginal.

Respondent's recognized six strengths: workforce training, basic skills programs, the diversity of courses, accessibility, affordability, and flexibility. 80.1 percent agreed that GTCC's technical training benefited the community and 71.3 percent said they would refer family, friends, colleagues, and employees to the College. However, those figures were offset by the more than 40 percent who knew little if anything about the Institution's eight top programs and the majority who knew little or nothing about 21 of 22 programs listed in the survey. The number one threat to GTCC was, as suggested, a lack of awareness about the College among influential business, civic and social leaders. More than 25 percent of the respondents did not know enough about GTCC to form opinions about the school's services. Glaring variances diffused the perception of quality programs, staff, marketing, and funding.

McNeill Lehman recommended a three-year campaign to raise business and community awareness to begin in August 2001. The promotion included direct mail, TV advertising, the formation of a speaker's bureau, and information sessions designed to develop strong community-business relationships. The marketing committee initially responded with a proposed 12 month direct mail campaign using provocative postcards that provided information about specific programs. The first mailing, "Creating, Changing and Achieving," promoted GTCC's new positioning statement:

> Guilford Tech has a broader, more profound, and more productive impact on business, professional, and personal lives in Guilford County than any other institution—by raising the standard of living, alleviating poverty, and helping people retool their lives.[14]

The postcard campaign elicited a positive response, but the state's economy suddenly soured and budgetary shortfalls delayed subsequent mailings for months. The marketing committee's request to the Board for $100,000 for a TV campaign fell prey to the statewide economic slowdown that forced the Community College System and the counties to the brink of fiscal survival. Undeterred, marketing developed a media presentation to sell the "Imagine Guilford County Without Guilford Tech" theme in a variety of community venues and generated an array of media stories about GTCC programs and student success.

The silver lining—if you can call it that—to this truncated marketing campaign materialized in February 2002 when WXII-TV partnered with GTCC and other Piedmont Triad-Southside Virginia community colleges to stage an opportunistic workforce training campaign titled "Putting the Piedmont Back to Work." This promotion, outlined in the following chapter, generated well more than $100,000 in TV advertising at no cost to the College. The print media also responded equally to the crucial unemployment situation (2001–03) that generated widespread anxiety aggravated by massive layoffs in the textile and apparel industries. Combined media coverage created a tremendous public relations bonanza for the College with thousands of inches of free advertising and TV news stories.

Most of the marketing department's financial resources during this era were allocated to the ubiquitous Institutional material, schedules, catalogs, brochures, and reports. The College web site was accessible, but far from adequately staffed and grossly underutilized as a major marketing tool. A revitalized Internet sub committee of the Technology Committee began reviewing the website in July 2001 at the same time the Community College System launched a massive computer system conversion.

NCCCS Software System

The North Carolina Community College System began the new century desperately needing to revamp its method of managing and distributing information. By 2000, all but 2 of the 58 institutions were using the state supported IIPS (Institutional Informational Processing Systems) system. GTCC had moved beyond the paper-driven era to develop its own student software module to compliment the IIPS finance and HR software modules. The challenge to convert the system was monumental since NCCCS processes more than 800,000 student records annually and manages over 25,000 full and part-time staff. The system desperately needed a technology infrastructure that would support a full range of educational entities, including curriculum and continuing education, financial and business related programs, human resources, general ledger, payroll, applicant tracking, and financial aid departments.

The five-year contract to install the Colleague single-solution standardized computer-software program, originally estimated to cost $42 million, was awarded to Virginia based Datatel and its partner Affiliated Computer Systems. NCCCS decided to introduce the plan to the 58 colleges in three stages, beginning with a group of eight pilot schools, including GTCC. Marcia Daniel, an experienced community college administrator, most recently vice president of educational programs and student services at Randolph Community College, was named CIS project co-manager for the NCCCS, while Chief Information Officer Sandie Kirkland managed the project for GTCC. Datatel's rollout of the Colleague software system across the system represented the largest implementation of information technology in the company's history and in higher education. Fully implemented, the installation took six years and cost more than $80 million.[15]

Business and Industry Services

I've been sitting on the policy-setting side for a long time, and now I have an opportunity to be in on the implementation process. This is a way I feel I can personally contribute to the community by helping individuals receive better opportunities for career enhancement and personal growth and enrichment. I will also be able to assist new and expanding industries and corporations by offering their employees additional training and skills while in the workforce.[16]

Former GTCC Trustee Leroy Stokes brought 35 years of experience at Lucent Technologies to GTCC when he was appointed to the newly created position of Vice President of Corporate and Continuing Education in January 2001. Stokes assumed responsibility for Focused Industrial Training (FIT), the New and Expanding Industry Training program (NEIT), Inplant Training, Continuing Education, and the operations of GTCC's Small Business Center.[17]

His arrival coincided with the division's renewal of its five-year relationship with Banner Pharmacaps to launch a year-long Pharmaceutical Technician certificate program to cross train 29 employees in all production areas. The GTCC Chemical Processing Technology program scheduled classes in the encapsulating plant for eight different departments to teach employees both job and employability skills in process operations, environmental health and safety, and machine maintenance. The College also instituted an Associate Degree Business Education program at the north High Point pharmaceutical maker's plant and began conducting on site English as a second language (ESOL) classes.[18]

Marshall "Sonny" White, Ph.D.

The retirement of community college legend and GTCC executive vice president George Fouts in July 2001 provided Dr. "Sonny" White an opportunity to begin a new career in education. The newly retired CIBA Specialty Chemicals, Inc., executive had taught at the undergraduate and graduate levels at North Carolina State University, Virginia Tech, and UNCG, and had served as a member of the Guilford County Schools Enrichment Board. White was well acquainted with GTCC having supported the College with a tremendous workforce preparedness grant, membership in the GTCC Foundation, and a seat on President Cameron's Advisory Board. White's credentials included a doctorate in chemistry from Clemson University and a stint at Harvard University's Advanced Management School. White brought an unequaled brand of enthusiasm to the College for five years before resigning on March 31, 2006, to accept the presidency of Midlands Technical College in Columbia, South Carolina.[19]

GTCC Foundation

James S. "Jim" Belk was another high-profile retired business executive Cameron hired in 2000 to change the culture at GTCC. Belk brought a distinguished fund-raising record as a civic volunteer to the executive director-ship of the GTCC Foundation. Charged to increase the wealth of the College from $3.8 million to $10 million, Belk began by staging the Foundation's first annual gala at the Grandover Resort for members of the President's Society, who had contributed at least $1,000 to the College.

Charitable gifts of money, time, equipment, and services from industry and individual donors supplement the operating budget of the College and fund scholarships, program start-ups, equipment acquisitions, and professional de-velopment for faculty and staff. For example, in 2001 Old Dominion Freight Lines, Inc., established a scholarship to assist diploma- or degree-seeking stu-dents studying Heavy Diesel Maintenance.

Retired astronomy professor Aaron Martin and wife Ruth contributed $10,000 to launch the Aaron and Ruth Martin Astronomy Endowment Fund.

A $150,000 grant from the Weaver Foundation, the largest ever received by GTCC at the time, funded a three-year pilot program to provide work expe-rience for adult high school students. The grant honoring Charles "Chuck" Hayes, the Guilford Mills, Inc., CEO who received his GED from GTCC in 1996, required students to work at least 80 hours for a business or non-profit agency and give 50 hours of volunteer service.[20]

September 11, 2001

He found some socks
She chose his tie
And when he left for work that morning, he was just another guy
Going to work
He'd have to fly
Out to a meeting in L.A., so she had kissed him twice goodbye.
"Little Did She Know, She'd Kissed a Hero," Kristy Jackson

The September 11, 2001, terrorist attack on the United States profoundly changed the universe and skewed the destinies of its various populations. Whatever transpired before those dreadful airliner crashes and the deaths of thousands of innocent people belongs to an irretrievable world. Each living American of a responsible age remembers what she or he was doing at the mo-ment of the assaults on the World Trade Towers and the Pentagon, and can re-call the agonizing vapor trail of horror accompanying that dreadful crash of Flight 93 in the Pennsylvania countryside.

The GTCC campus community responded immediately to share the grief and offer prayers for the victims. A regularly scheduled Red Cross blood drive underway on the Jamestown campus was boosted by dozens of donors from the community. The continuing wave of contributors, including many first-timers, encouraged GTCC and Red Cross personnel to remain at their posts past 10 P.M. to collect more than 500 pints of life-saving blood.

Fire Science instructor Mel Doggett, a member of one of the four National Medical Response Teams (NMRTs) organized under the United States Public Health Service, responded immediately to the terrorist attacks. Doggett's Special Operations Response Team (SORT) was assigned to provide medical support and decontamination resources to protect first responders and civilians.

The College convened a memorial service for the 9/11 victims on Friday following the attacks. Executive Vice President Sonny White moderated the service in the Koury Hospitality Center auditorium; GTCC counselor Edna Hurley explained the process of coping with pain and anger. Professor Ibraheem Kateeb reviewed Islamic beliefs and practices and Dr. Jeff Kinard addressed the historical implications of the attacks. The service concluded with an audience question and answer period and the singing of "God Bless America," soon to become the thematic 9/11 hymn.

Randy Owens, Welding Technology Department Chair, voluntarily participated in the 9/11 Sculpture Project created by Greensboro steel sculptor Jim Gallucci. The immense undertaking involved two gates incorporating 16 tons of steel from the demolished World Trade Center. The first gate standing about 21 feet high and weighing five tons was completed by the first anniversary of the terrorist attacks. The second gate is about 50 feet high and weighs between 60–65 tons. The gates were personalized by the "Pages of Expression," thoughts, poems, prayers, and anecdotes composed by mourners that were transferred to bronze plaques and affixed to various parts of the gates.

Entertainment Technology instructor Kristy Jackson, Nashville composer-vocalist and author of the Reba McEntire hit "Take it Back", was profoundly touched by the 9/11 tragedy. She writes about the inspiration to compose "Little Did She Know" (She'd Kissed a Hero) in her book by that title (2004). While Jackson sat at the piano following a moving memorial service, "a new song poured out inspired by the heroes of Flight 93," the airliner that crashed in Pennsylvania. A Greensboro DJ turned Jackson's self-produced CD into an immediate local, then national hit. She spurned a major record company's offer to sign a contract and produced the record under her own "Fever Pitch Music" label. Internet sales of the number one requested song on the major New York City radio stations raised $26,000 for 9/11 charities. During the next two years Jackson performed "Little Did She Know" free in venues all over the U.S. including the CBS "Early Show." Kristy's compassionate ballad brought a new wave of media attention to GTCC's Entertainment Technology program even as it encapsulated the shock of the 9/11 tragedy for millions of Americans.[21]

A year later (September 2002), President Cameron led the first anniversary commemoration of the terrorist attacks in a ceremony on the Jamestown campus where a tree was planted to honor the victims. Dr. Cameron shared the storied history of America and the dreams and sacrifices of our individual citizens as a way of memorializing those who died in New York, Washington, and Pennsylvania. Reminding his audience that the Jamestown campus stands along one of the major colonial routes stretching across the Piedmont, he reiterated that "while we may sometimes believe individually that we are overlooked in the great scheme of events, history inevitably touches us all." He asked the audience to "remember their responsibilities as citizens of the world's greatest democracy, to work in all instances to guarantee the sanctity of their nation and bond in all endeavors to comfort and nurture their fellow citizens."[22]

Summary

Don Cameron concluded his first decade as GTCC's president determined to empower the transition of the Guilford County workforce from its traditional base of textile, furniture, and apparel manufacturing to the new era of biotechnology, nanotechnology, informational technology, and new medicine. Aware that industry would come and go at an accelerated rate, his faculty and staff positioned the College to train a workforce to meet every shift in employment. Good intentions and planning aside, no one could have foreseen the economic setbacks extending from September 11 that exacerbated the fiscal distress already affecting the nation and North Carolina.

GTCC's enrollment skyrocketed at the same time a budget deficit of nearly one billion dollars confronted the state (June 30, 2002). Once again, Guilford County's most unique educational institution found itself on the front line in the war against plant closings, massive layoffs and state budget reductions. The man in the Medlin Campus Center third floor presidential suite sat at his desk and began to fashion a plan for survival.

Campus Notes

The international faculty exchange between GTCC and the Danish technical college Erhvervs Uddannelses Center (EUC) in Sonderberg, Denmark, began with the Culinary Technology Program in spring 2000 and expanded to the Automotive Department in 2001.[23]

GTCC graduate Nickie Doyal, a speech communication major and grandmother of six, won a Phi Theta Kappa International full-ride scholarship valued at $13,150 per semester to attend High Point University

Doyle and Brenda Rae Haynes won Academic Excellence Awards in 2001. The award recognizes excellence and encourages scholarship among the more than 760,000 students of the NCCCS.

Certified Nursing Assistant (CNA) Instructor Doxie Whitfield received the 2001 Distinguished Service Award presented by the City of Greensboro. Whitfield was honored for collaborating with the Bell House of Greensboro to meet the growing demand for qualified nursing assistants and to provide specialized training for disabled individuals.

High Point's Education 2009 Committee in collaboration with the High Point Partners, GTCC, Leadership High Point, and the High Point Chamber of Commerce generated an award-winning gift program. PCs for GEDs in 2001, originally championed by Ed Parks, had rewarded 556 GED recipients with used personal computers by December 2006.[24]

Chapter 31

2002–03:
Managing in Tough Times

The situation is dire for many colleges. State funding is being cut at a time when enrollment at many schools is at an all time high as the poor economy pushes laid off workers to community colleges for new skills. And this year (2002) students saw tuition increase from $31 per credit hour to $34.25.[1]

The Future Is Not What It Should Be!

As the 20th century shuttered to an end, Don Cameron was clearly aware that the millennium was unlikely to begin on a positive economic note. By 1998, the state's 76,855 trade-related job losses, 1.9 percent of the total workforce, led the nation.[2] The loss of traditional manufacturing jobs in textiles, tobacco, furniture, and some related industries swelled the unemployment ranks in Guilford County to 14,782 in 2002–03 and 13,845 in 2003–04.[3] The state totals were even more startling with 281,437 individuals unemployed in 2002–03 and 269,400 in 2003–04. This recapitulation of the economic collapse that seriously impacted GTCC's resources during the nightmare-budget years 2002–03 dresses the stage for a description of the institutional strategy administrators created to survive and grow despite budget restraints and job training demands.

The President's 2002 New Year greeting warned the Guilford legislative delegation that incapacitating budget restraints forced on the state's community colleges would foster irreparable damage. The fact that these institutions, the state's first defense against unemployment and poverty, were forced to wait for funding until the economy recovered unleashed this forceful admonition from Cameron.

Guilford Tech and its fellow community colleges are under immense pressure. We are on the front line in the war against the plant closings and massive layoffs which have left thousands of workers unemployed and technically adrift. Yet, 2002 finds us victimized by perpetual underfunding, a condition intensified by debilitating reversions to our operating budgets.

Guilford Tech is committed to educating and retraining the Piedmont's workforce and our success speaks louder than words, but forcing community colleges to do more with less is not a fiscally responsible strategy.

We are accomplishing our mission in spite of budget constraints and punitive reversions. Our teachers have accepted additional students because it is the right thing to do. Our faculty and staff work for reasons other than money, but the fact is, we can only reward these servants of the people with a "pat on the back" for so long.[4]

GTCC had previously reverted 2 percent of its budget when, in February 2002, it was ordered to return another $685,000; at the same time its full-time paid student enrollment jumped 6 percent (8,357) in the fall of 2001 and 11 percent in spring 2002.[5] In April 2002, the College faced a possible base budget reduction for 2002–03 that could range from four percent ($717,617) to ten percent ($2,210,991).[6] While contingency measures were instituted to prevent possible faculty and staff layoffs, Board Chair J. Patrick "Pat" Danahy (2001–04) shared President Cameron's concern for the Institution's fiscal vitality as the state budget shortfall, then approaching $2 billion, prodded the General Assembly to consider $695 million in education budget cuts for fiscal 2002–03. For the first time in history, North Carolina's community colleges were unlikely to receive enrollment growth estimated at $52 million, a projection that would, under normal circumstances, earmark as much as $2.7 million for GTCC.

Vice President of Administrative Services Rae Marie Smith sketched two possible scenarios; the first projected a six percent reduction in the base formula with a two percent mid year reversion costing the College $1.7 million. The second projection was based on a situation whereby GTCC might receive 50 percent of its enrollment growth while absorbing a ten percent budget cut restricted to non instructional dollars. While this scheme promised a better budget, it lacked the flexibility to provide the support services necessary to assure student success.[7]

GTCC eventually received $1,861,790, roughly 69 percent of its enrollment growth, in new formula funding, and the Community College System $41.5 million of its $51 million enrollment growth. The State Board of Community Colleges was further ordered to identify an additional $5 million reduction and did so by eliminating one clerical position from every institution's base and increasing the average class size. The $3.2 million cut in instructional funding forced GTCC to increase class sizes from 19 to 20 students and raise tuition from $31 to $34.25 per credit hour translating to $39 per semester more for students enrolling for 12 or more credit hours.[8] By 2007–08, in-state tuition totaled $39.50 per semester hour for a maximum of $632.00 per semester (16 credit hours). Out-of-state tuition was $219.50 per credit hour for a maximum of $3,512.00 (16 credit hours) per semester.[9]

The Enrollment versus Funding Dilemma

The curriculum enrollment and FTE totals for 1997–2001 indicated that, while there had not been a major growth in enrollment, the annual FTE had steadily increased indicating that students were taking more hours. The 7,645 FTE tally for 2001–02 reflected an increase of 649 over 2000–01.[10] Curriculum enrollment for 2001–02 reflected a 9.3 percent growth in headcount during a period when manufacturing was slipping in Guilford County. The unduplicated headcount enrollment for Continuing Education, including Basic Skills, Community Service, Business & Industry, Occupational Extension, and Self-Supporting for 2001–02, totaled 30,064. This 5.5 percent boost over the previous year increased the FTE by 7 percent.[11]

In lieu of funding a salary increase for professional faculty and staff for the fiscal year 2002–03, the General Assembly directed the State Board of Community Colleges to establish guidelines allowing the colleges to make their own decisions about funding raises from their existing budgets. Increases not to exceed 1.84 percent could include one time salary bonuses, a maximum of 10 days additional leave, or a combination of all three. GTCC awarded its professional faculty and staff 10 days additional leave, a 1.84 percent increase, two additional paid holidays, and a $500 one-time bonus.[12]

The obsolete "funding in arrears" process that annually weakens the mission of North Carolina's community colleges was cobbled together in the 1980s when enrollment projections were poorly executed. This faulty anachronism that should have been revised when technology improved reporting in the 1990s still forces community colleges to base their future funding requests on the previous year's verifiable enrollment numbers. Dr. Cameron strenuously objects to this dilemma that flies in the face of common sense.

> If I am being funded based on last year's budget and I have a 5 percent enrollment increase this year, where do I get the money to pay for that? We either need to get it from the private sector, or shift things around internally to make things work. This isn't the best way to run an operation."[13]

The disparity extends to a per capita student funding policy that equally funds nursing students and liberal arts students. For example, in 2002–03, it cost GTCC approximately $1,000 a year to educate a liberal arts student compared with $5,500 per year to train a nursing student and $7,900 to train a physical therapist. Since the state was then funding the College at $3,795 per year per student, the College needed to enroll as many liberal arts students as possible to finance the greater demand for the fewer health care student slots.[14]

As the state and its counties wavered on the cusp of economic collapse, GTCC reassured Guilford County taxpayers that, regardless of the crisis, they were getting a high return on their investment. Vice President for Instruction, Linda Thomas-Glover and Kathryn Baker Smith, Vice President for Educational Support Services, analyzed the cost of the school's programs and correlated their findings with the value of the programs to the community. They ranked the programs by cost per full-time equivalent (FTE) and matched them to areas of high employment demand and the key employment clusters identified in economic development studies. Their scholarly analysis confirmed Cameron's argument that low-cost general education programs enabled the College to "earn" the money necessary to fund the more expensive technical programs. The study further revealed that GTCC's programs were in concert with the local economy's high demand sectors.[15]

The statewide economic crunch knifed into spring 2003 when the College was ordered to prepare for a 15 percent decrease in its May state allocation and a 25 percent cut in the June allocation for a total of about $216,000. Those funds were originally budgeted to buy a wide range of instructional supplies including specific materials for welding and dental hygiene classes. The College immediately scaled back its purchases and cancelled unfulfilled orders.[16] As funding evaporated, the enrollment soared to 9,800 in fall 2003, the largest headcount in the school's history.[17]

GTCC Trustees learned the devastating extent of the bludgeoning budgetary restrictions at their November 7, 2003, work session; full classes had prohibited 661 students from enrolling. A wide range of programs and introductory classes quickly reached capacity after sizes were increased, but the College was unable to offer 110 classes that could have been scheduled had funding been available. The inability to hire teachers, plus the lack of qualified teachers, classroom space, workstations, and labs severely impacted enrollment. An additional 657 students were dropped for non-payment, or left within the first week of school due to financial problems, schedule conflicts, family and personal reasons.[18] Dr. Cameron reported that since 2000 enrollment in the North Carolina Community College System had grown by 30,000 students while the system had suffered $36 million in permanent cuts; the outlook for 2003–04 was hardly promising.[19]

Perceptions and Misconceptions

The budget dilemma and the inability to meet enrollment demands put the marketing department's three-year promotion to educate the public and the business community about GTCC and close the information gap presumed by the McNeill Lehman survey (2002) on hold. However, positive media coverage emanating from GTCC's frontline offensive to quell the disastrous effects of a major unemployment crisis exemplified by the highly effective "Putting the Piedmont Back to Work" promotion on WXII-TV, more than compensated for the restriction on marketing dollars.[20]

The business community's perceived lack of knowledge about GTCC, as gauged by the McNeill Lehman (2001) and the Herman (2005) studies, is difficult to reasonably substantiate when you consider the major College Tech Prep and apprenticeship programs Don Cameron and Guilford County School's superintendent Jerry Weast instituted in the mid 1990s at the invitation of these self-same industrialists. Beyond the fact that some of these industries had significantly declined by 2000, the Business & Industry division still posted significant numbers in workers trained and programs delivered. Since more than 450 business and industry leaders belonged to GTCC program advisory boards, the information gap, "GTCC is Guilford County's best kept secret," presumably prevailed at the volatile CEO level; a fact revisited by the Herman Group Report (2005).

Massive changes in corporate leadership, multiple plant closings, and a proliferation of new and smaller firms challenged the marketing department to find innovative success stories to sell the College to the targeted CEO segment. The author remains convinced that the perceived information gap was centered in Greater Greensboro where the historic absence of a significant collegiate image, coupled with the lack of signature programs, contributed to the lack recognition for GTCC's training mission. The general public in Guilford County could not have been unaware of GTCC since thousands of them attended various credit and non-credit classes.[21]

Putting the Piedmont Back to Work

A Triad media executive with personal and professional ties to GTCC through a long standing relationship with the author found the downturn in the economy so alarming that he committed his company to a major job training promotion. Henry E. "Hank" Price, President and General Manager of WXII-TV (NBC, Hearst-Argyll), provided a spectacular workforce preparedness partnership in late 2001. Concerned by North Carolina's 17-year high jobless rate and the fact that Guilford County led the state in claiming jobless benefits, Price offered to televise a series of four segments produced by GTCC that explored training opportunities at the community college. WXII-TV aired the segments on its 6 and 11 pm newscasts and repeated them on its morning news show during the all important February (2002) Nielsen rating period. In a concerted campaign titled "Putting the Piedmont Back to Work," Price expanded the project to include 11 community colleges in the Piedmont Triad and southern Virginia.

GTCC's initial segment (February 5, 2002) focused on the demand for workers in skilled trades including welding and carpentry and explored the College's extensive catalog of continuing education courses. Contact information was provided at the conclusion of each segment plus GTCC staff and faculty manned a call center to answer inquiries during and immediately after the broadcasts throughout the month-long campaign.

The second segment emphasized Basic Skills, GED, and adult high school diploma programs. By publicizing the availability of remedial classes for less prepared students, GTCC sought to convince the region's unschooled "hands-people" to enroll for classes. Segment three highlighted Health and Public Safety programs including GTCC's exceptional Surgical Technology program plus a variety of emergency medical science opportunities. The fourth segment profiled GTCC "Distinguished Alumnae" Judy Miller, President and CEO of RSVP Communications. Miller's meteoric rise from unemployment to CEO through GTCC's Secretarial Science program (now Office System Technology, OST) served as a creditable endorsement for the College and as an inspiration to potential applicants.

"Putting the Piedmont Back to Work" was a tremendously successful venture for the public, the community colleges, and WXII-TV. As is often the case with media phenomena, competing TV stations, seeking to profit from the campaign, gravitated toward the topic and presented additional stories illuminating community college possibilities for unemployed and untrained workers. This unprecedented promotional exposure heightened public interest in area community colleges and generated a residual effect in on-going media coverage of workforce preparedness programs and issues through the first seven years of the 21st century.[22]

GTCC Expansion

The plan to improve and increase GTCC's presence and services in Greensboro did not miss a beat during the economic downturn. The availability of a large, reasonably priced tract of land on East Wendover Avenue attracted Cameron's attention in the aftermath of the Carolina Circle Mall debacle and was quickly targeted as a campus possibility. The project moved a step closer to reality in early 2002 when architect Ken Mayer (Moser, Mayer, Phoenix, Inc) presented a master plan projecting a set of four buildings including a central energy plant and perimeter parking. The Technical Education Center (TEC), formerly proposed for the Jamestown campus, was transferred to Greensboro to join an Adult Education Center (AEC) and a Continuing Education Center (CEC).[23]

But first, it was High Point's turn to get a campus upgrade. A large crowd gathered on a sun-swept, bitterly cold Valentine Day morning in February 2002 to celebrate the ground breaking for the first of the 2000 Higher Education bond buildings. The $9.25 million Entertainment Technology Center would house acoustically insulated recording studios, multiple electronic music labs, a large production studio, plus a 600-seat amphitheater. By the time construction began on the state-of-the-art facility, 104 students were taking courses in the program.[24]

New and Expanded Programs

Programs grew and prospered in spite of the economic downturn. The Associate Degree Nursing program began offering evening classes in 2002 in an attempt to alleviate the ongoing nursing shortage as hospitals and care facilities expanded their services. New programs included Agricultural Systems to train John Deere Service Technicians; Construction Management Technology; Esthetics, to provide competency based knowledge associated with the art of skin-care; Human Services/Mental Health offered an understanding of the culturally and emotionally challenged, developmentally disabled, and addicted clients. A new Plumbing certificate became a precursor to the plumbing apprenticeship program. Turfgrass Management Technology was instituted to train students to manage golf courses, build sports fields, and specialize in lawn care, irrigation design, and sod production.[25]

The Developmental Quandary and Customer Service

The massive loss of traditional manufacturing jobs forced GTCC to reexamine its workforce preparedness mission. While the College was capturing some of the high school Tech Prep graduates, it was losing far too many students who registered, but dropped out in the developmental process that would have prepared them to enter technical programs that could have assured them productive employment. President Cameron was additionally concerned when 2,000 of the 2,665 students who enrolled for the fall 2000 semester did not return in fall 2001.[26] He scheduled developmental education on the Board work session agenda (November 1–2, 2002) and enlisted two of GTCC's most experienced educators, George Fouts and Kathryn Baker Smith, to explore the issue.

Retired Executive Vice President George Fouts, then an instructor in the developmental education division, argued that the exceptional diversity present in their classes forced instructors to teach individuals as opposed to the entire group. Fouts found students were less prepared than those of the late 1980s and, while the majority had graduated from high school, some could not test above the sixth grade. They were less capable of critical understanding and sought shortcuts to solve problems without exercising an analytical approach to grasp the true nature of the challenge. Classroom discipline was a huge problem among students who were uninterested in culture, civics, and media. International students posed the biggest challenge. Fout's distressing conclusion indicated that approximately 40% of GTCC's entering students needed some type of developmental education.[27]

Smith identified seven risk factors impacting GTCC students: (1) delayed entry into college, (2) part-time enrollment, (3) full-time employment, (4) financial independence, (5) dependents, (6) single parenthood, and (7) the lack of a high school diploma. Smith based her presentation on a study compiled by Dr. Pat Abell, Director of GTCC's Institutional Research and Planning Office, and Sociology instructor Dr. Carol Schmid. Their research indicated that "highly non-traditional students were on average less integrated into college life and less likely to participate in study groups and clubs or speak with faculty outside the classroom." They concluded:

> Unless well-designed policies are able to identify and provide support for these highly non-traditional students, the completion of a college education for many of them would remain a "diverted dream."[28]

These expert observations and scholarly reports generated substantial planning grants that empowered GTCC to mediate challenges to students through two high profile programs, "Achieving the Dream" and "The Learning College."[29]

Smith's Educational Support Services division was equally involved in solving six major issues extending from a "Student Needs Report" in February

2003 that revealed glaring deficiencies in GTCC's customer service. Registration was a semi-annual challenge on the Jamestown campus where students were obligated to move between floors in two major buildings to complete the process. Academic advising was understaffed and there was no way to insure that students were choosing appropriate courses, learning how to develop good study skills, or taking advantage of services provided by the College.

Record enrollments had aggravated an already stressful registration-counseling scenario compounded by overwhelming telephone traffic, the lack of strong internal communications, and the absence of training for frontline customer service personnel. Long lines of waiting students contributed to confusion complicated by "tremendous numbers" of speakers of languages other than English and changes in immigration laws. The lack of mentoring and career planning support for students with personal issues, inherent weaknesses in the basic skills program, and a cumbersome website painted a dismal picture of customer service at GTCC.

The multiple causes of this dilemma were embedded in exceptional growth and gross inefficiency, outmoded paper based procedures, lack of trained personnel, and the absence of proper funding for a vital college operation. Guided by Smith, a spatial study, "Restacking the Medlin Campus Center," reconfigured the Medlin Campus Center to provide students with a realistic "Front Door Experience" on Level Two. Level One was redecorated to make it more appealing to students. Determined administrators revamped the Basic Skills programs in High Point and Greensboro, an experienced web designer was hired to redesign the website, and a committee was organized to improve customer service.[30]

NCCCS 40th Anniversary

The North Carolina Community College System commemorated this significant milestone on the evening of July 11, 2003, honoring W. Dallas Herring, one of the founders of the North Carolina Community College System. System President H. Martin Lancaster reminded the audience of Herring's immortal vision.

> The only valid philosophy for North Carolina is the philosophy of total education. That is why the doors to the institutions of North Carolina's system of community colleges must never be closed to anyone of suitable age who can learn what they teach. We must take people from where they are and carry them as far as they can go within the assigned functions of the system."[31]

Herring's admirable philosophy garnered accolades of respect from members of the North Carolina House and Senate who praised the system in recognition of its anniversary on June 3, 2003. A few weeks later when the General Assembly passed the state budget those "warm and fuzzy feelings" did not translate into more funding for the system that lost $10.5 million the previous year. Many in the system wondered why their expectations had been so high given that, even in good economic times, the General Assembly failed to adequately finance the Community College System.[32]

Summary

At the conclusion of its 45th year (2003), GTCC faculty and staff were determined to see the Institution regain its strength after three years of massive budget cuts and reversions. Funding shortfalls aside, they would determinedly launch the "Quick Jobs with a Future" job training initiative in February 2004.[33] Productively, GTCC achieved a superior success rating when 93 percent of its basic skills students continued their studies or graduated; 100 percent of its graduates reportedly met their goals at the College; 100 percent of the 2000–01 graduates had jobs within a year of graduation and 94 percent of the graduates attending a four-year institution were averaging at least a C.[34] Amidst these positives planning was proceeding to broaden the school's public image by strongly marketing the dedication of the new Larry Gatlin School of Entertainment Technology's $9.25 million High Point home.

Campus Notes

James S. "Jim" Belk, Executive Director of the GTCC Foundation, Inc., received the 2002 Brotherhood/Sisterhood Citation Award presented by the Piedmont Section of the National Conference for Community and Justice. The tribute recognized Belk's significant contributions during more than 40 years of civic volunteerism for an almost endless list of humanitarian groups. Belk was also chosen to chair the Piedmont Triad Partnership Foundation (2003–04), a subsidiary of the Piedmont Triad Partnership regional economic development group.[35]

Sociology Professor Dr. Carol Schmid was named a Fulbright Scholar and spent a year teaching in the Baltic republic of Latvia.[36]

GTCC's first librarian and Dean of Learning Resources Mertys Ward Bell died May 28, 2003, at her home in Sedgefield, a short drive from the Jamestown campus where she was first employed in 1962. The library component of the LRC was named for her when she retired in 1984.[37]

Cuyler McKnight, III was named Dean of the High Point Campus on September 15, 2003. The former business executive and U.S. Army Lt. Colonel (Ret.) was subsequently promoted to Executive Vice President on April 1, 2006.[38]

John Turner Davis, 81 (Davis Hall), the CEO of Davis Furniture Industries, High Point, and former GTCC Board Chair (1969–81), died Thursday, December 5, 2003.

The Miller Brewing Company's Tools for Success program presented tool kits to four GTCC students (2003) increasing their contribution since 1999 to $61,500.[39]

Chapter 32

2003–04:
Part I: Quality Enhancement and Expansion

I've just become a community college enthusiast. It helps a tremendous amount of people and helps them go as far as they want to go. I've never seen an organization try to be all things to all people like the Community College System does. It tries to teach people how to read or carries them all the way up to college transfer.

Dr. Stuart Fountain[1]

Engaging the Future

The academic year 2003–04 evolved as a benchmarking platform for GTCC as the College created and implemented initiatives that would guide it to the end of the 21st century's first decade. The prestigious Legacy Campaign, SACS reaccredidation, a review of teacher articulation agreements, the drive to pass a major local bond issue, the race to jumpstart a fast-track workforce retraining program, the initiative to implement a planning grant to improve student services and retention, elicited a cascade of media attention. GTCC spun in a remarkable public orbit at the same time it struggled with contractors to complete the Entertainment Technology Building in High Point and erect a new campus in Greensboro.[2]

The Legacy Campaign

GTCC launched its first ever capital campaign in February 2003 to raise $6 million in the midst of a state budget shortfall that in three years had slashed the school's annual equipment budget in half to about $500,000. The timing was crucial given that the College was in the midst of a construction program and the new buildings coming on line needed equipping. Undeterred by the economic challenges, Foundation executive director Jim Belk refused to delay the campaign;

> It's an opportunity we feel like we have to take advantage of. This is the time to do it. Because we've got the $58 million in new buildings (and need to equip them), we've got to go.[3]

The campaign was chaired by three high-profile civic leaders: Foundation Chair James F. "Jim" Morgan of High Point, and Greensboro residents Hayes Clement, retired Arthur Anderson Managing Partner, and community volunteer Shirley Spears. They identified $2 million for new buildings and $1.75 million in additional endowments for scholarships; $1 million was earmarked for faculty and staff support including six endowed teaching chairs at $100,000 each plus endowments to support innovative instructional technology, projects, programs, and professional development. An additional endowment of $750,000 for academic support would enhance classrooms, provide equipment funds for existing programs, and start-up money for future programs; a $500,000 unrestricted endowment would satisfy the Institution's greatest needs as determined by the Foundation Board of Directors and GTCC's Trustees. The campaign started positively when 125 members of the President's Society contributed $251,398 during 2002–03 when specific gifts to the $6 million Legacy Campaign totaled $602,687.[4]

The Foundation celebrated the first major gift of the Legacy Campaign in June 2003 by dedicating the Dr. Stuart B. Fountain Dental Science Building. The naming recognized Fountain's two decades of service as GTCC Trustee and Board Chair and his nomination to membership on the State Board of Community Colleges. It further acknowledged a generous commitment of $250,000 through personal contributions and those from family, friends, dental colleagues, and fellow Rotarians.[5] The Percy H. Sears family endowed GTCC's first teaching chair, the *Gladys S. Sears Endowed Teaching Chair in Business Technologies.* The fountain on the esplanade before the Percy H. Sears Applied Technology Center was officially dedicated to recognize this contribution on August 28, 2003.[6]

The SACS Accreditation Process

Accreditation by the Commission on Colleges of the Southern Association of Colleges and Schools (SACS) is a self-regulatory, peer-evaluated process.

GTCC is required to evaluate its operations and effectiveness every ten years to prove to a professional review board that it is providing its students a sound education with sufficient resources, programs, and services. Accreditation further signifies that GTCC maintains clearly specified educational objectives consistent with its mission and the degrees it offers, and is demonstrating institutional success in achieving its stated objectives.

Dr. Kathryn Baker Smith, GTCC's SACS liaison, directed the Accreditation Review Project comprising a Leadership Team and the SACS Compliance and QEP committees that began the process in January 2003. The Compliance Audit compelled the College to review its mission, structure, key policies, procedures, and stated objectives. The compliance team was charged to prove that SACS' core requirements, comprehensive standards, and federal mandates, were in place, working, and consistently scrutinized.

In 2004, SACS added a new dimension to the accreditation process when they asked GTCC to create a comprehensive quality enhancement plan (QEP) specifically related to student learning. GTCC's QEP team suggested improving internal communications, sharpening customer service, and developing strategies to raise student expectations by improving behaviors and academic achievement. The objective was to transform GTCC into a student-centered college and to improve the specific measurement of student-attained employability skills that did not have an extensive history of assessment: Teamwork, Responsibility, Communication, Problem-Solving, Information Processing, and Adaptability. The QEP created and promoted a college-wide consciousness about the importance and regular practice of assessment and the use of those statistics to continuously monitor the collective quality of work at the College.

The QEP provided guidelines to insure that the College met and sustained its goals. Why? Because educators are aware that the repetitive nature of instruction institutionalizes routines that should be consistently analyzed to insure that the changing needs of students and the workplace are constantly addressed by planning objectives. These objectives are determined through a reflective process that asks (1) what frustrates a teacher, (2) what behaviors need to change, (3) am I (teacher-staff) part of the problem, (4) what can we help others learn and how can we teach it; (5) how will we know if behavior has improved and how do we measure it? The peer review that forms the heart of the SACS process is the public's greatest assurance of institutional accountability.

Prior to this self-study, Dr. Cameron warned Smith's team that he was not prepared to accept more than single-digit recommendations (suggestions for improvement) from SACS. He was not disappointed; the lone suggestion forwarded by the visiting evaluators (September 20–22, 2004) was resolved before they filed their final report in June 2005.[7] In congratulating the staff and faculty on a stellar performance, President Cameron revealed that Dr. Dwyer, the SACS representative assigned to GTCC, had suggested that GTCC's study could serve as a model for other colleges: "The SACS committee was exceptionally impressed with our Quality Enhancement Plan. They further indicated that the plan we outlined is 'on the cutting edge.'" Dr. Smith and Dr. Carolyn Schneider, Division Chair, Arts and Sciences, were commended for their leadership.[8] While the SACS process is complicated and bureaucratically burdensome, it is absolutely vital to insure the credibility of the College. In this case, these exercises set new directions for student services that were to have a major impact on enrollment and retention.

Teacher Education

In 2003, North Carolina was under extreme pressure to educate as many teachers as possible to fulfill the need for 90,000 K–12 instructors across the next ten years. Four-year institutions were producing only about 3,000 to 4,000 per year and intimidating state licensure requirements were forcing some candidates to forego the profession; a 22 percent turnover rate and 17 percent attrition contributed to the imminent crisis. GTCC re-examined and strengthened its articulation agreements with four-year institutions to efficiently facilitate transfer options that would more conveniently enable students with associate degrees to enroll in teacher education programs.

Dr. JoAnn Buck, Professor/Department Chair, English/Humanities, directed GTCC's pre-education program development and faculty advising. Buck was determined to insure that the College over-achieved in meeting the state's teacher crisis with productive training initiatives including the Faculty in Training Program (FIT); the proven 2 plus 2 Program, GTCC's Early Childhood Education Program, and UNCG's B–K Certification. The College introduced a Pre-elementary education program for K–6 certification and preparatory programs for secondary content disciplines in English and History. Meetings with administrators from UNCG, NC A&T, Greensboro College, High Point University, Guilford College, and Elon University identified advising issues and course requirements for prospective teachers.

Buck and her colleagues, notably Pamela R. Herndon, who eventually implemented the necessary changes as program director, pursued articulation discussions with local transfer institutions to update the curriculum in 2001–03. Research disclosed that some agreements with four-year institutions had never been formally articulated. One university required pre-education

majors to complete 12 hours at the transfer institution to accumulate the required grade point average before admittance to a teacher education program.
There were major concerns about GTCC students passing the Praxis Level I
examination as a qualification for acceptance to a teacher education program.
Discussions with UNCG resulted in a formal cooperative agreement that allowed pre-education majors to rehearse the Praxis exam prior to officially taking it. The UNCG School of Education strengthened its articulation agreement by creating a community college liaison position to coordinate the
transfer process.[9]

GTCC was in the vanguard when community colleges were approved to provide teacher education. By 2007–08 the College offered two routes for those seeking a career in education. The Teacher Education Network (TEN) assisted students who planned to complete teacher training after completing their 2 plus 2
AA degree as a pre-education major at GTCC. The TEN enabled them to pursue a seamless transition to one of the College's four-year partners to complete
their teacher education. The Lateral Entry Program offered courses for bache-
lor's degree holders teaching in the Guilford County Schools to help them meet
the Department of Public Instruction general pedagogy competencies.[10]

Quick Jobs with a Future

This is not really designed to be a program for everyone. It will be aimed
at people who have been laid off from textile and manufacturing jobs and
have few transferable skills or job options in their fields. Quick Jobs empowers them to step forward and think about retooling and what they
are going to do for the rest of their lives.

Philip King, GTCC Dean
Business and Industry
Quick Jobs with a Future[11]

One of GTCC's most successful "back to work" programs emerged after a
presidential visit to Greenville Technical College, Greenville, S.C., in late 2003.
Dr. Cameron, Executive Vice President, Dr. Marshall "Sonny" White, and
Foundation Director Jim Belk, were extremely impressed by the "Quick Jobs"
program Greenville Tech launched in 2001 to retrain displaced workers and
return them to the workforce as quickly as possible. Greenville Tech's impressive record offered GTCC a possible solution to revitalize the productive
prospects for an estimated 14,000 unemployed workers in Guilford County.

Greenville Tech had trained over 3,000 people in two years and 75 percent
had found jobs in 60 days or less. GTCC's forthcoming *Quick Jobs with a Fu-*

ture program would offer specific training in a variety of courses at affordable prices, convenient times, and locations. Many programs could be completed in three months or less.

To launch the project, Cameron, White, and Belk negotiated partnerships with area social services providers and drafted a "Quick Jobs Proposal for Guilford County." This "Coalition for the Dislocated Worker" included the Greensboro and High Point Chambers of Commerce, the Employment Security Commission, Department of Social Services, Job-Link, the Women's Resource Center, Goodwill Industries, Greensboro Urban Ministry, Moses Cone-Wesley Long Community Health Foundation, Salvation Army, United Way of Greater Greensboro, United Way 211, the Welfare Reform Liaison Program, the Workforce Development Board, and several training providers.[12]

Since GTCC's operating budget could not provide funding for start-up programs, financing was contingent on community support. E. S. "Jim" Melvin, CEO of the Joseph M. Bryan Foundation and the titular leader of the six-foundation *Action Greensboro* provided $260,000 to jumpstart the program. This enabled Philip King, GTCC Dean of Business and Industry, to assemble the infrastructure to select and package existing courses that correlated with job needs and to market the program.[13]

Quick Jobs with a Future was designed to become self-sustaining within three years as the offerings presumably expanded to a projected 50 targeted jobs and 3,500 participants. GTCC and its industry partners identified jobs with high vacancy rates in Healthcare, Supply Chain-Logistics, Information Technology, Construction, and Engineering Technology. Students would have to pay for the fast track classes, but grants and scholarships were available to those who needed tuition assistance. The founding coalition was determined to have more than 70 percent of the participants back at work by June 30, 2004.[14]

Nearly 1,000 possible applicants appeared at the first *Quick Jobs with a Future* information session on January 16, 2004. The 435-seat Koury Hospitality Center auditorium was filled by the two o'clock pm start time and a second session was immediately scheduled to accommodate the overflow; 600 students were served during the first six months of the program. While the unemployment numbers declined, many unemployed or displaced individuals regularly attend the free information sessions hosted by GTCC on the first Friday of each month, at publication, with the unemployment rate in Guilford County peaking at 4.5 percent (October 2007). *Quick Jobs with a Future* offered more than 20 programs and more than 2,000 completers had been returned to the workforce.[15] The specialized training is based on a proven demand for trained employees in Guilford County. The classes implement skills that are taught to address specific employment needs to expediently prepare individuals for the workforce. Additional programs are offered when research targets areas where training is needed.[16]

The 2004 GTCC Bond Issue

Planning for this referendum began in 2003 after the inability to buy the Carolina Circle Mall forced the College to consider a series of alternatives to more firmly establish GTCC's image and services in Greensboro. Dr. Cameron had previously pegged GTCC's "true needs" for facilities at an astounding $76 million, but at the spring 2003 work session the Board asked the staff to draft a bond proposal not to exceed $20 million.[17] The $19 million issue they reviewed in June 2003 targeted $5 million for a proposed new Allied Health building at Jamestown; $5 million for renovating three buildings on the Jamestown campus; $5 million for new instructional equipment; $1 million for new biotechnology classrooms, and $3 million to purchase land for a new campus in northwest Guilford County.[18] The Board, chaired by Pat Danahy, stuck to that scheme through November 2003 even as they asked the administrative services division to formulate yet another priority list of needs for speculative issues of $25, $30, and $35 million.[19]

The political climate is historically a major factor in developing a bond issue in traditionally conservative Guilford County. GTCC's Board never publicly endorsed a figure without intensively lobbying the county commissioners who, in 2004, allocated at least 14.3 percent of the Institution's annual operating expenses.[20] The Board ultimately approved a $47 million request based on need and the obvious factor that the College was an economic driver of major proportions. Facilities expansion was critical if the Institution were to successfully train a high tech work force for the county. GTCC was a tremendous enterprise distributing $30 million in annual salaries at a time when every dollar invested by state and local governments generated $1.25 in salaries and benefits. The College was a boon to its students who realized a return of $12.90 for every dollar invested in training.[21]

After a majority (six to four) of the commissioners endorsed the $47 million request, the College formalized its strategy to win the electorate's approval.[22] Dr. Cameron named retired Executive Vice President George Fouts to chair the bond promotional committee's ninety day campaign. Fouts confidently decided to forego hiring a consultant and opted to fill his campaign chest through the time proven corporate and private donation process.[23] Thematically, the "Friends of GTCC 2004" campaign projected the College as a nationally recognized leader in workforce preparedness as evidenced by the

Wall Street Journal article and the fact that the number of people using the College's services had increased 25 percent in four years.[24]

The referendum targeted eight major projects: (1) $5 million for an Allied Health building to consolidate programs and provide desperately needed training space, (2) $10 million for a Business & Industry/Biotechnology building, (3) $5 million to install instructional equipment and technology updates in all buildings, (4) $4.5 million for classroom renovations and HVAC updates, (5) $3.5 million for an Aviation/Transportation building, (6) $8 million for a classroom building at the High Point campus, (7) $3.5 million for expansion land acquisitions, and (8) $8 million for a new Greensboro classroom building.[25]

Editorialists endorsed the GTCC bond as "a wise investment in the community's future." Noting that "the state's community colleges get by with less than they need or deserve," the editorialist implored voters to "help remedy that inequity by approving money to end the current crunch as well as plot the future."[26] TV news coverage was consistently positive and College officials promoted the bond issue during expanded interviews on the Triad's early morning news shows. Time Warner Cable donated, produced, and frequently broadcast, a thirty-second commercial promoting the proposal. Promotional postcards reached every mailing address in Guilford County.[27]

GTCC prevailed when 63.49 percent of the voters approved the $47 million issue on November 3, 2004, by a tally of 116,251 to 66,823. With almost 64 percent of the vote, the College won all but ten of the county's 159 precincts with the margin tightest along the distant Guilford County borders. Campaign chairman Fouts priced each vote at a mere 6 cents. Fresh from this resounding victory, GTCC acknowledged that it had accumulated $105 million in bond financing in the first four years of the 21st century.[28]

Summary

At this point, it should be obvious that the vortex GTCC's planners had created with a plethora of initiatives represented a near perfect example of the energy properly administrated community colleges can generate, but there were challenges particularly for the building program. In High Point, the Entertainment Technology project was exceptionally troublesome due in part to weather delays and completion issues with contractors and architects; challenges the Trustees saw first hand during a tour on February 19, 2004.

That same wintry month in Greensboro, carpenters began fabricating the interior of the Adult Education Center, the first of four buildings scheduled for the new Greensboro campus. Across the ragged landscape along East Wendover Avenue underground piping was snaking out from the Central Energy Plant to connect three major facilities. The footings were down at the Continuing Education Center and pre-construction meetings were taking place on the mammoth Technical Education Center. At Jamestown, site work had started for a service building at the Public Safety Service Complex.[29]

Chapter 33

2003–04:
Part II: Visionary Programs

It (the Larry Gatlin School of Entertainment Technology) is not going to ensure that they (the students) ever sing on the "Tonight Show," "American Idol," or in Carnegie Hall. That is not what it is about. It's going to give them the tools and equip them for a fighting chance.[1]

The Larry Gatlin School of Entertainment Technology

More than 200 students reported to Entertainment Technology's $9.25 million home in High Point in January 2004.[2] Ranging in age from 16-year-old home school graduates to senior citizen retirees, they pursued a variety of goals. Some sought career development while others focused on specific technical skills to validate their "on-the-job" experience. Personal intentions aside, they bonded to organize the instructional equipment in six state-of-the-art production studios and the assortment of specialty labs, classrooms, rehearsal rooms, and offices for faculty and staff that comprised the facility.

The premier performance venues included a major production studio with flexible seating for an audience of 225 and an outdoor amphitheater accommodating more than 600.[3] When Program Coordinator Todd Dupree, who had co-authored the technical curriculum with Arts and Sciences Division Chair Carolyn Schneider resigned to pursue a full-time career as a theatrical production manager, the College launched a national search for the program's first department chair. In the words of President Cameron; "You have heard of angels dropping down from heaven? Well, that's what happened when we hired Jeff Little."

The Boone, N.C., native and Appalachian State University graduate joined GTCC in April 2004 at the apex of a remarkable show business career.[4] An accomplished pianist, who debuted at 6 with the renowned folk artist Doc Watson, Little created a successful musical reputation in Nashville by adapting folksy Appalachian fiddle tunes to the piano. His quarter-century career as a professional musician included a parallel background in production and artist management for John Michael Montgomery and Grammy Award winner Keith Durban. Little had honed his production experience on Grammy Award Shows and in recording studios producing compact discs. His exceptional background in performing, managing, and producing tailored the perfect Department Chair for the Larry Gatlin School of Entertainment Technology's four-track curriculum; his arrival coincided with the dedication of the school's new home.

Cuyler McKnight chaired the committee that organized the four-day dedication of The Larry Gatlin School of Entertainment Technology on April 28 through May 1, 2004. The extensive program was designed to introduce the public, and GTCC's six sister Guilford County institutions of higher education, to Entertainment Tech's exemplary facilities and to set the stage for possible future partnerships. Musical groups from these neighboring colleges and universities were invited to perform on Thursday and Friday evenings and during Saturday's 10 am–4 pm open house.[5]

The celebration was graciously underwritten by a generous $40,000 grant from BB&T (Branch Banking and Trust Company, Inc.) presented by CEO Robert E. Greene. The major dedicatory event "An Evening with Larry Gatlin" on Wednesday, April 28, 2004, opened with a GTCC Foundation Reception Gala in the "Jim and Ann Morgan Community Room" and tours of the building. In his opening monologue, Gatlin, a University of Houston English major and perennial educator, confessed his original skepticism to Don Cameron's dream of a "school of country music" when he encouraged the visionary president to broaden his concept to entertainment technology. Charlie Greene, former GTCC Board Chair and Chair of the Facilities and Finance Committee that supervised the building's construction, grounded the audience in the practicality of the community college vision.

> Don't look at the buildings. Look at what comes out of the buildings. Look at the students, whether they are 60, or whether they are 20. They come here because they want to. They came here for a second chance. The facility is great and we hope it entices them through the doors, but watch what comes out, that is the future.[6]

Government officials, Trustees, foundation Board members, and college officials lined up across the amphitheater's proscenium stage to cut the ribbon officially dedicating the facility. Following Gatlin's nostalgic concert, Dr.

Cameron inducted the entertainer into the *Larry Gatlin School of Entertainment Technology Hall of Fame.*

> Guilford Technical Community College will henceforth present the Hall of Fame Award to professional performers, producers, technicians, and songwriters who have achieved special recognition in their chosen fields. The recipients who may, or may not be a native or resident of Guilford County, would receive a personal and appropriate symbol of recognition and have their names inscribed on a plaque to be located in a significant location in the school.[7]

The inductions continued during the Saturday, May 1, 2004, open house when Dr. Cameron posthumously installed founding Entertainment Technology Advisory Board members Kay Saintsing and "Big Paul" Franklin Fuller, Jr. Saintsing, who died suddenly on June 7, 2002, served as the Executive Director of the North Carolina Association of Festivals and Events (NCAFE) and was best known as the longtime producer of the award winning "Lexington Barbecue Festival." Fuller, a top rated country disc jockey for Clear Channel's WTQR Radio, died in a motorcycle accident that seriously injured his wife Susan on May 5, 2002. Widespread public respect for these two show business icons contributed immeasurably to the community's acceptance of the Entertainment Technology Program.

Achieving the Dream

GTCC was consistently judged to be an exemplary college by North Carolina's Critical Success Factors and Performance Measures. However, these data exposed a complex enrollment issue: GTCC and its sister community colleges were established as "open door" institutions, but low graduation and retention rates indicated that they too often were "revolving door" colleges. Students left and returned at surprising rates and many who had not graduated had attended GTCC off-and-on for years. GTCC's 36.1 percent minority enrollment in degree/diploma programs and 74.8 percent in basic skills and continuing education programs earned the College eligibility to compete for a $50,000 "Achieving the Dream: Community Colleges Count" planning grant (to be followed by a $400,000 four-year investment grant) from the Lumina Foundation[8] and its partners, the AACC (American Association of Community Colleges) and MDC, Inc.[9] Dr. Kathryn Baker Smith convened a group to develop a winning proposal. GTCC was awarded the planning grant in July 2004.

"Achieving the Dream" is a data-driven, outcomes-directed project designed to foster access and success, particularly among underserved students. To participate in the study, community colleges commit to developing a "culture of evidence," that is, to develop their capacity to accumulate and analyze data, and to make using data to influence decision-making, evaluation, and resource allocation standard practice. The award enabled GTCC to plan a major multi-year initiative to increase success for the growing number of students for whom community colleges are the point of entry into higher education. The $400,000 award validated GTCC's plan.

GTCC, through Achieving the Dream, is particularly focused on improving student success, including graduation and transfer rates, among low-income students and students of color.[10] The grant enabled the faculty and staff to focus on outreach, advising, success in gateway courses, and mentoring to improve student success.

Standing committees institutionalized the requested "culture of evidence" by supporting increased data collection and analysis. Additional data were incorporated through the regular planning process. Next, plans were made to welcome students to the College with a special "front door experience:" SOAR (Student Orientation, Advising and Registration) introduces new students to college culture, requirements, and registers them with program advisors. Learning communities, long desired, were started. "Gateway Courses"—the ones all students have to take to go very far into their programs—were identified and strategies to support student success in them were explored: A study skills class was piloted as a requirement in several programs; supplemental instruction is being piloted; training in cooperative learning, long a college focus, was provided to more faculty and reinforced with others. A College Transfer Advising Center was established, and faculty participation in advising increased.

Statistics indicated that the SOAR sessions were a successful retention strategy. Nearly 2,000 participants in the fall of 2005 and spring of 2006 attended the SOAR sessions where they met instructors from their programs and were briefed on learning styles and employability skills. The withdrawal rates of students who participated in the orientation (13.6 percent) were substantially lower than those who did not (23.7 percent). Among those taking a full load of 12 credit hours, only 12.1 percent who participated in orientation dropped out while 55.5 percent completed their full 12 hours. By comparison, 21.3 percent of the non participants dropped out and only 41.8 percent completed the 12 hour course load.[11]

For those who did not attend SOAR, 64.3 percent persisted from fall 2005 to spring 2006 and 44.4 percent from fall 2005 to fall 2006. Comparatively, the 78.7 percent who attended orientation persisted from fall 2005 to spring 2006 and 55.9 percent persisted from fall 2005 to fall 2006. By fall 2007, statistics indicated that fall gateway course success rates college-wide had increased from

61.1 percent to 62.6 percent and the institutional fall-to-fall persistence rate had increased from 49 to 51 percent.

Smith reported that the 2006–2007 annual unduplicated headcount topped 13,000 curriculum students. For the period 2006–07, the College counted more than 1200 completers receiving associate degrees, diplomas and certificates, an increase of 7.8 percent over 2005–06. Achieving the Dream has enabled GTCC to help students succeed in greater numbers. The College is building momentum in its continuous effort to improve student retention and graduation.

Biotechnology: 2004

Biotechnology: The unlocking of DNA life sciences and the impact of genomics on healthcare, life extension, and medicine.[12]

By 2002, the collapse of North Carolina's traditional manufacturing economy, based on tobacco and textiles, had forced the state and county leaders to identify new industrial clusters. Biomanufacturing, which had been exceptionally successful in the Research Triangle Park (RTP), emerged as the model for future job creation in the Triad and across the state. The N. C. General Assembly established a Piedmont Triad Office of the North Carolina Biotechnology Center in Winston Salem in 2003 to promote biotech commercialization in an area containing a high concentration of learning institutions and research facilities. Forecasters predicted that the Piedmont Triad Research Park, anchored by a new campus of the Wake Forest University School of Medicine, could provide 5.7 million gross square feet of developed space for a "growing cadre" of new pharmaceutical companies.

According to various estimates (2004), 30 to 80 life science, or biotech companies were then operating in the 12 county Piedmont Triad Partnership region. Industry experts, most notably Dr. Marshall "Sonny" White, GTCC's executive vice president, believed that GTCC and its sister community colleges could support this cluster by training technicians for these small, venture capital biotech labs including five in north High Point's sprawling Piedmont Center.[13] Noting that 67 percent of all biomanufacturing jobs required more than a high school degree, but less than a four-year degree, White suggested training candidates through GTCC's Chemical Processing/Biotechnology program.[14]

The College eventually received several biotechnology grants from the North Carolina Community College System and the Golden Leaf Foundation. GTCC and neighboring Forsyth Technical Community College were approved by the BioNetwork to share the General Pharmaceutical Training Center (PMET) in the Piedmont Triad Research Park. The BioNetwork is a statewide initiative connecting community colleges as a way of providing specialized training, curricula, and equipment to develop a world class workforce for the biotechnology, pharmaceutical and life sciences industries. This facility is responsible for developing expertise in clean room skills, sterile techniques, fill and finish operations, general biotechnology bench techniques, and pharmaceutical skills including introductory Quality Assurance/Quality Control, validation, and GMP/SOP. The collaborative venture also works with economic development leaders to help recruit new firms to the region and the state.[15]

By 2006–07, the Chemical Process Technology program that had successfully supported Banner Pharmacaps had disappeared from GTCC's curriculum. However, three certificate and associate degree programs trained students for a variety of biotech industries including pharmaceuticals, medical devices, home and personal care products, specialty chemicals, foods and flavorings, agrochemicals, technical and engineered textiles, government and clinical laboratories. A BioWorks program instituted in August 2004, prepared process technicians to work for life science companies.

By 2007–08, the Piedmont Triad Biotechnology Center was working to develop five economic sector initiatives: Regenerative Medicine, Medical Technology and Devices, Nanotechnology, Genomic Medicine, and Industrial Biotechnology. While about 400 bioscience companies employing around 48,000 people were operating in the state, GTCC had been relegated to a secondary educational role offering "pre-major" courses that prepared students to pursue AA degrees at Alamance Community College and Forsyth Technical Community College, or to enroll for B.S. degrees at four-year institutions.[16]

Summary

A highly successful bond referendum, SACS accreditation, the dedication of the new Larry Gatlin School of Entertainment Technology and the introduction of the "Quick Jobs with a Future" program define 2004 as one of the great years in GTCC history, but as time and events would prove, 2005 was in the running for its own share of institutional glory. A new Greensboro campus was rising on East Wendover Avenue with dramatic implications for the future of Eastern Guilford County. Another research project (The Herman Report) dissecting GTCC's reputation and credibility would spur a new set of initiatives and deadly Hurricane Katrina would force the College to review its emergency contingency plan.

GTCC's total expenditures for operating and equipment during the fiscal year 2003–04 totaled $53,536,328. The school spent $23,598,003 in capital construction funds; State expenditures totaled $30,488,563 and Guilford County operating expenditures $7,777,529.[17]

Campus Notes

The GTCC Foundation Inc. reported cash and pledges totaling $617,484 plus $466,381 designated to the Legacy Campaign.

Federal Express, the world's largest express transportation company, donated "Destiny," a Boeing 727-100 freighter, to serve as a "classroom with wings."

Aviation student William H. Joyce received the first Tony Coble, Jr. Endowed Scholarship.[18]

President Don Cameron chaired the United Way of Greater Greensboro's successful campaign and received the prestigious Charles Duncan McIver Award from the University of North Carolina at Greensboro.[19]

Associate Professor of English Dr. Caramine White participated in a Fulbright Teacher Exchange Scholarship in Banska Bystrica, Slovakia, and Culinary Instructor L. J. Rush was selected Chef of the Year for the Piedmont Triad.[20]

The Nursing Department implemented a Practical Nursing Diploma program, achieved a 100 percent pass rate for the 2004 RN licensing exam, and was granted accreditation for 8 years by the N.C. Board of Nursing with no recommendations.

Retired GTCC art instructor Fred T. Jones was the featured artist for the African-American Atelier's 13th Annual Founding Members Invitational Exhibit and the 17th annual African-American Arts Festival.[21]

The Mary Perry Ragsdale Family YMCA, adjacent to GTCC Jamestown, opened officially with a gala ribbon cutting on May 3, 2004, bolstered by a charter membership of 1,800.[22]

The GTCC Middle College, a high school option in the Guilford County Schools System, was named one of Governor Easley's "Learn and Earn" schools. GTCC staff member Jane Pendry was chosen to coordinate the workforce preparedness incentive program that allows selected students to take a fifth year of high school in exchange for a free community college degree.[23]

Campus Notes continued

GTCC automotive technology student DeVane Burnette won first place at the SkillsUSA National Leadership and Skills Conference. The Terry Labonte Chevrolet (Greensboro) service technician was a second-year student in the General Motors ASEP program.

MY GTCruiser, a powerful new communication tool, premiered (fall 2004) for students, faculty and staff. The internet-based portal allowed 24/7 access from any place that has an internet connection and enabled the College to assign email addresses to students.

The GTCC Children's Center, a high-quality daycare provider that doubles as a major educational component of the College, celebrated its silver anniversary in 2004 by serving 61 children, ages infant to 5, at a cost of $515 to $600 per month. Since its inception (1979) as an on-campus training area for students in the Child Care Worker and Early Childhood Specialist programs, the center had cared for more than 5,000 children.[24]

GTCC Profile 2003–04

Faculty and Staff	
Full Time	530
Part Time	680
Curriculum Students	
Total	11,791
Employed	66%
Female	56%
Male	44%
Minority	40%
Students By Age	
18–24	57%
25–34	24%
35–44	12%
45–older	7%

Chapter 34

2004–05:
Part I: Evaluation and Regeneration

GTCC's new campus on East Wendover Avenue provides an eye-catching eastern gateway to the city. More importantly, the $31 million project should serve as an economic engine for east Greensboro and eastern Guilford County.[1]

The Herman Report

The end of the 20th century collapse of North Carolina's traditional manufacturing base of textiles and tobacco, coupled with the vision of futuristic industrial clusters, broadly challenged GTCC's mission as Guilford County's number one workforce trainer and economic developer. As traditional manufacturing companies shut down or were assimilated, many established executives, long relied upon for their knowledge and support of GTCC, disappeared in the flux. Their absence created a knowledge gap between GTCC and business and industry that was most noticeable in the Greater Greensboro community. It was apparent that, while GTCC was nearing 50 and had served hundreds of thousands of residents, many new and influential leaders in business, industry, and politics lacked sufficient information about the school's strength as an economic developer and workforce trainer.

Cameron and Executive VP "Sonny" White commissioned futurist Roger Herman's study in the wake of the aforementioned "McKinsey Report," (1999)[2] and McNeill Lehman's "Marketing Action Plan" (2001). The latter's compilation of casual observations and statistical analysis gleaned from questionnaires returned by citizens, politicians, and corporate leaders had embarrassingly indicated that GTCC was either "not on their radar," or that, "while they knew about GTCC, they had no clear idea about what the College did, or could do."[3]

As previously noted in Chapter 30, GTCC's attempt to immediately accelerate its marketing in response to this study was blunted by the state budget crisis.

By late 2004, the College was recovering fiscally, but still lacking the strategic focus to serve evolving 21st century industrial clusters. College administrators desperately needed to understand the business models and strategies the county's top CEOs were pursuing; more importantly, GTCC needed to reexamine its reputation in the corporate community. These factors convinced Cameron to ask the futurist Herman Group to develop a realistic appraisal of GTCC's future as it related to specific key business clusters in biotechnology, supply train logistics, and health technologies through a set of critical questions.

Should the College strengthen its Chemical Processing program to train lab technicians for biotech companies? Should it create courses in logistics with the advent of a Federal Express hub at Piedmont Triad International Airport? Should it consider building a new campus near PTIA in booming northwest Guilford County and create a two plus two partnership there with UNCG? Herman and his staff personally quizzed 117 Guilford County business executives for their opinions about Guilford County's present and future economy, resultant workforce requirements, and the need for specific training to support economic development. The participants provided perceptions of the regional economy and reviewed their corporate plans for growth and employment needs during the next 15 years. They were queried about their knowledge, use, and expectations of GTCC's training and service programs, and provided with detailed information about the College.

The forthcoming "Preparation of Tomorrow's Workforce—Guilford County, North Carolina: A Report of Research Observations, and Forecasts" recommended expanding outreach efforts at multiple levels in employer organizations; promoting specialized training programs through HR, operations managers, and training supervisors; and creating strategic planning workshops to guide companies in workforce development as a way of marketing the training products provided by GTCC's Business and Industry Services Division. The report suggested a departmental review of job placement capabilities, a statistical report on placement figures and tracking studies, and a revitalization of GTCC'S student recruiting program. Herman's report inspired new marketing initiatives to publicize the value and range of GTCC programs available to companies employing 200 or fewer workers. Initiatives like Achieving the Dream and the Learning College would address additional workforce preparedness issues.[4]

Later that year, the High Point Economic Development Corporation commissioned the Herman Group to produce "The High Point Work Force Preparedness Study" (2005). This research revealed "tremendous deficiencies in the abilities of local workers including, as GTCC was sadly aware, "many with fresh high school diplomas." Herman concluded that "prospective employers would be hesitant to bring higher level jobs to High Point."[5] Writing at the time, an editorialist noted a recent trend by local governments to entice industries with tax incentives as opposed to suggesting that the corporations consider allowing the local community college to train their workforce with state money, at no cost to them or the county.[6]

Dell Arrives in the Piedmont

GTCC's need to revamp its services was additionally motivated by Dell Inc.'s sudden interest in building a computer assembly plant near PTIA in addition to the projected arrival of a FedEx package sorting hub, and a variety of interstate and local highway construction projects, citizens could literally "feel" the county rising to a new plateau in its industrial and transportation history as the northern gateway to North Carolina. GTCC administrators first met with Dell Inc. officials in April 2004 to discuss training employees for this plant the firm established in Forsyth County's Alliance Science and Technology Park (December 2004).

Enriched by $37 million in incentives from Forsyth County alone, Dell anticipated needing 700 trained workers in its first year and at least 1,500 over 5 years.[7] The State of North Carolina sweetened the incentive pot with $242 million in tax breaks and training funds. While Forsyth Technical Community College became the lead institution managing job-training for the $100 million, 500,000-square-foot plant, GTCC aided in the employee interview process by making its huge open computer lab available. The College also introduced an eight-week *Quick Jobs* course to train workers in skills applicable to a variety of manufacturing venues (January 2005).[8]

Undocumented Students

In 2004, the lack of a national immigration policy convinced the North Carolina Community College System to allow its institutions to make local decisions about admitting undocumented residents. The policy was driven by a controversial bill that, had it passed, would have allowed in-state tuition for illegal immigrants. Forsyth Technical Community College decided in April 2005 to allow undocumented students to study in degree programs as out-of-state students provided they paid out-of-state tuition. GTCC adopted an identical policy a few weeks later. Out-of-state tuition in May 2005 totaled $211 per credit hour, or a maximum of $3,376 per semester. According to the new policy, undocumented students wishing to enroll in curriculum programs at GTCC were required to have attended a U.S. high school for at least three years and graduated; they were not eligible for financial aid and they were automatically restricted from some professional programs by federal licensing statutes. Ironically, this undocumented population could freely access a wide range of community college continuing education courses including the vital ESOL program.[9]

In November 2007, the colleges were informed that the Attorney General had ruled that they must admit undocumented students without conditions as out-of-state students. The law was interpreted to mean that conditions not specified in the law could not be added. Thus colleges must admit "all applicants who are high school graduates or who are at least 18 years of age."[10]

Embry-Riddle Aeronautical Aviation University

GTCC's strategy to define itself through prestigious partnerships was measurably reinforced on June 27, 2005, when Dr. Cameron signed an articulation agreement with Embry-Riddle Aeronautical University. The world's oldest, largest, and most prestigious university, specializing in aviation and aerospace, committed to accepting associate degree graduates from GTCC's Aviation Management and Career Pilot Technology program and the Aviation Systems Technology program. The articulation enabled junior-year students to complete undergraduate degrees at GTCC's T. H. Davis Aviation Center at Piedmont Triad International Airport (PTIA).

The agreement signified a major step toward establishing programs in transportation, logistics, and supply chain management. By May 2006, the Embry-Riddle program offered four quarters (eight courses) with enrollment averaging 13–14 students and a projected enrollment of 17 for summer 2006. Transportation Technologies Division Chair Ed Frye reported that the partnership complimented the follow-on education plans of GTCC graduates and the enrollment figures for the Pilot and Management AAS courses.[11]

The Davis Aviation Center was strategically located to serve a $500 million PTIA project including the 600,000-square-foot FedEx Mid-Atlantic Hub due to open in 2009. At the time, Honda Aircraft was testing the small commercial jet that it later decided to build at the regional airport in 2007. Meanwhile, the airport authority had built a hangar for Comair (Delta Airlines) that would become one of the company's major repair facilities employing as many as 60 technicians.[12]

Hurricane Katrina: August–September 2005

Mother Nature's cyclonic forces pounded the south and southeast relentlessly during the early years of the 21st century. President Cameron and GTCC administrators spent most of Labor Day weekend September 2–5, 2005, planning for arrival of an undermined number of evacuees fleeing the aftermath of Hurricane Katrina, the vicious storm that slammed the Gulf coast on August 29. When Greensboro and Guilford County responded to a request from federal and state authorities to house about 300 evacuees in the Greensboro Coliseum complex, authorities designated the T.H. Davis Aviation Center as a processing center for the projected entourage.

GTCC Police Chief Jerry Clark and his staff were assigned to provide security for the evacuees and Transportation Technologies Chair Ed Frye was tasked to organize their reception at the Aviation Center. While the airlift did not materialize, the preparatory exercise demonstrated that GTCC was prepared to respond immediately to emergency situations. The College had previously joined other institutions in offering assistance and free tuition to displaced college students in the Gulf region.

Katrina disrupted the flow of gasoline through Gulf pipelines to North Carolina forcing President Cameron to issue severe travel restrictions; out-of-state travel was prohibited; in-state travel was restricted to activities related to law enforcement, public safety, public health, due process hearings, and emergency situations; and *essential travel* was defined as instructional and clinical.[13] The Katrina disaster prompted the North Carolina Community College System to order its 58 units to develop a Business Continuity Plan.

GTCC Greensboro

The opening of GTCC Greensboro's Campus at 3505 East Wendover Avenue was the Institution's pre-eminent historical event of 2005. The initial four building complex was built, and to a degree equipped, with funds allocated from 2000 and 2004 county bonds and GTCC's portion of the 2000 state higher education bonds.

The 54,000-square-foot Adult Education Center (AEC) opened first in January 2005. Built for $7,654,491, the AEC accommodated Adult High School,

GED, Adult Basic Education, Compensatory Education, and ESOL (English as a Second Language) programs formerly located at the Washington Street campus. The 107,000-square-foot, $18,057,412 Technical Education Center anchored most of the Industrial, Construction, Electrical, and Technical (ICET) programs. The 41,000-square-foot, $5,694,168 Continuing Education Center (CEC) housed the bookstore and administration offices. These three major structures, supported by a $2.4 million Central Energy Plant, completed the first round of construction at a cost of $37,340,488 million.

The Greensboro Campus Dedication Committee worked for more than six months to prepare for the marathon three-day dedication. The celebration debuted Thursday evening October 6, with showcase presentations in the TEC and the CEC. Guests enjoyed tours, displays, and demonstrations at the Industrial, Engineering, and Construction showcase in the Technical Education Center. Nearby, the Continuing Education showcase highlighted many of the division's popular programs including Business and Industry demonstrations, personal enrichment classes, and information sessions.

Heavy rain, a factor in campus construction from day one, forced the official dedication ceremony at 11 A.M., Friday, October 7 to move from a tent erected at center campus into the TEC's atrium-lobby. The "building that teaches" provided a dramatic location for the event. For graciously introducing the campus to her constituents, Greensboro District 2 Councilwoman Claudette Burroughs-White was recognized as the dedication's Honorary Chairperson.[14]

North Carolina A&T Chancellor Dr. James Renick pledged to partner the University's Engineering School with GTCC's ICET program, a commitment Renick honored by assigning an A&T counselor to the TEC for the spring 2006 semester.[15] On behalf of Governor Mike Easley, State Senator Kay Hagan, a Greensboro resident and staunch GTCC supporter, presented GTCC Trustee and former Board Chair Charles A. Greene with *The Order of The Longleaf Pine*, the highest honor the state awards for public service. The brief but memorable dedication concluded with a light lunch and tours of the Technical Education Center.

On a wet, raining Saturday, October 8, the tent sheltered those who came for free Commemorative T-shirts and prizes awarded by three radio stations. TV journalists roamed the major buildings with their cameras as entire families were introduced to a major new educational presence. Tours of the Technical Education Center, a Basic Skills "Coffee House" poetry reading in the Adult Education Center, and demonstrations and displays in the Continuing Education Center attracted an appreciative audience and dozens of media stories. The College waived GED test fees and provided those who signed up for the program and completed their GED a chance to win a $100 WalMart Gift Certificate. Community attendance, the GTCC faculty and staff's commitment to the event, significant media coverage, and distinguished accolades from educators and industry leaders prompted Dr. Cameron to characterize the three-day event as "a resounding success."[16]

2005: A Distinctly Presidential Year

Don Cameron's obsession to elevate GTCC's reputation as Guilford County's number one economic developer and workforce trainer and to institute corporate and educational initiatives to insure greater student success emerged as a mighty river fed by seven futuristic initiatives to stream the Institution toward its 50th anniversary in 2008. Some of them were based on Roger Herman's futuristic study, while others specified the creation of new business models to engage, process, and retain students through technology and conceptual planning.

The College sharpened its focus on teaching, learning, and improving performance measures. Faculty and staff applied the SACS- mandated Quality Enhancement Plan (QEP) with its emphasis on employability skills. In concert with the institutional determination to focus on accountability to its students and the citizens of Guilford County, the College wrangled with campus expansions, dealt with the vagaries of instituting a system-wide computer information system, struggled to meet the needs of business and industry, and promoted the GTCC Foundation's Legacy Campaign.[17]

Don Cameron's calendar may have been clogged with a heady combination of crisis and chaos, but the energy and leadership he had committed to the College was publicly recognized and suitably proclaimed. The accolades actually began in late 2004 when *The Business Journal of the Triad* named him one of the "Triad's 10 to Watch." In a "two for one" selection, the paper cited Cameron and Forsyth Technical Community College President Gary Green as "leaders of institutions retraining the Triad's new work force in preparation for the arrival of Dell Computers, Inc." Cameron was credited for ramping up efforts to train unemployed factory workers for jobs in logistics and transportation and working with Forsyth Tech to create a biotech training campus. Both presidents were additionally cited among the "Triad's 50 Most Influential People."[18]

North Carolina, the organ of the North Carolina Citizens for Business and Industry (NCCBI), and the organization that represents itself as the state's Chamber of Commerce, portrayed Cameron as "a tireless promoter of not only GTCC, but the entire Community College System," The article referenced the front page story in the *Wall Street Journal* (1996) that credited Cameron with "developing a model program for workforce preparedness."[19]

The Joseph M. Bryan Foundation of Greater Greensboro, Inc., acknowledged Cameron's civic profile by naming him the *2005 Unsung Hero* for community service. Shirley Frye, Bryan Board Chair, GTCC Trustee and future Chair, saluted Cameron for creating the *Quick Jobs with a Future* program underwritten by the Foundation. Acknowledging his leadership in establishing customized courses for companies, creating the Larry Gatlin School of Entertainment Technology, and supervising the construction of a new Greensboro Campus,[20] Frye commended his civic commitment to the communities served by GTCC including his chairmanship of the most recent and successful Greensboro United Way Campaign and his leadership of the High Point Chamber of Commerce.[21] Jim Melvin, CEO and President of the Bryan Foundation, added that "Dr. Cameron has truly made a difference in the communities the College serves."[22] In accepting the award, which included a $25,000 check to the GTCC Foundation, Cameron remarked that he was fortunate to have the support of his staff and faculty at GTCC:

> There's only one way you can become an unsung hero and that's by having 300 to 400 people working with you who are committed to changing the community by helping citizens grow their lives and careers.[23]

Summary

Never in its history had Guilford Technical Community College, its President, staff, and faculty, received such an amazing degree of positive public and press attention, but Cameron didn't miss a step as he prepared for an increasingly unstable future. The Board, chaired by High Point industrialist David M. Miller (2004–07), aggressively focused on expanding the new Greensboro campus, designing the Health Technologies building, and renovations and additions to the High Point and Jamestown campuses. Program expansion continued with approval of the Practical Nursing program and the request to establish a two-semester Pharmacy Technology diploma program. GCS superintendent Terry Grier expressed interest in attaching an Entertainment Technology Middle College to the Larry Gatlin School of Entertainment at GTCC High Point, and Don Cameron continued surveying northwest Guilford County for a location to build a new campus, a mission he completed in late summer 2007.

Chapter 35

2004–05:
Part II: Refocusing on Learning

What has come to be known as the learning college movement, the learning revolution, or the learning paradigm was born and evolved in American community colleges in an environment of decreasing resources, increased calls for accountability and attention to institutional effectiveness.[1]

New Strategies for Success

The Board's historic November 2005 work session, chaired by David Miller, touched on three major issues that would conceivably influence the direction of the College through the end of the decade. First, the physical aspects of master planning addressed an ongoing construction program including new construction, the reemployment of existing buildings and cosmetic and environmental adjustments. Second, an institutional objective emanating from the work session, and discussed later in this chapter, promoted the Learning College concept as a complement to Achieving the Dream.[2] This ambitious program challenged colleges to reform their methodology of teaching and focus on student outcomes to improve retention and graduation rates. A third tactic to redefine GTCC for the 21st century, and one that extended from the 1990s, involved the pursuit of entrepreneurial partnerships with business, industry, and other educational institutions.

Creating a climate of intellectual change, spurred by the Learning College concept and the Achieving the Dream initiative, were idealistic models critical to enhancing GTCC's workforce preparedness mission. However, as the Herman Group's "High Point Workforce Preparedness Study (2005)" indicated, GTCC was under tremendous pressure to elevate the competencies of thousands of ill-prepared high school graduates.[3] This chapter continues to explore the trials incumbent in this climate of change when the College sought to dramatically improve its retention and graduation rates. As is the case in institutional settings, successful outcomes extend from functional facilities.

The Jamestown Campus Master Plan, 2005–2011

This document presented by Moser, Mayer, Phoenix Associates, PA addressed the major factors that limited expansion on the Jamestown campus. They posited watershed and traffic implications, the condition of existing facilities and their possible redeployment, and program/curriculum development against the challenge to create a sense of community by enhancing the existing physical and natural beauty to support the "Learning Centered" concept. Ken Mayer and Robert Grill concluded that the maximum "build out" of the campus could provide 500,000 more square feet of building space estimated at $125 per square foot for a total of $62,500,000 (in 2005 dollars) plus 2,500 additional parking spaces.[4]

This comprehensive blueprint emphasized the need for a Student Services Center, offices for facilities management, and a central storage area. The plan proposed four three-story buildings, a new maintenance building, a central energy plant, a parking deck, a seven-and-a-half-acre recreational area, and several vehicular circulation improvements. The scheme to more densely develop the main body of the campus proposed inserting several three-story "infill" buildings into the empty spaces between major buildings.[5]

GTCC High Point

Architect Robert Grill's new design for GTCC High Point recommended closing Hamilton Street to create an expanded campus stretching from South Main to Centennial. Revitalization projects the City of High Point was pursuing in the area convinced the Board to purchase additional property adjacent to the campus. Campus Dean Cuyler McKnight expanded on the architectural vision by proposing a full-service campus offering workforce preparedness training and two-year college transfer programs. McKnight strengthened his argument with impressive statistics indicating that enrollment in GTCC High Point's ESOL programs had increased 40 percent in a year and Adult Basic Education (ABE) was up 26 percent. 117 students were enrolled in the new Guilford County Schools' Entertainment Technology Middle College, and the Human Services Technology program had posted a 38 percent enrollment increase.[6]

The signature Larry Gatlin School of Entertainment Technology had doubled its enrollment in two years, enrolling 241 students in 2005. The campus was serving more than 5,300 students through 17 satellite locations and offering on-site basic skills courses to employees on company time at a local firm. Program expansion accelerated when the new Pharmacy Technician program welcomed its first thirty students in spring 2006. McKnight, soon to be succeeded as Dean by Janette McNeill, asked the Board to consider adding an International Studies program and a Culinary Entrepreneurial program to the High Point campus.[7]

Learning versus Instruction

The futuristic architectural plans addressed GTCC's physical potential in terms that supported the *Learning College* academic concept introduced by Vice President of Instruction John Chapin at the November 2005 Board work session.[8] Theoretically this model empowered community colleges to improve retention and graduation rates by examining the way faculty and staff *think* about their institutions and then decide what *they* can do to substantiate the values *they* wish to inculcate in their students. Predicated on strategies to provide students with the most constructive opportunities to develop their employability skills, these exercises positively nurtured the learning paradigm theories that emerged in the early 1990s.

The transformational change reflects a self-conscious shift from teaching to learning. Educators subscribing to the Learning College theory assumed responsibility for developing and improving learning outcomes. By committing to processes that narrowed the disparity between job requirements and employee skills, they could ultimately judge their effectiveness on the quality of student learning they produced.[9]

GTCC elected to adopt this theory to change the ways in which students succeed by making school relevant, competitive, accessible, and accountable. The process to improve retention and graduation rates began with a decision to increase a student's sense of "personal engagement" from the first moment of contact with the college. The decision to put learning, instead of teaching, at the heart of academia mandated an overhaul of the conceptual, procedural, and curricular architecture of the college.

Historically, the learning paradigm, challenged traditional education as "time-bound, place-bound, bureaucracy-bound, and role-bound," inspired the establishment of 12 Vanguard Learning Colleges in 2000. These institutions addressed five strategic objectives across a three-year period: organizational culture, staff recruitment and development, technology, learning outcomes, and programs for unprepared students.

By 2004 GTCC was already pursuing various initiatives aligned with the learning movement to improve the success of its underserved students. Student Services revamped its orientations and instructors explored strategies to shift from traditional teaching methods, replacing lectures with learning groups. They considered increasing web based classes and developing assessment techniques to discover the most effective ways of enabling students to learn. The critical problem centered in Developmental Studies, where the odds for student success rested somewhere between 40 and 60 percent. The average success rate in GTCC's top ten developmental courses was a dismal 58.7 percent in the fall of 2004. By 2005–06, the college was spending $2.5 million more to meet the demand for remedial course work.[10]

GTCC's Learning Leadership Team and the Learning College LEAD Task Force confronted the reality that thousands of students who enrolled at GTCC failed to experience minimal success. This problem had to be efficiently addressed if the college were truly determined to sustain its mission to develop a viable 21st century workforce for Guilford County. This crucial challenge emerged as U. S. high school graduation rates plummeted from number one in the developed world to 17th. At the same time our nation slumped from first to seventh in numbers of students entering college and became the only developed country where the literacy levels of older adults exceeded that of young adults.[11]

GTCC faculty and staff believed that by adhering to the learning paradigm they could remedy the idealistic fallacy of community college accessibility, the myth of the Open Door. While the Open Door policy did not require an SAT score, it did require placement testing that exposed flagrant learning deficiencies. The thousands of GTCC applicants possessing high school diplomas, sullied by 6th grade competencies in reading and math, desperately needed help if they were to build productive lives.[12]

Herman Group researchers (2005) discovered that the demand for remedial education had increased 14 percent at GTCC. Approximately 25–33 percent of entering GTCC students needed help in either reading, English, or mathematics; as many as 20 percent required help in two or three areas. Fifty-four percent of Guilford County high school students tested two levels below college in math and 41 percent tested one level below. President Cameron revealed that the College was spending $2.5 million in 2005–06 to meet the demand for remedial coursework.[13]

Some students are not motivated to take more challenging courses in high school, especially math. If the students are not prepared, we have to give them the background they need. We have to work on that a great deal. Math does require the most attention. Many students do not realize that even to fix cars you need to be an electronic technician. You have to be able to solve problems.[14]

The lack of a properly trained workforce was a major concern to High Point's perpetually motivated leadership even though more than 2,300 jobs were created or announced in 2005 when more than 20 companies either expanded existing operations or relocated to the city.[15] The emerging and widely promoted Las Vegas Furniture Market evolved steadily as an obvious menace to High Point's International Home Furnishings Market (renamed the High Point Market). This "competitive desert storm" pressured the city to strengthen its economic diversity by seeking to develop a highly skilled work force to attract emerging industry clusters.

High Point's long struggle to raise the literacy level among its residents and become North Carolina's best educated municipality pressured GTCC to support the city with a traditionally strong basic skills program and a steady stream of GED recipients. High Point's plight, coupled with Board Chairman David Miller's advocacy for literacy and Don Cameron's high leadership profile, compelled the College to retain and graduate as many students as possible. This is a critical mission for community colleges where students consistently move in and out of programs. The route to retention demanded compliance with the principles of the learning paradigm, plus support from *Achieving the Dream* and adherence to the SACS mandated Quality Enhancement Plan to insure that students acquired the necessary technical and employability skills to succeed in the work place.

The learning paradigm's strictures demanded a rigorous self-critique that exceeded even the ubiquitous SACS process. The Learning College Task Force (David Billings, John Chapin, Tom English, Donald Forbes, Cynthia Graves, Pamela Herndon, and Janette McNeill), challenged the faculty and staff to promote the six key principles; (1) to create substantive change in individual learners; (2) to engage learners as full partners in the learning process, (3) to condition learners to assume primary responsibility for their own choices; (4) to create and offer as many options for learning as possible; (5) to assist learners to form and participate in collaborative learning activities, and (6) to define the roles of learning facilitators by the needs of the learners.

Beyond these objectives, the ages-old question emerged: could this initiative succeed through energetic prosecution by staff and faculty, or would it slide onto the "cold case" shelf with the plethora of well-intentioned programs discarded for lack of continuous supervision, stated outcomes, faculty-staff turnover, and inconsistent review? The Learning College would be deemed successful when, and only when, improved and expanded learning was institutionally documented.[16] Presumably, GTCC's institutional commitment to its Quality Enhancement Plan insured that documentation since the QEP sought to improve the College's specific measurement of student attainment of employability skills: Teamwork, Responsibility, Communication, Problem Solving, Information Processing, and Adaptability.

The contrast between the learning college and the instructional college demands a practical comparison of their differences and a realistic appraisal of the task GTCC faced in recreating its institutional self. The College had to (1) transform its mission from providing instruction to producing learning; then, (2) transition from producing student credit hours to achieving student learning outcomes. Instructors had to forego organizing classes in 50 minute lecture blocks to devise flexible learning arrangements, or whatever worked best for the class. Instructors were counseled to change their perception of students as the passive recipients of lecture material and consider them as constructors of active knowledge participating in learning groups. This intentional strategy to base the institutional mission on student outcomes as opposed to inputs, enrollments, and resources positively addressed the objectives of the Quality Enhancement Plan.[17]

The GTCC-GCS Early Middle Colleges

> Each superintendent has his own agenda based on his experience and the needs of the school system. Regardless of what projects were accomplished with the previous public school administrator, I have found that I can best build trust with a new superintendent by listening to and responding to his agenda.
>
> GTCC President Don Cameron[18]

Don Cameron foresaw a bright future for business and education partnerships in the U. S. Department of Labor's prediction that there would be 10 million more jobs than people to fill them by 2010. Based on a projected decrease in males, women were forecast to comprise 48 percent of the workforce by 2015. Troubled by the skills gap, the National Association of Manufacturers predicted a shortage of 12 million skilled workers by 2020. Workplace demographics for 2025 indicated a 15 percent increase in working age adults and children, and an 80 percent increase in the elderly population with Hispanics, African-Americans, and Asians representing nearly 40 percent of the workforce.

By 2006 GTCC and its sister community colleges faced a formidable challenge to train the 75 percent of America's current workforce aged 25 to 34 who had not completed college. Furthermore, indicators predicted that 70 percent of the next decade's workforce would not graduate from college and 75 percent of the workers in that era would need retraining. Three factors appeared on a collision course: the dumbing-down of America, the declining supply of human capital, and the unrelenting need for skilled workers. The key to Cameron's belief that business and education partnerships provided the best strategy to confront this workforce preparedness challenge was collaboration, a shared responsibility that crossed industrial lines from skilled manufacturing to health care and biotechnology, from construction technologies to transportation and supply train logistics.[19]

GTCC's partnership with the Guilford County Schools, beginning with College Tech Prep, is thoroughly documented as an imminently successful collaboration that the *Wall Street Journal* described in 1996 as a model for other school systems. According to Dr. Cameron, this partnership was "first and foremost a personal relationship with Superintendent Jerry Weast." When Terry Grier succeeded Weast in 2000, the new GCS superintendent expanded the partnership by establishing a series of Early Middle Colleges to retain disengaged students who were potential dropouts.[20]

When Grier first introduced the middle college concept, he asked GTCC to partner in a program specifically designed for students who had the ability to do greater academic work, but needed an alternative academic environment in order to perform successfully. The first Middle College program premiered at GTCC Jamestown in 2002 with 125 students, a principal, 8 faculty, a counselor, and classes scheduled from 11:00 o'clock in the morning to 5:00 in the afternoon. The curriculum consisted of Honors courses and students were free to enroll in college classes before and after their high school classes. N.C. Governor Mike Easley visited the Jamestown campus on March 20, 2006, to meet with administration, faculty, and students from the Early Middle College, a 2004 recipient of an Accelerated Learn and Earn grant. The program enables students to enroll in courses for dual high school and college credit while providing an opportunity to incorporate career exploration in their academic curriculum. At publication two additional programs were operating on GTCC's Greensboro and High Point campuses. By August 2007, Learn and Earn Early Colleges were located on 41 community college campuses, with 77 projected by the end of 2008.[21]

The 2006–07 Learn and Earn Grant was directed toward GTCC's Industrial, Construction and Technology Programs.[22] Learn and Earn coordinator Jane Pendry reported that the initiative has demonstrated its effectiveness by getting at-risk students with potential back on track. Statistics indicated that 84 percent of the students graduate in 4 years; of the 28 students who took 45 GTCC classes, 68 percent completed with a C or better and 40 percent received A's. The fact that 75 percent of the 98 percent of earlymiddle college graduates who enrolled in college choose GTCC proved that Don Cameron's vision of an earlymiddle college program on a GTCC campus would serve as a tremendous recruiting tool was right on target. Notably, a 2005 graduate ranked first in his class at NC State University after his junior year, and a 2006 graduate transferred 42 credit hours to UNC Chapel Hill. [23]

When the Guilford County Schools established an Entertainment Technology Early Middle College at GTCC High Point in fall 2005, 105 students enrolled to pursue classes in TV production. The third Early Middle College opened on the Greensboro campus in fall 2006.

GTCC Welcomes Eastern Guilford High School

The Greensboro campus served as a temporary campus for more than 500 Eastern Guilford High School juniors and seniors when their school was destroyed by fire on November 1, 2006.[24]

President Cameron answered the first call GCS Superintendent placed for help. Six days later, Cameron, Grier, and school board officials greeted the students when they arrived at the East Wendover Avenue facility to begin their first noon to 6:00 P.M. day. Their schedule complemented GTCC's heavy early morning and evening class schedule. The College designated six classrooms, two computer labs, and two administrative offices in the Adult Education Center for EGHS students, faculty, and staff. Lunch facilities to serve approximately 70 at a time were provided in the Continuing Education Center. For $7,500 per month through June 12, 2007, GTCC provided these facilities including parking and supervision by campus police.[25]

Operation Iraqi Freedom

Nearly two years after the George W. Bush Administration launched its major offensive to destroy the regime of Saddam Hussein (March 19/20, 2003), GTCC students like USMC reservist Lance Corporal Jason King found their education interrupted by active duty assignments. During 2004–05, 360 students used their VA/Military Education Benefits, in 2005–06, 388. While fewer than ten students were deployed during each of those academic years, GTCC accommodated its service personnel with tuition refunds and compensation for text books. Most of those forced to withdraw returned to their studies as soon as possible. At publication (2007) 315 military students and their dependents were enrolled at GTCC. Five were deployed to Iraq, one of whom was taking on-line courses.[26]

Summary

By the end of 2005, GTCC administrators were diligently pursuing the seven major initiatives developed to revamp the Institution as its 50th anniversary approached. One issue not in doubt was GTCC's impact on the Piedmont Triad region. Spurred by more than 500 full-time employees and a $47 million annual budget, the College pumped $515 million into Guilford and surrounding counties.[27] Don Cameron planned to celebrate his 15th year as President in 2006 by unveiling his longtime dream of a viable athletic program and planting GTCC's flag firmly into the psyche of the new Greensboro Partnership leadership group.

Campus Notes

Quick Jobs coordinators reported that 1,160 participants had successfully completed their course work by December 2005 with 2,529 registering for information sessions; the estimated walk-in, email, and telephone contacts totaled more than 3,000. One hundred eighteen classes had been offered since the program's inception in February 2003 with an estimated job-seeker success rate of 80 percent. As projected, the program began operating self-sufficiently in the 2006–07 academic year.

Dr. JoAnn Buck, Professor and Chair of the English Department, received the Distinguished Service Award from the Conference of English Instructors, one of the oldest professional organizations in the North Carolina Community College System.

Culinary instructor Al Romano was named *Chef of the Year* by the Triad Chapter of the American Culinary Foundation. Keith Gardiner, Department Chair, Hospitality, received the President's Medallion for outstanding service to the chapter.[28]

Campus Notes continued

GTCC Greensboro's Basic Skills program, directed by Patricia Freeman, won the 2005 Innovation Award for Continuing Education presented by the North Carolina Community College Adult Education Association. The award recognized Basic Skill's "Preparing for Success"orientation, a three-day program that helps students establish a mindset for success through career assessment, self-esteem, and values.[29]

The Kenneth O. Vaughn Award, honoring the retiring Accounting and Business Department Chair's 39 years of service, is presented annually to a Business Technology instructor exemplifying outstanding instruction, mentoring, advising, and role modeling to the division's students.[30]

The GTCC Political Science Club persuaded lawmakers to introduce a bill in the General Assembly that proposed adjusting how the state designated members of the Electoral College. The proposed bill would have provided two electors to the statewide winner with 13 apportioned on the basis of who comes out ahead in each congressional district. Under this plan, the state's electoral vote would more accurately reflect the popular vote.[31]

The Titans score again, beating the Guilford College Quakers 88–48 on December 3, 2006.

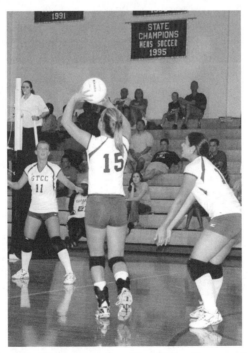

The Lady Titans battle it out against Blue Ridge Community College on September 16, 2006.

2007–2008 Baseball players for the inaugural team. From left to right: Brent Haynes, Jordan Pegram, and Kyle Boyan.

Chapter 36

2006–07
Part I: The Cameron Presidency:
Year Fifteen

In the war among the states over economic development, many states offer tax breaks to lure companies in, or dissuade them from leaving. But here in North Carolina, the secret, and often more successful weapon, is job training at community colleges. In Guilford County, halfway between Charlotte and Raleigh, Guilford Technical Community College turns out a steady supply of graduates in more than 50 fields while racing to update its curriculum and equipment as business needs change.

The Wall Street Journal, November 26, 1996

Retrospective: 1991–2006

Don Cameron celebrated his fifteenth year as President a decade after the *Wall Street Journal* proclaimed the Institution's workforce preparedness partnerships to the nation and the world. While the succeeding years were extremely productive in terms of bond money accrued, new campuses created, programs originated, and students graduated, critical issues at the turn of the century forced the College to continually reinvent its mission. The economic slump accompanying the massive collapse of North Carolina's traditional manufacturing base triggered a major unemployment crisis displacing an estimated 14,000 workers in Guilford County.

As GTCC struggled to retrain as many displaced workers as possible for the emerging industrial clusters, administrators found their mission blunted by legislative under-funding exacerbated by state-wide budget shortfalls. By 2006, the economy had improved. Legislative funding promoted by a Guilford

County delegation that was beginning to achieve committee longevity helped stabilize GTCC's fiscal position as the county's premiere work force developer. Honda Aircraft's eventual decision in 2007 to establish its corporate and manufacturing facility at PTIA would confirm GTCC as the county's number one economic developer and workforce trainer.

The genesis of the Institution's success is directly related to Cameron's first presidential message "GTCC and the Community: Working Together to Meet the Technological Challenge."[1] In this preamble to his historically successful community college administration, he thanked the citizens of Guilford County for approving the $18.5 million bond package in November 1990 that prefaced the $105 million GTCC would eventually accrue from county and state bond referenda in 2000 and 2004. Those funds empowered the College to fulfill segments of the building plan formulated in the 1990s and expand into underserved areas designated for tremendous growth.

The Board, chaired by David Miller, was planning another classroom building for the relatively new Greensboro campus. New programs and facilities had enlarged GTCC High Point and a groundbreaking for the new Hassell Health Careers Technologies Center at Jamestown was projected for 2007. A Northwest Guilford Campus to serve the PTIA-Heart of the Triad (HOT) region was in the planning stage.[2] The HOT was a largely underdeveloped area flanked by the FedEx Hub on the east and Dell Manufacturing in the west. Area chambers of commerce were encouraging planning and development to maximize the potential for job creation in this region.[3] Successful development of the HOT depended on the determination of Triad business and governmental bodies to accept and underwrite a conception of regionalism highlighted by the development of an Aerotropolis as opposed to continuing "the tricky balance of choosing to promote the region or their own municipalities."[4]

Further speculation about a productive cooperative future for the region focused on Guilford County's historical position as the "gateway" to north central North Carolina. The Heart of the Triad's arterial structure that linked Forsyth and Guilford with Interstates 40 and 85 and would eventually host I-73 and I-74 seemed the perfect spot to develop a transportation logistics cluster. Visionaries contemplated expanding this model into financial and insurance Services, health/life Sciences, and nanotechnology (defined as "the manipulation of matter at the atomic scale, producing new drugs, fuels, materials, and machines).[5]

Institutional Profile: 1991–2006

At the beginning of the Cameron Presidency in 1990–91, GTCC's headcount, then based on the quarter system, totaled 36,904 including 10,882 curriculum (4,100 FTE) and 25,666 extension (continuing education, 2,022 FTE).[6] The 2005–06 headcount of 44,166, based on the semester system, represented an annual curriculum enrollment of 12,804 (6,975 FTE) with continuing education at 25,508 (1,587 FTE) and basic skills enrollment at 5,854 (FTE 727).[7]

In 1991 GTCC offered 45 degree programs, 20 one-year diploma programs, and more than 40 certifications in addition to hundreds of literacy, continuing and occupational education programs.[8] In 2006 the College offered 94 degree programs (AA, AS, AFA, & AAS combined), 30 diplomas and 73 certificates.[9] Beyond the three main campuses and two centers, students were enrolled in more than 4,000 curriculum classes and almost 6,000 continuing education classes at hundreds of locations throughout Guilford County with thousands on line. The College graduated 609 students in 1991 compared with 1,006 in 2005–06. The latter figure included 659 degrees, 112 diplomas, and 235 certifications. GED and adult high school figures for 2005–06 included 258 (GED) and 34 adult high school graduates for a total of 292.[10]

Workforce Preparedness and Economic Development

The United States and its allies first went to war with Iraq in Cameron's inaugural year. In 1991, North Carolina's 2,235 textile and apparel plants employed 252,702 workers. By 2006, 1,402 plants, a 61 percent decrease, were employing only 97,525 workers. Thanks to GTCC's *Quick Jobs with a Future* and other retraining initiatives, the unemployment rate in Guilford County had dipped to 4.8 percent, leaving 11,738 of Guilford County's workforce of 241,322 unemployed at the end of 2006.[11]

The Greensboro Partnership

By 2006 Don Cameron's business and civic leadership commitments had elevated his reputation as one of Guilford County's most respected and innovative leaders. However rich the laurels in his public and administrative crown, he realized that he needed to demonstrate a greater awareness of his institution to the Greensboro Partnership, the Gate City's newest CEO consortium. It was again time "to sell the College to Greensboro."

The Greensboro Partnership was the latest in a series of economic develop-ment entities community leaders had orchestrated following an unfortunate loss of confidence in the Greensboro Chamber of Commerce. The Partnership was created in 2005 by merging the Chamber with Action Greensboro and the Greensboro Economic Development Partnership. In January 2006, Dennis Barry, retired Moses H. Cone Health Systems CEO and ardent GTCC supporter, sched-uled a landmark meeting of the Partnership in the Adult Education Center's *News-Record* Room on the GTCC Greensboro Campus. At this January 19, 2006 session, the group named industrialist and former GTCC Board Chair J. Patrick Danahy (2001–04) its founding President and CEO and welcomed Don Cameron to profile GTCC's programs and partnerships. From that moment none of the leaders present, including public officials, could claim ignorance about the school's mission. Observers were convinced that Cameron had succeeded in "sell-ing GTCC to Greensboro" where most of his predecessors had faltered.[12]

The GTCC Titans Debut

Many young people are looking for experiences. Athletics is just one more way of offering spectacular opportunities that make a whole student.

Dr. Donald W. Cameron
The Chronicle of Higher Education
June 6, 2007

The first indication that President Cameron was pursuing an athletic pro-gram surfaced in April 2003 when he touted the retention value of the project to the Board as a strategy to motivate students toward a broader involvement in college life; "The more you have students involved, the better the chance to retain them."[13] A little over four years later on July 6, 2007, Cameron's latest ini-tiative to increase and sustain enrollment was prominently featured in *The Chronicle of Higher Education*. According to the *Chronicle*, more than 40 ath-letic programs had joined the National Junior College Athletic Association since 2003, increasing the membership for men's and women's teams at 2-year schools to more than 1,000. Student fees and bookstore funds, plus a $80,000 gift to the GTCC Foundation, facilitated the debut of the men's basketball and women's volleyball programs in fall 2006. GTCC's athletic program cost about $165,000 in 2006–07 with the tab projected to increase by about $20,000 annually with the addition of a baseball team in 2007–08. According to Cameron, "The sports teams have really turned our student morale around. Our bookstore manager will tell you he cannot keep our sports paraphernalia in stock."[14] The GTCC Foundation organized the Titan Club to support the athletic program.

The Titans were not the school's first competitive teams. The *Green Hornets* represented GTI on the basketball court in fall 1968 (Chapter 13), but Cameron hoped the new edition Titans would introduce the school's most successful athletic program. That is the charge he presented Athletic Director-Head Basketball Coach Phillip Gaffney at the February 9, 2006, all personnel meeting. Gaffney launched his exceptionally successful coaching career as an assistant at his alma mater, SUNY Brockport, (Division III), in 1987–88. A year later he moved to Division I University of Maryland-Eastern Shore (1989). During his first head coaching job at Columbia-Greene Community College in 1993, his squads were nationally ranked for three seasons, reaching as high as #4 in 1994–95. The team set seventeen school records, including most wins in a season (22) and most points scored in a game (138). Gaffney's Mohawk Valley Community College team went 138–46 during a three-year period while their #2 national ranking (1999–2000) earned him Regional III and Conference Coach of the Year titles.

The inaugural men's basketball team included:

Edwin Agosto (G) .... Brooklyn, NY	Cornell Holland (G) .... Greensboro, NC
Kevin Atkins (F) .... Wallburg, NC	William Little .... High Point, NC
Charles Balan (F) .... Brooklyn, NY	Winston Loman (G) .... Greensboro, NC
James Crowder (G) .... High Point, NC	Ross Richardson (G).. High Point, NC
Joell Davis (G)............ Henderson, NC	Marcus Short (F) .... Woodbridge, VA
Vince Davis (G) .... Beaufort, NC	Cameron Tatum (G).... Raleigh, NC

Marque Walton (G) ... Jamestown, NC

Coach Gaffney was assisted by John Patty, Terail LeSane, and Dejuan Bowe with Ashley Williams as Manager and Dominique Ricci, Scorekeeper. The Titans concluded a highly successful season by going to the tournament finals and finishing with a 19–13 record.

Sabrina Johnson, a GTCC instructor and former varsity volleyball star at Appalachian State University, was named head coach of the Lady Titans Volleyball Team assisted by Debbie Hammond. The inaugural team included:

Diana Dau .... Medellin, Colombia	Michele Smith .... Gowanda, NY
Brooke Ellis .... Durham, NC	Heather Sapp........... Wallburg, NC
Ashelie Griffin .... Archdale, NC	Toressa Poole .... High Point, NC
Amanada Hubbard ..... Thomasville, NC	Kimberly Norman ..... Charlotte, NC
Jessica Hubler............ Mt. Holly, NJ	Maya Lea .... Reidsville, NC
Kaitlyn Spencer .... Sophia, NC	Chelsea Kuhl............ Wallburg, NC

The Lady Titans compiled an 8–16 season before losing in the second round of the tournament to number one seeded Pitt Community College.[15] GTCC added baseball to the athletic program in 2007 and appointed former Ragsdale High School (GCS) star John Barrow to coach the squad. During the fall 2007 practice season, the team posted a 13–4–1 record.[16]

The 2005–09 College Initiatives

Dr. Cameron set the stage for the Institution's march to its 50th anniversary in 2008 at the February 9, 2006, all personnel meeting. Noting GTCC's superior rating as determined by the State Board of Community Colleges, he reviewed the seven major institutional initiatives driving the College.[17]

(1) Achieving the Dream

Expanding on the strength of a series of projects during the 2005–06 academic year (Chapter 34), administrators created mentoring programs for minority male and female students.

(2) The Learning College

A number of Learning Communities were instituted for developmental and transitional students, almost 25 percent of whom were enrolled in remedial math and English courses.[18] The Division of Arts and Sciences made supplemental instruction available to students and created a College Transfer Advising Center. The concepts prevalent in "On Course," a nationally recognized program to help students gain skills necessary to be successful in college, were inserted in several curriculum departments. An annual class schedule was published to help students to plan their academic lives a year at a time.

(3) GTCC Foundation

The Foundation received $420,430 in cash and pledges for the Legacy Campaign and $337,210.25 in cash and pledges for the Annual Fund in 2005–06. The Haydon Harmon Foundation established a new endowed scholarship for High Point's Andrews High School graduates. Two major anonymous gifts in late 2005 included $100,000 to endow a Teaching Chair in the Culinary Technology Department and the aforementioned $80,000 that helped establish an endowment for athletic scholarships. The GTCC Greensboro campus library was named for Guilford Mills CEO and GTCC alumni Charles "Chuck" Hayes. The GTCC Jamestown Board Room was named for Williard and Evon Dean.

(4) Computer Information System

MIS installed a new server prior to fall 2006 registration and partnered with Clearwire Communications to provide four wireless access points on the

Jamestown, High Point, and Greensboro campuses. The bandwidth at Jamestown was upgraded from 6 to 20MB and from 1.5 to 10 MB at GTCC High Point.[19] E-commerce expanded to enable students to make on-line credit card payments. In the midst of a 2003–08 technology plan, Chief Information Officer Sandie Kirkland asked the College to consider a replacement cycle for computers; replacing desktops with laptops; organizing levels of users; exploring new technologies; designing a "classroom of the future, and (6) replacing the radiophone with the "Blackberry."[20] The College continued to implement the Datatel Colleague Solution, the North Carolina Community College System's new information system.

(5) Facilities Expansion

A ground breaking for the 70,000-square-foot $19 million Hassell Health Technologies Center approved in May 2006 was held on May 14, 2007. Named for Lillian Hassell Benton, the mother of donors Steve and Judy Hassell James of Greensboro, and built in the footprint of Furniture Hall on the Jamestown Campus is slated to open in January 2009. [21]

Another ground breaking at GTCC's Greensboro campus on July 25, 2007, heralded the construction of an $8.6 million 45,436-square-foot classroom building.[22]

(6) Succession Planning

The first indication that Succession Planning, a concept Dr. Cameron introduced by creating the Department of Organizational Development in 2004, could succeed at GTCC was realized with GTCC High Point Dean Cuyler McKnight's promotion to executive vice president. This strategy enabled two of his direct reports to move up the administrative ladder assuring organizational continuity.[23] Randolph County native Janette McNeill succeeded McKnight as Dean of the High Point campus. Stephany Cousins, the third administrator in this succession model, succeeded McNeill as Director of Basic Skills at GTCC High Point.

(7) Meeting the Needs of Business

The Business and Industry Division relied on several major research studies to redefine their mission; the Herman Group's "Preparing Tomorrow's Workforce in Guilford County;" the companion "Workforce Study for the City of High Point", and the Greensboro Partnership's "Strategic Plan for Greensboro."

B&I sponsored GTCC's first *Disney Institute Keys to Excellence* professional development program that utilizes the successful management principles and business philosophies of the Walt Disney World Resort. Nearly 400 people attended the unique one day event at Providence Place in High Point in September 2006. The program provided B&I with an opportunity to market courses and programs to a highly motivated audience.

In many respects, 2006 was a break-out year for the Business and Industry Division. According to Dean Philip King, B&I provided training for more than 600 employees through the New and Expanding Industry (NEIT) program. Funded by the largest Focused industrial Training budget ($111,447) in the state, the division trained more than 100 employees.

Business Continuity Plan

In addition to institutional initiatives, administrators pursued the need for a higher level of crisis organization. Precipitated by the Hurricane Katrina disaster that ravaged the Gulf states in August and September of 2005, the Business Continuity Plan they developed enabled GTCC to continue operating in the event of a catastrophe, including, but not confined to a disastrous fire, a worldwide flu epidemic, terrorist attack, or weather related disaster. After a comprehensive survey of institutional functions, the President's Council developed a strategic plan to mitigate risks and protect the school's operational infrastructure. The equipment and contents of each building were inventoried to provide data for costing-out replacement items that would help return the facility or program to normal operations. The exercise, based on a model developed by GTCC High Point, provided an instructional opportunity to think through a disaster and formulate a recovery plan. The process convinced administrators to hire Mark Soisson, a Chartered Property and Casualty Underwriting Associate in Risk Management, as the Institutions first risk manager.[24]

2006 N.C. General Assembly Session

Community colleges could get unexpected help in buying expensive industrial training equipment from North Carolina's lottery under a bill state Rep. Maggie Jeffus of Greensboro, and other House Democrats, filed Wednesday (May 17).[25]

President Cameron was frankly disappointed when only two of the ten members of the Guilford County legislative delegation attended GTCC's legislative briefing on April 20, 2006. After welcoming Maggie Jeffus (D) and

Laura Wiley (R), he briefed the legislators on salary upgrades, the GCS Early/Middle College program, construction plans, building utilization, and the College's operational efficiency. As the legislative session proceeded, Cameron was most appreciative when Jeffus introduced legislation that would have channeled taxes on the state's brand new lottery to community college instructional equipment budgets. Allocating taxes collected on winnings over $600 to instructional equipment could conceivably have increased the funds available for sophisticated training equipment and machinery to the NCCCS by as much as $25 million a year.

Noting that GTCC's entire equipment budget for 2005–06 was only $500,000, Cameron pointed out that the cost of sophisticated training equipment for the nurses program alone often exceeded GTCC's annual equipment budget. Representative Jeffus' tax set-aside to help community colleges stay abreast of the latest technology was among several lottery-related bills floating through the early weeks of the session that did not prevail.[26] However, the legislature attempted to right the shortfalls of previous sessions by providing the NCCCS with a generous budget and funds for salary increases.[27]

For many GTCC employees the biggest event of 2006 occurred on Monday, July 10, when Governor Mike Easley signed the $18.9 billion state budget giving state employees their largest pay raise in 16 years. The measure included a six percent base increase and a one time two percent bonus for faculty and professional staff; and a 5.5 percent increase for hourly community college employees. The College responded to the loyalty of the latter group by increasing their base raise to six percent with an additional one half percent bonus. By comparison, the General Assembly did not award any pay increases during Dr. Cameron's first presidential year (1991–92).[28] The 2007 budget provided a 5.0 percent increase for professional faculty and staff and a 4.0 percent raise for hourly employees, which the College graciously increased to 5.5 percent.

FTE funding reflected the improvement in North Carolina's economy with curriculum funded at $4,231.97 per FTE in 2005–06 as compared with a low of $3,858.48 during the recession-wracked 2003–04 fiscal year. Extension (continuing education) FTE improved from $3,409.41 in 2003–04 to $3,719.60 in 2005–06 and Literacy (basic skills) jumped to $4,750.96 in 2005–2006 from $4,255.54 in 2003–04. The curriculum calculation is based on the case of one student who takes 16 hours of class instruction per semester (16 weeks) for two semesters and generates 512 hours, or one annual curriculum FTE. Extension and basic skills FTE is calculated by adding 16 hours x 11 weeks for summer to equal 688 hours; in others words, a three-semester average.[29]

Summary

When Don Cameron assumed the Presidency in 1991, the College employed 166 full-time instructional faculty and 238 full-time staff. The 24 percent minority representation was 62 percent female and 38 percent male. By comparison in 2005–06, the College employed 582 faculty and staff full-time and 737 part-time (986); faculty employment totaled 249 full-time and 737 part-time.[30] Because state appropriations vary greatly according to the economic health of the state, GTCC carefully controls the employment of full-time staff and faculty as a hedge against layoffs due to budget cuts or revisions.

The total direct economic impact of GTCC on Guilford County's economy in 1990–91 was estimated at $30,195,691. College expenditures totaled $4,361,198; employee expenditures $5,310,303 with student expenditures equaling at least $20,424,150. The multiplier effect recommended by the Ryan-New Jersey model produced a total tangible economic impact of $60,391,302. GTCC received $25,456,840 in state, federal and county support in the 1990–91 fiscal year creating a ratio of GTCC's total tangible economic impact to tax payer support indicates that for every dollar spent by taxpayers in support of the College, $2.37 was returned to the county's economy.[31]

In the fifteenth year of Don Cameron's Presidency, GTCC's capital revenues totaled $65,274,338 and expenditures $71,876,558. New and improved facilities were planned for the three major campuses in Jamestown, High Point, and Greensboro and a new campus was in the developmental stage for northwest Guilford County. The "Achieving the Dream" initiative had improved the open door experience for students and a College Transfer Advising Center had opened to enhance the student experience in that program. The Aviation Transportation Technologies program hovered on the cusp of a major expansion thanks to its ongoing relationship with TIMCO and a forthcoming partnership with Honda Aircraft Co., Inc. GTCC's fiftieth anniversary celebration, April 3–5, 2008, promised a huge marketing opportunity as the College entered the most exciting period in its history, eclipsing even its elevation to a comprehensive community college in 1983.

Campus Notes

GTCC Greensboro Basic Skills director Pat Freeman's staff inaugurated a newsletter, introduced a revised brochure, and formed a community of learners to participate in the "One City-One Book Project" to read and discuss *The Diary of Anne Frank*. Enrollment in the Greensboro Basic Skills program totaled 2,135 in the spring and increased to 2,510 in fall 2006.

The LRC began lending wireless laptops and network cards for use in the center while serving 92,265 customers at its facilities on the Jamestown, High Point, and Greensboro campuses. 1,864 courses used Blackboard, which provided seats for 15,010 students.

Apple Computers, Inc. selected GTCC as the first NC community college to achieve status as an iTunes U campus. The media browser enables students and teachers to share audio and video content, and links the College with other academic institutions.[32]

GTCC accounting students Mary Neese, Carol Hamley, Denise Bulla and Edelmira Luna teamed to run the fictional company *Heel to Toe Footwear*, which reached the Global Top Twenty in *The Business Strategy Game*.

The Konica Minolta Manufacturing USA facility that President Cameron helped recruit to Guilford County in 1989 began closing its 150,000-square-foot paper production plant in eastern Guilford County, with an eventual loss of 258 jobs. However, efforts by company president Bob Harris resulted in the plant's sale to Zink Imaging in June 2007, retaining at least 60 jobs.[33]

The Greensboro Transit Service initiated a new Higher Education Access Transit program (HEAT) in August 8, 2006, to serve six area universities and colleges and approximately 60,000 students. The graphic design personalizing the new buses was created by GTCC Advertising and Design major Jennifer Homer.[34]

The 45 Associate Degree Nursing students who graduated in May 2006 passed the National Licensing exam and the entire 64th Basic Law Enforcement Training (BLET) class passed the state certification examination with a grade average exceeding 90 percent.[35]

GTCC and the Guilford County Schools received the Platinum Overall, Gold Promotion and Gold Partnership Awards at the annual College Tech Prep Conference.

The Physical Therapy Assistant program achieved a 100 percent pass rate for 2002–04 and Mark Hagenbuch, Director of the GTCC Small Business Center, won the Greensboro Chamber of Commerce "2006 Advocate of the Year" award.[36]

Data Trends
Comparison of Institutional Growth
Cameron Presidency
1991–2005

Enrollment			Programs		
	1991	2005		1991	2005
Curriculum	10,882	12,804	Associate Degrees	45	94
Extension	25,666‡	25,508*	Diploma Programs	20	30
Female	51%	58%	Certificates	40	73
Male	49%	42%			
White	78%	56%			
Minorities	22%	44%			

*Basic Skills, Continuing Education
‡Extension included Academic, 1,856; Avocational, 2798; Human resource Development, 397; Literacy, 4,446; New and Expanding Industry, 960; Occupational Extension 13,247; Practical Skills, 1608: PAR 1991–92, p. 16.

Graduates		
	1991	2006
Curriculum/Diploma	489	771*
Certificates	533	235
Adult High School (GED)	533	292
*Curriculum 659, Diploma 112		

Chapter 37

2006–07:
Part II: Envisioning the Future

Guilford Tech's really representing a changing community with changing needs; they're having to build facilities to accommodate needs for different things.

Kenon D. Briggs, Vice President Business and Finance, NCCCS.[1]

Planning the 2008 Bond Referendum

The calendar year 2007 comprising the latter half of the 2006–07 and the first half of the 2007–08 fiscal-academic years represents one of the most frenetic periods in the Institution's history. Planning for a 2007 bond issue initially emerged as a major priority for the Board chaired by David Miller but then the county commissioners postponed the referendum. The delay played into President Cameron's hand, giving him time to complete the purchase of a new northwest campus site and focus on training employees for Honda Aircraft's factory at PTIA. Since the projected 2008 bond issue figures significantly into GTCC's future expansion, the topic bears explication.

GTCC's success in securing the approval of the voters of Guilford County for local and state bond referendums in 2000 and 2004 convinced Dr. Cameron to speculate as late as 2006 that the school's next public issue could possibly be delayed until 2011. However, when talk of a statewide university referendum began to fade at the end of 2006, he gave serious consideration to rearranging GTCC's timetable to get an issue on the ballot in 2007.[2] His reasoning included the necessity to immediately strengthen the Aviation Technologies program to accommodate the Honda Aircraft and TIMCO training partnerships and buy or build a new facility to train dealer apprentices for

Volvo of North America and Mack Truck Company dealerships. These initiatives would be wrapped into Cameron's dream of a Northwest Campus then estimated to cost $10 million.[3]

Following tentative approval from the county commissioners, the Board approved $75 million, about one third of the "want" list devised by the President's Council at its July 2006 retreat. Existing bond funds were obligated and would be spent within the next three years. GTCC would be joining the Guilford County Schools who were on the ballot for $450 million and seek to maintain the College's unbroken streak of respectable wins in bond referendums.[4] The President's Council labored throughout May 2007 to pare their $216 million "needs list" to a prioritized $75 million package for Board approval. Their proposal emerged with approximately $44 million targeted for the proposed Northwest Campus plus $28 million to include a new B&I Corporate Training Center on that site.[5]

Aviation Building	Northwest Campus	$10.0 M
Land Purchase	96.677 Acres US 68	$6.5 M
Roads, Parking, Utilities	Northwest Campus	$4.5 M
Water and Sewer	Northwest Campus	$4.1 M
Two Buildings	Northwest Campus	$18.7 M
B & I Training Center		$28.0 M
Central Energy Plant	Northwest Campus	$3.0 M
HVAC and Renovations	Jamestown Campus	$9.2 M
Parking Deck	Jamestown Campus	$12.0 M
Classroom Addition	High Point Campus	$4.0 M
"Aviation and aero space technology may be the next big thing for North Carolina's economy and the Triad will likely play a key role as the industry expands."*		
*N&R, Mar. 19, 2007.		

When questioned about his intention to seek $75 million on the proposed November 6, 2007, ballot, President Cameron answered, "I'm not going to put the College in the position of saying we can't meet the needs of business and industry for the people of Guilford County."[6] Five days later when a reporter again questioned the need for three bond issues in seven years, Cameron pointed out that,

Three years ago we were not aware the Honda Aircraft announcement would be made. We were not aware that TIMCO would be doing some of the additional work they're doing. All this plays into things that have happened in our community since the last bond referendum.[7]

In 2004, 63 percent of those voting approved $47 million for new buildings, technology upgrades, and classroom renovations, but the proposed 2007 referendum would have placed GTCC on a crowded and possibly volatile ballot that included $440 million for controversial public school construction projects and $105 million issue for an equally controversial jail construction project. After surveying the public's attitude, the commissioners reconsidered the decision to place $640 million in bonds on the November ballot. While Greensboro and many of the county's smaller towns had scheduled municipal elections in November 2007, High Point and unincorporated areas had not. With nothing to vote on but the bonds, commissioners feared the electorate in those areas might be less motivated to visit the polls. In addition, opening polls in those areas would cost an additional $80 to $100,000.

According to Chairman Paul Gibson, "It's (the referendum) somewhat unfair, I think, to rural Guilford County voters. It'd be hard to get them out." Editorialists continued to promote the bond based on the critical need for a new jail and GTCC's plan to build a $75 million Northwest Campus to support the area's forthcoming growth in transportation and distribution.[8] The commissioners ultimately voted on June 21, 2007, to delay the four bond projects until possibly May 2008. President Cameron observed that the postponement, coupled with rising construction costs, would force the College to build less than originally proposed.[9]

Honda Aircraft Co., Inc. and the Piedmont Triad Aviation Industry

Led by President Cameron and Transportation Technologies Chair Ed Frye, GTCC played a strategic role in convincing Honda Aircraft Company executives to locate their new small-jet production facility near their corporate headquarters at Piedmont Triad International Airport. GTCC's relationship with the firm dated from 2000 when Michimasa Fujino, the chief engineer who directed the aircraft's development for 20 years, began creating the prototype in a private hangar at the airport. The radically designed "very light jet" was projected to sell for about $3.65 million when it appeared on the market in 2010.

Piedmont Triad Airport Authority Chair Henry Issacson noted early in the negotiations that Honda was attracted to PTIA because of its ample land and runway space and GTCC's T. H. Davis Aviation Technology Training Center.[10]

According to J. Patrick Danahy, CEO/President of the Greensboro Partnership, GTCC Trustee, and former Board Chair, "Nobody else Honda Aircraft had talked to in the southeastern U. S. had community college capability on the airport site that could do what GTCC could do." The College also benefited from its longtime partnership with TIMCO, an aircraft overhaul and mainte-nance company, and the two-plus-two articulation agreement with Embry-Riddle Aeronautical University that enabled GTCC graduates to pursue ad-vanced degrees in the aviation industry at PTIA.[11]

Speculation as to the number of employees Honda would hire initially ranged from 300 to 500 full-time and contract workers; Governor Mike Easley's office placed the number at 283 with an average salary of $70,000. At the June 27, 2007, groundbreaking of its new factory, Honda Aircraft Co., Inc. President and CEO Michimasa Fujino said the plant would employ about 350 when fully operational.[12] If the plane proved successful, some believed the em-ployment could jump to 1,000. In return for adding as much as $20 million annually to the Guilford County payroll, Honda incentives reportedly included $1.4 million from regional government and business groups and $7 million from the state.[13] The incentive package was signed, sealed, and delivered in February 2007. Incentives included $600,000 from Greensboro while High Point dolled out $100,000; another $100,000 was forthcoming from a private Winston Salem group, $600,000 from Guilford County, and $6.68 million from the N.C. Economic Investment Committee.[14] The Joseph M. Bryan Foun-dation of Greater Greensboro, Inc. directly supported GTCC with a $1 mil-lion grant to enable the Aviation and Transportation Logistics Program to buy the equipment to train workers for Honda and TIMCO.[15]

While Honda was projecting its first delivery for 2010, two additional Guil-ford County companies in this new industrial cluster were tuning up their pro-duction lines for vastly different products. Antilles Seaplanes in Gibsonville was recreating the Grumman Goose (c. 1945), a 10 passenger amphibian selling for between $1.3 and $2.2 million, while Opus Aircraft in Stoneville was develop-ing a $70 to $80,000 light sport two-seater. In 2007, GTCC began training TIMCO's top 20 managers in Spanish and planned to offer Airframe & Power Train Technician Training to 300 of the company's employees in fall 2007.[16] GTCC began training the first class of Honda employees in January 2008.

The Virginia Tech Massacre: April 18, 2007

The deadliest shooting in modern U. S. history occurred on the Virginia Poly-technic Institute and State University (Virginia Tech) campus in Blacksburg, Virginia. In two attacks, about two hours apart, Seung-Hui Cho killed 32 people and wounded many more before committing suicide. The South Korean senior who had moved to the U. S. at age eight had previously been accused in 2005 of stalking two female students and declared mentally ill by a Virginia special justice. At least one professor had asked him to seek counseling.[17]

After dedicating a moment to honor the victims of the massacre at the April 19, 2007, all personnel meeting, President Cameron reminded faculty and staff to familiarize themselves with the Institution's Emergency Response Plan. Since the Katrina disaster, Management Information Systems (MIS) had upgraded the College bandwidth and directed the development of a Business Continuity Plan and Disaster Recovery plan that included installing a backup data server on the Greensboro Campus.[18]

International Partnerships

Following a fact-finding mission to the Dominican Republic in February 2007, GTCC established a partnership with Daytona Beach Community College (DBCC) to help create a Community College System in the island nation. A $2 million grant awarded to DBCC by the Dominican Republic compensated travel expenses and provided stipends for GTCC faculty and staff participating in professional development activities there. DBCC has also invited GTCC to assist Daytona Beach CC with a grant funded project in the Bahamas directed toward technical program development.[19]

The College continued to participate in the Trans-Atlantic Technology and Training Alliance (TA3). This consortium of leading community and technical colleges in the U. S., Europe, and South Africa, promotes the efforts of community colleges to support their regional economies and endorses the importance of maintaining a global perspective on community college missions.

The international faculty exchange between GTCC and the Danish technical college Erhvervs Uddannelses Center in Sonderberg, Denmark, that originated with Culinary Technology in spring 2000 and expanded to the Automotive Department in 2001 continues at publication.[20]

Faculty-Staff Compensation

GTCC Senior Administrators addressed the perpetual need to review recruiting and retention concerns by implementing the findings of a faculty-staff compensation study prepared by Mercer Human Resources Consulting,

Inc. In 2004, a formula was applied to raise employees to the minimum of their recommended salary range. For example: a regular employee in a position identified by Mercer as earning below the minimum range of the pay grade established received an increase of up to 6 percent of his/her base pay — retroactive to Jan 2004 — to raise the individual closer to the minimum pay range. The process to elevate this class of employees to the minimum of their salary range was accomplished in two stages during 2004–05. In October 2006, another formula with attention to equity was instituted to move eligible employees to the midpoint (Phase II) of their salary range. This ongoing process is implemented in stages as budgetary conditions allow. Enrollment growth during 2006–07 empowered the College the implement another stage in the Mercer salary study for the fiscal year 2007–08.[21]

2007 Program and Service Reviews

Annual reviews of GTCC's programs and services enabled the Board to gauge the Institution's energy and achievement. By fall 2007, the college transfer program had grown from 2,588 in the fall of 2005 to 2,930 (unduplicated headcount).

The Business Technologies Division introduced a Global Logistics Program in fall 2006 and planned to offer Hospital Billing and Coding and Electronic Medical Records Certificates in fall 2007. A WIRED (Workforce Innovation in Regional Economic Development) grant the U.S. Department of Labor awarded to the Piedmont Triad Partnership in February 2006 resulted in a Focus Talent Development Grant awarded to GTCC in May 2007 in partnership with Forsyth Technical Community College. It enabled the institutions to begin preparing workers for high skill/high wage jobs in advanced manufacturing, logistics and distribution, creative enterprises/arts, and health care.

The Business Technologies Division also developed a comprehensive, competency based logistics curriculum with structured continuing education courses designed to meet specific short terms employer needs. These courses would additionally provide students a transparent route to pursue an associate degree in logistics plus an additional opportunity to continue to a four-year institution. This tiered instructional approach supported the increasing demands for skilled employees from firms seeking to improve their logistical efficiency in an extremely competitive field.[22]

The Financial Aid Office directed by Lisa Koretoff, awarded over $20 million in Financial Aid and reported a 50 percent increase in loans.[23] The Educational Support Services Division also introduced three 'Seeds for Success" enrollment information fairs (Spring 2007) on the Jamestown, High Point and Greensboro campuses.

Without restating the crisis Guilford County faced in graduating unprepared students, a new Developmental Education Division, chaired by Dr. Nwachi Tafari, was created to manage the overwhelming need for remedial courses in English, Reading, and Math that would enable students to qualify for college credit courses. The division's three departments were headed by Michael Murphy (Math), Elizabeth Renn (Reading) and Linda Whisnant (Writing).[24] The division's mission statement defined it as:

> A premier comprehensive teaching and learning center that creates learning opportunities and promotes lifelong learning for adult learners, an academic sister to Student Services, helps adult learners lay a foundation on which scholarship, responsibility and success in curriculum level courses and in life may be built. [25]

Noting that "less than 7 percent of the students in the lowest levels of developmental education ever made it to their graduations (National Center for Developmental Education, 2007), Dr. Tafari and High Point Campus Dean Janette McNeill fostered a collaboration between Basic Skills and Developmental Education in a *College Transition Program* designed to identify the weakest students from their placement test scores and move them more quickly to academic success, with less financial burden. Previously, students needing extensive developmental work were expending their financial aid before they could possibly attain a degree.[26] This free program with instruction and books provided at no cost to the students helps them reserve their financial aid until the following semester.

Dr. Beverley Gass, Dean of Learning Resources, reported that distance learning continued to expand across the college community. Over 5,000 students were enrolled in 252 web-enhanced or on-line courses; AV equipment had been installed in 125 of the Institution's 350 classrooms, and the library had fulfilled over 59,000 requests for journal articles or other material in an electronic format as well as having served over 4,000 students with electronic information and resources accessed remotely (2006–07).[27]

2007–08 Board of Trustees

When Shirley M. (Mrs. Henry E.) Frye, one of Guilford County's most dynamic women leaders, assumed the chairmanship of the GTCC Board on July 1, 2007, she became the first African-American and the first female to occupy that position.[28] The Board welcomed two new members appointed for full four-year terms, Susan Alt of High Point and G. Watts Carr III of Greensboro. Alt, the president of Volvo logistics of America, was appointed by Governor Mike Easley and Carr, a retired textile executive and civic leader, received his appointment from the Guilford County Board of Education. GTCC Student Government President Barry Haddon was named to serve as an ex-officio member of the 12 person Board.[29]

Community College Survey of Student Engagement

GTCC was a top performer in the Community College Survey of Student Engagement (CCSSE, 2007). This national survey focuses on teaching, learning, and retention in technical and community colleges. CCSSE surveys five factors as indicators of student success: Workforce Development, Diverse Populations, Learning Needs, Resources, and Technology and identifies what students accomplish in and out of the classroom. GTCC was also recognized for its active and collaborative learning efforts.[30]

The 2007–08 Community College Budget

Community colleges have tended to be the Rodney Dangerfields of higher education. They don't get no respect. That's wrong. They are powerful tools of economic development and democracy. We neglect them at our peril. Four-year colleges may get all the ink, but community colleges offer an affordable way to begin a college education for many, workforce training for many more. A recent report in this paper (*News-Record*) showed that many with college degrees return to community college for career training. A liberal education is a wonderful thing, but in a competitive world practical training in marketable skills is often essential for job seekers.[31]

For 58 community colleges, 9 cents of the educational dollar! How long will it go on? On the eve of GTCC's 50th anniversary, the *News & Record* editorial "Community Colleges Power Our Economy," reiterated one of this study's major themes, the perpetual legislative budgetary slighting and skimping that undermines the North Carolina Community College System. The figures are astounding when you consider that more than 268,000 students are reportedly pursuing a two-year or four-year degree, more than 576,000 taking a "mind boggling" range of continuing education courses, and additional 50,000 in collaborative workforce programs with a variety of industries.[32]

Epilogue

The State of Guilford County: 2007

Guilford County led the Piedmont Triad in industrial growth at 2.5 percent over 2006. While the employment rate in the county stood at 4.9 percent, level with 2006, compared to a national rate of 4.6 percent, the more than 236,831 employed registered a gain of 2.7 percent over the past year. By comparison, in 1958 the county's labor force totaled 103,600 with 5,700 [5.5%] unemployed.[1] Considering the industrial revolution driving Guilford County from its traditional manufacturing economy to a more sophisticated mix of goods producing, service industries, transportation-logistics, and technology firms, statistically the region appeared remarkably stable. While many factors contribute to this picture, GTCC's ability to react to economic fluctuations and industrial change, as in the case of *Quick Jobs with a Future* and the Honda Aircraft recruiting initiative, were credited in large measure for ensuring the country's future industrial productivity.

GTCC Profile: July 1, 2007

At publication, GTCC was ranked 21st in the nation among the top 50 fastest growing public two-year colleges with 5,000 to 9,900 students; the growth rate was pegged at 15 percent for the period 2005–07; 13,174 students were enrolled in curriculum (credit) programs and 27,591 in non-credit programs for a grand total of 40,765. The record fall 2007 headcount enrollment of 10,589 in curriculum courses represented an increase of 7.8 percent over fall 2006 [9,819]. The arts and sciences division grew by 423 students to total 4,789. The business technologies division expanded by 157 students to 1,706 and additional gains were reported in health sciences, industrial, construction, engineering technologies [ICET], public service and transportation. GTCC's total state operating allotment was up 11.3 percent in the fall of 2007.[2]

The College operated three major campuses in Jamestown, High Point and Greensboro; the T. H. Davis Aviation Center at Piedmont Triad International Airport and the Small Business Center in Greensboro. Various classes were taught at more than 300 locations in Guilford County. The Guilford County Schools operated three early middle colleges enrolling 325 students on GTCC campuses at Jamestown, High Point and Greensboro. Transfer agreements were in place at all the four-year colleges and universities in the county; more than 300 students transferred annually to continue their higher education. The institutional emphasis on outcome-based education was delivering viable re-sults. The Nursing program had achieved a 93 to 100 percent pass rate for five years; Dental Hygiene, a 95 to 100 percent pass rate for five years; Aviation, a 100 percent pass rate for five years; a student from the Culinary program placed second in the 2007 national SkillsUSA contest. 95 percent of GTCC stu-dents who were seeking employment found jobs.[3]

The powerful initiatives formulated earlier in the decade were driving the College toward its most productive period of growth. Achieving the Dream's success in elevating the level of customer service through "the front door ex-perience" with new points of contact; Enrollment Services, a Call Center and Processing, were, to varying degrees, positively affecting enrollment and re-tention, as were a variety of accelerated concepts.[4] Proposals to expand college transfer at the High Point and Greensboro campuses would surely attract more students and a broader marketing plan was already generating growth for the College. Land for expanding the High Point campus had been purchased and a new classroom building was rising on the Greensboro campus. Construc-tion at Jamestown was underway on the Hassell Health Technologies Building and building projects on the Northwest campus site awaited the outcome of the 2008 Guilford County Bond referendum.

Continuing Education, a major link to the community through GTCC's Corporate and Continuing Education Division, offered more than 1,000 courses in the fall 2007 *Live and Learn* catalog and online. Approximately 30,000 students were enrolling annually in one or more classes or seminars to pursue professional development, personal enrichment, or basic skills courses. The Biz2Go program enabled individuals to access job training at their conve-nience by providing more than 100 classes online. As of June 30, 2007, the *Quick Jobs With A Future* program had offered 37 programs with 2,399 partic-ipants completing 301 classes. More than 5,800 people had contacted the school about the program and 3,402 had attended the monthly information sessions.[5]

The GTCC Foundation

When James S. "Jim" Belk assumed the directorship of the Foundation in August 2000, the total assets including "promises to pay," totaled approximately $3,250,000. Through the Legacy Campaign, the Foundation sought to increase the giving to $10 million. As of June 30, 2007, its total assets including all "promises to pay" and a charitable remainder trust totaled $8,839,659. As the Foundation entered its fortieth year and the College prepared to celebrate its fiftieth, Belk was confident that the Foundation would reach and exceed its $10 million goal by July 1, 2008.

GTCC: The Second 50 Years

GTCC's growth foretold major challenges for the future in manpower, technology and facilities. The critical need to replace retiring faculty and staff was exacerbated by a need for additional faculty to handle the institution's unparalleled growth particularly as it related to ESOL students. The growth of the College in students and expanding campuses lengthened the race to stay on the cutting edge of technology and create the infrastructure for a virtual campus. At the same time new facilities were rising, older buildings were begging for renovation and space for growth was spatially and financially at a premium.

Throughout his tenure, Don Cameron has been continually frustrated by the media's failure to broaden the discussion of community college underfunding. While this narrative has referenced numerous articles and editorials explicating the problem, the 2007 documentary "Discounted Dreams" that focused on students at community colleges in New York, California, and Illinois raised some funding points about the NCCCS. While the situation differed from college to college, the issues remained the same; tremendous growth coupled with inadequate funding restricted the creation of additional classes to help students get the classes they need to graduate on time. The shortage of trained counselors often subjected students to inadequate or inaccurate advising. From a cultural standpoint, many students needed a wide range of services and counseling just to keep them motivated as they struggled through the developmental (remedial) courses that would qualify them to take technical courses that prepared them for a productive vocation.

During the administration of President Martin Lancaster, the NCCCS overall budget actually grew from $5.82 million (1997–98) to $1.08 billion, an increase of $498 million (86 percent).[6] While it was obvious that the retiring administration had worked diligently to keep up with the needs of students,

communities and industries during a decade punctuated with increased enrollment, permanent budget cuts and gubernatorial reversions (2002–04),
blunted the mission of the community colleges to train the state's workforce.[7]
Cameron contemplated how many pennies it would take to continue opening
the door to all of the people while giving every community college student the
tools to make them, as suggested by Thomas L. Friedman (2007), "employable
for a lifetime."[8]

In the final analysis, the future success of GTCC and her sister colleges rests
with a commitment from the North Carolina General Assembly to address the
community college funding issues through a series of new business models
that would enhance the state's productive industrial destiny by rewarding the
colleges for enrollment and graduation as opposed to compensating them for
trapping developmental students in a cycle of failure. Additional funding could
increase graduation rates by adding additional classes, teachers and counselors
enabling North Carolina's community colleges to enhance their responsibility
for student success.

In reviewing his administration (1991–2007), Don Cameron listed two
major accomplishments; the establishment of the signature Larry Gatlin
School of Entertainment Technology in a state-of-the-art $9.25 million build-
ing in High Point and the construction of four buildings on the new Greensboro campus at a cost of almost $39 million. He attributed GTCC's enviable
record of workforce preparedness successes to a cohesive, professional Board
committed to putting the needs of the students first. To underscore this point,
he quoted Trustee Charlie Greene's oft-used observation: "Don't look at the
buildings. Look at what comes out of the buildings. Look at the students,
whether they are 60 or 20. They come here because they want to. They come
here for a second chance." He praised the Guilford County Commissioners for
their ongoing endorsement and thanked the county's citizens for their consistent approval of the bonds that grew GTCC's facilities.

President Cameron framed his vision for the College as a covenant between
the institution and the community:

> We must make sure we are providing the work force with the skills nec-
> essary to effect the monumental transition between the declining age of
> traditional manufacturing and the new technology era that is expanding
> in the PTIA-Heart of the Triad area. We must have the facilities in place;
> in this case, our new airport campus, to support Honda Aircraft, FedEx
> and Cessna.[9]

But, as he reviewed the 2007–08 total education budget for community colleges ($1,160,299,014),and noted that it totaled 8 percent while the actual ap-

propriation ($938,106,160) amounted to only 5 percent of the general funds appropriation, he recalled the plea of former Governor and System President, Robert W. Scott who asked the legislature (1992), then funding the NCCCS with 7.9 cents of the higher education dollar, to increase their allocation to a dime on the dollar, Cameron's optimism for the future of GTCC and the System was tempered by reality.[10]

> The day has passed when other states envied our Community College System; they are catching up and passing us. At some point, the General Assembly is going to have to rediscover the diamond they have buried in the sand and fund the NCCCS appropriately.

When asked to comment on his decision to forego many opportunities to leave GTCC, nostalgia and confidence tempered his reply.

> We always think the grass is greener somewhere else, but for me and my family, the decision to remain at GTCC was the best I could have made. Jayne and I have enjoyed the opportunity to raise our children and grandchildren in Guilford County.

In the final analysis, Don Cameron proved to be exactly the leader Board Chair Stuart Fountain sought for the presidency of GTCC in 1990; "A dynamic individual who can lead us into the 21st century."[11]

A few months after Fountain's statement in 1990 and a few weeks before his death in July, Bruce B. Robert's family drove the stroke-ridden patient through the Jamestown campus. According to his wife Rachel with whom he lived on campus during his directorship of the GIEC (1958–65), he murmured, "proud, proud, proud." In Robert's case, as in Don Cameron's, GTCC was the marvelous intersection of "a job and a man well-met."

GTCC Profile 2006–07

Student Body	
Curriculum Students	13,174
Attending Day Classes	78%
Attending Night Classes	22%
Employed	66%
Female Students	57%
Male Students	43%
Minority Students	46%
Curriculum Students By Age	
18–24	49%
25–34	27%
35–44	13%
45 and older	9%
Student Enrollment	
College Transfer	26.32%
General Education	26.52%
Technical	47.16%

Finances: 2006–07 (unaudited)

Revenues	
Operating Revenues	$23,043,891
Nonoperating Revenues	$42,538,711
Capital Revenues	$26,771,441
Expenditures	
Operating Expenditures	$69,442,140
Capital Expenditures	$7,014,004

Appendix

GEIC, GTI, GTCC Board Members

Name		Term
Alt	Susan	2007–present
Amos	Harold L.	1979–1987
Amos, Jr.	H. Lindsay	1988–1990
Andrews	Lee D.	1974–1987
Bass, Jr.	Rev. Fredrick O.	1985–1993
Beerman	William L.	1967–1975
Bluethenthal	Joanne	1996–2003
Bodenheimer	F. P.	1968–1969
Bostic, Jr.	Joe E.	1998–2006
Bowden	R. Steve	2001–2003
Bowie	Joanne W.	1976–1985
Brady	Donald J.	1990–1998
Brewington	Dr. Janice	2001–2004 & 2005–present
Bruggeworth	Robert A.	2006–present
Carr	Watts	2007–present
Chance	Edith	2006–present
Chavis	Vance	1966–1971
Conrad	Willard O.	1963–1967
Covington	George A.	1969–1979

GEIC, GTI, GTCC Board Members *continued*

Name		Term
Culler, Jr.	Roy B.	1982–1987
Culp	Dr. Harry R.	2001–2007
Danahy	J. Patrick	1994–present
Davis, Jr.	John T.	1965–1981
Dean	Evon	1984–2006
Dorsett	Katie G.	1981–1993
Farlow	Gene M.	1985–1990
Foster	John R.	1963–1981
Fountain	Dr. Stuart B.	1981–2001
Fouts	Daniel W.	1977–1979
Froelich, Jr.	Jacob H.	1996–2003
Frye	Shirley	2001–present
Fulmore	Julius A.	1993–1997 & 2004–2005
Greene	Charles A.	1987–present
Hagan	Charles T.	2001–2007
Hall, Jr.	Russell F.	1963–1968
Harris	Jarvis	2003–present
Hinson	William P.	1967–1981
Irvin	Mary Elizabeth	1990–1996
Jarrell	Mary L.	2007–present
Johnson	Odell H.	1977–1985
Kelly, III	Edward W.	1997–2001
Kemp	E. Edward	1963–1967
Kistler	Robert O.	1965–1969
Koonce, Jr.	Arnold	1991–1995
Landreth	J. Robert	1975–1983
Low	Sidney	1969–1977
Manuel	Dr. Nan P.	1993–2001
Manzi	Jacqueline R.	1992–1996
McCachern	Jack G.	1988–1990

GEIC, GTI, GTCC Board Members *continued*

Name		Term
McGuinn, Jr.	J. William	1979–1987
Miller	David S.	1998–present
Millikan	James B.	1969–1977
Morgan	James F.	1990–1998
Page	Ronald L.	1990–1991
Patton, Jr.	Wendell M.	1963–1966
Payne	Katherine Lee	1991–1994
Ragsdale	Katherine A.	2003–2005
Reichard	Peter A.	1995–1999
Rives	Jefferson H.	1987–1988
Rochelle	Zalph	1963–1969
Saddler	Gordon	1971–1974
Sears	Percy H.	1963–1995
Shaw	Robert G.	2006–2007
Snitzer	Lois S.	1974–1975
Starling	H. Frank	1963–1973
Starr	Nina K.	1983–1991
Stokes	Leroy	1987–1992 & 1995–2001
Thompson	John W.	1965–1981
Williams	Elynor A.	1981–1984
Williams	James L.	1963–1977
Williard, Jr.	Coy O.	2003–present
York	Frank W.	1977–1990

GTCC SGA Presidents
Non-Voting Board Members

SGA Presidents	Term
Adria Zimmerman	1977
Nick Crawford	1978
Keith Livesay	1978
Charles Jones	1979
Patricia N. Bray	1980
William Hobbs	1981
Eddie Cockman	1982
Robert H. Bald, Jr.	1983
Spencer Smith	1983–1984
Diane Griffin	1984–1985
Mark Gilbert	1985–1986
Josh Dillingham	1986
Gina Lowe	1987
Michael Hawk	1987–1988
David Nantz	1988–1989
Allan D. Asper	1989–1990
Martin Purser	1990–1991
Patricia Howard	1991
Terry Powers	1992
Brian Baker	1993
Kenneth B. Dockery	1993–1994
Gregory A. Carter	1995–1996
Brian Gibson	1997
Okiemute "Tre" Arhagba	1997–1998
Paul Campbell	1998–1999
April Pierce	2000–2001
Kei–Shawn Prather	2001–2002
Charlene Green	2002–2003
Tanetta Kelly	2003–2004
Jessica Lowell	2004–2005
Todd Totherow	2005–2006
Kristen Lineberger	2006–2006
Barry Haddon	2007–2008

Board of Trustee
Teaching Innovation Award Winners

Jane Brandsma	1996
Sandie Kirkland	1997
Dr. Linda Thomas-Glover	1998
Dr. Carolyn Schneider	1999
Aaron Martin	2000
Dr. JoAnn Buck	2001
Shelia May	2002
Dr. Rick Foster	2003
L.J. Rush	2004
Dewayne Washburn	2005
Charles Toler	2006
Michael Sexton	2007

Teaching in Excellence Award Winners

1986
Mildred R. Mallard
Paul D. Sayers
Bobbie VanDusen

1987
Henrietta H. Andrews
A. Howard Millican
Walter J. Rouse

1988
Vickie M. Campbell
Rita C. Gress
Walter F. Hawn

1989
O. Henry Barber
Sarah Beale
JoAnn M. Buck
Susan Dalton
Lynda F. Hodge

1990
Paulette E. Agha
Jane Pendry
Vici Skladanowski
Nancy S. Summerell
Merilyn N. York

1991
David E. Craven
Sue G. Duff
Thomasine Gant
Fredrick N. Jones
Sandra I. Kirkland
Shelia D. May
David M. Reeves
Dr. George D. Ritchie
Paula S. Rosen
Kenneth O. Vaughn
Mary J. West

1992
Shanna M. Chastain
Shelly J. Lutzweiler
A. Howard Millican
Sharon L. Saunders
Carolyn A. Wells

1993
Sue Dick
Joan Moran
Aaron Martin
Linda Thomas-Glover
Terry Ward

1994
Richard Foster
Allison Nottage
John Pelot
Nancy Summerell
Ron Wolf

1995
Astrid Hoy Todd
Merilyn Linney
Mary C. Rose
Elenaor Simon
Kenneth Vaughn

1996
JoAnn Buck
Rita Gress
Sandra I. Kirkland
Sharon Pratt
Dr. George D. Ritchie
Mark Wheeler

1997
Dr. Carolyn Schneider
David W. Harris
David M. Reeves
Joan Moran
Kim Churchill

1998
Joyce Hill
Sue Canter
Shelia May
Steve Withrow
Cheryl Wood

1999
E. Trent Allen
Dr. JoAnn Buck
Dennis C. Hipp
Merilyn N. Linney
Rebecca S. Mann
Suzanne O. Shaut

Teaching in Excellence Award Winners *continued*

2000
Sue Duff
Shelly J. Lutzweiler
Joan Moran
Heather Robbins
Sharon Pratt

2001
Michael Dunklebarger
Richard Foster
Brenda Flippen
Concepion McNeal
Philip Vavalides

2002
Scott Burnette
Cheryl Fries
Shelia May
Charles Toler
Susan Barbitta

2003
Susan Dick
Megan Gurgon
Michelle Martin
Timothy Perry
Deana St. Peter

2004
JoAnn M. Buck
Pamela R. Herndon
Joseph N. Jeffers
David M. Reeves
Kenneth O. Vaughn

2005
Deborah Fondow
Rita Gress
James Lutzweiler
Shelly Lutzweiler
Elizabeth Renn
Joseph R. Yow

2006
Robbin Baker
Julie Evans
Kimberly Jordan
Joan Moran
Donald Ward
Tonya Welch

President's Leadership Seminar Participants

1997

Ernest Allen
Anne Buchanan-Hockett
JoAnn Buck
Art Clark
Herb Curkin
Denise Estridge
Rob Everett
Bill Geter
Sandie Kirkland
Ed Knight
Peter McCarthy
Jane Pendry
Jackie Pettiford
Gerald Pumphrey
Carol Schmid
Rae Marie Smith
Linda Thomas Glover
Mary West
Vincent Williams
Ruth Wooten

2000

Carole Albright
Denise Askew
Rhonda Foust
Jean Groome
Ron Hamilton
Michael Hester
Cindy Kane
William Lanning
Jan Mays
Joan Moran
Sandra Neal-Tuck
Timothy Perry
Graham Reaves
David Reeves
Linda Saunders
Carolyn Schneider
Shirley Sims
Rusty Smith
Jannette Whisenhunt
Teresa Wooten

President's Leadership Seminar Participants *continued*

2001
Pat Abell
Janet Barclay
Carol Butler
Jeff Faircloth
Mac Frank
Chris Halker
Joyce Hill
Dennis Hipp
Dave Hicks
Jean Jackson
Matilda Kirby-Smith
Lisa Kortoff
Tony Makin
Shelia May
Vivian McSwain
Marc Williams
Arimental Mosley
Margaret Reid
Steve Saunders
Dan Sitko
Lois Smith
Leroy Stokes
Lorraine Theilman
Stephanie Miller Wilson

2003
Roddy Akbari
Theresa Campbell
Connie Carroll
Angela Carter
Connie Cerniglia
Berri Cross
Larry Farrer
Pat Freeman
Keith Gardiner
Margot Horney
Sonia Johnson
Katherine Jones
Eugene Kearns
Susan Lowe
Joe McIntosh
Gwyn Riddick
Ken Rowe
San Juan Timmons
Philip Vavalides
Dwayne Washburn
Caramine White
Marshall White
Linda Whitlow
Paul Whittington

President's Leadership Seminar Participants *continued*

2005

Rankin Barnes
David Billings
Brad Burch
Patricia Cates
Jerry Clark
Kent Cowan
Tom English
Deborah Fondow
Donald Forbes
Barbara Goodman
Cynthia Graves
Jackie Greenlee
Mark Hagenbach
Pam Herndon
Cynthia Lewis
Jeff Little
David Mayers
Lenora McCandless
Elizabeth McKinney
Janette McNeill
Janell Miller
Steve Patton
Samuel Richardson
Jameson McCann

2007

Susan Barbitta
Larry Belton
Peter Boers
Morris Boswell
Stephany Cousins
Shawn Dee
Katherine Hill-Oppel
Michelle Hines
Tiffany Hunter
Ron Jones
Jeff Kinard
Frankie Lane
Sandra Lindsay-Hardge
Michelle Martin
Cuyler McKnight
Kathleen Rawls
Jennifer Ray
Karen Ritter
Demetria Siler
Nwachi Tafari
Joseph Yow

President's Award Winners

1985–1986
Thomas Bloom
Jane Cassady
Larry Dales
William Guill
Martha Hickey
Paul Sayers
Peggy Teague

1986–1987
Annie Banks
Phyllis Barber
Lynwood English
Thomas Freeman
Jeanette Harmon
Albert Lochra
David Schlosser
Mimi Stang
Dwight Whitesell

1987–1988
Robin Brewington
Ivonne Castillo
Grace Davis
Jay Hooper
Edward Knight
Arnold Oldham
Archie Ritter
Merilyn York

1988–1989
Homer Arrington
JoAnn Buck
Charles Creekmore
Kenneth Kirk
Frances Muller
Sylvia Nguyen
Charles Roach
Jean Trotter
Patricia Wood

1989–1990
Margaret Cain
Ralph Calhoun
Richard Dymmel
Ruth Frankena
Barbara Kazazes
William Lewis
J. C. Marshall
Jolane McCain
Arimental Mosley
Jane Pendry

1990–1991
Deborah Blackman
Edith King
Melissa Leonard
Mary Lockey
Rufus Short
Eleanor Simn
Angus Small
Lynda Snider
Nancy Summerell
Nancy Williams

1991–1992
Lynwood English
Amy Huffman
Monroe Kennedy
Sharon Pratt
Rachel Ruth
Lynn Rycroft
Jane Stilling

1992–1993
Barbara Badeau
Ann Carroll
Becky Chaney
Rob Everett
Rhonda Foust
Bill Geter
Betty Mabe
Renee Richnafsky
Carolyn Wells

1993–1994
Patti Banks
Scott Burnette
David Craven
Joyce Hill
Malinda Mebane
Elaine McLendon
Carolyn Schneider
Dick Statham
Randi Trollinger

President's Award Winners *continued*

1994–1995
Malinda Carmon
Carolyn Jordan
Sandie Kirkland
William Lewis
Al Lochra
Kitty Montgomery

1995–1996
Anthony Edwards
Richard Foster
Michael Harris
R. P. Hughes
Aaron Martin
Pam Philpott
Drew Rowe
Rae Marie Smith
Donna Streetman
Jean Williams

1996–1997
Anne B. Hockett
Karen Hartsoe
Betty Jones
Jerry Kinney
Janet Oldham
Kathy Pitts
Gerald Pumphrey
Wayne Vaughn
Doxie Whitfield
Brenda Wood

1997–1998
Charlie Daniels
Keith Gardiner
Pam Hawley
Barbara Ide
Joan Moran
Timothy Perry
Belinda Richardson
Phyllis Townsend
Sandy Wagner
Carol Webb
Bill Whitaker

1998–1999
Cheryl Davis
Jaynie Gibson
Shelia May
Barbara Pless
William Timpson

1999–2000
Berri Cross
Cheryl Fries
George Fouts
Dave Hicks
Rodney Mabe
Nancy Murchison
Randy Owens
Graham Reaves
Deborah Squirewell
Janette Whisenhunt

2000–2001
Janet Barclay
Cheryl Davis
Jean Groome
Matilda Kirby-Smith
Edward Knight
Lisa Koretoff
Cecelia Ray
Carol Rose
Shirley Sims
Kenneth Vaughn

2001–2002
Jerry P. Cooper
Kent Cowan
Jeanette Harmon
Tanya Herring
Stephanie Wilson
Charles Pitts
Carolyn Schneider
Nancy Sollosi
Charles Toler
Joshua Weaver
Linda Whitlow

2002–2003
Patricia Abell
Kimberly Cannon
Angela Carter
Donald Forbes
Katherine Jones
Lenora McCandless
Malai Prokopowicz
Carol Schmid
Dan Sitko
Jamie Soto

President's Award Winners *continued*

2003–2004
Constance Cerniglia
Bridget Gallimore
Pamela Herndon
Ednalyn Hurley
Debra Kelton
Kenneth "Randy"
  Ludington
Janell Miller
Carolyn Schneider
Aaron Smith
Beverly Summers
Mary West

2004–2005
Rankin Barnes
Jerry Clark
Cheryl Hemric
Claire Hunter
Melissa Leonard
Sandra Lindsay-Hardge
David Mayers
Janette McNeill
Jacqueline Pettiford

2005–2006
Patricia Bradley-
  Freeman
Shawn Dee
Deborah Fondow
Cynthia Graves
Christopher Halker
Joyce Hill
Renee Jones
Michael Sexton
Janet Williams

2006–2007
Morris W. Boswell
Amy L. Brown
Brad E. Burch
Stephany Cousins
Mark H. Highfill
Wesley M. Koonts
Sandra A. Neal
Karen R. Ritter
Patricia A. Spencer

Bibliography

Manuscripts

GTCC Archives, Mertys W. Bell Library
GIEC Advisory Committee Records
GTI, GTCC Board of Trustees Records
    Facilities and Finance Committee Records
    Curriculum and Personnel Committee Records
Director/Interim/President's Records [in chronological order]
    Bruce B. Roberts, 1958–65
    Herbert F. Marco, 1965–67
    Luther R. Medlin, 1967–75
    Woodrow B. Sugg, 1975–77
    [Interim] N. Jerry Owens, 1978
    Harold James Owen, Jr., 1978–80
    Raymond A. Needham, 1980–90
    [Interim] Donald W. Cameron, 1990–91
    Donald W. Cameron, 1991–Present
Annual Reports
    "A Proposal for the Establishment of an Industrial Education Center at the Guilford Sanatorium Site, Jamestown, N. C. 'Hub of the Piedmont;'" Piedmont Industrial Education Center Project Committee, March 24, 1958
    "The GTI Story," William Conrad 1967
    "Guilford Technical Institute 1958–71," Roy A. Carter, Jr.
    "Workforce Preparedness," Ned Cline, 1998
    Historical Briefs Archives
    Anonymous Monographs, circa, 1970, 1980, 1983
    Decades of Development: GTI 1958–78

"GTCC History," Shelly Lutzweiler, 1998
Oral History Series, Shelly Lutzweiler, 1998–99
"Iddings House," Shelly Lutzweiler
"Gazebo," Shelly Lutzweiler
"TB Sanatorium," Shelly Lutzweiler

Student Publications

"Tech Talk"
"Whispering Pines"
"The Guilford Technician"

Reports/Plans

A Comprehensive Study of Global Diversity, GTCC, 1992
Institutional Effectiveness Plan, 1991–92
GTCC Educating the Work Force 1998
Long Range facilities Plan, GTCC 1996–2006
GTCC Long Range Master Plan 2002–08
GTCC Jamestown Campus Master Plan 2005–11
GTCC High Point Campus Master Plan 2006–12
   "Preparation of Tomorrow's Workforce, Guilford County, North Carolina: A Report of Research Observations and Forecasts." The Herman Group, Feb. 2005.
   McNeill Lehman, Inc. "Research Report: Marketing Action Plan: GTCC, July 2001
   Fain, Lin and Brooks, Steven. "The Public Be Damned: A Question of Loyalty: A Study of GTI's Quest to Become a Community College.

Articles

Brandon, Lynne. "A Vital Link in North Carolina's Shifting Economy." Bizlife, March, 2004.
Cameron, Donald W. and Needham, Robbie Lee. "Policy for Instruction." AACC Journal, October 1994, pp. 38–39.
Cameron, Donald W. and Fouts, George M. "Reforming Workforce Preparedness" in The Leadership Dialogues: Community College Case Studies to Consider.

League for Innovation in the Community College, Phoenix 2004.

Shore, William. "Training: Going Against the Flow." Economic Development Review, Summer 1997, pp. 33–35.

Meekins, Kay. "GTCC: What Have They Done For You Lately?" Bizlife, May 2002, Vol. 14, No. 5.

Primary Published Works

Arnett, Ethel Stephens. *Greensboro North Carolina: The County Seat of Guilford*. Chapel Hill, University of North Carolina Press, 1955.

Batchelor, John. *The Guilford County Schools: A History*. Blair, Winston Salem, 1991.

Cash, W. J. *The Mind of the South*. New York: Vintage Books, 1991.

Chafe, William H. *Civilities and Civil Rights*. London: Oxford University Press,1980.

Cohen, Arthur M. and Brawer, Florence B. *The American Community College* San Francisco, Josey-Bass, 2003

Canton, James P. *The Extreme Future*. New York: Dutton, 2006.

Dickson, Paul. *Timelines*. New York: Addison-Wesley, 1991.

Friedman, Thomas L. *The World is Flat*. New York, Picador, 2007.

Herring, William Dallas. *What Has Happened to the Golden Door?* Rose Hill: Bedwyr Historical Press, 1992.

Hewlett, Sylvia Ann. *When the Bough Breaks*. New York: Basic Books, 1991.

Johnson, Clint. *Piedmont Triad*. Charleston, Atlantic Publishing Group, 2004.

Kinard, Lee W. Jr. *Good Morning*! Asheboro: Down Home Press, 1997.

Lefler, Hugh T. and Newsome, Albert R. *North Carolina: The History of a Southern State*. Chapel Hill: University of North Carolina Press, 1979

Lewis, Johanna Miller. *Artisans in the North Carolina Backcountry*. Lexington: University of Kentucky Press, 1995.

Marks, Robert. High Point: *Reflections of the Past*. High Point Historical Society.

McPhail, Christine Johnson, ed. *Establishing and Sustaining Learning Centered Community Colleges*. Washington, Community College Press, 2005.

Parnell, Dale. *The Neglected Majority*. Washington: Community College Press, 1985.

Powell, William S. *North Carolina Through Four Centuries*. Chapel Hill: University of North Carolina Press, 1989.

Robinson, Blackwell P. and Stoesen, Alexander R. *The History of Guilford County, North Carolina, U.S.A. to 1980 A.D.* Edited by Sydney Cone, Jr. Greensboro, 1980.

Sarason, Seymour B. *The Creation of Settings and Future Societies.* San Francisco, Josey Bass, 1972.

Smith, H. McKelden, ed. *Architectural Resources: An Inventory of Historic Architecture in High Point, Jamestown, Gibsonville and Guilford County.* NC Department of Cultural Resources Division of Archives and History. Raleigh 1979.

Thomas, C. Yvonne Bell. *Roads to Jamestown.* Fredericksburg: Bookcrafters, 1997.

Timblin, Carol L. CPCC: *The First Thirty Years.* Charlotte, 1995.

Trelease, Allen W. *Making North Carolina Literate: From Normal School to Metropolitan University.* Durham: Carolina Academic Press, 2003.

Wiggs, Jon Lee. *The Community College System in North Carolina: A Silver Anniversary History, 1963–1988.* Raleigh: N. C. State Board of Community Colleges, 1989

Woodward, C. Vann. *The Burden of Southern History.* Baton Rouge, LSU Press, 1993, 3rd. ptng.

Dissertations

Kinard, Lee W. Jr. "A Phenomenological Study of WFMY-TV's 'Good Morning Show' and Its Relationship to the Greensboro, North Carolina, Community," UNCG, 1998.

Lochra, Albert Putz. "The North Carolina Community College System: Its Inception, Its Growth, Its Legal Framework." UNCG, 1978.

Smith, Kathryn Baker. "The Role of the North Carolina Community College System in the Economic Development of the State's Communities." North Carolina State University, Raleigh,1996.

Wiers, Alison Joan. "A Partnership of Education and Entertainment: A Case Study of the Larry Gatlin School of Entertainment Technology at Guilford Technical Community College." The University of Texas at Austin, May 2007.

Newspapers and Other Periodicals

GIEC/GTI/GTCC Publications:
"The Guilford Technician"

"Tech Talk"
Greensboro Daily News [GDN]
Greensboro Record [GR]
News & Record [N&R]
High Point Enterprise [HPE]
Jamestown News [JN]
The Business Journal of the Piedmont Triad [BJ]
Greensboro Magazine
North Carolina Magazine
The Wall Street Journal [WSJ]
The Winston-Salem Journal
Bizlife Magazine

Notes

Preface

1. Bledsoe, a *New York Times* best selling author wrote one of his first investigative pieces on GTI; Benton eventually served as GTI-GTCC information director; Lewis became the first Public School Information *Specialist* in the U.S.; Davis built and managed the UNCG Information Office and worked for GTCC on a part-time basis in 2007–07.
2. Robinson, Blackwell P. and Stoesen, Alexander R. *The History of Guilford County, North Carolina, U.S.A. to 1980 A.D.* Edited by Sydney Cone, Jr. Greensboro, 1980, p. 216; hereafter, Robinson. Lefler, Hugh Talmadge and Newsome, Albert Ray. *North Carolina: The History of a Southern State.* The University of North Carolina Press, Chapel Hill, 3rd ed. 1979, pp. 522, 645, 648; hereafter Lefler. I. Epps Ready, "The Community College System in North Carolina;" Address to the North Carolina Association of Public Community College Presidents, Oct. 30, 1975.
3. Decades of Development: A Twentieth Year Report. GTI 1958–78;" hereafter GTI 1958–78; *GR*, June 30, 1972, from comments by Dr. Luther E. Medlin, President of GTI (1968–75). During the planning stage, the Guilford Industrial Education Center was referred to as the Piedmont Industrial Training Center (PIEC), or as the Industrial Education Center (IEC). The author has selected to refer to the school as the Guilford Industrial Education Center (GIEC).

Acknowledgments

1. Trelease, Allen. Making *North Carolina Literate; From Normal School to Metropolitan University.* Durham, Carolina Academic Press, 2003; hereafter, Trelease, 2003 ....

Introduction

1. Cohen, Arthur M. and Brawer, Florence B. *The American Community College,* San Francisco, Josey Bass, 2003, p. 5; hereafter, Cohen-Brawer.
2. Robinson, p. 216.
3. Lewis, Johanna Miller. *Artisans in the North Carolina Backcountry.* Lexington, University of Kentucky Press, 1995.
4. Robinson, pp. 223–25; "A Proposal for the Establishment of an Industrial Education Center at the Guilford Sanatorium Site, Jamestown, N. C. 'Hub of the Piedmont;'"Piedmont Industrial Education Center Project Committee, March 24, 1958; hereafter IEC, 1958.

5. Powell, William S. North Carolina Through Four Centuries. UNC Press, Chapel Hill, 1989, pp 132, 407; hereafter Powell, 1989.

6. IEC Proposal, 1958. History changed on October 4, 1957, when the Soviet Union successfully launched Sputnik I, the world's first artificial satellite precipitating the Space Age and the US-USSR space race.

7. Cash, W. J. The Mind of the South. New York: Vintage Books, 1991; pp. 203–06, 209–12. GDN, Feb 4, 1967.

8. Lefler, p. 688.

9. Ibid. 660; Cohen-Brawer, pp. 219–51.

10. N&R, March 23, 2006. The job loss from 70% to 65% of N. C.'s "less educated," or high school dropouts, was attributed to the employment of illegal aliens.

11. Lefler, pp. 642, 644, 648.

12. Powell, 1989, p. 407. "Most of the development in North Carolina was undertaken (after the Civil War) by son's of the upper or middle class. The upper class alone furnished 49.2 percent of the post-war business leadership, most of which came from the planter stratum."

13. Ibid. p. 660. Cohen, Arthur M. and Brawer, Florence B. The American Community College, San Francisco, Josey Bass, 2003, pp. 219–51; hereafter, Cohen-Brawer.

14. Lefler, p. 642.

15. N&R, Dec. 9, 2003; See "Quick Jobs with a Future," Chapter 31.

16. Chafe, William H. Civilities and Civil Rights: Greensboro, North Carolina and the Black Struggle for Freedom. New York: Oxford University Press, 1981, pp. 14–28; hereafter, Chafe, 1981.

17. IEC Proposal, 1958.

18. "Decades of Development: GTI 1958–78."

19. Wiggs, Jon Lee. The Community College System in North Carolina: A Silver Anniversary History, 1963–1988. NC State University, 1989, p. 1; hereafter Wiggs. "The Community College Movement in North Carolina;" Dr. I. E. Ready, Address to the North Carolina Association of Public Community College Presidents, October 30, 1975; GTCC Archives; hereafter: Ready, 1975; Cohen-Brawer, pp. 1–36. Lochra, Albert Putz. "The North Carolina Community College System: Its Inception, its growth, its legal framework." Unpublished Dissertation, UNCG, 1978. Lochra provides an excellent description of North Carolina's struggle to establish a community college system, pp. 26–32.

20. Wiggs, pp. 1–2; Ready, 1975: Timblin, Carol L. CPCC: The First Thirty Years, Charlotte, 1955, pp. 2–3; Powell, 1989, pp. 547–48; Wiggs, pp. 7–14.

21. Woodward, C. Van, The Burden of Southern History. 3rd Edition LSU Press, 1993, pg. 6.

22. Robinson, pp. 236–37. GTCC (GTI) maintained its Washington Street campus in this building acquired from the county in 1973 until 2005, Robinson, 238.

23. Wiggs, pp. 2–7; Powell, William S. North Carolina Through Four Centuries. Chapel Hill: University of North Carolina Press, 1989, p. 547–48; hereafter Powell, 1989.

24. Wiggs, pp. 232–33; Lochra, Albert Putz. "The North Carolina Community College System: Its Inception, its growth, its legal framework." Unpublished Doctoral Dissertation, UNCG, 1978, pp 26–32.

25. "Decades of Development: GTI 1958–78;" IEC Proposal, 1958; Executive Summary IEC Proposal in notes for Introduction.

26. IEC Proposal, 1958.

27. Regulations Governing the Establishment of Industrial Education Centers, GTCC Archives.
28. IEC Proposal, 1958.
29. "A History of Guilford Technical Institute: 1958–1971," by Roy A. Carter Jr. provides an exceptional record into the establishment of the college. Carter prepared the text between February 1, and May 21, 1971 while serving as an intern at GTI under the supervision of Dr. Luther R. Medlin, President and Nelson R. Wallace, Administrative Assistant. The paper is available in the GTCC LRC and in the College Archives.
30. In a rare decision, the commissioners cut $800,000 from the Institution's 2007–08 budget.
31. Wiggs presents an extensive record of budget cuts and shortfalls from 1963 to1988. Those between 1988 and the present are cited in the text from various sources.
32. Powell, 1989, p. 443 discusses the historical distribution of power in North Carolina that often, in the authors' opinion, disenfranchised Piedmont citizens.
33. *N&R*, Jan 21, 2007.
34. Carter, 1978 provides a structure for the progress of GTCC from 1958–78, p. 26.

Chapter 1

1. Robinson, p 129,237; the authors quote a 'woman interviewed during the 1930's Federal Writers' Project.
2. The Piedmont is defined as the central section of North Carolina, bordered on the east by the Coastal Plain and on the west by the Blue Ridge Mountains and its foothills. The Piedmont extends south to the South Carolina border and North to Virginia. GTCC is located in Guilford County in the north central Piedmont Triad Region; 12 counties anchored by the cities of Greensboro, Winston Salem and High Point.
3. Robinson, pp. 131, 216–217, Powell, pp. 410–14.
4. Robinson, p. 219.
5. "Decades of Development: GTI 1958–78."
6. Decades of Development; Lefler-Newsome, pp. 689–91. *GDN*, Feb. 5, 1967. Each furniture manufacturer pitched in $5.00 yearly for each upholster to be employed. The first class had eight students; the rent was $35 a month and the instructor earned $20 a week.
7. Kemp served three terms as a representative from Guilford County (1957–63) and two terms as a state senator (1957–63). Born Aug. 24, 1921, Kemp died at 78 on March 9, 2000.
8. Powell, William S. *North Carolina Through Four Centuries*. UNC Press, 1989; p. 546; Wiggs, p. 4; I. E. Ready, 1975.
9. Robinson, p. 249; Ed Kemp: GTCC Historical Video Series, GTCC Archives; Carter, pp. 1–5.
10. GTCC Archives May 8, 1958.
11. GTCC Archives, May 15; June 12, 1958.
12. GIEC minutes, 12 June, 1958 (GTCC Archives).
13. "Piedmont Industrial Education Center Project Committee Report," March 24, 1958; GIEC Archives.
14. Lefler-Newsome, p. 676.
15. In 1950, North Carolina reported 89.9 cases of TB for every 100,000 people; Public Health Division, N.C. Department of Health and Human Services.
16. Decades of Development, 1978; GTCC Archives: Detailed information about the hospital is available on the GTCC website through the Library-Archives link and includes

articles, photographs and oral histories. The hospital's former gateway, a gazebo, is the facility's sole remaining structure. It was remodeled and serves as the GTCC Foundation's emblem. The GTCC Oral History Video Collection includes a series of recollections related to the Sanatorium.

17. One of the administrators was counselor coordinator Edward K. Kimpton of Chicago, employed effective Sept. 1, 1958. Kimpton was mentioned as the administrator who held the school together during the alleged incapacitation of director Bruce Roberts in the spring of 1965; see GIEC Archives June 12, 26; Jul. 10, 24; Aug. 28 and Sept. 1, 1958 and GTCC Oral History Series, Smith-McClure interview; Decades of Development: 1978;GIEC Archives, Aug. 28, 1958.

18. The author: Interview with Rachel Roberts, Nov. 9, 2007.

19. Letter from Terry Sanford, Governor of N. C. to Bruce Roberts, May 31, 1962. Wiggs, p. 65; The Department of community Colleges began sponsoring programs for inmates through the State Prisons Department on September 15, 1965. For comments about the early students and the rehabilitation program at GTI, see the Smith-McClure interview and Monroe Kennedy interview in the GTCC Oral History Series.

20. Carter, p. 50.

21. *HPE*, Aug. 1961.

22. Carter, pp. 7–8. MDTA classes in Greensboro were taught in the Ingram Motor Company/Ford building at 315 North Elm Street.

23. Powell, pp. 522–23.

24. This correspondence is in Book I of the GIEC Archives, 1958.

25. Chafe, William H. *Civilities and Civil Rights*, Oxford, 1980; Wolff, Miles. *Lunch at the 5 & 10*, rev. ed. Ivan R. Dee, Chicago, 1970; Marks, Robert et al. *Reflections of the Past*. High Point Historical Society, Inc., pp. 70–72.

26. GIEC Archives: the application form requiring a photo was amended at the October 12, 1961, meeting of the Advisory Board.

27. Chafe, p. 108.

28. GIEC Archives, March 21; October 23. 1958. Complaints were lodged and protests were often staged by African-American groups to see if they could attract press coverage. See Kinard, 1988.

Chapter 2

1. Wiggs, p. 15; Lochra, Albert Putz (UNCG, 1978) "The North Carolina Community College System. Its Inception, Its Growth, its Legal Framework (ADI 39/07A, 4007). Hereafter Lochra, 1988.

2. Wiggs, pp. 15–16; Carter, pp. 6–7.

3. Carter, p. 7; The membership is listed by appointing authority and expiration of term; Guilford County School Board: Zalph Rochelle, High Point (June 30, 1971); John R. Foster, Greensboro (June 30, 1969), Willard O. Conrad, Greensboro (June 30, 1967), C. Edward Kemp, High Point (June 30, 1965), From the Guilford County Board of Commissioners: Dr. Wendell M. Patton, Jr., High Point (June 30,1971), Russell F. Hall, Jr., Greensboro (June 30, 1969), Percy H. Sears, Greensboro (June 30, 1967), and James L. Williams, Greensboro (June 30, 1963). GIEC Minutes, September 9, 1963. The sole female involved in founding GTCC was Mrs. O. Arthur Kirkman, appointed to the Industrial Education Center Project Committee by the High Point City Council; Carter, p. 37; Greensboro Record, Sept. 10, 1963; hereafter GR.

4. His contributions to the college were later recognized with the naming of the Percy H. Sears Applied Technology Center on GTCC's Jamestown campus. The Sears family has generously contributed to a memorial fountain and various scholarship programs; Greensboro Record, May 8, 1964.

5. GIEC Archives, September 9, 1963; Oct. 29, 1963. For further insight into Sears' personality and contribution to the college, see the GTCC Oral History Series. John T. Davis, Jr. Interview in the GTCC Archives. *N&R*, Apr. 2, 1997.

6. HPE; Oct. 22, 1963.

7. GDN; Sept. 1963.

8. HPE, April 12, 1964; For insights into Bell's career see her interview in the GTCC Oral History Series, Hicks, Hickey, Bell, Calhoun, Breedlove, Vestal.

9. GIEC Archives, Sept. 29, Dec. 8, 1964.

10. HPE, Dec. 19, 1964.

11. GIEC Board Archives, Sept. 29; Dec. 8, 1964.

12. GIEC Board Archives, Jul. 22, 1964, Carter, Appendix H.

13. GIEC Board Archives, July 22, 1964.

14. GIEC Board Archives, Apr. 2, 1965.

15. GR, August 4, 1965.

16. Wiggs, p. 20. Any community college established will offer college parallel, (and) technical, (and) vocational, (and) general adult and community service programs (NCSBE minutes, 1964).

17. See personal comments on Rochelle's characterization as the "Furniture Czar," charged with keeping the unions out of High Point's furniture plants, and a portrait of Marco as a "visionary educator in the Smith, McClure interview; GTCC Oral History Series, GTCC Archives.

18. *HPE*, May 7, 1965.

19. Author interview with Mrs. Roberts, Nov. 7, 2007. According to Mrs. Roberts, President Marco asked her and a friend to leave the campus after she returned to pick up a family heirloom she had used as a flower container.

20. Roberts and his wife resided in the home previously occupied by the TB sanatorium director; see Decades of Development, 1978. GTI Archives.

21. Decades of Development: 1978. Roberts reportedly dealt in real estate for two years after leaving GTI before becoming Coordinator of Non-Residential Projects for the High Point Redevelopment Commission. Bruce B. Roberts died Saturday, June 21, 1990 in High Point.

22. *HPE*, May 23, 1966.

23. GIEC Board Archives, April 2, 1965.

24. Wiggs, p. 44; GIEC minutes, May 11, 1965.

25. Wiggs, p. 44; Carter, p. 9; Appendix F Marco Biography.

26. GDN, Feb. 2–6, 1967.

27. Robinson, pp. 159–68.

28. GTI Board Archives, June 8, 1965.

29. GTI Archives, July 20, 1965. GTI Archives, Aug 10. 1965, Carter, p. 44. The Dental programs emerged as two of the Institution's most successful due in large measure to the consistent support of the Guilford County Dental Society. In appreciation GTI Trustees asked the Guilford County School Board to replace resigning Trustee Ed Kemp with a practicing dentist. Dr. William P. Hinson, Jr. succeeded Kemp in October 1967.

Chapter 3

1. Letter from Dr. Herbert Marco to Dr. Wendell Patton, Nov. 1, 1965, BOT, Nov. 9, 1965.
2. Ibid. Aug 2, 10, 1965.
3. *GR*, Aug. 4, 1965.
4. Lefler-Newsom, pp. 699–700.
5. *GDN*, August 20, 1965.
6. State Policy 2.0412: The institutions may continue to enroll high school students only at the request of the local public school authorities, such enrollment to terminate on June 30, 1964 was extended to June 30, 1965; GTI BOT, Jan. 17, 1966.
7. Ibid. Oct. 12, 1965. This official report varies from Bruce Roberts statement that when he left in 1965, the center had more than 3,000 students and a staff of approximately 60; Decades of Development, 1965.
8. BOT, Oct. 12, 1965.
9. For a complete list of programs see Carter, 1971.
10. Carter, pp. 10–11. BOT, Sept. 15, 1965; The Board placed Dental Hygiene under the MTDA to gain additional funding to alleviate the cost of equipment and the cost of the program per student hour.
11. Ibid. Sept. 15, 1965.
12. Ibid. Oct. 12, 1965.
13. GTCC Oral History Series; Smith-McClure interview.
14. Robinson, pp. 221–22.
15. From this moment, October 12, 1965, on there are no further references to union activity regarding the institution in the BOT minutes.
16. BOT, Oct. 12, 1965.
17. BOT, Nov. 9, 1965, Letter from Herbert Marco to Wendell Patton, Nov. 1, 1965.
18. Ibid. Nov. 9, 1965.
19. Carter, p. 44.
20. Liability insurance was an early priority at GTI where, as one administrator noted, "students are here at their own risk!" Coverage was available for students from the nearby Pilot Life Insurance Company (Sedgefield) for a $2.00 premium. GIEC Archives, May 11, 1965.
21. GTCC Oral History Series, Smith-McClure Interview.

Chapter 4

1. BOT, Feb. 8,, 1966, Book II, p. 4. This perception is attributed to a telephone conversation between Marco and Dr. I. E. Ready, Director of the Department of Community Colleges.
2. Material for this program update provided by Carter, pp. 11–12 and BOT, Jan. 11, 1966, and Feb. 8, 1966; see Carter Appendix H for a complete list of programs.
3. Machinery Hall (1959), a 15,050 square foot shop was the second new building constructed on the Jamestown campus at a cost of $103,000.
4. BOT, Jan. 11, 1966. Carter, Appendix I, p. 50, indicates that the original sanatorium property was 26.46 acres; 20 acres were added in 1966; at that time 105 acres owned by Guilford County were available to the east for expansion.
5. BOT, Jan. 11. 1966, Book II; Carter, pp. 11–12; see Carter Appendix I for a description of the physical plant.
6. BOT, April 8, 1966. The Board chose J. Hyatt Hammond and Associates as architect on May 10, 1966.

7. BOT, Feb. 8, 1966; Book II, letter (no date) from Dr. Wendell Patton.
8. He is apparently referring to the children of Gilbert and Barker (Gilbarco) executives who had resettled to Greensboro from New England.
9. BOT, Feb. 15, 1966, form letter returned by Dr. Wendell Patton.
10. BOT, Feb. 8, 1966; GTI Archives; letters from the AAJC dated Jan. 24 and April 20, 1966.
11. BOT, May 10, 1966; Letter, May 16, 1966, GTI Board Archives.
12. BOT, Mar. 8, 1966; Resignation letter from Dr. Wendell Patton, Aug. 9, 1966.
13. BOT, Mar. 8, 1966.
14. *GR*, May 13, 1966., Nov. 9, 1965.
15. *GDN*, April 11, 13, 1966; *GR*, Feb. 8, 9, 11, 12, 13.
16. BOT, April 12, 1966.
17. GR, May 13, 1966.
18. Ibid.
19. Ibid.
20. Ibid.
21. Ibid. May 17, 1966.
22. These letters are in BOT, May 18, 1966.
23. Gilbert and Barker Company (1966) manufactured gasoline pumps for service stations.
24. BOT, May 18, 1966.

Chapter 5

1. BOT, Aug. 2, 1966.
2. BOT, May 15, 1966, Dickson, p. 151.
3. *HPE*, May 23, 1966.
4. A copy of Marco's Inaugural Address, printed by the *Jamestown News*, is in his file in the GTCC Archives.
5. See Virginia Bangiola Interview (1997) in the GTCC Archives Oral History series.
6. BOT, Feb. 8. 1966.
7. Ibid. July 14, 1966.
8. BOT, July 14, 1966.
9. Ibid. July 14; Aug. 2, 1966.
10. Ibid. Aug. 2, 1966.
11. Ibid. Aug. 2, 1966; Report of GTI Executive Committee vote to submit a request for community college status to Dr. Ready and the State Board of Education, Aug. 3, 1966.
12. Dr. I. E. Ready to Zalph Rochelle, BOT, Aug. 4, 1966; also see Marco memo to the Board, Aug. 5, 1966 announcing conversion approval.
13. BOT, Wendell Patton to Dale Montgomery, Aug 9, 1966; Patton to Marco, Aug. 10, 1966; Patton to Rochelle, Aug. 10, 1966.
14. Patton to Marco, Aug. 29, 1966, BOT Archives.
15. BOT, Aug. 30, 1966.
16. BOT, Sept. 15, 1966; Sept. 30, 1966 Letter from G. A. Jones, State Budget Officer, to Dr. I. E. Ready Sept. 30, 1966, also BOT, Oct. 11, 1966.
17. Oct. 7, 1966 Letter from I. E. Ready to Zalph Rochelle.
18. BOT, Oct. 11, 1966.
19. Ibid. Sept. 15, 1966.
20. Carter, Appendix H, p. 47.

21. Marco to Ready, Jan. 20, 1966, BOT Archives.
22. Rochelle to Marco, Jan. 21, 1966.
23. Letters, Bryant to Ward, Jan. 17, 1966; Marco to Ready, Jan. 20, 1966; memo to the Institute, Rochelle, Jan. 21, 1966.
24. BOT, Oct. 11, 1966; Nursing Agreement with the M.H. Cone Healthy Systems, Nov. 9, 1966.
25. BOT, Oct. 11, Nov. 9. 1966.

Chapter 6

1. *GDN*, Feb. 6, 1967.
2. BOT, Nov. 9, Dec. 13, 1966.
3. Nov. 14, 1966 letter from Reba Embry to State Auditor Henry L. Bridges, GTI Board Archives, Nov. 9, 1966.
4. The GTI *Green Hornets* played their first game in the fall of 1968, GTI Archives.
5. BOT, Nov. 9, 1966.
6. *GDN*, Feb. 6, 1967; see McClure-Smith interview in the GTCC Oral History series.
7. *GDN*, Feb.5, 1967, GTI Board Archives, Dec. 13, 1966.
8. BOT, Dec. 13, 1966, Book III, pp. 35–38; See Letter Dec. 8, 1966 from Henry L. Bridges to President Marco, GTI Archives, Dec. 13, 1966; The sign change is in GTI Board Archives, Dec. 21, 1966. Bledsoe, *GDN*, Feb. 9, 1967, writes "The word college was not removed, however. It was covered up by the 'Register Now.'"
9. These abandoned machines were sold for junk with the proceeds transferred to local funds and thence to the GTI Foundation, Inc.; GTI Board Archives, Jan. 17, 1967.
10. BOT, Dec. 21, 1966; *GDN, Bledsoe*, Feb. 5–9, 1967.
11. *GDN*, February 6, 1967. The results of this anonymous opinion survey had not been made public when the *Greensboro Daily News* began its five-part series on the school's woes on February 5, 1967.
12. BOT, Nov. 9, Dec. 21, 1966.
13. Ibid. Feb. 5, 1967.
14. Ibid. Jan. 23, 1967.
15. Ibid.
16. Ibid. Jan. 23, 1967.
17. *GDN*, Feb 5, 1967; GTI Board Archives, Jan. 17, 1967.
18. The Dental Hygiene and Dental Assistant programs were MDTA programs until 1968; see Carter, pp. 46–47. Letter from Louise D. Bryant, Department of Community Colleges, to President Marco reference nurse refresher course, Feb. 21, 1967. The FTE (Full time Equivalency) formula for this period: one FTE was equal to 16 hours per week for 44 weeks, Wiggs, p. 31.
19. *GDN*, Feb. 6, 1967.
20. Wiggs, pp. 57–58 (NCSBE minutes, 1966f).
21. Ibid. p. 66; BOT, Jan. 17, 1967.
22. *GDN, Feb.* 4, 1967.
23. Ibid. Feb. 5, 1967.
24. *GDN; News and Observer* (Raleigh); hereafter *N&O*, Feb. 5, 1967.

Chapter 7

1. Ibid. Feb. 5–9, 1967.

2. Oral history interviews occasionally describe the school's earliest students in unflattering terms since many were unmotivated dropouts, delinquents, and inmates.
3. Powell, 1989.
4. See Chapter 28 for details about a project to establish a two plus two program with UNCG at GTCC High Point in 2001–02.
5. *GDN*, Feb. 5, 1967; Growth figures ranged from 500 students (1963) to 2000 (1967) and from a budget of $336,694 (1963) to approximately $1,757,954 (1967).
6. Feb. 6, 1967.
7. *GTI* Catalog 1965–66.
8. *GDN*, Feb 8, 1967, Carter, pp. 46–47; The Associate Degree in Nursing Program began as a part of the Institute's Technical curriculum in 1970; Dental Assisting began as an MDTA vocational program in 1966 and Practical Nurse Education as a vocational offering in 1965.
9. GTI Archives, Jul. 20, 1965.
10. *GDN, Feb.* 8, 1967.
11. *GDN*, Feb. 8, 1967, GTI Archives.
12. Letter from Louise Bryant to Mrs. Charles Ward, Jun 17, 1966.
13. BOT, Rochelle letter to Ready Jan. 20, 1966.
14. Rochelle to Marco, Jan. 21, 1966, BOT Archives.
15. *GDN, Feb.* 8, 1967; Carter, pp. 46–47.
16. GTI Archives, Feb. 8, 1966.
17. *GDN*, Feb. 8, 1967.
18. GTI Board minutes, May 10, 1966, page 12, Book II.
19. See the Alwayne McClure interview in the GTI Archives Oral History Series.
20. *GDN*, Feb. 9, 1967, GTI Archives. ·
21. Ibid.
22. *GDN*, Feb. 9, 1967.
23. *GDN*, Feb. 9, 1967.
24. *HPE*, Feb. 12, 1967.
25. Ibid.
26. *HPE*, Sunday, February 12, 1967. GTI Archives.
27. Letters to Herring and Moore, GTI Archives, 1966.
28. *HPE*, Feb. 12, 1967.
29. *GDN*, February 9, 1967. GTI Archives.
30. *GDN, Feb.* 15, 1967, GTI Archives.

Chapter 8

1. *GDN*, Feb. 15, 1967.
2. Ibid. Feb. 17, *1967*, "Rochelle Asked to Resign Post."
3. Newly appointed Trustee Vance Chavis did not fill Dr. Wendell Patton's seat until Feb. 23, 1967. Chavis attended his first meeting on March 14, 1967. Rochelle, Starling and Kemp did not attend this meeting. The details of this meeting rely exclusively on Jerry Bledsoe's Feb. 14, 1967, report in the *GDN*.
4. *GDN*, Feb. 17, 1967.
5. *GDN*, Feb. 17. 1967; Conrad told reporter Jerry Bledsoe that he had completed one phase of an audit of the Board's operating procedures which showed no chairman or vice chairman had been elected for the year beginning July 1, 1966.
6. Ibid. Feb. 17, 1967. Some information may be missing from the minutes; on

November 9, 1966, Chairman Rochelle informed the Board secretary that, "all statements made at the Board meetings would be included in the minutes unless the secretary was instructed not to include certain statements"; GTI Board Archives, Nov. 9, 1966.

7. This motion appears directly related to the North Carolina State Board Policy read into the minutes of the previous Board meeting by Dr. Marco on January 17, 1967, defining open door admission of both high school graduates and others who are eighteen years old or older, but are not high school graduates. This policy additionally warned that, since community colleges had been designed for this mission, aspiration to become a 4-year college would destroy the community college role. On Feb. 14, 1967, Marco inserted state policy 2.0411, which does not mention 16- to 18-year-olds and 2.0412, which allows institutions to enroll high school students only at the request of local school authorities and notes an extension of this policy only to June 30, 1965. See Wiggs, pp. 27, 62, 163, 243; The adult high school diploma program began in 1966. See *GR*, Feb. 14, 1967. Ironically, 35 years later (2002), the Guilford County Schools established the state's first Middle College at GTCC for students who did not perform well in the traditional high school setting. This led to Senate Bill 656 promoting the establishment of innovative high school programs"; *HPE*, Jul. 4, 2003.

8. GTI Board Archives, Feb. 14, 1967; William O. Conrad, "The GTI Story," GTCC Archives.

9. Feb. 14, 1967, GTI Archives; *GDN*, Feb. 15, 1967.

10. *GR*, Feb., 14, *1967*. GTI Archives.

11. *GDN*, Feb. 15, *1967*.

12. Ibid. Feb. 14, *1967*; James Wagner, the *High Point Enterprise*, February 15, 1967, GTI Archives.

13. Wiggs, p. 79.

14. *GDN*, Feb.15, 1967.

15. Ibid.

16. Ibid. also see Jim Hawkins, *HPE*, Feb. 15, 1967.

17. *GDN*, Feb. 15, 1967.

18. *GDN*, Feb. 15, 1967, GTI Archives.

19. *GR*, Feb. 15, *1967*, GTI Archives.

20. *GDN*, Feb. 17, *1967*.

21. *GDN*, Feb. 17, *1967*.

22. *GDN*, Feb. 14, *1967*.

23. Ibid. Feb. 18, *1967*.

24. *GR*, Feb 18, *1967*.

25. *HPE*, *GDN*, Feb. 17, 18, 1967; *GR*, Feb. 18, 1967.

Chapter 9

1. *GDN* editorial, *Feb.* 18, 1967, GTI Archives.

2. *GR*, Feb. 28, 1967.

3. *GDN*, Feb. 22, 1967, GTI Archives contains a list of Task Force members. *HPE*, Feb. 28, 1967.

4. Ibid. Feb. 28, 1967.

5. *GR*, Feb. 28, 1967.

6. *HPE* Feb. 24, 1967.

7. Dallas Herring to Charlene Hall, letter dated, Feb. 15, 1967. GTI Archives.

8. Tom Duncan to Dallas Herring, letter dated Feb. 15, 1967, including petition, "The

Need to Be a Community College," GTI Archives. Duncan's letter appeared in the *Greensboro Record*, Feb. 23, 1967.

9. Ibid.
10. *HPE*, Feb. 24, 1967; Letter from Jack Marshall; GTI Archives.
11. *GDN*, Feb. 14, 1967.
12. GTI Board Archives; Conrad's term ended June 30, 1967. Chairman Rochelle wrote the Superintendent of the Guilford County Schools on April 26, 1967, suggesting that the school board reappoint Conrad to the Board; see GTI Board Archives April 11, 1967.
13. President Marco had asked the State Board of Education and Dr. I. E. Ready, head of the Department of Community Colleges, to approve Associate in Arts degrees for the dental hygienists. GTI Archives, March 14, 1967.
14. GTI Archives, March 14, 1967.
15. *GR,* March 16, 1967.
16. Ibid.
17. W. O. Conrad, "The GTI Story," Mar. 22, 1967, GTI Archives.
18. *HPE*, April 12, 1967.
19. Ibid.
20. Ibid. At the November 9, 1966 Board session Chairman Rochelle instructed Secretary Rita Embry "that all statements made at the Board meetings would be included in the minutes unless the secretary was instructed not to include certain statements."
21. Letter, Marco to Montgomery, Apr. 28, 1967. GTI Archives.
22. *HPE*, May 3, 1967.
23. *GDN*, May 3, 1967.
24. *GDN*, May 10, 1967. The MDTA program instituted at a cost of $379,095 was still awaiting accreditation and Marco was reportedly to blame.
25. GTI Board Archives, May 2, 1967.The information from the Task Force Report is excerpted from "State Tells GTI: Correct Weaknesses, Mend Split," *GDN*, May 3, 1967. It substantiates claims made by Jerry Bledsoe in his *GDN* Feb. 5–9, 1967 expose.
26. BOT, June 13, 1967.
27. Marco was probably aware that a new chair and vice chair had been nominated, but his dismissal of Rochelle, who had voted confidence in him on several occasions, was the most subtle way he could express his displeasure with the chairman. Letter of Resignation, Herbert F. Marco, GTI Archives, 1967; *HPE*, June 3, 1967; June 14, 1967.
28. Carter, p. 14; The student newspaper *The Gateway* Vol. 1, Issue No. 3, June 1967, lists 24 graduates including 17 A.A.S. and 7 A. A. A. recipients.
29. GTI Board Archives, Sept. 11, Oct. 10, 1967. For insights into the Davis-Sears relationship, see John T. Davis Interview in the GTI Oral History Series, Archives.
30. BOT, June 13, 1967.
31. *HPE*, June 13, 1967. GTI Archives.
32. "Staff and Faculty" circa 1965–66, GTI Archives.
33. Ibid. GTI Archives. *GDN*, Aug. 12, 1967. Marco accepted a position as coordinator of the curriculum development laboratory of the Virginia Department of Community Colleges.
34. Manuscript, *GDN* Owen Lewis interview with Herbert Marco, GTI Archives, July 1967, hereafter, Lewis-Marco.
35. Ibid.
36. Ibid.
37. "Decades of Development: GTI 1958–78. GTI Archives.

Chapter 10

1. This version of the GTI alma mater was sung to the tune of Edelweiss from "The Sound of Music." An earlier version written by MDTA Steno IV student Judy Canter was sung to "Maryland, My Maryland;" BOT, June 1, 1965.
2. *HPE*, June 14, 1967.
3. Ibid. Aug. 24, 1967.
4. BOT, July 11, 1967.
5. Ibid. Medlin was evidently traveling with the renowned Page High School Choir when contacted about the job, *GR*, Sept. 23, Aug. 10, *GDN*, Aug. 11; Aug. 14;*GR*, Aug. 14, 1967.
6. Central School later served as a Greensboro campus for GTI before it was razed to provide a location for the Weaver Education Center.
7. The State Board of Education approved Luther Medlin as president of GTI on August 3, 1967; *GR* Editorial, Aug. 10, 1967.
8. Ibid.
9. The Board decided to relocate the program to the space utilized by a student lounge in Furniture Hall (November 14, 1967), and it was here that the author later interviewed the long term director of the program Claude Culp for a segment of WFMY-TV's "Good Morning Show."
10. Letter, July 25, 1967; BOT, Sept. 1967. The Thompson-Arthur Paving Company invoices were signed by E. S. Arthur; also October 10, 1967. The Board continued to deal with the construction of the new library classroom building and seek new quarters for the cosmetology program at its September 11, 1967 session.
11. 'Decades of Development, 1978; Medlin's 1967 contract is a part of his historical papers in the GTI Archives. His salary for the 1967 academic years as principal of Page High School would have been $14,820, *GR*, Aug. 9, 1967.
12. Ibid. Resolution honoring Ed Kemp and W. O. Conrad, BOT, Oct. 10, 1967.
13. J. Hyatt Hammond, "Proposed 1967 Building Program, "BOT, Sept. 11, 1967.
14. President's Report: Financial Status, BOT, September, 1967.
15. These reminiscences by Dr. Medlin are excerpted from Decades of Development, GTI: 1971.
16. (1967) Helen Medlin was the principal at Claxton Elementary School in Greensboro and Luther, Jr. taught at Aycock Junior High; *GR*, Aug. 9, 1967.
17. Medlin: President's Report to the Board, BOT, Oct. 10, 1967.
18. Robinson, pp. 165–68.
19. *HPE*, Aug. 13, 1967.
20. *HPE*, Aug. 6, 1967. *GDN*, Aug. 9, 1967; Wiggs, p. 70.
21. Cameron to Kinard, Oct. 16, 2007.
22. BOT; Embry's termination was approved by the Board on June 13, July 11, 1967.
23. "President's Report to the Board of Trustees," BOT, Oct. 10, Nov. 14. 1967; Medlin presented further details about staff and faculty responsibilities on Dec. 4, 1967, BOT; for salary details see Wiggs, pp. 69–70.
24. BOT, Oct 10, 1967.
25. Ibid. Nov. 14–30, 1967.
26. Trustees Committees Meeting, BOT, Dec. 4, 1967; the Board approved these recommendations on Dec. 12, 1967.

27. GTI Foundation Board Archives, Nov. 14, 1967. The BOT served as members of the Foundation board.
28. BOT, Curriculum Committee, Dec. 4, Dec. 12, 1967. The 2-year nursing and Electronic Data programs began in the fall of 1970; *GDN*, Oct 10, 1970.
29. BOT, Nov. 28, 1967. Administrators were also studying a sick leave policy.
30. BOT, Dec. 4, 1967.
31. "President's Report to the Board of Trustees," BOT, December 4, 1967.

Chapter 11

1. Luther R. Medlin, "President's Report: 1974."
2. GTI BOT, Feb. 13, 1968; The County Attorney also questioned the propriety of proxy votes. During the February 1968 session, the chairman recommended the presence of a quorum at all future meetings; presumably a simple majority. The BOT actually set 7 members as a quorum on September15, 1965; as of Feb 13, 1968 telephone votes and written proxies were not to be utilized and members absent without reason would be asked to resign. The BOT bylaws were amended in 1998 to define a quorum as a simple majority.
3. GTI BOT, Jan. 9, May 14, June 11, 1968.
4. GTI Board Archives, Jan. 9, 1968. The Trustees accepted President Medlin's new sick leave policy that, while it did not fix a certain number of days for sick leave, it did empower the administration to take discretionary action based on individual cases; *GR*. Jan. 10. 1968.
5. BOT, Feb. 13, 1968.
6. BOT, May 14, 1968.
7. BOT, May 14, June 11, 1968.
8. BOT, Mar. 12, Aug. 13, 1968.
9. BOT, July 9, Aug. 13, 1968; Carter, p, 19.
10. Chafe, pp. 178–82.
11. Ibid. GR, Jan. 10, 1968.
12. Mar. 8, 1968; Enrollment Report; *HPE*, Mar. 15, 1968.
13. BOT, Oct. 8, 1968.
14. BOT, April 9, 1968.
15. BOT, April 9, 1968.
16. Medlin, Adult Education Report to the Board, BOT, April 23, 1968.
17. BOT; Enrollment Report, Mar. 8, 1968; Richard L. Waldroup, Jr., Dir. of Instruction.
18. BOT, April 9, 1968.
19. Carter, p. 17.
20. Carter, p. 17.
21. Carter, pp. 17–18; GTI Archives, Nov. 19, 1967.
22. BOT, Aug. 7, 13, 1968, See "Project One Hundred" revision; Carter, 1971, pp. 19–20.
23. BOT, July 1968 budget.
24. BOT, Jan. 16, 1969.
25. BOT, Feb. 13, 1969; Carter, p. 50.
26. Dickson, p. 169.

Chapter 12

1. "Decades of Development," 1978.
2. BOT, Sept. 1966.

3. Ibid. May 14, 1968; Oct. 8, 1968; see Carter, 1971, Appendix L for GTI's "Statement of Purpose."
4. GTI, "Report of Visiting Committee, Nov. 18–21, 1968," p. 22. GTI Archives.
5. *HPE*, April 23, May 8, 1969; *GDN*, May 5, 1969.
6. *GDN*, Dec. 4, 1969; GTI BOT, Sept. 11, Dec. 11, 1969.
7. *GDN*, *GR*, Dec 4, 1969. There is no mention of any attempt to change the name to GTI in the BOT minutes for this period. Nelson Wallace had replaced George Finley as Administrative Assistant (Executive Vice President) on July 1, 1969; BOT, "President's Report to Trustees," July 10, 1969.
8. *HPE*, July 10, 1969.
9. *N&R*, Feb. 9, 1987.
10. Carter, pp. 21–22, 46. "Provisional accreditation" was simply a precursor to unqualified accreditation. For detailed discussion of new programs see BOT, May 25, 1969; *GDN*, March 6; Oct. 9, 1970. BOT, Aug. 14; Sept. 11, 1969. Approved Registered Nursing, Data Processing, Aviation Administration, and Career Pilot Training. For details about approved aviation programs see BOT, Nov. 19, 1970.
11. Medlin to Charles Holloman, DCC, Sept. 10, 1969; also BOT, Dec. 11, 1969.
12. BOT, Aug. 14; Sept. 11, 1969; Oct. 9. 1969; The Cosmetology account totaled $4,495.05 on Aug. 31, 1970.
13. BOT, Dec. 11, 1969.
14. Carter, p. 22; also Appendix I. GTI negotiated to buy the Guilford College Evening Division building on Washington Street in Greensboro in 1970. This campus was transferred to the Guilford County Schools in 2004 when the Adult Basic Education Center opened on the new Greensboro-East Wendover Campus.
15. Ibid. May 7, 1970, Carter, pp. 21–22.
16. *GDN*, Apr. 13, 1969. BOT, July 10, 1969, Oct. 8, 1970.
17. BOT, Aug. 14, 1969; April 9, 1970.
18. BOT, Aug. 13; Sept. 10, 1970.
19. BOT, Apr. 9, 1970.
20. BOT, March 12, 1970.
21. BOT, Apr. 9, 1970.
22. BOT, May 15, 1970, I.E. Ready letter to Luther Medlin.
23. Some students paid activity fees to use the library at 4-year institutions, but there is no indication that the students paid a higher tuition for these courses than for identical technical courses.
24. BOT, May 20, 1970.
25. BOT, June 11, 1970.

Chapter 13

1. The President's Annual Report, 1972; hereafter PAR, 72.
2. Medlin Oral History, GTI archive.
3. Ibid.
4. Carter, pp 25–26, Appendix M, p. 58.
5. PAR, 1972.
6. BOT, Feb. 11, 1971.

7. Letter from Luther Medlin to John Witherspoon, Feb. 17, 1971, BOT Archives; BOT Bond Resolution for $5,231,000, Mar.24, 1971.
8. Carter, p. 24.
9. 3 TV stations served Guilford County with over-the-air signals in pre-cable 1971.
10. BOT, Apr. 27, 1971.
11. GTCC Bond History, Archives.
12. BOT building committee notes, Nov. 17, 1971.
13. BOT, Nov. 1972. This became the Washington Street campus of GTI until the Basic Education and Adult High School programs moved to the Greensboro Wendover Campus in August, 2004.
14. Ibid. p. 23.
15. The Library Classroom was renamed Business Careers. The ground floor was renovated to house the Entertainment Technology Program in 2000. Health-Science eventually became the Stuart Fountain Dental Health Center, and Technical Laboratories was renamed Gerald Hall.
16. The Airport Authority had assured the Board that land would be available for a fixed base operation if the property acquisitions they were negotiating materialized; however the Board's negations were momentarily interrupted when the FAA ordered the Airport Authority to forego discussions with GTI in favor of Atlantic Aero, Inc., a fixed base operator. GTI supporters demanded an investigation into the decision. GTI Archives, Nov. 16, 1972.
17. BOT, Aug. 13, 1970. The cost of operation was set at 10 cents a mile or $40 an hour and the craft was additionally available for school business. For a description of the aircraft and regulations governing its use, see BOT Sept 9, Oct. 31, 1971.
18. Carter, p. 23; PAR 72; GR, March 1, 1971. Enrollment figures and program statistics varied from publication to publication during this period of furious expansion with the President's Annual Report the most reliable (in all probability).
19. GR, Mar. 5. 1971.
20. Ibid. Mar. 5. 1971.
21. BOT, March 10, 1971. *GR,* Mar. 1–6, 1971.
22. BOT, April 27, May 13, 1971. Low was appointed by the Governor to replace Robert Kistler and served from August 1969 until June 30, 1977.
23. BOT, Sept. 9, 1971.
24. BOT, April 13, May 11, 1972; see Exhibit C; also BOT, June 13, 1972. On Mar. 8. 1973, the Board approved transfer of Fore-See component of the Model Cities Program to a separate board effective May 1, 1973.
25. Carter, p. 47.
26. For background on law enforcement programs in the NCCS, consult Wigs, p. 128. BOT, Feb. 10, April 13, 1972, "A Proposal to the Piedmont Triad Criminal Justice Training Unit," and "Law Enforcement," a curriculum description.
27. BOT, April 13, 1972.
28. Vaughn retired in 2005 after 39 years of service.
29. PAR, 72.
30. Ibid.

Chapter 14

1. PAR, 1973; BOT, Jan. 17, 1974.
2. "VII Years of Vision and Progress: 1973–74;" hereafter PAR, 1973–74.
3. PAR, 1972–73; BOT, Sept. 13, 1973, Sept. 12, 1974; Kinard, 1988, 1997; The "School Days" segment originated on WFMY-TV NEWS2's "Good Morning Show" in 1971 to support the desegregation of the Greensboro Public Schools by presenting positive interviews and features. Coverage was later extended to other school systems, colleges and universities.
4. BOT, July 12, 1973.
5. Ibid. March 14, 1974.
6. Ibid. June 27, 1974.
7. PAR, 1973–74.
8. "A Report to the Community 1974–75;" Hereafter PAR, 1974–75.
9. BOT, March 8, 1973.
10. Ibid. August 9,16,23,25, 1971.
11. Ibid. May 1974, Jan. 3, 1975.
12. Site of the current Marriot Hotel.
13. PAR, 1972–73.
14. Administrative Information for the Board, Jan. 17, 1974. SACS confirmed GTI's accreditation in December 1973. The American Council on Dental Education approved the Dental Hygiene Curriculum in May 1973. The N.C. State Board of Nursing approved the Associate Degree Nursing and Practical Nursing Curricula in February 1973.
15. PAR, 1972–73.
16. During the early 1970s, four private colleges and two universities offered liberal arts programs in Guilford County, but their size, characteristics, entrance requirements and enrollment restrictions made it difficult for many "stay-at-home" students to gain admission.
17. PAR, 1973;" "VII Years of Vision and Progress, 1967–74."
18. *HPE*, May 30, 1973.
19. Ibid.
20. PAR, 1973–74. 1974–75.
21. PAR, 1974–75.
22. *GR*, Jan. 26, 1974.
23. *Whispering Pines*, 1972–1973.
24. *Whispering Pines*, 1974.
25. Medlin to the Board, Aug. 1, 1974.
26. *GR, HPE, GDN*, August 1, 1974.
27. BOT, Mar.18, April 10, 1975.
28. PAR, 1967–74.
29. *PAR, 1974–75.*
30. *N&R*, Jan 8, 2000.
31. *N&R*, Jan. 8, 2000. An interview with Dr. and Mrs. Medlin recorded Jan. 1999, a year before his passing, is in the GTCC Archives. By this time, Dr. Medlin was unable to communicate and most of the dialogue is provided by his wife Helen.

Chapter 15

1. GTI Archives 1975–76; Ken Sanford, Building a History from the Past: A History of Gaston College, 1999.
2. *GDN*, Aug. 7, 1945.
3. BOT, July 10, 1975. Sugg came to GTI fully cognizant of the 1975–76 budget since he had assisted retiring president Medlin in preparing it; Lutzweiller Oral History Series (LOHS), GTI Archives, 1999.
4. *GDN*, Aug. 7, 1975.
5. BOT, Oct. 1975; "Remarks Made to the Guilford Technical Institute Staff at the Opening of the 1975–76 School Term, Thursday September 4, 1975."
6. Ibid.
7. BOT, Sept. 4, 1975.
8. BOT, Dec. 12, 1974. Sugg's salary was $38,000 plus a $10,000 annual supplement.
9. *GDN*, Dec. 13, 1974.
10. *HPE*. Undated article (1976); BOT, Nov. 11, 1975.
11. "Your Technical Institute and the Challenges of Today's Economy," BOT Archives, 1975–76.
12. North Carolina's four-year public colleges and universities are funded through a separate governing board.
13. PAR, 1975–76.
14. PAR, 1975–76.
15. BOT, Oct. 10, 1975. 34% more students (3,627 curriculum) as compared with the previous year's 2,704, enrolled for fall 1975. Con-Ed was up 12% and 12,647 students were taking one or more courses during the quarter.
16. LOHS, PAR, 1975–76.
17. PAR, 1975–76.
18. Ibid.
19. GTI Board History; BOT, Aug. 14, Sept. 4, Oct 10, 1975. Powell, 1989; Governor James E. Holshouser, Jr., was the first Republican elected governor of North Carolina in the twentieth century.
20. Ibid. Nov. 13, 1975, Feb. 12, 1976.
21. BOT, July 15, Aug 1, 1976.
22. BOT, June 12, 1975.
23. BOT, May 13, 1976, also see Gerrald's biography in BOT 1976.
24. Wigg, p. 164. For example, Dallas Herring, Chairman of the State Board of Education, addressed the 30 percent increase in community college enrollments in light of the General Assembly's 4.2 million dollar budget reduction. Herring pointed out that the reduction to community colleges allowed for an equivalent increase in tuition grants for students attending private colleges. Herring argued that the tuition these extra community college students paid should be used to pay directly for their instruction, as opposed to being forwarded to the state.
25. PAR, 1975–76.
26. Ibid.
27. PAR, 1975–76.
28. "*Tech Talk*," Vol. XI No. 13, Jan. 9, 1976.

Chapter 16

1. *GR*, April 22, 1977.
2. *GDN*, April 23, 1977.
3. *GR*, April 22, 1977.
4. Wigg, p. 189. (NCSBE minutes, 1978c).
5. LOHS, GTI Archives, March 1998.
6. BOT, Oct. 27, 1977.
7. BOT, November 17, 1977. An interim committee composed of Dr. N. J. Owens, Dr. Ray Lane, and Chairman John Davis was designated to serve as an interim management team until a successor for Dr. Sugg was selected.
8. *GDN*, Oct. 26, 1977. Sugg's resignation letter, GTI Archives, Oct. 27, 1977.
9. *HPE*, Jan. 1, 1978.
10. PAR: 1976–77.
11. Ibid.
12. 1970 census; the Guilford County's total population exceeded 300,000. By 2005, the figure had declined to less than 47,000 while the population had increased to 424,000.
13. Wiggs, p. 158–59; PAR 1976–77.
14. BOT, Sept. 15, 1977; PAR 1976–77.
15. Ibid. Sept. 27, 1977; PAR 1976–77.
16. PAR 1976–77.
17. Ibid.
18. Ibid.
19. BOT, Jan. 20, 1977; April 21, 1977 (Exhibit C); Aug 18, 1978.
20. Percy Sears, Dec. 27, 1977.
21. *GR*, Dec. 27, 1977. In addition to Sears, the search committee included Trustees John Davis, George Covington, John Foster, Frank York, and Robert Landreth. Wiggs, p. 189; Dr. N. J. Owens, Sr. was approved as Acting President of GTI by the State Board of Education effective January 1, 1978.
22. GR, *GDN*, Jan.10, 1978; BOT, Jan. 19, 1978.
23. BOT; Presidential search, Jan. 19; Feb. 16; Mar. 10; May 1, 1978.
24. GTI Archives, Dr. Jerry Owens, letter to Dr. Jim Owen; Memo to GTI faculty and staff, May 24, 1978. *HPE*, June 15, 1978.
25. GTI Archives, LOHS interview, March 1998.
26. *GDN*, June 16, 1978.
27. See Gazebo in GTI Archives.
28. Ibid. GTI Archives, 1983 note to GTCC President Dr. Needham from Jane Smith; also see various articles including Jane Smith interviewed by Shelly Lutzweiler, LOHS, 1998.
29. OT, Dec. 8, 1977.
30. "*Tech Talk*," Vol. XIV, No. 23, May 15, 1978.

Chapter 17

1. BOT, May 1, 1978; *GR*, May 31, 1978.
2. *GDN*, May 30, 1978.
3. *HPE*, May, 2 1978.
4. *GR*, May 31 1978.
5. *HPE*, May 2, May 5, May 31, 1978.

6. *GDN*, May 2, 1978.

7. Wiggs, p. 195.

8. Ibid. p. 203. Dr. McLeod was the former vice president of instruction and development at Piedmont Technical Institute in Roxboro.

9. BOT, April 27, 1978, April 30, 1978, Dec. 20, 1979.

10. *GR, GDN*, Sept. 29, 1978.

11. BOT, July 19, 1979. See Exhibit E.

12. GTI Archives, LOHS, 1988.

13. "Five *Very* Good Reasons to VOTE YES on Bond Issues, November 6, 1979," GTI Archives, N. J. Owen file.

14. Margaret Wheaton, *Codename-Greenkil: The 1979 Greensboro Killings*, U. Of Georgia Press, 1987, provides the most complete early review of this tragedy.

15. The author hosted the "Good Morning Show" on WFMY-TV (CBS Greensboro) from 1956 until 1999 and was uniquely familiar with GTI from its founding as the GIEC.

16. BOT Executive Committee Archives, Jan 18, 1979.

17. Ibid. Aug. 16; Sept. 20, 1979; Jan. 17, 1980.

18. Ibid. Dec. 20; May 27; June 21, 1979.

19. BOT, July 19, 1979.

20. Ibid. Oct. 19; Dec. 21, 1978; Letter from Frank York to Dr. H.J. Owen, Oct. 4, 1978.

21. Ibid. Sept. 20, 1979.

22. Ibid. Feb. 15; June 21, 1979.

23. Ibid. Exhibit B, Mar. 15, 1979.

24. *GDN*, Jan.18, 1980.

25. Ibid. Jan. 18, 1980; *GR*, Jan.17, 1980' BOT, Jan. 17,1980.

26. Wiggs, p. 201.

27. Memorandum Nov. 7, 1979. GTI Archives, Owen file. LOHS interview, 1998.

28. Wiggs, p. 207.

29. Ibid. pp. 203–05, 207–08, 218.

30. *GR*, June 5, 18, 1980.

31. Ibid. June 18, 1980.

32. Ibid. Mar 15, 1979.

33. Ibid. July 19, 1979.

34. Ibid. July 19, 1979, Oct. 16, 1980 at a cost of $20,100.00, which bankrupted the contractor.

35. *Tech Talk* "Special Edition," probably Aug. 1977.

36. Ibid. Jan. 30, 1978.

37. Wiggs, p. 187. The Visiting Artist program was a partnership between the State Board and the North Carolina Arts Council.

Chapter 18

1. *GR*, July 1, 1980.

2. Ibid. *GDN*, June 22, 1980. Actually, the state numbers quoted in the press ranged from $29,322 (*GR* June 18, 1980) to $32,160 (*GDN*, June 22, 1980).

3. Ibid.

4. *GR*, July 1, 1980.

5. Ibid. *GDN*, June 7, 1980.

6. *GR*, July 1, 1980.

7. LOHS, Ray Needham videotape interview recorded June 1999.

8. Ibid. *GDN*, June 7, 1980; *N&R*, June 18, 1980. Needham discusses the role Trustee Percy Sears played in creating the special salary fund.

9. *GDN*, June 22, 1980.

10. *GDN*, June 22, 1980.

11. Ibid. July 2, 1980.

12. *HPE*, June 18, 1980.

13. *GDN*, June 6, 1980.

14. *HPE*, June 18, 1980.

15. *HPE*, July 1, 1980.

16. *HPE*, July 7, 1980.

17. Ibid.

18. Ibid. July 1, 1980.

19. BOT, Sept. 18, 1980; *HPE*, Aug. 22, 1980.

20. *HPE*, Aug. 24, 1980.

21. BOT, July 31, 1980.

22. Ibid. Aug. 21, 1980; *GR*, Aug. 21, 1980; BOT, Sept. 9, Nov. 18, 1980.

23. BOT, Four standing committees were established on Aug. 21, 1981; Buildings and Grounds, Finance, Personnel and Policy and Curriculum.

24. *GDN*, 01-21-81. LOHS, GTI Archives, Needham alluded to campus criticism of Percy Sears in an interview noting that he was accused of snooping around, but in the final analysis Sears' ability to influence the operation of the College was controlled by the fact that he was never elected chairman of the Board.

25. BOT, Aug. 21, 1980.

26. *GR*, July 31, 1980.

27. Ibid. LOHS interview, GTI Archives.

28. *GR*, July 31, 1980.

29. *GDN*, Aug.22, Sept. 13, 1980.

30. BOT, Mar. 24, 1981. *The Greensboro Daily News* reported on November 26, 1980, that the school would have to revert $51,199, as a result of the audit exception.

31. GR, Nov 18, 1980.

32. BOT executive committee Archives, Sept. 20, 1979; *GR*, Nov. 18, 1980.

33. *GDN*, Nov. 18, 1980.

34. GTCC Management Manual, IV-2.021, .5.

35. GR, Jan. 21, 1981.

36. BOT, May 21, 1981; "*Tech Talk*," May 11, 1981; *GDN*, Jan. 21, 1981. LOHS interview with Don Cameron, GTI Archives.

37. BOT, Sept. 18, 1980.

38. "GTI Annual Report: 1981–82."

39. Ibid.

40. BOT, Feb. 19; Aug. 20, 1981.

41. BOT, May 13, 1981.Greensboro Educator Julius Fulmore served the remainder of Dorsett's unexpired term.

42. Ibid. July 1, 1980.

Chapter 19

1. Wiggs, p. 256.
2. "The Public Be Damned: A Question of Loyalty," Lin Fain and Steven Brooks, (A paper prepared for EDSP291 (Dr. George) Dec. 1, 1983; hereafter, Fain, 1983; See "Background of Guilford Technical Institute's College Transfer Program." Courses were transferred on an individual basis. When the author decided to resume his undergraduate education at UNCG in 1971, he was encouraged by the UNCG Admissions Director to take Algebra I and II at GTI and the courses transferred with no problems.
3. Fain, 1983, Appendix A.
4. Ibid. see "Activity Summary", p. 2.
5. BOT, Nov 19, 1981; Fain, 1983; Activity Summary, p. 2.
6. BOT, Jan. 21, 1982.
7. Ibid.
8. Ibid.
9. *GDN*, Jan. 21, 1982.
10. *HPE,* Jan. 24, 1982.
11. Ibid. The author recalls that most media reports tended to focus more on GTI's problems than its programs. The media Archives support this analogy.
12. BOT, Mar. 11. 1982; See "Request for the Addition Of A College Transfer Program, Book I, Formal Request, effective July 1, 1982, Archives.
13. Wiggs, pp. 256–57.
14. Fain, 1983.
15. Wiggs, p. 256; Fain, 1983.
16. Wiggs, p. 256.
17. Wiggs, p. 256.
18. Wiggs, pp. 256–57; "Private Schools Fear Growth of Community Colleges," *N&O* 3/8/82.
19. BOT, April 15, 1982.
20. *NR*, May 1, 1983.
21. *NR*, May 1, 1983.
22. Fain, 1983.
23. *NR*, Sept, 3, 1982.
24. *GDN, GR, HPE*, Dec. 17, 1982.
25. Wiggs, pp. 268–69.
26. *GDN*, Jan. 14, 1983.
27. *GR*, Jan. 28, 1983.
28. Ibid. Feb, 2, and *HPE*, Feb. 11, 1983.
29. *GDN*, Needham Archives.
30. Fain, 1983; BOT, June 16, 1983.
31. Further background on the process is contained in the BOT Archives for January and February, 1983.
32. *JN*, June 30, 1983.
33. BOT, Feb. 17, 1983. The GHG Corporation continued to build houses through this period.
34. Ibid. Jan. 20, 1983.
35. Ibid. June, October, 1982.

36. Ibid. Mar. 17, 1983.
37. On Sept. 8, 1983, the BOT approved remodeling the Service Careers Building for the new Culinary program.
38. Ibid. Jan. 20, Feb. 17, 1983.
39. *LOHS*, Virginia Bangiola interview, GTCC Archives.
40. *JN*, June 30, 1983. LOHS interview with Ray Needham, GTCC Archives, 1998.

Chapter 20

1. *GR,* Sept. 27, 1983.
2. *HPE,* July 29; *GDN,* July 30; *HPE,* Sept. 26, *GDN, GR,* Sept. 27, *JN,* Sept 30, 1983.
3. Wiggs, p. 273.
4. Ibid. pp. 200–01.
5. Ibid. 273–74.
6. *HPE,* July 7, 1983.
7. "GTCC and Guilford County: Twenty-Five Years of Growing Together," 1983, Needham Archives.
8. BOT, Feb. 7, 16, 1984.
9. "This Is Your Life, Guilford Tech High Point Center," Dec. 8, 1982, GTI-Needham Archives.
10. BOT, Sept. 15, 1983.
11. Not be confused with the Associate in General Education non transfer degree still offered (2007–08).
12. Ibid.
13. Donald W. Cameron, "Entrepreneurial Partnerships," in John E. Roueche and Barbara R. Jones, *The Entrepreneurial College,* Community College Press, Washington, D. C., 2005.
14. Ibid. also BOT, Sept. 15, 1983 see exhibit D.
15. "The Guilford Technician," hereafter TGT, Mar. 28, 1984; *HPE,* Oct. 18, 1984; BOT, Oct. 21, 1983.
16. *GDN,* June 27, 1984.
17. Ibid. Dec. 14, 1984.
18. Ibid. Dec. 14, 1984; BOT, Jan. 24, 1985.
19. Ketcham, Inc. study, Sept. 1983, BOT, 1984.
20. BOT, Dec. 134, 1984.
21. BOT, May 10, 1984.
22. BOT, July 11, 1984; The General Assembly allocated $1.8 million to build the Transportation/Electronics Complex and the county contributed $835,000, GTCC 1984–85 Annual Report.
23. BOT, Sept. 20, 1984, "The Financial Structure of North Carolina Community Colleges," Exhibit I. Figures for the GTCC budget therein differ from those the author selection from the GTCC Annual Report: 1984–85.
24. FTE values for 2001–05. GTCC.
25. Ibid. Figures appear in BOT, Sept, 20, 1984. Exhibit I.
26. BOT, March, 15, 1984.
27. TGT, April 18, 1984.
28. BOT, April 19, May 10, Sept. 14, 1984; GTCC Annual Report: 1984–85.
29. TGT, May 22, 1984.

30. BOT, Sept. 15, 1983.
31. Ibid. Aug. 23, 1984.
32. Ibid. Mar. 14, 1985, exhibit N; BOT, Dec. 12, 1985; A salary supplement proposal was being developed.
33. BOT, Oct. 22, Nov. 19, 1987.
34. GTCC Annual Report: 1984–85. The material in this update is provided in this report.
35. BOT, June 28, 1984.
36. Ibid. May 5, 1984.
37. *GDN*, Sept. 21, 1984; BOT, Sept. 20, 1985; In contrast to national figures, GTCC's enrollment increased.
38. BOT, Mar. 14, 1985.
39. *HPE*, Sept. 20, 1984.

Chapter 21

1. GTCC: 1986–87.
2. Halstead resigned in June 1987 and was replaced by Dr. Paula Garber, President Needham's assistant and Bruce Nolan, Director of Public Information ....
3. This "relational gap" is attributed to divisive personal and professional points of view on the part of the leadership in both communities and to the competitive nature and personalities of the two cities. Down through the years the relationship has been often soured by Greensboro's inclination to pursue certain initiatives and then inviting High Point to participate as an (perceived) after-thought; BOT, Mar. 14, 1985; *HPE*, Mar. 28, 1985.
4. Ibid. 09/23/86.
5. BOT, Sept. 25, 1986; GTCC: 1987–89.
6. BOT, July 18, 1985; Exhibit B.
7. GTCC Annual Report: 1985–86; hereafter, GTCC: 1985–86.
8. Ibid.
9. BOT, Oct. 17, 1985; GTCC: 1985–86.
10. Ibid.
11. *NR* article Exhibit D in BOT, August 28, 1986; GTCC: 1985–86.
12. GTCC: 1985–86.
13. GTCC: 1986–87.
14. GTCC: 1985–86.
15. Ibid.
16. Ibid.
17. GTCC: Needham Archives, 1986.
18. GTCC: 1985–86; "Community College Study, Sept. 11, 1985," in BOT, Oct. 11, 1985.
19. GTCC: 1986–87; GTCC: 1987–89.
20. Ibid.
21. GTCC: 1986–87.
22. Sylvia Ann Hewlett, *When the Bough Breaks*, Basic Books, 1991, p. 41. Hodgkinson Report, BOT, Sept. 8, 1986.
23. GTCC: 86–87; BOT, June 22, 1989.
24. GTCC: "Reflections: President's Report to the Community: 1987–89;" hereafter, GTCC: 1987–89.
25. Ibid. p. 8.

26. GTCC: 1986–87; BOT, June 25, July, 23, 1987. Konica Minolta Manufacturing USA ended the production of photographic paper at its Whitsett plant in 2007 with a loss of approximately 260 jobs. *N&R*, Jan. 3, 2007.
27. GTCC: 1986–87.
28. BOT, Dec. 11, 1986; Feb. 26, 1987.
29. BOT, Nov. 19, 1987.
30. *NR*, Sept 8, 1989.
31. GTCC: 1987–89. *HPE*, Oct. 18, 1984, Jan. 24, 1985; *GDN*, June 27, 1984; *N&R*, Dec. 14, 1984; *JN*, Dec. 18, 1986.
32. GTCC: 1987–89; BOT, June 23, 1988; *The Business Weekly*, Mar. 9, 1987.
33. BOT, April 4, 1989.
34. BOT, June 22, 1989.
35. GTCC: 1987–89.
36. Ibid.
37. Letter to Sherwood Smith, Chairman, Commission on the Future of the Community College System from GTCC Board Chair Stuart Fountain, BOT, April 4, 1988; *GDN*, Jan. 5, 1988.
38. *GDN*, Jan. 5, 1988.
39. GTCC: 1987–89.
40. *JN*, Mar. 15, 1989.
41. Ibid.
42. BOT, April 30, 1987.
43. Ibid. July 20, 1989; GTCC: 1987–89.

Chapter 22

1. *N&R*, May 1, 1990.
2. BOT, Feb. 15, 1990, Exhibit G; "Vision for the 90"s," May 10, 1990 in BOT, May 17, 1990.
3. *N&R*, Feb. 16, 1990.
4. Lutz-Cameron interview: 1999. According to Cameron, the proposed communications building was telescoped into the third floor of the Sears Applied Technology Building.
5. BOT, Feb. 15, 1990, Exhibit G.
6. Ibid. May 17, 1990.
7. *N&R*, May 1, 1990, *JN*, May 9, 1990, *HPE*, May 1, 1990.
8. BOT, May 17, 1990.
9. Resignation Memorandum, Needham Archives, May 1, 1990.
10. *N&R*, *HPE*, May 1, 1990.
11. *N&R*, May 1, 1990.
12. Ibid. May 14, 1990.
13. Ibid. *N&R*, Sept. 8, 1989.
14. BOT, June 21, 1990.
15. Ibid. Aug. 9, 1990.
16. *N&R*, May 14, 15, 1990; Community College Weekly, April 12, 1997;Needham retired from Tacoma Community College in July 1997.
17. *HPE*, Oct. 10, 1991; Parker resigned June 30, 1994, to join the Kellogg Foundation and later returned to the North Carolina Community College System as Vice President of Student Services.
18. BOT, Feb, 15, 1990.

19. LVHS, Needham, 1998.
20. BOT, Feb.15; May 17, 1990; *HPE*, May 17, 1990; *NR*, Feb. 16, 1990.
21. *N&R* May 1, 1990. The Board met with presidential search consultant Jim Tatum during a special called meeting On May 25, 1990.
22. BOT, May 17, 1990. Memo Fountain to the Board re: "Presidential Search, May 25, 1990 in BOT Archives May 1990.
23. The decision to select Cameron as interim president occurred on a motion by Percy Sears and was unanimously approved at the May 17, 1990, Board session effective Aug. 1, 1990.
24. See biographical information on Dr. Donald W. Cameron in the GTCC Archives.
25. BOT May 17, 1990; See "Presidential Search Update," BOT, Aug. 9; Sept 27; Dec. 13, 1990.
26. BOT, Sept. 27, 1990.
27. *HPE,* Feb. 8, 1991; also see "1990 Bond Issue," GTCC Archives; "Vision for the 90's,: GTCC Bond Update and LVHS, interview with Dr. Cameron (1999).
28. BOT, Sept. 27, 1990.
29. BOT, April 23, 1992.
30. Ibid. June, 18, 1992. The Tech Prep concept originated with the publication of The Neglected Majority, by Dr. Dale Parnell, President of the American Association of Community Colleges (AACT).
31. BOT, Feb 21, 1991. The State Board of Community Colleges approved Cameron's presidency on Feb. 14, 1991.
32. *GDN*, May 19, 1981; *JN*, Feb, 2, 1991; *N&R, HPE*, Feb. 2, 1991.
33. Donald W. Cameron and Robbie Lee Needham, "Policy for Instruction," AACJC Journal, October. 1984, pp. 38–39; BOT, Feb 17, April 21, 1994.
34. Wiggs, 1988; BOT, June 27, 1991; *HPE*, Oct. 10, 1991. Fouts left GTCC in 1994 to serve as Executive Vice President at Wayne Community College before reoccupying his Medlin Campus Center office in 1997. He retired in 2001 and reverted to his beloved role as a Developmental Studies instructor.
35. Consult the Cameron Archives for details about the program and BOT, Aug. 8, 1991 for planning details and Oct. 24, 1991 for the Board's positive reaction to the ceremony.
36. *N&R*, Oct. 10; Nov. 1; *HPE*, Oct. 10, 1991.
37. Cameron Archives, GTCC. See "Gaining the Competitive Edge: The Challenge to North Carolina's Community Colleges," MDC, 1989, GTCC Archives.

Chapter 23

1. Remarks at GTCC, Oct 8, 1991.
2. BOT, Feb. 27; April 23; June 18, Oct 8, 1992.
3. BOT, Dec. 19, 1991.
4. BOT, Feb. 21, 1991, "GTCC Special Projects: 1991–96.
5. BOT, Feb. 21, 1991.
6. Donald W. Cameron and George M. Fouts, "Reforming Workforce Preparedness," in *The Leadership Dialogues: Community College Case Studies to Consider*, edited by Lawrence W. Tyree, Mark David Milliron and Guardo E. de los Santos. League for Innovation in the Community College, Phoenix 2004; hereafter, Cameron-Fouts.
7. BOT, Dec. 19, 1991; Dr. Gerald Lord made his initial visit to GTCC on Dec. 12, 1991 and scheduled the self-study committee visit for Mar. 21–24, 1994.
8. Cameron-Fouts.

9. *"President's Report to the Community: 1991–92,"* hereafter PAR, 1991–92.

10. Ibid. p. 7; Calculated on a three quarter average for curriculum and a four quarter average for continuing education.

11. Ibid. p. 8.

12. Ibid. p. 9; *BOT*, Feb 21; April 25, 1991.

13. PAR: 1991–92. p. 10.

14. Ibid. p. 11.

15. Ibid. p. 11.

16. Ibid. p. 11; BOT, Aug. 8, 1991; Cameron-Fouts.

17. BOT, June 18, 1992; "PAR, 1991–92;" Ben Hill and Jason White were introduced as an Ambassadors to the Board on June 18, 1992, but were not included in the 1991–92 annual report.

18. BOT, Dec. 19, 1991; Cameron-Fouts.

19. By 1994, GTCC had sent three classes totaling 62 people through the program.

20. BOT, December 12, 1991; *HPE*, Jan. 1, 1992; BOT, Oct. 8, 1992. LVHS, Cameron 1999; Cline report,1–8.

21. Cline 1.

22. BOT, Oct. 8, 1992; PAR: 1991–92. Cameron discusses Eaton in LVHS-Cameron, 1999.

23. BOT, Oct. 8; Dec. 13, 1992; PAR: 1993–94.

24. BOT, Dec. 17, 1992.

25. Memorandum from North Carolinians for Community Colleges, Feb. 2, 1993; BOT, Feb 18, 1993.

26. PAR: 1993–94.

27. *N&R,*May 31, 1992.

28. Dheeraj Mehrotra, "Applying Total Quality Management in Academia," at www.isixsigma.com/library/content.

29. GPAC Recommendations, BOT, Feb. 18, 1993; *JN*, July 12, 1995, "GTCC President responds to recent editorial (GPAC); *JN*, July 12, 1995.

30. Cameron and Weast commissioned former Greensboro *N&R* editor Ned Cline to write a book about the Guilford County Workforce preparedness model. Cline delivered the manuscript in 1998 and it remains unpublished. Chapters 23–24 and 25 make extensive use of Cline's information; the document is lodged in the GTCC Archives and hereafter noted as Cline with numerals indicating the chapters.

31. BOT, August 19, 1993; Cline 1.

32. The guide was adopted as a model by the Community College System Office.

33. "Joint Policy Statement, BOT, May 12, 1993.

34. BOT, Dec. 16, 1993; Feb. 17, 1994; PAR 1991–92, p. 6.

Chapter 24

1. *N&R*, April 22, 1994.

2. Ned Cline, "Untitled Paper," 1998, GTI Archives. Foreword and six chapters designated numerically as indicated in the text; hereafter, Cline. Donald W. Cameron and George M. Fouts. "Reforming Work Force Preparedness," in Lawrence W. Tyree, Mark David Milliron and Gerado E. de los Santos, The Leadership Dialogues: Community College Case Studies to be Considered. League for Innovation in the Community College, Phoenix 2004; hereafter Cameron-Fouts.

3. BOT, Feb. 27, 1994; "BDO Seidman 1994: Pulse of the Piedmont Triad" supported Dr. Cameron's statement that "the cooperation between the public schools and the community college working together on the Tech Prep initiative is of great importance."
4. Cline-1.
5. For background on the civil and social history of Guilford County and its municipalities consult Robinson, Chafe and Kinard (unpublished dissertation, 1988).
6. Cameron-Fouts; Cline, Foreword.
7. PAR: 1993–94; Cline-1.
8. Cline-1, Cameron-Fouts.
9. Ibid. Cameron Fouts; Robinson, pp. 237–38; also Chafe and Kinard (unpublished dissertation).
10. Cameron-Fouts.
11. Ibid. Cline-1.
12. Ibid.
13. Ibid.
14. Cline-1.
15. "Preparing Guilford County's Workforce: President's Report to the Community: Guilford Technical Community College: 1994–96, p. 4; hereafter PAR 1994–96.
16. BOT, May 12, 1993; Proposed Tech Prep Associate Degree Program Update.
17. PAR: 1993–94, p. 7; Apprenticeship program instituted with AMP, Inc., BOT, Oct. 19, 1994.
18. Cameron-Fouts.
19. Ibid.
20. BOT, Feb. 17, 1994.
21. BOT, June 16, 1994; "President's Report to the Community: 1993–94;" hereafter PAR 1993–94; p. 5.
22. Ibid. p. 6.
23. BOT, Feb. 17; April 21, 1994; N&R, April 22, 1994.
24. Memorandum to BOT Finance & Facilities Committee from George M. Fouts, May 6, 1994 re: State Budget Update—Fiscal Year 1994–95.
25. BOT, Feb. 17; April 21; Memo: George Fouts to Finance and Facilities Committee, Board of Trustees, May 6, 1994; Subject: State Budget Update: FY 1994–95; BOT, June 16.
26. Ibid. p. 8.
27. BOT, Oct. 10, 1993.
28. PAR 1993–94, pp. 9–11. Source 1993–94 Annual Registration Report, N.C. Department of Community Colleges.
29. BOT, Aug. 18, 1994; PAR 1993–94, p. 17;UNCG News Bureau, July 22, 2002.
30. PAR 1993–94, p. 17.

Chapter 25

1. BOT, April 21, 1994; Feb. 16; April 20; Aug. 17; Oct. 19, 1995. Sears died April 1, 1997.
2. BOT, Dec. 15 1994; N&R, Jan. 29, 1995; "Incidents may force Teens out of GTCC;" see BOT, Feb.16, 1995.
3. Jan. 29, 1995.
4. Ibid.
5. BOT, Dec. 15, 1994.

6. Ibid. JTPA, Job Training Partnership Act (1983–2000) directed and funded the largest Federal employment training program in the nation, serving dislocated workers, homeless individuals and economically disadvantaged adults, youths and older workers. It was replaced by WIA on July 1, 1, 2000.
7. Ibid.
8. During the 2006–07 academic year, 385 Early Middle College students attended classes on three GTCC campuses in addition to more than 500 Eastern Guilford High School juniors and seniors taking classes on the Greensboro Campus in the aftermath of the fire that destroyed their school.
9. Email from Pat Freeman, August 23, 2007 (LEIS).
10. Cline-1; Also see "Tech Prep Youth Apprenticeship Metals Project' and "Tech Prep/Associate Degree," in BOT, Feb. 16, 1995.
11. "Preparing Guilford County's Workforce: President's Annual Report to the Community: Guilford Technical Community College: 1994–96," p. 4; hereafter, PAR; 1994–96.
12. Dr. White retired from CIBA in 2001 to become GTCC's executive vice president, a position he held for almost five years before assuming the presidency of Midland Technical College in Columbia, S.C. (April, 2006).
13. PAR 1994–96, p. 5.
14. Ibid.
15. Ibid.
16. Ibid. p. 6. See "GTCC and Workforce Preparedness: A GTCC Faculty Guide," prepared by the CIBA Specialty Chemical Company Grant Cadre in notes for Chapter 25.
17. PAR 1994–96, p. 6.
18. Ibid.
19. Ibid. p. 7; Cameron-Needham, 1984.
20. PAR 1994–96, p. 8.
21. Ibid. pp. 8–9.
22. Ibid. p. 18.
23. BOT, June 20, 1996.
24. BOT, June 15, 2006; "Friends of the Cline Observatory Newsletter," Spring 2006.
25. BOT, April 17; October 19, 1995 and June 20, 1996.
26. PAR 1994–96.
27. PAR 1985–86; 1994–96, p. 12.
28. PAR 1994–96.
29. BOT, April 20. 1995.
30. *JN*, July 12, 1995.
31. Cline-3.
32. Ibid. p. 10.
33. Ibid. p. 11.

Chapter 26

1. Cline-4.
2. Feb 15, 1996. During this same period, the College was pursuing a cooperative program in auto maintenance with Ford and GM and would add Volvo in 1996, but that model had not been expanded to other industrial skills.

3. Oct. 23, 1997; PAR 1996–98. Dr. Cameron hosted a GTCC delegation that joined a similar group from UNCG to visit Wuhan University March 3–13, 2006 to discuss a tourism and related disciplines project.

4. Feb. 15, 1996.

5. Feb. 15, 1996; Cameron introduced Pumphrey to the Board.

6. Cline-4.

7. Ibid.

8. 1993 General Assembly appropriated 3.5 million to the Board of Governors of the UNC System to finance PTCAM an applied manufacturing facility to be owned and controlled by N.C. A&T State University (Piedmont Triad Center for Advanced Manufacturing).

9. was named President of South Puget Sound Community College on June 19, 2006.

10. Cline-4.

11. June 20, 1996.

12. The Facts 1997 in PAR 1996–98.

13. Dec. 18, 1997.

14. August 22, 1996; December 18, 1997; Email Bill Eversole, GTCC Director of Workforce Preparedness, to Kinard, Jan. 31, 2006.

15. President's Report: 1996–98;" hereafter PAR 1996–98.

16. Cline-2.

17. State Board of Community Colleges awarded GTCC $37,000 to develop a model to track CTP students and their outcomes, BOT, Oct. 23, 1997.

18. *Community College Times*, April 9, 1996.

19. *N&R*, Oct. 11, 1996.

20. LVHS-Cameron, 1999.

21. *Florida Times Union*, 10-06-96, *N&R*, *HPE* 10-11-96.

22. *N&R*, Oct. 11, 1996.

23. *WSJ*, Nov. 26, 1996.

24. Ibid.

25. *N&R*, Nov. 27, 1996.

26. BOT, Dec.19, 1996.

27. Ibid. Aug. 21, 1997.

28. *N&R*, May 7, 1997.

29. Ibid.

30. *Community College Times*, April 9, 1996.

31. *N&R*, May 7, 1997.

32. Ibid. Guilford County School Superintendent Jerry D. Weast resigned in 1999 to become superintendent of the Montgomery County Maryland Public School System.

33. *N&R*, May 17, 1997.

34. Ibid. also see *HPE*, May 7, 1997, May 15, 1997 & May 17, 1997.

35. BOT, Feb. 27, 1992; *N&R*, August 20, 1997.

36. PAR, 1996–98.

37. George Fouts returned to GTCC on March 3, 1997.

38. PAR, 1996–98.

39. Ibid. p. 14.

Chapter 27

1. BOT, Feb. 19; Aug. 20, 1998.
2. Ibid. Oct. 15, 1998.
3. Email Don Cameron, June 10, 1998.
4. Ibid. Aug. 20, 1998.
5. GTCC Media Luncheon Presentation, June 8, 1998.
6. BOT, Feb. 19, April 16, 1998. A $15,000 grant from GenCorp Foundation (OMNOVA) supported the Chemical Manufacturing Process Technology program by financing the purchase of specialized chemistry equipment including four Spectronic-20-Genesys Spectrophotometers, an Electronic Analytical Balance, two Melting Point Apparatus and a Gas Chromatograph with data collection software.
7. "President's Report 1996–98," hereafter, PAR 1996–98, pp. 5–6.
8. BOT, Feb. 19, 1998.
9. Ibid. p. 7; BOT, April 16, 1998.
10. PAR 1998–2000, p. 5; The groundbreaking for these facilities occurred on March 16, 2000.
11. Ibid. April 16, June 18. Aug. 20.
12. BOT, Feb. 19; Aug. 20; Oct. 15; Dec. 17, 1998; Dec. 16, 1999. Donald W. Cameron, "Entrepreneurial Partnerships," in John E. Roueche and Barbara R. James, The Entrepreneurial Community College, Washington, Community College Press, 2005. Dr. Cameron was awarded the facility's first lifetime membership for his support in bringing the project to fruition at the September 2002 groundbreaking.
13. *Winston-Salem Journal*, Oct. 10, 1999. Source, NCCFA.
14. BOT, Feb. 18; May 6, 1999.
15. BOT, May 6, 1999.
16. Vision 2030 is discussed in Chapter 29.
17. BOT Spring Work Session, May 6, 1999.
18. BOT, June 17, 1999.
19. *N&R*, Aug. 4, 1999.
20. Source: Chief Jerry Clark, GTCC Police Department.
21. PAR 1998–2000, p. 4.
22. BOT, Oct. 14, 1999.
23. *Triad Business* News, Oct. 15, 1999.
24. *JN*, Nov.10, 1999; PAR 1998–2000, p. 7.
25. PAR 1998–2000, p. 7.
26. Ibid. pp. 8–9.
27. Ibid.
28. BOT, Oct. 14, 1999; Oct. 12, 2000.
29. Donald W. Cameron, "Entrepreneurial Partnerships," 2005.
30. *JN*, Oct. 20, 1999; *The Business Journal,* Oct. 29, 1999; *Triad Style*, Dec.8, 1999.
31. *N&R*, Dec. 12, Dec. 5, 1999 ....
32. BOT, May 6, 1999; PAR 1998–2000.
33. BOT, June 17; Work Session, Oct. 29, 1999. 2000 Bond Resolution adopted Dec. 16, 1999.
34. BOT, Oct. 29, 1999.
35. *Triad Business* News, July 23, 1999.
36. PAR 1996–98, p. 5.
37. Ibid. June 18, 1998.

38. These awards appear in PAR 1996–98.
39. BOT, Dec. 16, 1999.
40. *HPE*, Nov. 7, 1999.
41. The award was presented by the North Carolina Division of Child Development.
42. BOT, April 15, 1999.

Chapter 28

1. *HPE*, Aug. 5, 1999.
2. *N&R*, Aug. 29, 1999.
3. BOT, Oct. 12, 2000.
4. *N&R*, Aug. 10, Jul. 8, 1999; BOT, Dec. 17, 1999.
5. *HPE*, Aug. 5, 1999; *N&R*, Aug. 6, 1999.
6. *N&R*, Aug. 10, 1999.
7. *N&R*, *HPE*, Aug. 6, 1999; *N&R*, Mar. 3, 2006.
8. See BOT, Dec. 16, 1999.
9. *HPE*, Aug. 5, 1999; *N&R*, Aug. 6, 1999; ibid. Aug. 10, 1999.
10. Ibid. Aug. 6, 1999; ibid. Aug. 11, 1999.
11. See BOT Oct. 29, 1999, " Carolina Circle Mall Briefing Paper;" also *The Business Journal*, Oct. 29, 1999; *HPE*, Nov. 11, 1999. Six years later (2005) many of these programs would form the core of GTCC Greensboro's new campus at 3505 East Wendover Avenue.
12. *The Business* Journal, Oct. 29, 1999.
13. *N&R*, Nov. 18.1999.
14. *HPE*, Nov. 21, 1999. At this point, (*N&R*, Nov. 23, 1999) some Greensboro leaders began to consider redeveloping the land the county would vacate downtown when they moved to the mall. This idea eventually came to fruition, but not in the sense of this early speculation. A consortium of Greensboro foundations (Action Greensboro) led by Jim Melvin, CEO of the Joseph F. Bryan Foundation, Inc., purchased land beyond the downtown and built offices to relocate selected county departments. The former county offices became the site of Greensboro's new minor league baseball stadium.
15. *N&R, Nov.* 23, 1999; ibid. Nov. 24, 1999; ibid. Nov, 26.1999. *HPE*, Nov. 24, 1999.
16. *N&R*, *Dec.* 5, 1999.
17. BOT *Archives*, Greene to Cotton, Dec. 14, 1999.
18. BOT Dec. 16, 1999; Greene to Cotton, Dec. 16, 1999; *HPE*, Dec. 5, 1999; ibid. Dec. 17, 1999, *N&R*, Dec. 17,1999.
19. BOT, Feb. 17, 2000.
20. *HPE*, Feb. 1, 2000; June 4, 2003, Rae Marie Smith (GTCC) to Brian Byrd (Smith Moore, L.L.P; BOT, June 12, 2003, BOT Feb. 19, 1998.
21. *N&R*, Jan. 5. 2000.
22. *N&R*, Jan. 28, 2000.
23. Ibid. April, 25, 2000; April 28, 2000; May 1, 2000, May 3, 2000.
24. BOT, *Oct.* 12, 2000.
25. *HPE*, Nov. 27, 2000.
26. This optimistic October 23, 2000, memo to the Board assumed passage of the November State Bond package. Cameron dated his 10 years from his appointment as interim President in July 1990.
27. GTCC "Vision for the 90's" summary, GTCC Archives.

28. *HPE*; Sept. 10, 1999.
29. "The Role of the Community College System in The Economic Development of the State's Communities;" Unpublished Dissertation, N. C. State University, Raleigh, 1996. Dr. Kathryn Baker Smith received the 2002 NCCCS System Staff Award endowed by BB&T for outstanding service to the community college system.
30. *N&R*, Sept. 10, 1999.
31. Cline, 6-4.
32. (The author) Cameron quickly learned that Grier had his own ideas about alternative education when the new superintendent invited him to visit the prototype of an Early-Middle College in Tennessee.
33. Remarks; ET dedication, Wednesday, April 28, 2004.
34. Cameron to the author, 2000.
35. The author (Lee Kinard) reported to work at GTCC on February 28, 2000; Cameron immediately introduced him to Schneider and Dupree, informed him that he was the marketing anchor of the program and walked away. It is the author's opinion that the team succeeded from mutual respect and the abject fear of failing Don Cameron's dream. From this point on much of this document includes the author's experience in projects as Executive Assistant to the President and supervisor of the GTCC Marketing and Information Department.
36. Franklin was the first inductee into The Larry Gatlin School of Entertainment Technology Hall of Fame when the Larry Gatlin School of Entertainment Technology was dedicated in 2004 shortly after Franklin was killed in a motorcycle accident.
37. International Association Technical Stage Employees.
38. *The Business Journal*, Dec. 31, 1999.
39. *HPE*, Oct. 16, 1999; ibid. Oct. 20, 1999; *N&R*, Oct. 16, 1999.
40. Dr. Carolyn Schneider asserts that had a snow storm not cancelled classes at GTCC January 25–28, 2000, the curriculum might not have been written. Both she and Dupree were heavily engaged in their normal activities, but the snowstorm gave them time to write the curriculum through an exchange of emails. Schneider to Kinard, Oct. 9, 2006.
41. BOT, Aug. 24, 2000.

Chapter 29

1. *The Business Journal*, May 12, 2000.
2. N.C. Board of Science and Technology, hereafter NCBST in author's notes for Chapter 29.
3. *The Business Journal*, May 12, 2000.
4. *HPE*, Dec. 11, 2000.
5. *The Business Journal*, Feb. 11, 2000.
6. NCBST.
7. Piedmont Triad Partnership Focus Group, Aug. 3, 1999.
8. NCBST.
9. "High-Tech Clusters in North Carolina, North Carolina Board of Science and Technology, 2000, pp. 18–19.
10. Vision 2030, Board Archives, June 15, 2000.
11. *HPE*, Aug. 30, 2000. The College employed 205 full-time and 200 part-time instructors.
12. Melvin to Charlie Greene, March 19, 2001.

13. The GCS also established an Early College at Guilford and Middle Colleges at Bennett, Greensboro College, and NC A&T.
14. GTCC Board Archives, Oct. 28, 2000; NR, Nov. 27, 2000; *N&R*, Nov. 27, 2000.
15. *HPE*, Mar. 17, 2000.
16. *JN*, Mar. 15,2000; *N&R, HPE*, Mar.17, 2000.
17. President's Annual Report 2001–02; p. 5.
18. GTCC Board Archives, April 25, 2000; *HPE*, Feb. 14, 2000.
19. *HPE*, Friday, Dec. 8, 2000; *JN*, Dec. 20, 2000.
20. *N&R*, Mar. 6, 2000.
21. Dr. Macgregor Frank to the author, March 14, 2006.
22. HPE, Apr. 7, 2000; *JN*, Apr 12, 2000.
23. Ibid. June 9, 2000, *HPE*, Aug.30, 2000.
24. The author maintained extensive files on the correspondence surrounding the High Point Education Alliance. These documents are available in the GTCC Archives under that title. GTCC and UNCG later partnered in a Fusion program in the PTIA region.
25. *Triad Business News*, Mar. 10, 2000.
26. Email report from Terri Shelton, UNCG, Nov. 12, 2007.
27. *N&R, HPE*, Sept. 14, 2000.

Chapter 30

1. *JN*, Feb. 1, 2001.
2. *N&R*, Mar. 12, 2001.
3. *BOT*, Feb. 15, 2001.
4. Ibid. *N&R*; Mar. 12, 15, 2001.
5. *The Business Journal*, Apr. 3, 2001.
6. *HPE*, May 23, 2001; ibid. June 6, 2001, ibid. Nov. 15, 2001; *N&R*, Nov. 16,2001. GTCC Archives Board minutes, Oct. 26, 2001.
7. *JN*, Jan. 10, 2001. The amendments were passed in June 2000 and January 2001.
8. *N&R*, Jan. 27, 2001; HPE, Jan. 27, 2001; Minutes of Closed Session of Board of County Commissioners of Guilford County, Feb. 1, 2001. AYES; Commissioners Barber, Dunovant, Yow, Arnold, Landreth, Alston, Dorset, Shaw, Wade and Thigpen. Noes: Commissioner Rakestraw. *N&R*, Feb. 2, 2001.
9. Board , Feb. 15, 2001.
10. *HPE*, Feb. 2, 2001; *N&R*, Feb. 3, 2001.
11. *N&R* Feb. 10, 200; ibid. Feb. 17, 2001.
12. The *The Business Journal*, Mar. 30, 2001; HPE, Mar. 17, 2001; ibid. Board of Commissioners of Guilford County, April 19, 2001. Apr. 21, 2001.
13. Board, April 12, 2001.
14. "Research Report: Marketing Action Plan: GTCC, July 2001. McNeill Lehman, Inc. High Point.
15. *N&R*, Jan. 25, 2001; Marcia Daniel to the author; *N&R*, Mar. 18, 2001. The Datatel Project cost an extra $40 million when the software had to be rewritten to change the cash basis system to an accrual basis system; Sandie Kirkland to the author July 18,19, 2007.
16. *N&R*, Jan. 14, 2001.
17. Ibid. *JN*, Jan. 17, 2001. Stokes was first appointed as a Trustee by The Guilford County Commissioners in 1987 for what became an extended term that expired in 1992. The commissioners named him to replace Percy Sears in 1995 for a four-year term ending June 30, 1999.

18. *HPE*, Jan. 29, 2001; *N&R*, Apr. 8, 2001.

19. *HPE*, June 15, 2001. White was succeeded as Executive Vice President by Cuyler McK-
     night, Dean, GTCC High Point.

20. *HPE*, Apr. 21, 2001.

21. www.Littledidsheknow.com.

22. Remarks prepared by Dr. Cameron: see notes for Chapter 30.

23. Board, Dec. 13, 2001.

24. *HPE, Aug. 5, 2002; N&R*, August 7, 2002; Jul. 25, 2003; *HPE*, Jul. 13, 2003. *HPE*, Nov.
     16; Dec. 20, 2004 High Point Chamber of Commerce, July 2007. In 2004, the Carolina
     Association of Chamber of Commerce Executives (CACCE) named the program one
     of their "Good to Great" projects and the NC Community College Adult Educators As-
     sociation (NCCCAEA) selected it for their 2004 Innovation Award. 556 total email from
     Sam Terry to Lee Kinard, Dec.19, 2006.

Chapter 31

1. *HPE*, Oct. 10, 2002.

2. The State Board of Community Colleges 2003–05 Expansion Budget Request, October
    2002.

3. Employment Security Commission, www.ncesc.com.

4. Cameron to Guilford Delegation, Jan. 15, 2002.

5. BOT, Dec. 13, 2001; Feb. 14, 2002.

6. BOT, Apr. 11, 2002.

7. Rae Marie Smith to Board of Trustees, May 16, 2002.

8. *HPE*, Oct. 10, 2002; *JN*, August 7, 2002.

9. GTCC Catalog. 2007–08.

10. BOT, Apr. 11, 2002. HPE, Aug. 12, 2002.

11. BOT, April 10, 2003.

12. Ibid. Oct. 17; Nov. 1–2, 2002.

13. *The Business Journal*, Sept. 12–18, 2003.

14. Ibid. In 2007–08, The cost to train a nurse was $6,365. Email Kathy Phillips to Lee Ki-
    nard, Oct. 22, 2007.

15. BOT, Nov. 7, 2003.

16. *HPE*, May 21, 2003.

17. *HPE*, Aug. 24, 2003.

18. "Student Enrollments Fall 2003," Dr. Kathryn Baker Smith, Dr. Linda Thomas-Glover,
    BOT, Nov. 7, 2003.

19. BOT, Nov. 7, 2003.

20. PAR 00–02, p. 8.

21. BOT, Nov. 7, 2003.

22. BOT, Dec. 13, 2001; Feb. 14, 2002; PAR 00–02.

23. Ibid. Dec. 13, 2001. GTCC broke ground for four buildings on its new 65 acre Greens-
    boro Campus at 3505 East Wendover Avenue on Tuesday, June 10, 2003.

24. BOT, Feb. 14, 2002; Entertainment Technology Program Data, GTCC IR 2006.

25. President's Annual Report 2000–02, p. 6; hereafter PAR: 00–02.

26. Abell-Schmid study, 2002.

27. BOT, Nov. 1–2, 2002.

28. Ibid.

29. Ibid.

30. BOT, April 11, 2002; Feb. 20, Nov. 7, 2003. The project was completed and opened to students in the fall of 2006. See minutes from President's Council Retreat, July 30, 2007, Chapter 36 and Epilogue for outcomes from these initiatives.

31. "The Community College Connection," Summer 2003 Vol. 6, No. 1.

32. Durham *Herald-Sun,* Aug. 6, 2003.

33. BOT, Nov. 7, 2003.

34. www.ncccs.cc.nc.us/Publications/Publications/csf/2003.pdf.

35. *N&R,* July 30, 2003.

36. BOT, Feb. 20, 2003.

37. *JN,* June 4, 2003.

38. *HPE,* June 30, 2003; McKnight replaced Dr. Graham Reaves.

39. BOT, April 10, 2003.

Chapter 32

1. *HPE,* June 22, 2003.

2. BOT, Feb. 19, 2004.

3. *N&R,* Feb. 23, 2002.

4. GTCC Foundation Legacy Campaign Goals, BOT, Feb, 20, 2003. *N&R,* Feb. 23, 2003; BOT, Nov. 7, 2003; PAR 00–02, pp. 11–12.

5. Ibid.

6. BOT, Aug. 28, 2003; *HPE, N&R,* Aug. 29, 2003.

7. BOT, Aug. 19; Oct. 21, 2004.

8. Information filed in Board minutes for 2003; Additional information is available about SACS under that button at www.gtcc.edu and at sacs.org; Sept. 27, 2004, Cameron letter to BOT. GTCCAll, Sept. 27, 2004.

9. "The Teacher Shortage," BOT, April 10, 2003; April 15, 2004; email from JoAnn Buck to Lee Kinard, July 26, 2007. Paper: Pamela Herndon: Highlights From the Last ¾ Years of the UNCG Relationship (2004–05), GTCC History Archives (Ch. 31).

10. www.gtcc.edu/teacherEd/ July 2007; See GTCC Archives for minutes from All Personnel Meeting, Feb. 9, 2006.

11. *N&R,* Dec. 9, 2003.

12. *N&R* Jan. 14, 2004; *JN.* Jan. 17, 2004.

13. GTCC Foundation Report, Nov. 6, 2006.

14. *N&R,* Dec. 9, 2003, ibid. Dec. 23, 2003; ibid. Dec. 24, 2004; *HPE,* Dec. 9, 2003., Triad Business Journal, Dec. 19, 2003.

15. State of the Community College, Don Cameron, Oct. 2007; *N&R,* October 27, 2007.

16. *N&R,* Jan. 9, 2004;*JN,* Jan. 21, 2004; *HPE* Jan. 11, 2004, ibid. Jan. 17, 2004.

17. BOT, April 10, Nov 7, 2003.

18. Ibid. June 12, 2003

19. Ibid. Nov. 7, 2003.

20. Year ended June 30, 2003.

21. BOT, April 10, Nov. 7, 2003; *N&R,* June 11,15, Dec. 30, 2003; *Triad Business Journal,* Dec. 26, 2003; *HPE,* June 10, 2003; Jan. 5, 2004; *JN,* June 18, 2003; Jan. 14, 2004.

22. *HPE,* Jan. 5, 16, 2004.

23. BOT, Nov. 7, 2003.
24. BOT, Aug. 19, 2004; *HPE*, Oct. 24, 2004.
25. BOT (work session) April 15, 2004; Nov. 7, 2004.
26. *N&R*, Oct. 17, 2004.
27. BOT, Oct. 21, 2004.
28. BOT, Aug. 19, Oct. 21, 2004; *HPE*, Oct. 18, 22, Nov. 3, 2004; *N&R*, Nov. 1, 2004.
29. Ibid. April 15; June 17; Aug.19; Oct. 21, 2004; completed in December 2004.

Chapter 33

1. Excerpted from a rerecording of the dedicatory performance, GTCC Archives.
2. Enrollment totaled 242 in 2003–04, 214 males, 27 miles and 19 students aged 45 plus; source GTCC IR.
3. *N&R*, Jan. 5, 2004.
4. *N&R*, Apr. 4, 2004; *HPE*, Apr. 8, 2004ibid, Apr. 9, 2004.
5. *N&R*, Apr. 26, 2004.
6. Ibid.
7. *HPE*, Apr. 29, 2004.
8. Philanthropyjournal.org, NC: Grants/Gifts, Aug. 22, 2005.
9. MDC was established in 1967 by the North Carolina Fund to help the state transition from a segregated, agricultural workforce to an integrated, industrial work force (North Carolina Manpower Development Corporation) www.mdcinc.org; AACC (American Association of Community Colleges).
10. BOT, Feb. 20, 1999; HPE, Jul. 9, 2004; "Community College Weekly," July 5, 2004; BOT, June 17, 2004.
11. GTCC AtD Newsletter, June 2006.
12. Canton, James M. *The Extreme Future*. New York, Dutton, 2006.
13. *HPE*, Aug. 28, 2003, *N&R*, Aug. 29, 2003, Triad Business Journal, Sept. 4, 2003.
14. Brandon Lynne, "A Vital link in North Carolina's Shifting Economy," *BizLife*, March 2004.
15. NCCCS Press Release, June 3, 2004; PAR 2002–04, p. 11; *N&R*, May, 7, 2004; *Triad Business Journal*, May 7; Jul. 9, 2004. *Winston-Salem Journal*, May 9, 2004. See www.ncbionetwork.org for a description of this program and its allied centers.
16. *N&R* August 5, 22, 2004, PAR 2002–04, p. 11. Email to the author from Barry Teater/Gwyn Riddick, Aug. 1, 2007. In September 2007, Forsyth Tech and Alamance Community College reported "a slight oversupply of biotechnology graduates" inferring that the industry had not matured to expectations: *Winston-Salem Journal*, Sept. 16, 2007.
17. BOT, July 22, 2004.
18. PAR 2002–04, p. 6.
19. *N&R*, Nov. 28, 2004.
20. BOT, April 15, 2004.
21. *N&R*, Jan. 16, 2004.
22. *JN*, Apr. 28, 2004; ibid. May 4, 2004; ibid. May 19, 2004; *HPE*, Apr. 4, 2004; ibid. Apr, 28, 2004; ibid. May 4, 2004; *N&R*, Apr. 30, 2004.
23. BOT, Aug. 19; Nov. 5–6, 2004; *N&R* Sept. 9, 2004; *Triad Business Journal* Oct.8, 2004. *JN*, Sept.15, 2004; *HPE*, Sept. 21, 2004.
24. BOT, April 15, 2004.*HPE*, Apr. 17, 2004.

Chapter 34

1. *N&R*, Mar. 18, 2005.
2. See Chapter 29.
3. McNeill Lehman, Inc. "Research Report: Marketing Action Plan: GTCC July 2001.
4. BOT, Feb. 17, 2005; "Preparation of Tomorrow's Workforce, Guilford County, North Carolina: A Report of Research Observations, and Forecasts," provided by the Herman Group Consulting Futurists for GTCC, Feb. 2005; hereafter Herman-GTCC 2005; BOT Work Session, April 21, 2005.
5. The High Point Economic Development Council began developing a strategy to deal with these issues in mid 2007.
6. *N&R*, Nov. 28, 2006. Dr. Cameron warned the EDC shortly after the study was released that if the city of High Point did not take action, the findings would remain just another expensive research project relegated to a shelf.
7. The company was employing 1000 by May 10, 2005.
8. *TBJ*, Nov. 12–18; Dec. 31, 2004.
9. HPE, April 16, 2005;*N&R*, Mar. 22, 2005; April 27, 2005; May 6, 2005, May 10, 2005; GTCC BOT, Apr 21; June 16, 2005.
10. CC07-275; NCCCS numbered memo. November 7, 2007.
11. *The Business Journal*, Aug. 5, 2005; GTCC Archives, BOT June 16, 2005;, email from Transportation Division Chair Ed Frye, May 5, 2006.
12. *Greensboro Magazine*, 2006, Vol. 3.
13. Sept. 2, 2005; Don Cameron to GTCC Staff and Faculty.
14. Claudette Burroughs White represented Greensboro City Council District #2 from 1994 to 2005. She succumbed to cancer on Sept. 16, 2007.
15. Renick resigned from NC A&T State University on May 31, 2007. He was replaced by interim deputy Chancellor Lloyd V. Hackley on June 1, 2006. Hackley was replaced by Dr. Stanley F. Battle on July 1, 2007.
16. *N&R*, Mar. 11, 18, 2005; BOT, Aug. 18, 2005. There is an extensive videotape history of the opening in the GTCC Archives
17. BOT Work Session, Nov. 4–5, 2005.
18. *The Business Journal*, Dec. 31, 2004; Feb. 8, 2005; hereafter, *TBJ*.
19. North Carolina, Dec. 2004.
20. *TBJ*, Feb. 8, 2005.
21. Cameron chaired both organizations.
22. Ibid.
23. Ibid.

Chapter 35

1. Christine Johnson McPhail, ed., Establishing and Sustaining Learning Centered Community Colleges, Washington, Community College Press, 2005, p.v, hereafter, McPhail.
2. BOT, Nov. 4–5, 2005.
3. "The High Point Point Workforce Preparedness Study," The Herman Group, 2005.
4. "Jamestown Master Plan: 2005–11," Moser, Mayer, Phoenix, Pa; hereafter MMP-05.
5. The Student Services Center was immediately addressed (see Chapter 33) by restacking the Medlin Campus Center (2006–07).
6. BOT, Nov. 4–5.

7. BOT, Nov. 4–5.
8. Vice President, Instruction, John Chapin resigned in July 2007 precipitating a reorganization introduced by Cuyler McKnight at the President's Council Work Session, July 30, 2007.
9. McPhail, p. vi.
10. *HPE*, Jan. 4, 2006.
11. Dr. Donald W. Cameron Presentation, Univ. Texas, Nov. 2003.
12. *HPE*, Jan. 4–6, 2006.
13. Ibid. Jan. 4, 2006.
14. Ibid. Jan. 4, 2006.
15. *N&R*, Mar. 2, 2006.
16. BOT, Nov. 4–5, 2005; William J. Flynn, "The Learning Decade," Learning Abstracts, Jan 2003, Vol. 6, No. 1.; Ibid. "What the Learning Paradigm Means for Faculty," June 1999, Vol. No. 4; ibid. "Becoming a Learning College," March 2003, Vol. 6, No. 3.
17. Establishing & Sustaining Learning Centered Community Colleges, ed. Christine Johnson McPhail, Community College Press, 2005, p. 18.
18. Don Cameron, 2005, University of Texas presentation.
19. Ibid.
20. Close scrutiny indicates that most of Don Cameron's successful partnerships evolved from personal relationships.
21. Jane Pendry, "Early Middle Colleges at GTCC," 2007; Email from Audrey Bailey, NCCCS, Aug. 17, 2007; email from Chancy Kapp, NCCCS, Aug. 27, 2007.
22. Ibid. Mar. 21, 2006.
23. BOT, May 15; June 15, 2006; *Newsweek*, June 12, 2006.
24. *N&R*, Feb 26, 2005; Mar. 1, 2005; *HPE*, Mar. 2, 2005, Jul, 5, 2005; Northwest Observer, June 3, 2005. BOT, Aug. 18, 2005.
25. The Eastern Guilford High School fire received extensive media coverage from the beginning of the conflagration on November 1, 2006; Email: Nov. 2, 2007, Cuyler McKnight to Terry Grier, GTCC President's Council, Nov. 6, 2006; videotaped (DVD)news conference at GTCC Greensboro with Don Cameron and Terry Grier, GTCC Archives, plus extensive TV footage from local channels; *N&R*, Nov. 7,9, 25, 27,28, 30; Dec. 1, 2, 8, 15, 20, 25; Jan. 5, 20, 2007.
26. Email from Flora Taylor, GTCC Veteran's Affair coordinator, Sept. 19, 2007.
27. *Triad Business Journal*, Feb. 4, 2005.
28. *Winston-Salem Journal*, Feb 23, 2005; GTCC BOT Archives April 21, 2005.
29. BOT, Oct. 27, 2005.
30. *N&R*, June 3, 2005
31. *N&R*, Mar. 6, 2005.
32. *HPE*, Apr. 29, 2005; BOT, Apr 21, 2005.
33. BOT, Dec. 20, 2005.

Chapter 36

1. GTCC President's Annual Report 1991–92.
2. President Cameron signed the papers transferring this northwest Guilford farm to GTCC on Friday, August 24, 2007.
3. *N&R*, Dec. 17, 2006; BOT Feb. 15, 2007.

4. *The Business Journal*, June 22–28, 2007. The "Aerotropolis" concept was presented to the Piedmont Triad Partnership by Dr. John D. Kasarda, Director of the Kenan Institute of Private Enterprise and Kenan Distinguished Professor of Entrepreneurship, Kenan-Flagler School of Business, UNC-Chapel Hill.
5. *N&R*, Jan. 7, 2007; Canton, 2006, p 73.
6. GTCC Office of Institutional Research and Planning, Jan. 11, 2007.
7. Email: Claire McCaskill to Lee Kinard, Jan. 5, 2007; hereafter, McCaskill,
8. PAR 1991–92, p. 16. Source: 1991–92 Annual Registration Report, NC Dept. of Community Colleges.
9. McCaskill.
10. Ibid. Nov, 15, 2006, GTCC 2005–06 Speerings.
11. Source: NC Employment Security Commission.
12. Greensboro Partnership, Jan. 20, 2006; *N&R*, Jan. 24, 2006.
13. BOT, April 10, 2003.
14. *The Chronicle of Higher Education*, July 6, 2007.
15. Source: GTCC Athletic Department, Phil Gaffney, Director; email from Sabrina Johnson to Lee Kinard, Dec. 19, 2006.
16. Email from Wilson Davis, Oct. 25, 2007.
17. BOT, Sept. 21, 2006.
18. *N&R*, May 17, 2006.
19. GTCCALL, Sandie Kirkland, Aug. 21, 2006.
20. BOT, Jan. 19, 2006; President's Council Retreat, July 31, 2006.
21. Through the generosity of Steve and Judy Hassell James of Greensboro, the building was named to honor Mrs. James' mother Lillian Hassell Benton. Mrs. Benson grew up in Jamestown, attended Woman's College (UNCG} and taught for 33 years in the Cabarrus County, N. C. Schools.
22. BOT, Feb. 23; April, 20 and May 15, 2006; The "Business Case for Funding the Project," Oct. 9, 2006, indicates that Health Technologies was down sized from 115,000 square feet due to escalating construction costs. (May 15, 2006) Priorities in order of commitment included (1) Health Technologies and the Greensboro classroom; (2) GTCC High Point classroom. The John Deere and Volvo programs were the impetus for pursing land for the northwest campus and the parking deck at Jamestown had the lowest priority.
23. Quoted from All Personnel Meeting, Feb. 9, 2006.
24. See "Data Incident Response Plan," June 30, 2006; Mark Soisson hired, GTCC press release, May 22, 2007.
25. *N&R*, May 18, 2006.
26. *N&R*, May 17, 2006.
27. BOT, June 15, 2006. Senator Kay Hagan is GTCC Trustee, Charles "Chip" Hagan's spouse.
28. North Carolina General Assembly Budget Record on Legislative Increases, pp. 10–20.
29. Source: NCCCS, Program Audit Services, May 1, 2006.
30. PAR 1991–92. These figures differ to some degree based on information provided in Speight, Lowell, *The Economic Impact of GTCC on Guilford County: 1990–91*; GTCC Archives.
31. Speight.
32. Selected Number 3 in the "Top Ten Community College News Stories in North Carolina in 2006; source NCCCS. 1182.

33. *N&R*, Jan. 20, 2006, June 14, 2007.
34. "Passenger Transport," Vol. 64, No. 32, Washington, Dc, Aug. 7, 2006;*N&R*, Aug. 8, 2006.
35. GTCCALL, Sept. 29; Dec. 20, 2006.
36. BOT, April 20; June 15, 2006.

Chapter 37

1. Ibid. June 19, 2007.
2. BOT, Jan. 17 Work Session; Feb. 17, 2007.
3. These issues were envisioned during the BOT Jan. 17, 2007 work session.
4. BOT, Feb 19; April 19, 2007.
5. President's Council, April 30, 2007.
6. *N&R*, June 14, 2007.
7. *N&R*, June 21, 2007.
8. *N&R*, June 21, 2007.
9. Ibid. June 22, 2007.
10. Ibid. Aug. 9, 2006.
11. GTCC Press release, May 8, 2007.
12. Ibid. June 22; 28, 2007.
13. Ibid. Jan. 25, 2007.
14. Ibid. Feb. 9, 2007.
15. Bryan Foundation Gift, BOT, Mar. 22, 2007; GTCC Press Release, April, 5; May 14, 2007. Across a five-year period $744,000 would support Honda and TIMCO training with the remainder supporting a dealership technician apprenticeship program for Volvo Trucks North American and Mack Trucks, Inc.
16. BOT, Feb. 15, 2007.
17. Wikipedia.org, June 12, 2007.
18. BOT Mar. 8, 2007.
19. BOT, April 19, 2007.
20. President's Council Work Session, July 30, 2007; email Ed Frye to Marcia McClaren, July 27, 2007; email GTCCALL from D. W. Cameron, Aug. 27, 2007.
21. BOT-CPPC, May 3, 2007; GTCCAll, Don Cameron, Aug. 27, 2007.
22. *N&R*, Feb. 2, April 4, 2006; May 17, 2007; BOT, Mar. 8, 2007; The $15 million WIRED (Workforce Innovation in Regional Economic Development) grant the U.S. Department of Labor awarded to the Piedmont Triad Partnership (PTP) in February 2006 was designed to promote global competitiveness at the regional level. The futuristic initiative supported innovative approaches to education and workforce development designed to prepare workers to compete and succeed in the US and globally.
23. Email from Lisa Koretoff, Nov. 1, 2007).
24. Email: John Chapin, Jan. 10 2007.
25. BOT, May 3, 2007.
26. President's Council Work Session, July 30, 2007.
27. Ibid.
28. Mrs. Frye is the wife of the former Chief Justice of the N. C. Supreme Court (1999–2000), Henry E. Frye. When Mr. Frye was elected a state representative in 1968, he was the only black legislator and the first elected in the 20th century. He concluded his career in public service as the first African-American Chief Justice of the N.C. Supreme Court; Wikipedia.

29. GTCC Press Release, Aug. 21, 2007.
30. PAR, 2005–06.
31. *N&R*, June 27, 2007. NCCCS Press Release, Aug. 17, 2007.
32. Ibid.
33. *N&O*, June 27, 2007.
34. Email from Kennon Briggs, VP Business and Finance, NCCCS, Sept. 25, 2007.
35. *JN*, Aug. 21, 2006, GTCC Press Release, June 14, 2007.
36. GTCC Press Release, Aug. 13, 2007.
37. Ibid. Aug. 23, 2007.

Epilogue

1. G. Donald Jud, www.uncg.edu/-juddon; also "A Proposal for the Establishment of an Industrial Education Center, 1958." GTCC Archives.
2. GTCC Press Release, Sept. 14, 2007. NCCCS 2006–07, Oct. 15, 2007.
3. Cameron, Don, "State of the Community College," Oct. 19, 2007.
4. Email from Brad Burch, Registrar, Oct. 18, 2007.
5. GTCC Press release, Aug. 7, 2007, email from Bob Plain, Nov 7, 2007.
6. Email from Kennon D. Briggs, VP, Business and Finance NCCCS, Oct. 17, 2007.
7. BOT, Nov. 7, 2003.
8. Herring, p. 156; Friedman, Thomas L. *The World Is Flat*. New York, Picador, 2007, p. 383.
9. These comments, and those that follow, extend from a November 8, 2007, interview with Dr. Cameron conducted by the author.
10. Herring, p. 223; Email from Chancy Kapp, Asst. to the President for External Affairs, NCCCS, Aug. 27, 2007. It is notable that Guilford legislators worked extremely hard to win $60.2 million for a nanotechnology school to be operated jointly by UNCG and NC A&T State University; Email Hoyt Phillips, president, Greensboro Chamber of Commerce, Sept. 20, 2007. For Robert W. Scott comments, see Chapter 23. The General Assembly appropriation for community colleges actually totaled 9 percent in 2005–06 and 2005–07.
11. *N&R*, May 1, 1990.

Index